D1496006

CHILDREN OF THE YELLOW EARTH

PLATE I

Iron ore deposit at Yen Tung Shan. The black line marks the ore seam

[*front*

CHILDREN OF THE YELLOW EARTH

STUDIES IN PREHISTORIC CHINA

J. GUNNAR ANDERSSON

THE MIT PRESS
CAMBRIDGE, MASSACHUSETTS

This volume is dedicated to the memory of my charming friend Davidson Black (†March 15, 1934), Professor at the Peking Union Medical College, who with such penetrating genius identified and described *Sinanthropus pekinensis*.

Translated from the Swedish by
Dr. E. Classen

Originally published in Great Britain in 1934 by
Kegan Paul, Trench, Trubner & Co., Ltd.

First MIT Press paperback edition, February 1973

Library of Congress Cataloging in Publication Data

Andersson, Johan Gunnar, 1874–1960.
Children of the yellow earth.

Translation of Den gula jordens barn.
Reprint of the 1934 ed.
1. China—Antiquities. 2. Man, Prehistoric—China. 3. Excavations (Archaeology)—China. I. Title.
DS715.A52 1972 913.31 72–8672
ISBN 0–262–51011–1 (pbk)
Printed and bound in the United States of America

CONTENTS

CHAP.		PAGE
	Foreword	xvii
I	The First Signs of Life	1
II	Prehistoric Swamp Forests	17
III	The Giant Saurians in Shantung and the First Mammals	32
IV	How the Mountains came into being	54
V	Dragons and Dragon-bone Mines	70
VI	The Peking Man	94
VII	The Yellow Earth	127
VIII	Pleistocene Man in the Ordos Desert	146
IX	The Face of the Earth Giant	156
X	We discover the First Prehistoric Village	163
XI	A Cannibalistic Sanctuary	188
XII	Ancient Implements and Vessels	200
XIII	We follow the Yang Shao People to Kokonor	224
XIV	The Gift of the old Madman	234
XV	Archaeology takes charge	244
XVI	The T'ao Valley	251
XVII	The Living in the Valley and the Dead in the Mountains	264
XVIII	Fecundity Rites, Hunting Magic and Death Cult	277
XIX	Aphrodite's Symbol	294
XX	The Symbolism of the P'an Shan Graves	313
XXI	The Yang Shao Civilization	330
	Index	339

LIST OF PLATES

PLATE — FACING PAGE

1. Iron ore deposit at Yen Tung Shan . . . *Front.*
2. The *Collenia*-bearing limestone in the gorge of the Hun River . . . 8
3. Landscape of the age of the Kaiping flora. Reconstruction, under the direction of Prof. T. G. Halle, by the artist Sven Ekblom . . . 18
4. "Bad Lands". Dinosaur area at Meng Yin in Shantung 34
5. *Helopus Zdanskyi*. Reconstruction, under the direction of Prof. C. Wiman, by Sven Ekblom . . . 40
6. *Samotherium sinense* from the Hipparion strata at Pao Te Hsien. Reconstruction, under the direction of Prof. C. Wiman, by Sven Ekblom . . . 88
7. Landscape at Chou K'ou Tien . . . 96
8. *Sinanthropus* site at Chou K'ou Tien. The man on the extreme left is Dr. Zdansky. Dr. Walter Granger is standing in the lower centre . . . 98
9. The San Men formation on the Yellow River, Yuan Chü Hsien . . . 140
10. Loess Terraces at Erh Liang Kou, Honan . . . 144
11. The Ma Lan Valley at Chai T'ang . . . 158
12. The Hun River Canyon . . . 160
13. Yang Shao Tsun: View from the most northerly part of the modern village . . . 166
14. Loess dwellings at Yang Shao Tsun . . . 168
15. Ravine landscape: Yang Shao Tsun . . . 170
16. The cultural deposit at Yang Shao Tsun . . . 172
17. Shao Kuo T'un cave . . . 190
18. Shao Kuo T'un cave, near view . . . 192
19. Man spinning with a distaff. Hsi Ning Ho, Kansu . 216
20. Pointed bottom vessels. Yang Shao civilization . . 220
21. Tripods. Yang Shao civilization . . . 222
22. The Lo Han T'ang dwelling site . . . 240
23. Excavations at the burial-place at Chu Chia Chai . . 246
24. Bone armour and bone knife from Chu Chia Chai graves . 248
25. The T'ao Valley . . . 256
26. Terrace landscape, Hsin Tien . . . 258
27. Excavations at Ch'i Chia P'ing . . . 262
28. Dwelling site. Ceramics of the Yang Shao Period, Kansu 264

LIST OF PLATES

PLATE		FACING PAGE
29.	The P'an Shan hills. To the left Wa Kuan Tsui, in the centre P'an Shan, and on the right Pien Chia Kou	268
30.	The Pien Chia Kou grave	272
31.	Two of the painted urns from the Pien Chia Kou grave	274
32.	Two painted urns from the Pien Chia Kou grave	276
	Map: Prehistoric sites in North China	346

LIST OF FIGURES

FIG.		PAGE
1	Amadeus W. Grabau, First palaeontologist of the National Geological Survey of China and Professor at Peiping University, a scholar of genius, an enthusiastic teacher and a delightful man	1
2.	Stromatolitic ore. Hsin Yao	3
3.	Section through Yen Tung Shan	6
4.	Section through the series of strata at the northern edge of the Kaiping coalfield. (By Sun and Grabau)	12
5.	Cambrian brachiopods. *a*, *Obolus luanhsiensis* Grabau; *b*, *Lingulella dimorpha* Sun. (3 times magnified)	13
6.	Cambrian trilobites. *a*, *Changshania conica* Sun; *b*, *Agnostus hoi* Sun. (7 times magnified)	13
7.	Ordovician cuttle-fish. *Actinoceras tani* Grabau. (Natural size)	14
8.	Ordovician shells. *a*, *Lophospira morrisi* Grabau ; *b*, *Pagodispira dorothea* Grabau. (Magnified double size)	15
9.	*Pseudomonotis Mathieui*. Mussel from Permocarboniferous formation of the Kaiping field	15
10.	The Kaiping tip	17
11.	Reconstruction of *Gigantopteris* by Halle	21
12.	Jurassic plants from Chai T'ang. *a*, *Coniopteris tatungensis* Sze (n. sp.); *b*, *Cladophlebis cf. whitbyensis*; *c*, *Phoenicopsis speciosa* Hr., related to *Gingko*	24
13.	Tertiary plants from the Fushun coalfield near Mukden. *a*, *Alnus kefersteinii* Ung.; *b*, *Sequoia langsdorfii* Brongn.	28
14.	Professor T. G. Halle, who described the *Gigantopteris* flora of Shansi	30
15.	Professor Wiman and the rear part of the *Helopus*	32
16.	Reconstruction of *Helopus*, with an indication of those parts of the skeleton found in Shantung. (*After Wiman*)	41
17.	Plant fossils from the Cretaceous deposits at Lai Yang in Shantung. *a*, *Sphenolepis arborescens* Chow; *b*, *Zamites sp.*; *c*, *Thinnfeldia sp.*; *d*, *e*, *Brachyphyllum multiramosum* Chow; *f*, *Palaeocyparis cf. flexuosa* Chow; *g*, *Baiera cf. australis* M'Coy	43
18.	Insects from the Cretaceous formation at Lai Yang. 1, *Samarura gregaria* Grabau; 2, *Laiyangia paradoxiformis* Grabau; 3, *Sinoblatta laiyangensis* Grabau; 4, *Proteroscarabaeus yeni* Grabau	45
19.	Tilted Eocene strata at Yuan Chü Hsien	50

LIST OF FIGURES

FIG.		PAGE
20.	Lower jaw of *Amynodon sinensis* Zdansky, from Eocene deposits at Yuan Chü Hsien in Honan . . .	51
21.	Professor Carl Wiman, who organized the study of the fossil vertebrate material from China and himself described the dinosaurs	52
22.	Dr. Wong Wen-hao, Chief of the National Geological Survey of China, a charming and wise little gentleman, author of several important treatises on mountain folding in the Pacific region	54
23.	Section through a part of the mountains north of Kaiping	58
24.	Section through the coalfield at Chang Kou Yü in the Peking Western Hills. (*V. K. Ting and H. C. T'an*) .	59
25.	Section from west to east through the ore-field at Hsin Yao	61
26.	North-Southern section through the Eocene area of Yuan Chü	62
27.	Mountain section at Hsi Ning Ho showing steeply inclined deposits of old crystalline rocks–*a*, less steeply inclined red Tertiary deposits–*b*, superimposed on them a slightly inclined cap of loess, with gravel deposits at its base–*c*	65
28.	Model showing the mountains between the Peking plain and the Mongolian plateau. Notice especially the valley of the Hun River. (*After Barbour*) . .	68
29.	Dragon design on a tile from a grave of the Han dynasty	70
30.	*a*, *b*, *c*. Zdansky's three sketches. For explanation see the text	83
31.	A Chilotherium family. Reconstruction by the artist Sven Ekblom under the guidance of Professor Wiman	86
32.	*Samotherium sinense*. Reconstruction of male skull. (*After Bohlin*)	87
33.	Skull of *Metailurus minor*. (*After Zdansky*) . . .	89
34.	Snout of sabre-toothed tiger, *Machairodus palanderi*, with the terrible knife tooth, in natural size . . .	90
35.	Dr. Otto Zdansky, now Professor at the University of Cairo, who with extraordinary skill excavated our most important vertebrate fossils and who later described large parts of this vast material	93
36.	Block diagram showing the situation of Chou K'ou Tien. (*After Professor George B. Barbour*)	94
37.	The Chou K'ou Tien cave, seen from the north-east. (*After Barbour*)	100
38.	Foremost molar in the left half of lower jaw of *a*, ten-year-old Chinese child ; *b*, *Sinanthropus* ; *c*, young chimpanzee. (*After Black*.)	107
39.	Section of the foremost molar in the left half of the lower jaw of *a*, ten-year-old Chinese child ; *b*, *Sinanthropus* ; *c*, chimpanzee. (*After Black*)	108
40.	Front portion of lower jaw of *a*, *Sinanthropus* ; *b*, a child of the latest Stone age in China ; *c*, a modern Chinese child ; *d*, a young chimpanzee. (*After Black*) . .	109
41.	Section of cave. (*After Teilhard, Young and Pei*) . .	114

LIST OF FIGURES

FIG. PAGE

42. *Sinanthropus* skull (SE): *a*, seen from above; *b*, seen from the right side 117
43. The genealogical tree of the Hominidae. (*After Keith*) . 119
44. Section through one of the layers (*e*) containing skeletal remains of *Sinanthropus*, together with stone implements. 1 & 2, jaws of *Sinanthropus*; 3, fragments of skull. (*After Pei*) 120
45. Stone implement from the deposits in the Chou K'ou Tien cave 121
46. Lower jaw of *Sinanthropus*. (*After Black*) 122
47. Stone implement from the Chou K'ou Tien cave. (*After Teilhard and Pei*) 124
48. Dr. Davidson Black at Chou K'ou Tien 126
49. The loess basin at Hsin Yao in the mountainous region north of Peiping. In the background are visible hills which contain the iron ore deposits. The valley in the centre is occupied by the loess formation, with its dark, gaping ravines 127
50. Section through the Ching Ho valley, Eastern Kansu . 129
51. Section across the course of the Yellow River at Shan Pai Wan in Kansu 132
52. *Struthiolithus* egg from the loess formation in Honan. The size is shown by comparison with a match-box of ordinary size 134
53. The old woman and the elephant, both invisible . . 139
54. The loess village of Su Chia Chiao, near Kalgan. (*After a drawing by Professor George B. Barbour*) 144
55. Father Emile Licent, the great collector and founder of the Huang Ho-Pai Ho Museum 146
56. Section through the Choei Tong Keou basin. (*After Teilhard and Licent*) 148
57. Stone implements from Choei Tong Keou, presented to the Museum of Far Eastern Antiquities by Licent and Teilhard 149
58. Stone implements from Choei Tong Keou, presented to the Museum of Far Eastern Antiquities by Licent and Teilhard 149
59. Section at Sjara Osso Gol. (*After Teilhard and Licent*) . 150
60. Stone implements from Sjara Osso Gol. (*After Teilhard and Licent*) 153
61. Bone object from Sjara Osso Gol. (*After Teilhard and Licent*) 153
62. Professor Pierre Teilhard de Chardin, the eminent French palaeontologist, who, together with Father Licent, discovered the traces of Old Stone-age man in the Ordos desert 154
63. The ancient Pao Te surface with the superimposed beds of gravel, 200 metres above the present bottom of the Chai T'ang valley. In the foreground later erosion valleys 156
64. The P'an Chiao valley with terrace formations of the Ma Lan age which have become broken by erosion during the P'an Chiao age, which has even reached into the solid rock 160

LIST OF FIGURES

FIG. PAGE

65. Section through the T'ao valley in Kansu 161
66. The P'an Chiao valley with Ma Lan terraces and later erosion during the P'an Chiao stage 162
67. During the excavation at Yang Shao Tsun. From left to right: P. L. Yuan, Andersson, old Wang, the father of the village, and the evangelist Wang 163
68. Wall profile of the site of the central portion of the Yang Shao dwellings 166
69. Kellergruben. *a*, Yang Shao Tsun; *b*, *c*, Achenheim in Alsace. (*After Forrer*) 172
70. "Well" during excavation 175
71. Ravine topography, Yang Shao Tsun. My assistant, Mr. Yuan, is standing on a small ridge between two ravines. Immediately below him is a small patch of cultural soil. The picture shows clearly how the ravine topography is later than the Stone-age village, the deposits of which have been dismembered and partly destroyed by erosion 176
72. Erosion topography from the southernmost part of the dwelling-site 177
73. Section through the southern part of the Yang Shao site, showing how erosion has intersected the cultural deposit and the deposits made by the water-course which at one time flowed on the surface of the unbroken plateau . 178
74. Diagram showing the fall of the water level from the Stone age to the present day 180
75. Greenstone axe from Yang Shao Tsun . . . 181
76. The asymmetric adze of stone, Yang Shao Tsun . . 182
77. *a*, *b*, arrowheads; *c*, sewing needle of bone; *d*, spinning whorl of stone; *e*, bracelet of clay; *f*, stone knife . 183
78. Comparison between painted ceramics from Honan and Anau 185
79. Painted bowl from Chin Wang Chai in Ho Yin Hsien, Honan 186
80. Figurine of marble. Sha Kuo T'un cave 188
81. Longitudinal section of the cave. The horizontal line in the roof of the cave is the base measurement line; the perpendicular line shows the position of the cross-section in Fig. 82 190
82. Cross-section through the cave 191
83. *a*, scraper; *c*, drill and *b*, arrowhead of chalcedony . 192
84. Polished stone axe 192
85. *a*, fragment of marble ring; *b*, reconstruction of thin marble ring. (Natural size) 193
86. Fragment of a mussel ring 194
87. Outline of a jar with narrow neck (¼ natural size) . . 195
88. Cylindrical vessel with pendulum decoration (½ natural size) 196
89. Showing the forms of development of the written character "Ko". *a–d*, archaic forms from inscriptions on bronze vessels and bronze weapons, all undoubted pictographs of the Chinese dagger axe; *e–f*, transition forms to modern written character *g* 200

FIG. PAGE

90. Stone knife formed from a flake broken out of a large pebble. The back is thickened, the sides provided with two incisions for securing a string (⅔ natural size) . 202
91. *a*, crescent-shaped, and *b*, rectangular polished stone knife 203
92. Japanese stone knife from Prince Oyama's collection . 204
93. *a*, crescent-shaped, and *b*, rectangular modern iron knife . 205
94. Iron knife with leather covering on the back and a loop for the thumb 205
95. Knife-grinder's rattle 206
96. Knives, *a*, from Anhui; *b*, from the Kalgan district (⅛ natural size) 207
97. Stone knife, probably from An Yang (½ natural size) . 208
98. Bronze scythe with clear marks of the shaft (½ natural size) 209
99. Chinese lumberman's pen (1/10 natural size) . . . 210
100 Illustrations showing the assumed connection between the asymmetric stone adze (1a and b), the bronze adze (2a–c), and the modern iron adze (3a–c) (½ natural size) 211
101. Development of the Chinese dagger axe, Ko. Fig. 1a–b of stone, 2–6 of copper and bronze 212
102. Method of attachment for *a*, stone ko; and *b*, bronze ko 213
103. Triangular arrowheads: *a*, of bone; *b*, of stone, both of the Yang Shao age; *c*, of bronze, early Iron age; and *d*, modern arrowhead of iron 214
104. Peasant farm in Kansu, reminiscent of the models in the Han graves 218
105. Pointed-bottom vessels: *a*, modern lemonade glass bottle; *b*, clay vessel from the Yang Shao dwelling site; *c*, modern clay vessel found on a boat on the Yellow River . . 220
106. Archaic characters for vessels with pointed bottom, from inscriptions upon oracle bones (end of second millennium B.C.) and bronzes (first millennium B.C.) (*After Karlgren*) 221
107. Development of written character li, *a*, an archaic form, a pictograph of the Li tripod; *b*, *c*, transition forms to *d*, the modern character 223
108. Camp on the northern banks of Kokonor 224
109. "The Pillar", the last remains of a Stone-age deposit, in which we found painted fragments of jars and bone knives 229
110. Tibetans on the southern shore of Kokonor . . . 231
111. The site of prehistoric discoveries at the eastern end of Kokonor 233
112. The old madman and his companions 234
113. Winged stone knife 242
114. Disc-like stone slab, coarsely hewn out of a rubble stone . 243
115. Writing tablets of bone (⅔ natural size) 250
116. We ride to the T'ao valley 251
117. Urn with a high collar and large handles (⅓ natural size) . 262
118. Fragment of "comb" ceramics 263
119. Old Ma says "stop" to our excavations in the P'an Shan hills 264
120. Objects from Ma Chia Yao: *a*, bone awl; *b*, clay rattle; *c*, stone bracelet; *d*, ibex (horn-shaped clay ring); *e*, bone finger ring (½ natural size) 266

LIST OF FIGURES

FIG. PAGE

121. Jade ring ($\frac{2}{3}$ natural size) 272
122. Pendant ornament (natural size) 273
123. Greenstone axe. Pien Chia Kou grave ($\frac{2}{3}$ natural size) . 274
124. Small urn with chessboard pattern 275
125. Rest during the transport of the P'an Shan vessels to Ti Tao 276
126. Chinese symbol combining the male principle *Yang* and the female *Yin* 277
127. Holy Tree. Province of Hupei. At the foot of the tree is a table for offerings, and on the trunk are secured tablets with invocations to the tree 283
128. Chinese Bronze-age jar, of which the neck is decorated with zig-zag signs, which are the archaic forms of the Chinese character "lightning" 289
129. Bronze rattle, with sun-wheel on top and bull's head on the base. (*Crown Prince of Sweden's Chinese collection*) . 290
130. Dragon Boat. (*After Allom, "China"*) 293
131. A woman's cap with cowrie shells, used by the Hottentots 294
132. Chinese axle-mounting in bronze, decorated with rows of cowrie images (natural size) 297
133. Chinese bronze lid with copious cowrie embellishments. Probably Han dynasty ($\frac{2}{3}$ natural size) 303
134. "Easy birth" shell used in Japan ($\frac{2}{3}$ natural size) . . 305
135. Chinese buckle of bronze, with cowrie ornament (natural size) 311
136. Burial urn from the New Stone age in Denmark . . 313
137. Death pattern; the red central band is dotted . . 315
138. Female-shaped mortuary urn, Egypt 316
139. Painted urn. Egypt. 317
140. Cowries from China: *a*, from the Stone-age dwellings at Pu Chao Chai; *b*, unknown Chinese origin; *c*, cowrie imitation in bone; *d*, imitation in bronze . . . 323
141. Details of an urn with cowrie pattern. Ma Chang period, Kansu 324
142. Whirlwind 325
143. Dragon in the clouds. (*After an original which in his day belonged to the Klaes Fåhraeus collection*) 326
144. Ceramic piece, probably a lid, crowned by a human head, on the top and neck of which a snake is coiled. It is decorated with the typical P'an Shan pattern and certainly belonged to this group 328
145. Stone pick from the Kalgan district ($\frac{1}{3}$ natural size). As this type has never been found in the Yang Shao dwellings, it may possibly belong to an earlier stage of the Stone age 330
146. Stone blade from the Kalgan district ($\frac{1}{2}$ natural size). Since this type has never been found in the Yang Shao dwellings it may possibly belong to an earlier stage of the Stone age 333
147. Ivory carving from An Yang (about 1500–1000 B.C.), one of the earliest historical relics of China. 336

FOREWORD

FIFTEEN years ago we knew very little of the course of events which gave birth to modern China, and nothing at all about the history of the Chinese people prior to the earliest legendary dynasties.

During these fifteen years epoch-making discoveries have been made and vast collections have been brought to light by numerous energetic workers. Research has erected a number of milestones, by the guidance of which we can safely journey to certain nodal points in the history and development of the country and its people.

But, nevertheless, research into the prehistory of China has only just begun, and it will require the systematic work of generations before our knowledge of that part of the world is in any degree complete.

When I sat down to write an account of my own studies in the prehistory of China, intended, not for experts, but for the general public, which may possibly interest itself in so remote a subject, I was fully conscious of the gaps in our knowledge. Certain stages of development appear in the full daylight, but in others we can only grope our way to the truth! At other times there is impenetrable darkness.

Under these circumstances I was able to choose one of two methods of presentation. I might endeavour to fill out synthetically the voids in our knowledge. Proceeding from a certain group of ascertained facts I might seek to reconstruct the most probable course of development to the next known point.

But I am convinced that it will be possible to make a presentation of the kind just described more easily and with better claims to reliability in about fifteen years' time, when the arsenal of ascertained facts will doubtlessly have been increased manifold.

I therefore chose the second method, of relating only what I had myself observed, whilst endeavouring to give to the reader such a survey as would enable him to fill in, according to his taste, the unwritten pages. It has therefore been my ambition to allow my own discoveries to speak for themselves and to present them in an easily comprehended form and without any tiresome detail.

But it was also my wish to give something more—something which in fact I alone can give : an account of how the discoveries were made whenever I and my collaborators turned over a new page in the prehistory of China.

By a series of fortunate circumstances I was on several occasions the pioneer. In 1914 I was the first to stumble upon the organic origin of stromatolite ore. In 1918 I discovered the Collenia nodules and recognized their connection with similar "fossils" in the pre-Cambrian area of North America. In the same year we discovered the first Hipparion field in China made known to science. In 1919 we found the beaver fauna at Ertemte in Mongolia. 1921 was a red-letter year : the Neolithic dwelling-site at Yang Shao Tsun, the Eocene mammals on the Yellow River, the Sha Kuo T'un cave deposit in Fengtien and the still more remarkable cave discovery at Chou K'ou Tien, which became world-famous by the work of those who followed after us.

Nobody but I can relate how these discoveries were made; how we groped our way forward by many routes, how we failed in many of our efforts, but held fast to one promising clue or another and, with it as a starting point, advanced further and further, till our discoveries became numerous, with rich and varied material, as, for example, in the case of the dwelling-sites and burials of the Yang Shao age, and the long succession of civilizations which we were able to point out in the province of Kansu. I feel it to be my duty to relate how all these investigations began on a small scale, how they grew and branched out, because I alone am in possession of the whole development of the story.

In another respect, too, my narrative is subjective in character. I have only touched in passing certain questions which many an expert would wish to see answered, as, for example, the age of the Yang Shao civilization, and the cultural exchanges which during the late Stone age were effected right through Central Asia, and of which the painted ceramics are certainly only a small part—even if the most striking one to the field archaeologist.

My view of these great and difficult problems is in many respects the same as it was in 1923, when I wrote " An Early Chinese Culture ". But I have determined to return to these subjects in all seriousness only when the whole of the material has been studied in detail.

On the other hand I have devoted no less than three of the final chapters (XVIII–XX) of this book to an interpretation of the painted designs of the P'an Shan ceramics as magic symbols, a view which I have developed in collaboration with Dr. Hanna Rydh and Professor Karlgren. I have devoted so much space to this subject partly because it is now in the forefront of my own research and partly because these investigations seem to disclose the possibility of glimpsing in the background the conceptions and the belief which the objects symbolize. If these surmises are correct, they place a powerful weapon in our hands in our final attack upon the supreme and most difficult problems of the chronology and the migrations of these ancient civilizations.

As I come to relate the results of ten happy years in the field out in the East and of seven years in the study at home, my thoughts naturally turn with gratitude to those who rendered this work possible.

In the first place I think of our honoured China Swede, Professor Erik Nyström, who gave the impetus to my visit to China and who in many ways promoted my scientific work.

Next in order I would thank my old friend Dr. Axel Lagrelius, who created the Swedish China Research Committee in order to assist me and who, through this organization, still labours with the same high courage for my benefit and that of the East Asiatic Collections. My humble thanks are also due to the State Authorities which founded the Museum of Far Eastern Antiquities in 1926 in order to provide for my archaeological collections a home and for my work a scientific laboratory which foreign colleagues rightly envy me.

Especially do I thank His Royal Highness the Crown Prince who, as Chairman of the China Research Committee, in questions of organization piloted us through many rocky channels, and who during his stay in China in 1926 gave me many fruitful suggestions.

The two directors of the National Geological Survey of China, Dr. V. K. Ting and Dr. Wong Wen-hao, opened the way for my collecting activity by arrangements which were both beneficial to Chinese science and generous to the Swedish museums. On me personally these admirable gentlemen bestowed a friendship which never failed, despite many strains.

Many of the young Chinese geologists worked together with me in the field for long periods, prominent among them being Professor P. L. Yuan, who with admirable care executed a number of topographical maps for my work on the prehistoric sites of Northern China.

H. C. T'an, who travelled with me through Shantung in 1922, was a splendid companion and a first-class field geologist. T. O. Chu, who camped with me in 1918 among the Hsüan-Lung ores, is now Director of the Geological Survey of the two Kuang provinces. I received some time ago some of his latest publications, together with a letter in which he reminded me of the happy days when, in snow and frost, we completed our map of that ore-field.

But I also had lesser helpers out there. Yao, Liu, Chang and Chin, Chen and Pai, Chuang and Li were, most of them, originally my personal servants, who were gradually absorbed into our great collecting activities, in which they displayed great zeal, skill and personal devotion. There pass through my mind also an almost interminable series of still more humble collaborators —porters, guides, diggers. Almost all of them gave testimony to the good qualities of the Chinese race; endurance, contentment and, under normal conditions, a peaceful frame of mind.

Among the missionaries who assisted us, I would especially mention Maria Pettersson in Hsin An, Joel Eriksson of the Swedish Mongol Mission, and George Findlay Andrew in Lanchow. General Munthe in Peking and Mr. Doodha, Postal Commissioner in Lanchow, also assisted me at critical moments in their respective towns.

Professor Davidson Black holds an honoured place as a scholar and a friend. Nobody could have worked better than he on my large collection of skeletons of the Yang Shao age and of other later prehistoric finds. But his most eminent distinction is the brilliant feat of raising the Peking man from the dead.

In preparing this book Professor Wiman has assisted me with the fossil vertebrates and Professor Halle with the fossil plants.

I stand in a special debt of gratitude to Professor B. Karlgren. He not only furnished to me all the data I required from the ancient Chinese records, and very kindly read my manuscript, but he also discussed with me during the course of years all the problems which occupied my mind, and thereby gave me both inspiration and necessary criticism.

The volume forms a popular summary of numerous scientific monographs published by the National Geological Survey of China in its *Bulletin*, *Memoirs*, and, before all, *Palaeontologia Sinica*. Every student who intends to make himself thoroughly familiar with the prehistory of China should read these original monographs. A complete list of the publications of the National Geological Survey of China will be sent on application to the Publishers of this book, who are the English Agents.

FIG. 1.—Amadeus W. Grabau, First Palaeontologist of the National Geological Survey of China and Professor at Peiping University, a scholar of genius, an enthusiastic teacher and a delightful man.

CHAPTER ONE

THE FIRST SIGNS OF LIFE

IT was a little piece of stone which from the very beginning gave a definite direction to my work in China, and from this beginning my fate unfolded throughout a decade of varied and shifting change, in which the milestones bear the inscriptions : mining expert—fossil collector—archaeologist.

At the beginning of 1914 I had accepted an appointment as adviser to the Chinese Government to arrange a survey of its coalfields and ore resources, and on May 16th I began my work in the Department of Agriculture in Peking.

In the ever-changing foreign colony, with its various elements of diplomats, agents of high finance, technical experts, missionaries and adventurers, I made the acquaintance of a Danish mining engineer of the name of F. C. Mathiesen, who earned his living by doing all sorts of odd jobs, principally the investigation of coal seams and galena deposits for Chinese speculators. One day Mathiesen invited me home, and it was there that I was to see what was to prove my lucky star. On his table lay a piece of hematite ore. It was unlike anything I had ever seen before, but it resembled most the curious kind of ore which is known in English as " Kidney ore ". On examining it more closely I found that it was composed of pear-shaped bodies, consisting of thin laminae of red iron oxide, and between these large pear-shaped bodies the interstices were filled with small grains of ore, as large as linseed, and also composed of layer upon layer of iron oxide. It was a kind of hematite ore entirely new to science, and it looked rich. If there existed much of this beautiful and curious ore, it should prove a very valuable asset.

Mathiesen did not seem to know very much about this piece of ore. He had got it from his boy, whose home was in a small mountain village some tens of miles to the north of Peking. The boy declared that there was plenty of this remarkable red stone in the hills around the village where his parents lived.

This sounded extremely tempting, and I immediately began to ponder what I should do in order, very quietly, to set things moving. I could not go there without asking permission of my Chinese superiors, and I did not want to do so until I knew something certain about the ore, which might be quite valueless.

It fortunately happened that the Swedish Diamond Drill Boring Company had sent out with me a very clever and skilful man, a drilling foreman, C. F. Erikson, who knew everything between heaven and earth, from the art of finding water in solid rock to the wonderful method of reading human character from the bumps and dents of crania. I knew that, in addition to his other accomplishments, Erikson was very good at essaying ore discoveries, and I therefore proposed to Mathiesen that he and Erikson should go with the Chinese boy to the hills and examine the wonderful hematite ore *in situ*.

It turned out to be a very fortunate expedition. When Erikson returned, he reported that the beautiful red ore was a regular layer lying between sandstone, shale and limestone, and that it could be traced from hill to hill for a distance of several miles.

It was evident that we had discovered ore resources of at least one or two million tons.

I then went to the Director of the Mines Department, Mr. Chang Yi Ou, a pleasant and amiable little mining engineer, who had received his technical training in Belgium. Mine was a delicate errand, for just as I desired to find an opportunity to

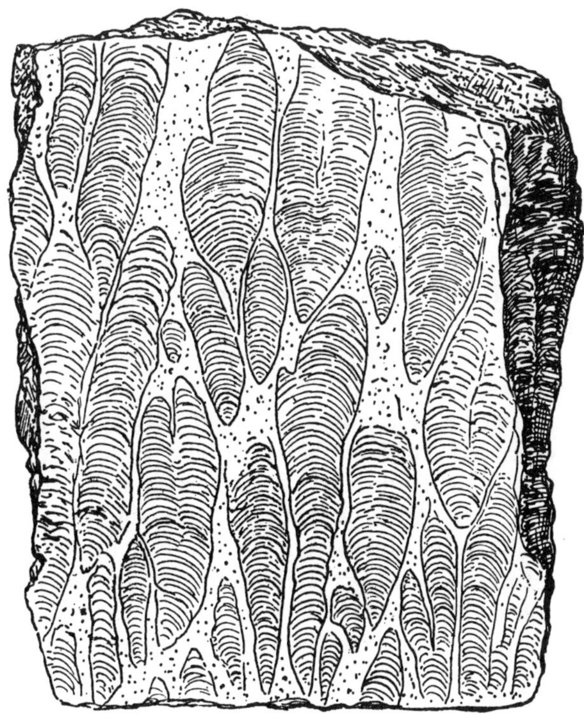

FIG. 2.—Stromatolitic ore. Hsin Yao.

examine this ore on behalf of the Chinese Government, so also it was my duty to protect as far as possible Mr. Mathiesen, on whose desk I had found the piece of stone which gave rise to the whole investigation.

"Mr. Chang", I said, "a foreigner, whose name I cannot disclose, has shown me some ore specimens which I believe to be of great interest. I cannot even tell you what kind of ore it is, nor where it is to be found. If you have confidence in me, you must first promise to give this foreigner 500 dollars if, after examination, I find that the ore is good."

He sought to draw me, but I appealed once again to his confidence.

" Very well ", said Mr. Chang, " I accept your proposal without asking you for any details."

I then placed before him the specimens of ore which Erikson had brought back. Chang's kindly eyes beamed with delight when he heard what was at stake. Half an hour later he had submitted the matter to His Excellency the Minister of Agriculture, and it was resolved that we should immediately institute an official investigation of the ore-field at Hsin Yao. A few days later I, Mathiesen and Erikson were *en route*, together with porters, for the hills, and at the end of October I was able to report to the Minister that there were in the Hsin Yao hills at least 17 million tons of fine hematite ore conveniently situated for mining.

But this was not all. We had reason to suppose that the ore-field was much more extensive than our investigation had shown. Our distinguished countryman, Dr. E. T. Nyström, now took over the work, and on November 18th he discovered very large new ore deposits at P'ang Chia Pu, about 12 miles south-west of Hsin Yao. Here the quantities of available ore probably amount to about 50 million tons, and in certain parts of the field the seam of ore shows a thickness of 3 metres. These new discoveries of iron-ore were left untouched during the following years, but towards the end of the Great War, when prices of ore had risen to the skies, it was proposed to exploit the ore in the Hsüan-Lung field, as I have named this district.

In the spring of 1918 a company was formed for mining in the great P'ang Chia Pu field, but difficulties were immediately encountered in the organization of the transport of the ore from the rugged hill districts where the thick and rich beds of ore break the surface of the ground. At the beginning of May I was ordered by the Chinese Government to assist the new company with a report on this transport problem, and for this purpose I departed for Hsüan Hua Fu, a fairly large town on the Peking-Kalgan railway, from which it was proposed to construct a branch line to P'ang Chia Pu.

I had, however, my own little secret plan for the solution of the ore problem. As early as 1914 I had observed certain geological conditions which seemed to indicate that the ore-bearing formations extend westward from P'ang Chia Pu in the direction of the railway, and I therefore conceived the possibility of finding ore in the Hsüan Hua Fu district. My eagerness to set out in search of ore was increased by the fact that just at that time I had bought from my countryman F. A. Larson a large and magnificent horse, which had come all the way from remote Ili in Central Asia, and I was full of impatience to see how this splendid animal would acquit itself in the hilly district north-east of Hsüan Hua Fu.

But in point of fact nothing very much came of my riding tour on that occasion, for I succeeded beyond all expectation in the rapidity of my search for iron-ore deposits. I had scarcely proceeded more than a few miles beyond the northern town-gate of Hsüan Hua Fu before I found in the river bed the first pieces of ore, and some hours later I found a fine complete section through the new ore-field, which I named Yen Tung Shan after one of the hills.

This unexpected discovery of workable iron ore quite near to the railway aroused no little attention in Government circles in Peking, and I received out in the field a present from the Minister of Agriculture which I have preserved as a most treasured souvenir of an interesting and eventful period of my work. Most amusing, however, was the survey and sampling of the new ore, which work I conducted during the early summer, when the mountain flora at 800 metres altitude was first flowering.

My idyllic quarters in an old water-mill, the rides to and from work, the mountain slopes with their wealth of flowers, the warm and beautiful weather, and the sense of doing productive work—all these make a singularly beautiful memory of this period.

My new discoveries at Hsüan Hua Fu agitated the minds of Peking. Two very high officials vied with each other to obtain concessions to mine this new ore, situated so conveniently near the Peking-Kalgan railway that a branch line of only a few miles length was all that was required to begin shipments of an ore which could be mined on the surface. In a short time the

Lung-Yen Company was formed to exploit the ore, and during the autumn of 1918 40,000 tons of ore were sent 1,250 kilometres to Hanyang on the Yangtse River, where large-scale smelting experiments were made with very great success. In November, however, came the armistice, accompanied by a rapid fall of prices in the ore market. Mining at Yen Tung Shan was discontinued and has never been resumed since, owing to the political disturbances in China.

The iron deposits of Yen Tung Shan occur in strata, just like coal seams. The mountain strata are only slightly inclined, and it is therefore possible to trace the ore as a connected band in the mountain cliffs for stretches of miles (Plate 1). Indeed, owing to the stratified formation of the ore it was possible for me and my collaborators to trace the seams, with some interruptions, over a distance of 82 kilometres and to show that one

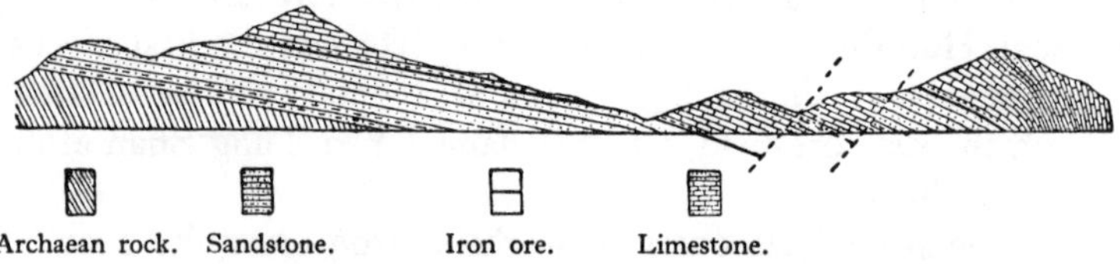

FIG. 3.—Section through Yen Tung Shan.

of the largest iron ore deposits of the world had once existed in this area, even though movements of the earth-crust, combined with destructive geological forces, have left only some tens of millions of tons of ore available for mining.

The Hsüan-Lung ore is loose and easily crumbles in the fingers to a red powder. For the greater part it is oolitic, i.e. it consists of grains of the size of linseed, which on examination prove to be composed of thin laminae, one beneath the other, in much the same way as an onion is built up.

There is, however, another type of ore, which constitutes whole seams at P'ang Chia Pu, and this ore shows a structure which places it in a class apart and without parallel in any other part of the world. It was a piece of this curious ore which I had seen on Mr. Mathiesen's desk and which had been the cause of the discovery of the Hsüan-Lung ores.

This type of ore has been called " Kidney ore ", but this

designation is very unsatisfactory, and another term, *stromatolitic ore*, somewhat difficult for laymen, has gained recognition among experts.

Stromatolitic ore (Fig. 2, p. 3) consists to a large extent of pear-shaped bodies, which appear very clearly in a vertical section through the ore seam. These pear-shaped structures are at most 5 cm. long and 1–2 cm. broad. The pears are always vertical in the seam, with the tips downward, and the tips themselves consist of a large oolitic grain, made up of layer upon layer of the red iron oxide. The pear also reveals the same structure of thin layers of iron oxide, which are all domed on top, and it is evident that the stromatolite or pear, as we shall for convenience sake call these bodies, has been formed by the further growth of the oolitic grain, which, when it reached a certain dimension, became so heavy that it could no longer be lifted by the iron depositing forces and therefore grew only in an upward direction.

In this description I have purposely used the expression " grew up " in order to indicate that the " pears " are probably *fossil remains* of a primitive vegetable or animal form, or that in any event some kind of organism contributed to the development of these characteristic bodies. If this interpretation be correct, than with the discovery of the Hsüan-Lung ores we also discovered the earliest traces of organisms in the Chinese mountain strata.

The ore seams in the Hsüan-Lung field (Fig. 3, p. 6) are embedded in sandstone and shale, and above this formation rests a limestone formation several hundred metres thick. Whilst surveying at Yen Tung Shan in the summer of 1918, I observed in this limestone some lumpy formations, with a high percentage of silica, of some centimetres section and consisting of concentric layers, which gave the whole the appearance of a large onion.

In the same vast limestone formations, which are very extensive in Northern China, I made numerous discoveries of these onion-shaped bodies in another district, and this under circumstances which deserve to be told.

In the middle of September 1920, after I had returned from a summer journey in Mongolia, I received in my home in Peking an interesting and welcome visit from two young fellow-countrymen. They were the engineer Gösta Richert, the son of the famous hydraulic engineer Professor Richert, and his young wife.

The Richerts were on a holiday tour after a period of duty in Shanghai. In their Chinese programme was also included a journey to the Yangtse River through the famous gorges which, together with the canyon of the Colorado River, belong to the most magnificent phenomena of erosion in the world.

These young Swedes, however, had too little time before their return to Sweden to undertake this very prolonged journey. It was under these circumstances that I proposed that I should be their guide to a canyon which, though it certainly could not compare with a journey through the Yangtse gorges, yet offered instead the excitement that it was uncertain whether any white man had yet made at one stretch the dangerous and difficult tour which I now proposed. Since the canyon which I proposed to visit was quite near Peking and since my programme would, according to circumstances, be either a success or a failure in a maximum period of ten days, Mr. and Mrs. Richert accepted my proposal.

In order that the reader may understand what was in my mind when I proposed this plan, it is necessary for me briefly to describe the topographical conditions north and west of Peking.

Whereas the ancient Chinese capital looks out to the east and south over an absolutely flat alluvial plain, which slopes down invisibly to the ocean, it is surrounded to the north and west by sharply broken mountainous regions with peaks rising to over 1,500 metres. Through these mountains run many rivers, which have cut deep and narrow canyons through the mountain strata, and especially through the vast limestone formations. The most important of these rivers is the Hun River, or Hun Ho, to use the Chinese name.

The course of the Hun Ho north-west of Peking is very peculiar. It flows across the 500-metre-high Huailai plateau, but turns south against the barrier of limestone mountains and breaks through them in a narrow, wild canyon gorge, several hundred metres in depth.

The lower part of the Hun Ho canyon is easily accessible, and I have, together with some Chinese geologists, made a detailed map of this part of the river. Regarding the upper part of the

PLATE 2

The Collenia-bearing limestone in the gorge of the Hun river

[*face page* 8

canyon, on the other hand, information was scarce, though it pointed to extreme inaccessibility. It was said that one could penetrate some distance into the canyon from the Huailai plateau, but that subsequently there were only steep, inaccessible mountain walls, which nobody had ever been known to pass.

This was the tempting project which the Richerts and I soon agreed to attempt together. The risk was slight, for nothing worse could happen to us than the humiliation of having to turn back.

On September 20th we departed from Peking by train for Huailai station, which was the starting point of our excursion. Two days later we entered the section of the Hun Ho valley, which is one of the most curious and exceptional of erosion valleys. Characteristic of such valleys is the curious and apparently abnormal circumstance that from a relatively low plain the river forces a way, in the form of a deep gorge, right through the mountain masses which obstruct its course. The explanation of the origin of these valleys is that they are very ancient, so ancient that the whole of the topography of the district has changed, whilst the river obstinately sticks to its old bed, and slowly, inch by inch, cuts its way through the mountain chain in proportion as the latter rises in its course. Owing to this curious origin these valleys are often very deep, steep and inaccessible.

For two days we wandered through a part of the canyon in which there were scarcely any human dwellings and where scarcely a path could be seen, so that we were obliged to scramble forward as best we could along the steep canyon walls, holding on to bushes and tree-roots.

We spent the night in a lonely cottage. Around us we had only the cliffs, several hundred metres in height, which rose up steeply and in fantastic forms above us. Below us the rushing river raced in numerous small rapids (Plate 2). In many places the precipices pushed out in perpendicular buttresses, so that we had to cross to the other side and were frequently compelled to wade the river. Fortunately we always found a fordable place and were thus able to keep our small equipment dry and in good condition.

It was during this adventurous excursion to the Hun canyon

that I found that certain strata in the several hundred metres thick limestone are full of the silicious, onion-like bodies which I had first observed on the slopes of Yen Tung Shan.

As early as 1918, when I first discovered the concentric structures in the limestone strata above the Hsüan Lung ore, I knew that similar structures had been found in mountain strata of approximately the same age in America and Europe, which in those countries had been described as remains of prehistoric coral-like animals or calcareous algae, under the generic name of *Gymnosolen*, *Cryptozoon* and *Collenia*. It thus seemed probable that in these onion-like bodies in the silicious limestone of Northern China, as also in the pear-shaped stromatolites of the hematite ore, we have to do with the earliest traces of organic life in this part of the world.

When the famous American geologist and palaeontologist A. W. Grabau came to Peking in 1920 as a teacher of his sciences at the Peking University and as a palaeontologist to the Geological Survey of China, he applied himself to an investigation of these ancient formations. To the material collected by me in the Hun Ho canyon was added other material collected by Grabau and his pupils in the Nankou pass north of Peking, and on the basis of this material Grabau described the three forms, *Collenia sinensis*, *C. cylindrica* and *C. angulata*.

We have already indicated that *Collenia* and *Cryptozoon*, etc., are very differently regarded by different writers. Some consider them akin to certain coral-like animals (*stromatopores*); others, such as Grabau, regard them as calcareous algae.[1] Holtedahl does not consider them real fossils but rather structures arising from the precipitation of lime by algae or bacteria. But even on this interpretation they yet remain what we called them in the title of this chapter, *the earliest traces of life* in Northern China.

The great German traveller, Ferd. von Richthofen, who by his expeditions during the 'sixties and 'seventies laid the foundations of our knowledge of the geology of China, differentiated

[1] Grabau, "The Sinian System", *Bulletin of the Geological Society of China*, Vol. I, 1922.
Grabau, *Stratigraphy of China*, Peking, 1923–4.

in his monumental work *China, 1877–1885*, a series of formations of old stratified rocks to which he gave the name " Sinian system ", thereby designating its rôle as a fundamental element in the rock structure of China.

Since then, it is true, it has been shown that Richthofen also included in this Sinian formation younger strata, which we now call Cambrian, but Grabau in his work, *The Sinian System*, published in 1922, has suggested that the term " Sinian " should be restricted to the pre-Cambrian formations, which other writers have called neo-Proterozoic, Algonkian, etc. He further considers that this term should be introduced as a term applying to the whole earth, similar to the names of later formations, such as Cambrian, Silurian, etc.

Thus in Northern China the Sinian system consists of a quartzite sandstone overlaid with shale containing iron-ore seams. Above them there is a thick silicious limestone with Collenia-like formations, such as we have already encountered in the Hsüan-Lung field in the Hun canyon.

A very well-known and significant development of the Sinian system is to be found in the north-western states of North America in the so-called " Belt " district, where, in a series of more than 10,000 metres thickness, are to be found not only *Collenia* but also remains of a Crustacean of the Eurypterus type, *Beltia danai*.

In Europe the Sinian series is represented by the Torredonian sandstone in Scotland, the red Jotnian sandstones of Fenno-scandia, and the stromatolitic dolomites in northern Norway.

All these primeval mountain strata in different parts of the world are characterized by the fact that fossils (with the exception of the doubtful *Collenia*) are entirely absent or very rare, as in the Belt formation of North America.

In this respect the Sinian formations are in sharp and inexplicable contrast with the next succeeding formation, the Cambrian, in which limestones and shales are often covered with fossil impressions, thus indicating an already highly developed and varied animal life.

We shall now examine some of these Cambrian and later fossil-bearing strata of Northern China.

When Ferd. von Richthofen, during one of his long expeditions in China, travelled along the shores of the Yellow Sea from Manchuria to the province of Chihli, he came to a rich coalfield at Kaiping, which first became better known to science by his account of it. In his day the coal was mined only by old-fashioned Chinese methods in small and irregular pits. When a modern company, the Kailan Mining Administration, under Anglo-Belgian direction, acquired control of this rich coalfield, the mining was completely rationalized and concentrated in a few large mines at Tongshan, Machiakou, Chaokochuang and Linshi, situated along the edge of the great trough-like structure in which the coal formation is enfolded.

In the late summer of 1914, a few months after my arrival in Peking, I had an opportunity of visiting the Kaiping basin and

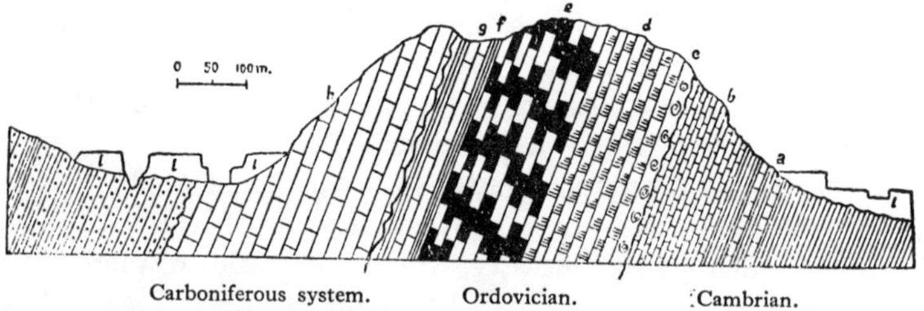

FIG. 4.—Section through the series of strata at the northern edge of the Kaiping coalfield (*By Sun and Grabau.*)

was able in an essential point—the age of the so-called Carboniferous limestone—to correct Richthofen's view of the geology of the district.

In the spring of 1916 I was sent by the Ministry of Agriculture to Kaiping to conduct final practical tests with students of the school of geology, which was training young men for appointments to the Geological Survey of China. I then spent ten days in this district with my twenty-two students, and we explored the whole of the coal basin in various directions.

After Dr. Grabau had taken the direction of palaeontological studies in China into his strong and expert hands, he instituted a more thorough investigation of the series of strata and fossils of the Kaiping area. The data which are given below are for the most part derived from his work, *The Stratigraphy of China*, Part I, 1923–4.

The mountain-forming forces, of which we shall have more to say in a succeeding chapter, have here compressed the originally horizontal strata, so that they now form a trough-like structure which the geologists call a synclinal fold. Towards the sea, in a southerly direction, the rock strata sink down under the later strata, which here cover the whole of the bed-rock, and form a low-lying plain as far as the Yellow Sea in the south.

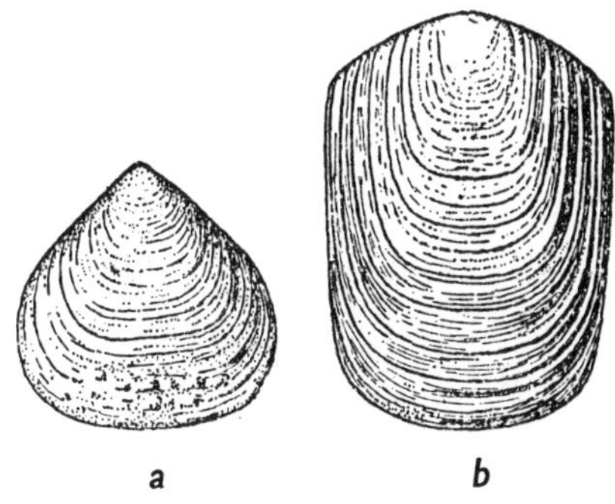

FIG. 5.—Cambrian brachiopods. *a, Obolus luanhsiensis* Grabau ; *b, Lingulella dimorpha* Sun. (Three times magnified.)

North of the coal basin itself, on the other hand, we find an undulating landscape consisting of silicious limestone. In this district we did not find any of the formations which we described under the name of *Collenia* and found north of Peking, but it is probable that further research will show that they exist here too. In any case it is quite certain, judging by the character of the rock formation, that we are dealing here with the same Sinian formation as yielded us the fossil formations in the Peking district.

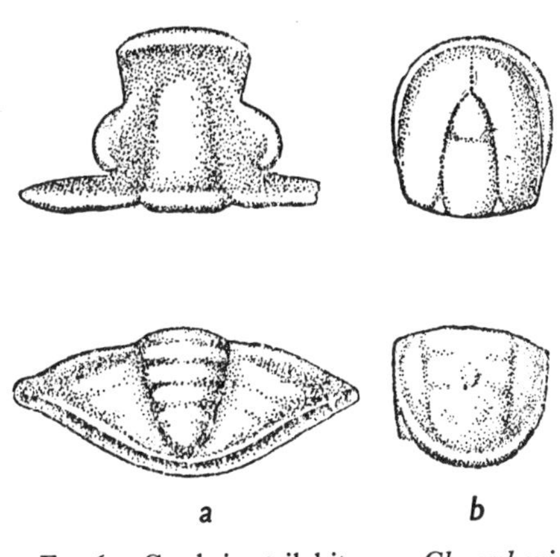

FIG. 6.—Cambrian trilobites. *a, Changshania conica* Sun ; *b, Agnostus hoi* Sun. (7 times magnified.)

Upon the Sinian limestone rests a thick and varying series of later rock strata. The lower ones are shown more in detail in Fig. 4, which is taken from the above-mentioned work of Grabau. Immediately above the Sinian formation follows a series of shales in different colours, and shale-like thinly laminated limestone. In these strata, which are known throughout the world as *Cambrian*, we find in large quantities the first absolutely indisputable fossils, brachiopods such as *Obolus luanhsiensis* and *Lingulella dimorpha*, and trilobites such as *Changshania conica* and *Agnostus hoi*. *Obolus and Lingulella* have near relations in the seas to-day, whereas the trilobites constitute a class long extinct. It is certain, in any case, that these animal forms, and many others which have been described by the young Chinese palaeontologist, Y. C. Sun, lived in a shallow marine area and that they belong to the oldest fossil-bearing formation, the Cambrian.

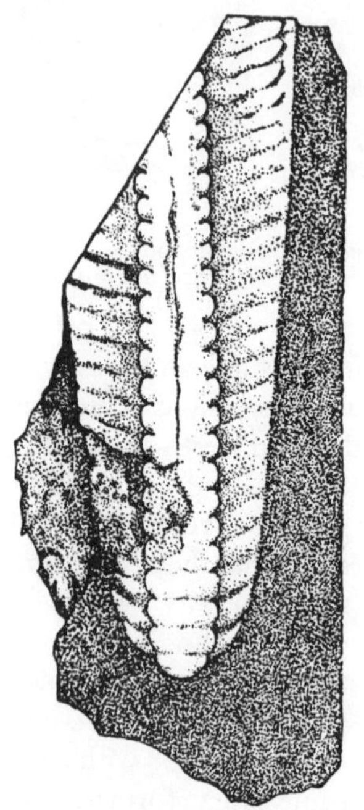

FIG. 7.—Ordovician cuttle-fish. *Actinoceras tani* Grabau. (Natural size.)

Above the Cambrian series there is a limestone formation some hundred metres thick. This limestone is of great practical importance. Especially in Tongshan, in the western part of the Kaiping field, it is quarried on a large scale and is hewn for building stone or is burnt, and during the last decades it has acquired further importance as one of the raw materials in the production of the great cement works at Tongshan. In this limestone series we observe among the fossils especially sections of *cephalopods*, such as *Actinoceras Tani*, a remote relation of the cuttle-fish of the modern seas. Also small spiral sea-shells, such as *Lophospira morrisi* and *Pagodispira dorothea*, are found in this limestone, which is again a marine deposit. This *Actinoceras* limestone belongs to the geological system which is commonly called *Ordovician*.

The Ordovician *Actinoceras* limestone is covered in turn by a stratum, 85 metres thick, of shale and sandstone, probably deposited in rivers and lakes, but there follows a marine stratum, a limestone rich in corals and brachiopods, such as *Lithostrotion kaipingense* and *Spirifer mosquensis*[1]. This coral limestone is included in the Carboniferous system. On the Carboniferous limestone rest beds of sandstone and shale, indicating continental conditions, but 35 metres above the coral lime-stone there lies a thin marine stratum with brachiopods, *Productus* and *Spiriferina chuchuani* as well as a mussel, *Pseudomonotis Mathieui*. This marine fauna belongs to the transition from the Carboniferous system to the next succeeding Permian formation. Above this thin marine stratum there succeed the continental formations, containing no less than twelve to thirteen coal seams of varying thickness.

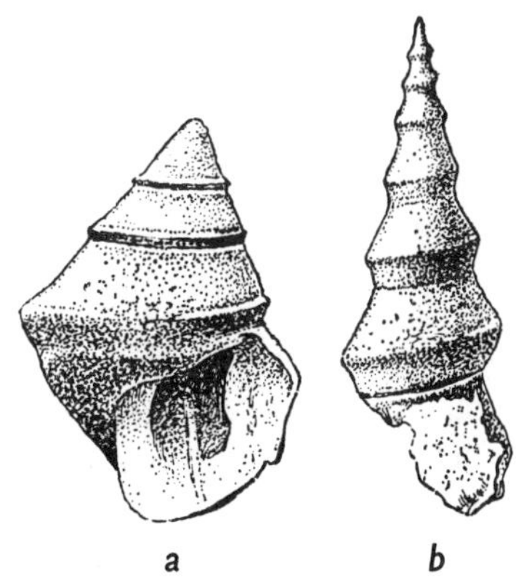

FIG. 8.—Ordovician shells. *a*, *Lophospira morrisi* Grabau ; *b*, *Pagodispira dorothea* Grabau. (Magnified double size.)

We have now rapidly surveyed a series of strata of some hundred metres thickness and have found no less than four successive marine formations, which in order of succession from the latest to the earliest are :

Permocarboniferous, with *Productus* and *Spiriferina*.

Carboniferous, coral limestone with *Lithostrotion*.

Ordovician, *Actinoceras* limestone.

Cambrian, with *Obolus*, *Lingulella* and *Changshania*.

This story would not be completely told if

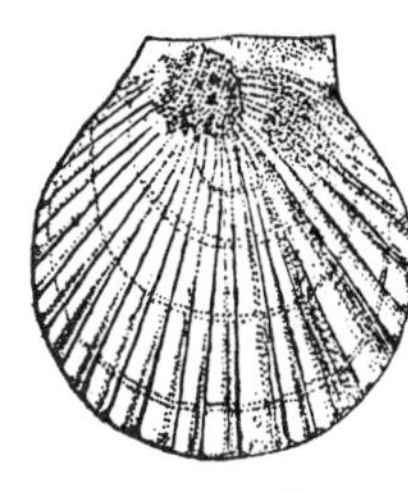

FIG. 9.—*Pseudomonotis Mathieui*. Mussel from Permocarboniferous formation of the Kaiping field.

[1] Mathieu, Delépine, Pruvost, " Observations sur le terrain houiller de Kaiping," *An. Soc. Géol. du Nord*, T. LII, p. 159, 1928.

Mathieu, who conducted exhaustive investigations in the Kaiping district, has found in the fresh-water strata a number of fish remains belonging to the genera *Megalichthys*, *Rhizodopsis*, *Rhadinichthys*, as well as a number of insect remains. So also arthropods of the *Merostom* group were first found by me, *Eurypterus chinensis*, afterwards also found by Mathieu.

I omitted to mention that Dr. Grabau's keen eye discovered several disconformities in these marine formations. It looks as if the district had on three, and possibly four, or more, occasions, lain above the sea-level and that at certain stages destructive, or as the geologists call them, erosive, forces had destroyed the exposed strata. We thus encounter here a repeated interaction between the depositing and erosive forces, and we see how the land time after time has sunk below the sea level, receiving new marine strata containing the living organisms of a new period. We are justified in giving here two quotations which Dr. Grabau employed as a motto for his *Stratigraphy of China*.

The first was written by Ko Hung in the fifth century and reads, " Three times I have seen the Eastern Ocean transformed into land with mulberry trees."

The second Chinese author, Chu Hsi, writes in the twelfth century, " I have seen shells and mussels in the high mountains, some of them appearing in stones. This shows that the stones are primitive earth. Shells and mussels belong to the water, so the low has been made high and the soft has been changed into hard."

If we read carefully the above account of the history of the Kaiping neighbourhood we shall see that the sea predominated during the Cambrian and Ordovician periods. With the appearance of the Carboniferous period continental conditions prevailed. Only during two short intervals did the district again fall below the sea level, but the *Productus*-bearing stratum under the coal seams is the last trace of marine activity. From the beginning of the Permian period until our own time this district has, so far as we know, been firm land, even if in modern times the Yellow Sea is almost within sight of Kaiping.

FIG. 10.—The Kaiping Tip.

CHAPTER TWO

PREHISTORIC SWAMP FORESTS

LET us now return to the Tongshan mine. It is a morning in the beginning of June and the dry heat is thrown back from the walls of the houses and from the pavements. The chimneys belch forth their black smoke, the engine-house roars, and the pit lifts deliver empty trucks to the depths and return others filled with coal. But it is not only coal that is thrown up from the depths. It is inevitable that as work proceeds some part of the surrounding black, thin shale should also be hewn and brought up. This useless material is carried up to an immense tip, which rises up like a pyramid and is visible far around. All day long the small trucks glide up to the end of the track which projects from the top of this pyramid of stone. There the contents are tipped, and with a thundering noise, accompanied by dust, roll down the steep side, often with long leaps.

At twelve o'clock the shrill sound of a steam hooter cleaves the din of work. Then the trucks stop on the top of the pyramid and its sides become populous instead with dirty little boys who have been waiting for the midday signal to climb up the steep sides in search of any bits of coal which may have been left in the masses of stone delivered from the mine. These are the children of the miners, who try in this manner to collect a little fuel for their poor homes.

When I first came to Tongshan in August 1914 I soon found that the coal shale of the great tip was full of plant imprints and I engaged the small boys to collect them for me. In this way I was enabled to sit at the foot of the pyramid and make a selection and for a few pence to acquire all I wanted.

Our first collections from the Kaiping district were unfortunately lost in the Swedish steamer *Peking*, which went down in a typhoon in September 1919 on the south coast of China. But I made a new collection in the following year. On the basis of this collection, and of his own observations on the spot, as well as with the guidance of Mathieu's investigations, Professor T. G. Halle has kindly given the following account of the Kaiping flora :

> The fossil plants of the Kaiping area originate in the latter part of the Carboniferous age and the beginning of the succeeding Permian period. They are on the average somewhat later than the Carboniferous flora in England and the rest of Europe, but they have the same general character. At that time there were still no deciduous trees, flowering herbs or grass, and in the Kaiping area scarcely any coniferous trees either. The vegetation consisted mainly of vascular cryptogams and a few groups of primitive gymnosperms. Among the vascular cryptogams we notice *Equisetum*, a species related to the modern *Lycopodium* and ferns as well as an extinct class (*Sphenophyllales*). Our modern *Equisetum*, *Lycopodium*, *Selaginella*, etc., are all herbs and usually small and inconsiderable, but the closely related forms of the Carboniferous age were as a rule large trees with trunks sometimes reaching two metres in diameter. Ferns, which played an even greater rôle, also differed greatly from those of to-day. A considerable part of the fern-like leaves are, however, now regarded as having belonged to the *pteridosperms*, which resemble ferns superficially, but had real seeds on the leaves. Furthermore we note *Cordaites*, an extinct class of large and beautiful trees with long, thin, often band-like leaves. Finally there are a couple of forms of *cycadophytes*, a division of the vegetable kingdom which is now represented, among others, by the species *Cycas*, whose leaves are commonly used in wreaths. The cycadophytes otherwise belong principally to the succeeding periods of the earth's history.
>
> At the time when the Kaiping coal deposits were formed, the geographical conditions of the earth were very peculiar, not to say abnormal. Over the whole of the northern hemisphere, except

Landscape of the age of the Kaiping flora. Reconstruction, under the direction of Prof. T. G. Halle, by the artist Sven Ekblom

[*face page* 18

Lower India, the luxurious Carboniferous flora predominated, which is evidence of a warm and damp climate (Plate 3). In Lower India and all parts of the world south of the Equator there extended vast coverings of inland ice, and when it melted away there developed a vegetation of a peculiar character. The Permo-Carboniferous flora of the Kaiping area and the rest of China belongs to the northerly province, but shows some peculiar features which may possibly indicate that the line of division was not very remote. This peculiar character is more pronounced in the somewhat later deposits, which were the special subject of our study in Shansi.

In the summer of 1919 I sent two of my collectors, Yao and Chang, to Shansi in order to look for various kinds of fossils. In a little village named Chen Chia Yü, situated only five miles east of the provincial capital Taiyuanfu, they discovered plant-bearing strata. From these they brought some fine specimens in which, among other forms, I recognized *Gigantopteris nicotianaefolia*, a peculiar, very large-leafed, fern-like plant (pteridosperm ?) which was also discovered by Richthofen in the province of Hunan and was described by the German scholar Schenk.

At this time a young Swedish geologist of the name of Erik Norin visited Professor E. T. Nyström, the founder of the Nyström Institute for Scientific Research in Shansi, at Taiyuanfu. He had already won a reputation by his geological research in Shansi, embodied in a very important model treatise on certain alkaline eruptive types of rock. I proposed to Norin to undertake a systematic investigation of the coal-bearing formation in the district of Taiyuanfu, in order, beginning with the remarkable and well-preserved plants from Chen Chia Yü, to investigate the chronology, stratum by stratum, of the Permo-Carboniferous floras.

The two works which Norin published as a result of the investigation thus initiated placed their author in the front rank of younger geologists—a distinction which he subsequently confirmed by his brilliant investigations in the Himalayas, and as a member of the Sven Hedin expedition.[1]

Norin not only surveyed and investigated in detail a series of deposits almost a thousand metres thick, but also reported on

[1] E. Norin, "The late Palaeozoic and Early Mesozoic Sediments of Central Shansi", *Bull. Geol. Survey, China*, No. 4, 1922. Norin, "The Litological Character of the Permian Sediments of the Angara Series in Central Shansi", *Geol. Fören. Stockholm Förh.*, Bd. 42, 1924.

the climatic conditions under which these rocks were formed. He also collected from a large number of successive series an immense and singularly well-preserved mass of largely unknown and extremely remarkable plant forms.

The field of fossil plants disclosed by Yao's discovery of the Chen Chia Yü flora, and investigated in detail by Norin, is one of the richest and most remarkable hitherto made known to science. Fortunately the botanical work on this copious and well-preserved material has been as superb as the field work. In a handsome volume *Palaeozoic Plants from Central Shansi* in the series " Palaeontologia Sinica ", 1923, Professor T. G. Halle has presented the results of his many years of work on this immense material. The flora comprises, in addition to some thirty incompletely represented forms, 103 species, which are sufficiently well represented to be capable of classification, and of these no less than 70 are new to science and have been named by Halle in this work.

The most striking feature of this ancient plant world is that, especially in the topmost part of the plant-bearing series of deposits, by far the largest number of species is known only in Eastern Asia, and many of them only in central Shansi. Such forms are the horsetail plants of the *Annularites* class, the ferns *Chansitheca*, *Emplectopteris*, and especially *Gigantopteris*, as well as certain of the new genera set up by Halle, *Norinia*, *Astrocupulites*, *Nystroemia* and the peculiar *Tingia*, of which the position in the plant system is not yet clearly established.

A very special interest attaches to *Gigantopteris*, which has given its name to the whole of the flora, and whose structure and manner of growth have been interpreted in a most fascinating manner by Halle in an essay published in 1929, " On the habit of the Gigantopteris ", in the *Transactions of the Geological Society of Stockholm*.

Gigantopteris was probably a fern-like *pteridosperm* of immense size (Fig. 11). It had double-bladed composite leaves, and in the earliest known form the folioles were so like tobacco leaves that Schenk gave the species the name *G. nicotianaefolia*. These folioles attain surprising dimensions, and Halle considers it probable that the whole leaf may sometimes have been more than one metre broad.

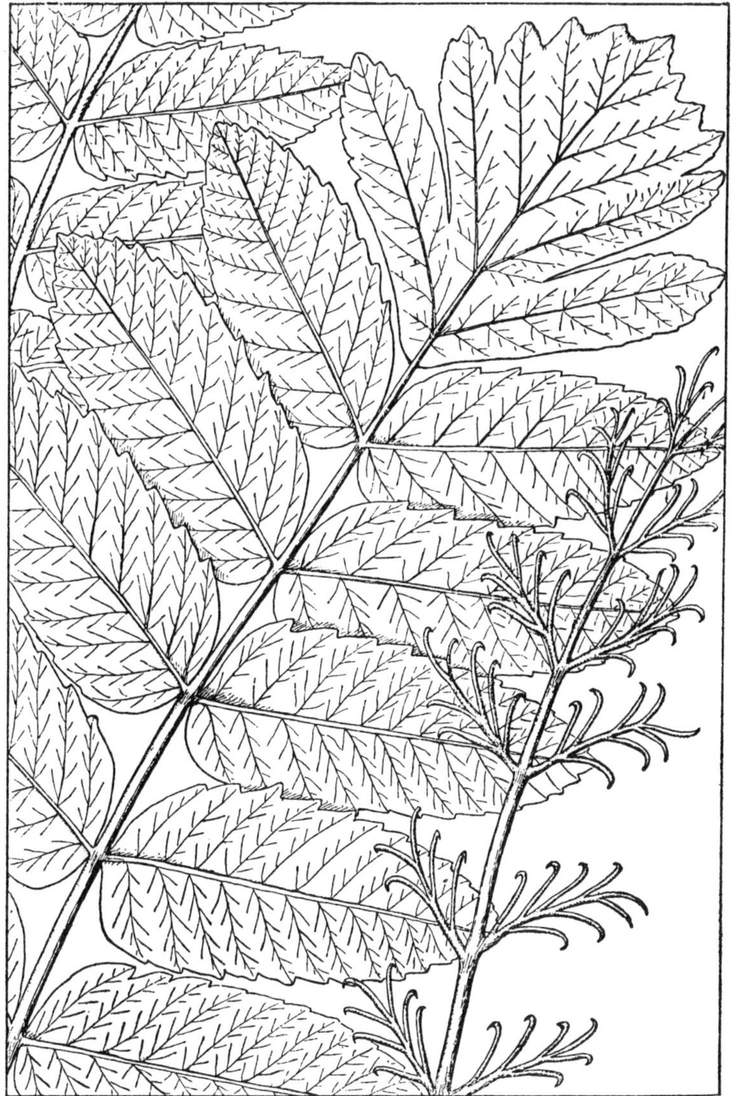

FIG. 11.—Reconstruction of *Gigantopteris* by Halle.

In certain *Gigantopteris* leaves the folioles were transformed into narrow strings with sharp crooks at the tip. From this remarkable structure, which Halle has admirably revealed in a schematic drawing, which is here reproduced by his permission, he concludes that the plant was a creeper, a kind of liane, of which the immense leaves crept up to the tops of the *Codaites* and other arboreal forms. Such a plant as *Gigantopteris* can scarcely have existed under other conditions than those of a tropical climate, and the latter is also indicated by the studies which Norin has made of chemical weathering in the rock series in which these plants lie embedded.

I shall now revert to modern times and address myself especially to those who have visited the great and beautiful imperial city of Peking. No visitor to Peking can have neglected to take an evening walk along the town wall above the Wagons Lits Hotel.

He will certainly remember how beyond Shui Men, the Water Gate, there runs a broad, rather steep, road up to the summit of the mighty wall. We are now standing on the broad tiled footpath which runs between the two great gates of the neighbouring Chien Men, in the west, and remote Hata Men, far away in the east. Up here the noise of the streets comes to us only as a distant hum; only an occasional puff of its dust reaches us, and the thousand odours of the city lie below in the depths. Peking lies beneath us like an immense park, with the yellow glazed roofs of the imperial palaces embedded in green, and down to the south the blue-violet top-hat of the Temple of Heaven rises up above the panorama of the city.

But far away to the west the horizon is formed by a blue mountain range. The almost complete absence of river or lake in Peking is very agreeably compensated by the presence of this mountain frame, the Western Hills, which lie at a convenient distance for excursions of a day or more.

The imperial city itself lies on a plain which is only about 50 metres above the sea level. This semi-circular plain is a depression within which the rocks have sunk along great fault lines into the depths and have subsequently been overlaid by deposits, during the Tertiary and subsequent periods, of clay, gravel and the peculiar fine dust, brought by the wind, which the learned call loess. On this loose earth the capital city was built.

But, as has been said, around this great depression rise the Western Hills, with peaks reaching to 1,500 metres in height.

On the first foothills of these mountains, where a spring surges out from the limestone cliff, lies the Summer Palace, and beyond, in the mountain valleys, we find famous temples, which afford rest and recreation to the visitor and delight the eye athirst for beauty.

This outer ring of the Western Hills is known to everybody who has sojourned in Peking. But what lies within the mountain ranges has been seen by only a few foreigners.

Certain places in these mountains possessed in ancient times a special reputation for the mineral wealth which they furnished to the capital. Thus the limestone hills around Hun Ho and at Chou K'ou Tien supplied all the lime required for building the palaces and houses of the city. One little mountain valley furnished slates, and far away in the south-west there are some low mountain ridges from which were quarried the immense blocks of white marble which, modelled into columns, fabulous monsters and balustrades, adorn the Forbidden City.

But the most valuable gift of the Western Hills to Peking is coal, which now reaches the city by the Hankow or Mentoukou railways, though it was formerly hauled out of the mountain valleys by hundreds of sooty and weary camels, which in endless succession tramped their way along the dusty roads.

Most famous of the coalfields of the Western Hills was Chai T'ang, which supplied excellent anthracite to the Imperial household. It was my first commission as the Government's mining expert in 1914, during the blazing hot days of June, to visit this coalfield. I was there on two subsequent occasions in 1918 and 1920, once during the spring and once during the late autumn, so that I know the country in all its varying garbs.

Most memorable were the April days of 1918, when the apricot groves were in blossom. But the spring colouring was not infrequently veiled by dust storms, which obscured the sun and filled the air with fine dust, so that it became impossible for us to work for the rest of the day.

It was here in Chai T'ang that I made my first acquaintance

with the curious Chinese method of mining coal. Wherever signs of coal are seen on the surface the Chinese dig themselves in through a narrow downward passage, in which they can only move on all fours. Bending low, or on hands and feet, I have crawled through these narrow passages, in which the air is smoky from the sooty oil lamps and stinks of the perspiration or excreta of the workers. Some of the mines of the Chai T'ang coalfield produce a highly esteemed anthracite, but the deposits are irregular and the coal-bearing formation is traversed by volcanic rocks.

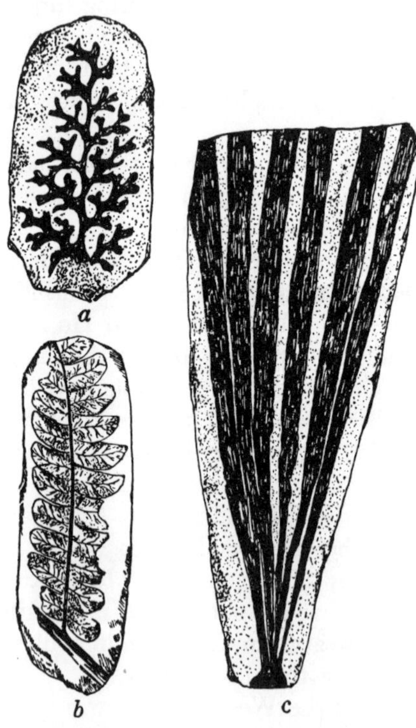

FIG. 12.—Jurassic plants from Chai T'ang. *a*, *Coniopteris tatungensis* Sze (n. sp.); *b*, *Cladophlebis* cf. *whitbyensis*; *c*, *Phoenicopsis speciosa* Hr., related to *Gingko*.

Just as at Kaiping, there are also here, in the deposits surrounding the coal seams, and especially in the loose sandstones, masses of plant imprints, mostly of ferns. These deposits belong, however, to much later stages in the world's history, to the Jurassic period, and the flora which we find there is of quite a different kind. The considerable collections which I made at Chai T'ang in 1914 and 1918 were unfortunately lost in the steamer *Peking*, the foundering of which I have already related. I therefore returned for the third time in 1920 and, together with my Chinese boys, made a new collection, of which Professor Halle has kindly given the following account:

The fine collections from Chai T'ang reveal a typical Jurassic flora. The large arboreal cryptogams which occurred in the earlier fossil floras of the Kaiping district and of Shansi are now extinct, as also are the pteridosperms and cordaites, as well as other peculiar plant types of the Palaeozoic era. But the flora is still very unlike that of modern times. Deciduous trees, flowering herbs and grass are still missing. Ferns are represented by several large and beautiful forms, all belonging to now extinct genera. The greater part of the flora consists, however, of *cycadophytes*, *conifers* and *gingko* plants.

During the Jurassic period the whole earth possessed a uniform vegetation. The climatic differences which existed between the northern and southern hemispheres when the above described fossil flora of Kaiping and Central Shansi flourished were now obliterated, and in China, Europe and India and the Antarctic much the same kinds of plants grew. During the succeeding periods this uniformity of vegetation was broken down and the modern floral areas began to develop.

The last retreat of the remains of the Jurassic flora was to be found just in Eastern and Southern Asia. Especially interesting is the history of the gingko plants. They are perhaps more plentiful in Chai T'ang and in other contemporary deposits in China, Siberia and Central Asia than in other Jurassic floras, and they probably survived longest in Eastern Asia. Even as late as the Tertiary period—the period which immediately preceded the ice age—these forms existed in Europe, North America and even the Arctic regions, but now there only remains one species, the *Gingko biloba*, which is found in China and Japan. The Gingko tree is not even authentically known in the wild state, but it has been cultivated since time immemorial round the temples. Thanks to this circumstance it is still to be found as a living fossil, which fact has made it possible to interpret the remains, preserved in rock deposits, of a large plant group which was characteristic of the flora of the Jurassic age in the same districts.

The reader and I will now journey to a new district of Northern China. We travel by one of the great railway lines from Peking to Tientsin. We have seen the outer harbour of Tientsin and the salt works at Tongku, where the dry air and constant sunshine of Northern China dry out masses of salt from the sea water, which is pumped by curious windmills into shallow basins. We have also travelled through the Kaiping area, with its rich peasant villages, its branch lines, power transmission and chimneys, which indicate to us the well-known coal-mines. Then, over a railway bridge, on which many a struggle took place during the recent wars, we pass across the memorable Luan river to the watering place Peitaiho and the great coaling port of Chin Wang Tao.

At Shan Hai Kuan we see the Great Wall, the mightiest structure on earth, sinking down to the sea from the last of the hills. And now the train rolls on over the Manchurian plain, so near to the sea that we can glimpse its blue gleaming surface from time to time, whilst on our left we perceive the low hills over which in ancient times ran the palisades, a bulwark intended to keep back the wild nomads of the steppes from the imperial road along the coastal plain.

Up there in one of the limestone mountains is the grotto where the people of the Stone Age practised their ritual cults, including human sacrifice—a story which I shall relate in Chapter XI.

Now we are approaching the fertile agricultural land of Manchuria, the immeasurably rich seed land from which, during the last fifteen years, Chang Tso Lin took money and natural resources for his campaigns in China Proper. At the Liao River, over which we now roll on, he checked Kuo Sung Lin, the young general who rebelled against him, and soon we shall have a view of the real capital of Chang, Mukden, on the outskirts of which in 1928 a mine explosion of terrific violence, caused by an unknown hand, tore the old robber general to shreds on the last occasion on which he approached the town from which he derived his strength.

Mukden, or Fengtien as the Chinese call it, is memorable blood-drenched soil. Here the Manchus built their first capital where, like the later Chang, they forged the weapons with which they conquered China. Here are their early imperial tombs, round which Russians and Japanese in 1905 fought out a trench warfare which in duration and manslaughter foreboded the horrors of the Great War.

It was not, however, the extensive old imperial city with its Japanese colony and the great arsenal erected by Chang Tso Lin which drew us to this territory. Our journey continues by a branch-line to Fushun, a famous coal mine which, under Japanese direction, vies with the Kaiping field in supplying Eastern Asia with good coal. To the miner, Fushun's chief merit is a great coal seam, which is no less than 40 metres thick, which is certainly unique and, though it makes hewing difficult, yet on the other hand concentrates a vast quantity of coal in a small space.

For us, whose mission it is to explore the fossil floras of China, the dark shales superimposed on the coal deposits are the goal of our long journey, for these black coal shales are a gigantic herbarium in which we can learn of a third and later stage of the history of Chinese plant life.

The first plant remains from Fushun were collected by the Russian geologist J. Edelstein, and his collection was described in 1906 by J. V. Palatin in the *Transactions of the Russian Mineralogical Society*.

In a mining journal published by Japanese geologists in Dairen in Manchuria a description was given of the Fushun coalfield and a number of additional fossil denominations were given.

In the summer of 1919 the geologist T. O. Chu, of the Geological Survey of China, undertook at my request a collecting expedition to Fushun and assembled some excellent material, which is described by Dr. R. Florin in a treatise, *Zur alttertiären Flora der südlichen Mandschurei*, in "Palaeontologia Sinica", 1922. It is from Dr. Florin's expert disquisition that I have drawn all the information here given concerning the Fushun flora.

In the study of this Manchurian coal flora we advance to a stage in the history of the development of the earth in which the plant world has already in its main features assumed a modern character. We should remember that the older floras which we have already studied, the Permian flora of Kaiping and Taiyuanfu, as well as the flora of Chai T'ang, belong to very remote eras, the earliest and the middle, of the earth, during which the lower plant forms, related to our modern mosses, horsetail plants, ferns, and conifers, predominated.

With the transition from the Cretaceous age, which marks the end of the middle period of the development of the earth, to the Tertiary age there occurred a rapid and comprehensive change in the living organisms of the whole earth. In our next chapter we shall see how our investigations and our collections in China reveal that in that part of the world also the higher animal forms of life developed rapidly. The giant saurians, the dinosaurs, which had hitherto been lords of the earth, rapidly died out. In their place the modern kings of beasts, the mammals, which until then had existed in small-sized forms, as it were in obscurity, rapidly assumed the power which the vanishing dynasty of saurians had left behind.

It is perhaps not altogether inconceivable that this radical change in animal life is connected with an equally profound and synchronous development of plant life. Animal life is of course entirely dependent upon plant life, and it seems possible that the dinosaurs did not thrive on the new flora which developed at the end of the Cretaceous age.

In any case it is well known that at the beginning of the Tertiary period, the age of mammals, a new era began also for the flora, which was greatly enriched by the higher flowering plants and deciduous trees.

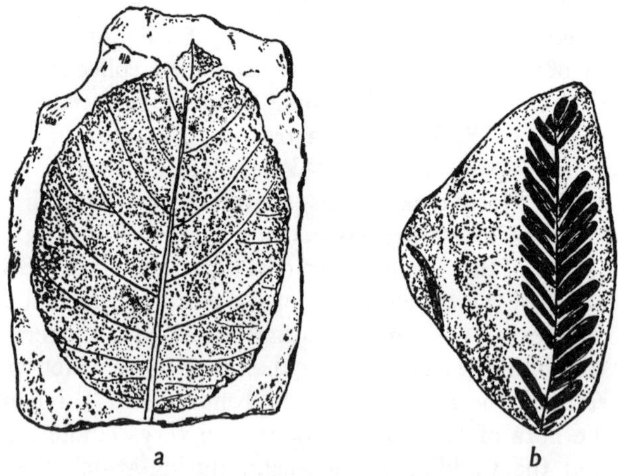

FIG. 13.—Tertiary plants from the Fushun coalfield near Mukden. *a*, *Alnus kefersteinii* Ung.; *b*, *Sequoia langsdorfii* Brongn.

It is such a Tertiary flora which, for the first time in our studies of Chinese plant life, we encounter on examination of the coal shale slabs from Fushun. It is true that we find ferns, such as the climbing *Lygodium* and the *Osmunda* and *Dryopteris* shooting from the ground. In addition, two remarkable conifers, one a near relation to the modern redwood, *Sequoia langsdorfii*, and the other the Tertiary marsh cypress, *Glyptostrobus europaeus*, are of special importance in the Fushun flora, though the majority of the plant forms found belong to the foliiferous trees. Among them we find a poplar, *Populus glandulifera*, a relation of our walnut tree, an alder, two forms which remind us of the hornbeam and the hazel, two members of the beech family, one related to the Japanese keakin, an elm-like tree, and one related to the Swedish water elder. Commonest among the leaf impressions are the beech, *Fagus feroniae*, and one of a conifer, *Sequoia*. Of other forms there are only isolated leaves. Dr. Florin assumes that the *Sequoia*, not only by its numbers, but also by its probably gigantic stature, dominated the landscape, whilst the other conifer, *Glyptostrobus*, like its modern descendants, flourished best by marshy river beds. Similarly other forms, such as *Osmunda* and the elm, seem to point to damp soil.

On the whole, the Fushun flora shows considerable indications of the old world temperate zone and nothing points to really tropical, or even sub-tropical, conditions. It is interesting, however, that we can also observe elements of an American type among which the *Sequoia* should especially be mentioned. From the general composition of the flora Dr. Florin concludes that it existed under conditions somewhat similar to these now prevailing on the west coast of North America.

This South Manchurian Tertiary flora is related to certain plant associations of about the same age, but from widely separated parts of the earth, such as the flora at Menat, by Puy-de-Dôme in France, which is regarded as belonging to the transition between Eocene and Oligocene, just as in the case of the flora at Vršovic, by Laun, in Bohemia. Many old Tertiary floras of the United States and Canada have much in common with the Fushun plants, but most striking is the resemblance to the probably Eocene flora of Alaska, which has no less than nine species in common with that of Fushun.

It is also of great climatological interest that many of the Fushun plants have long been known in Spitzbergen and Greenland. It was one of the most remarkable discoveries of the Swedish polar expeditions that the sandstone deposits in those polar regions, where nowadays ice rules and the flora is limited in the main to herb-like plants, are specked with magnificent impressions of fossil forests, in the tree forms of which we should especially notice the *Sequoia langsdorfii*, with which we are so familiar in Fushun. This Tertiary conifer has its modern counterparts in North America, and these two sequoia forms are by far the largest of all modern growths. The redwood, *Sequoia sempervirens*, grows in the Californian coastal regions, where it sometimes reaches a height of 115 metres and a diameter, breast high, of 5 metres. The age of some of these trees has been put at 1,300 years.

The second modern species, *Sequoia gigantea*, also belongs to the Californian flora, but grows high up on the western slopes of the Sierra Nevada, 1,500–2,600 metres above the sea level. This

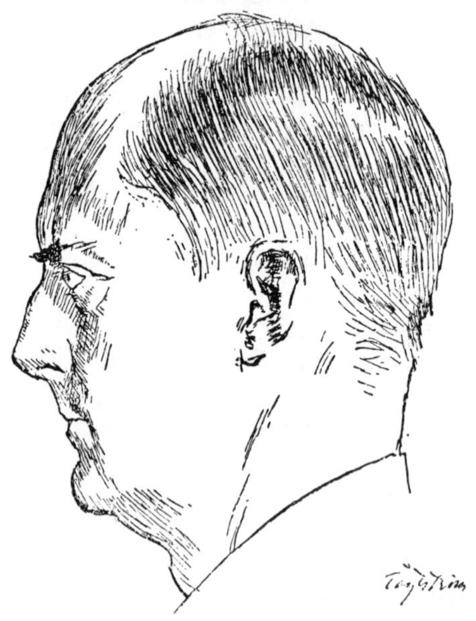

FIG. 14.—Professor T. G. Halle, who described the *Gigantopteris* flora of Shansi and who preserves in his department of the Riksmuseum, Stockholm, part of the fossil plants collected by us in China.

form also has a height of 100 metres or more, and the diameter near the ground may be as much as 12 metres. Their age has been estimated at 3,000 years for the oldest trees, and in one case it was possible by counting the annual rings to determine the age with a fair degree of accuracy at 3,148 years.

The extension of the rich and lofty Tertiary flora over the northern hemisphere right up to the polar regions is a climatological problem of great interest, and the phenomenon gained in universality when Otto Nordenskjöld, during the Swedish Antarctic expedition, 1901–3, found on Seymour Island a Tertiary flora with abundant foliiferous trees.

Many scientists have endeavoured to solve this riddle of fossil climates. Some have supposed that the axis of the earth in former ages was differently inclined through the globe than in modern times and that consequently the position of the poles was different. Others have sought a solution in the changes of the composition of the atmosphere, others again in the variation of intensity of the sun's rays or in periodic changes of other astronomical factors. But we must humbly confess that our knowledge is still too incomplete to solve this riddle of antiquity.

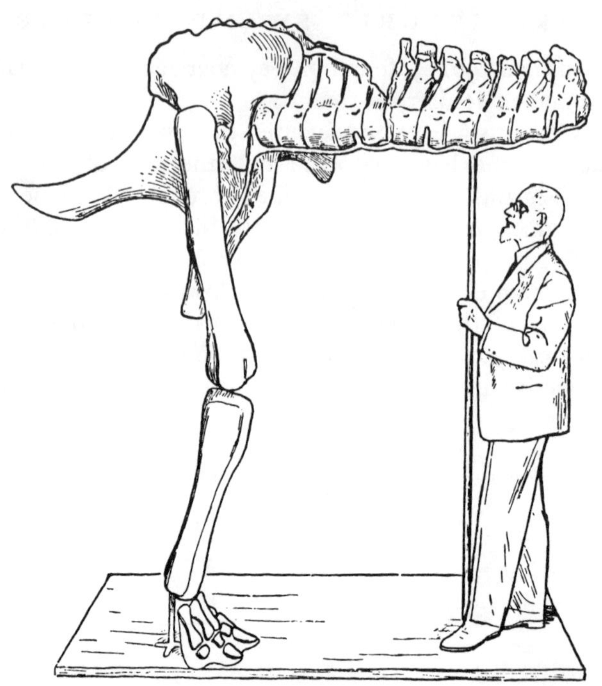

FIG. 15.—Professor Wiman and the rear part of the Helopus.

CHAPTER THREE

THE GIANT SAURIANS IN SHANTUNG AND THE FIRST MAMMALS

As I sit here and look back on the years of collecting in China it is amusing to remember how on two occasions during my work a bit of stone furnished the impulse to an advance into a new field of inquiry.

First, at the beginning of everything, it was the little bit of hematite that I saw on Mathiesen's desk and of which I have spoken in my first chapter.

Then, many years later, it was a block of sandstone in the Geological Museum in Peking which led us into entirely new paths of research.

During one of the first years of the Geological Survey a German mining engineer, W. Behagel, contributed to the collections a block of sandstone, about 50 cm. long, and containing three large vertebrae of some prehistoric animal. He also gave us the important information that the block had come from the Meng Yin district of the province of Shantung.

At first we were not quite sure what kind of vertebrate it was which had left a small portion of its skeleton in this block of sandstone, but when my collaborator, Dr. Zdansky, saw it, he thought it probable that it belonged to a giant saurian, a dinosaur, and when we had an opportunity of showing the block to Dr. Walter Granger, chief palaeontologist of the great American expedition to Mongolia, he fully confirmed Dr. Zdansky's opinion.

There was a great attraction in this discovery, which pointed the way to finds of a kind unknown to us and to geological deposits, probably belonging to the Cretaceous system, which was unknown at that time in China. I therefore agreed with Dr. Wong, the Director of the China Geological Survey, that I should, together with the geologist T'an, carry out a reconnaissance in Shantung towards the end of 1922.

We left Peking on November 28th by train via Tientsin and arrived at Taianfu about midnight. Tai An is quite a large town, situated on the Tientsin–Pukow railway, and is principally famous as the meeting-place of the thousands of pilgrims and tourists who come every year to make the ascent of the most important of China's five sacred mountains, Tai Shan, which rises to a height of 1,450 metres due north of the town, with the pilgrim's road clearly visible all the way to the temple-crowned summit.

In travelling around China we soon found that every district has its own method of transporting the traveller. In Southern China one travels by boat on the innumerable rivers. In Mongolia horses and camels are the mode of locomotion. Over a large part of the rough roads of Northern China one is shaken up in the small Peking carts or one lies and dozes in a palanquin borne between two mules. But if one wishes to travel in Shantung one is conveyed in push-carts. The native of Shantung is tough, hardy and ready to do any kind of coarse and heavy work which will provide for himself and his family. This hardened and thrifty people has very few domestic animals. All that the soil can produce is absorbed in feeding the population, with the natural consequence that the Shantung coolie is willing to harness himself to a cart, one in the traces and one pushing behind. If the wind is favourable the economical coolie likes to rig up a small sail to assist him. Two travellers can sit in the large and broad cart, or else one lays one's luggage on one side and occupies the other side oneself. It is a rough and bumpy conveyance until one becomes accustomed to it, but it moves quickly, so that one must almost run if one wishes to take exercise by following it instead of riding in it.

In this manner T'an and I made our entry into the vales of Shantung on a push-cart.

From Tai An we were conveyed south and south-east, first over the plain and afterwards over a simple but monumental landscape consisting of mountain ridges running in a north-west and south-east direction and separated from each other by broad and fertile valleys.

For several days we looked for dinosaur bones in the Meng-Yin district without finding any traces of them, but December 3rd was our red-letter day, when we found the rock formation which was to furnish us with the finest monsters of the whole of our six years of collecting. We were then living in a village of the name of Ao Yen Chen in the Meng Yin valley. I had gone out in the morning to reconnoitre the northern slopes, whilst T'an made inquiries in the villages of the plain towards the south. When I returned to our quarters at midday I found a note from T'an informing me that he had found " dragon's bones " in the neighbourhood of a little village called Ning Chia Kou.

The dinosaur bones appear in a series of deposits of green-grey sandstone, which forms a very curious landscape of small rounded hills, entirely without vegetation, and which thus look like a piece of desert country right out on the Shantung plain (Plate 4). It is principally the rapid crumbling of the rocks by weathering which prevents vegetation from gaining a hold. This desert landscape at Ning Chia Kou reminds me in a high degree of the so-called " bad lands " of North America, which, together with our district and the desert of Mongolia, have the common feature that the barren rock deposits easily expose to the scientist their contents of the bones of prehistoric monsters.

We had extraordinary luck when in Ning Chia Kou we met

"Bad Lands." Dinosaur area at Meng Yin in Shantung

[*face page* 34

the Catholic missionary of Meng Yin, Father Alfred Kaschel, who reported to us that another German Father, R. Mertens, had observed and recognized ten years previously the first dinosaur in China. Subsequently discoveries of the utmost importance had been made in other places in Chinese territory. Thus the Russian palaeontologist, A. N. Krystofovich, had discovered in 1914 in the extreme north of Manchuria (in the province of Heilungkiang) by the Amur River a dinosaur deposit which was systematically worked during the summers of 1915–17 by expeditions sent out from Petrograd. By these noteworthy investigations, too little noticed outside Russia, owing to the confusion of the war, three or four species, representing widely different groups of dinosaurs, were added to our knowledge.

In the summer of 1922 Roy Chapman Andrews, as representative of the Natural History Museum in New York, began the series of great expeditions to Mongolia which were crowned with unique success and may rightly be characterized as the most important field research of modern times. On one of the very first days, the palaeontologist of the expedition, Dr. Walter Granger, made the earliest discovery of Mongolian dinosaurs, and thanks to this honoured scientist and his technical assistants we now know a number of forms, of which one, the comparatively small *Protoceratops andrewsi*, has won singular distinction owing to the fact that not only was its skeleton found, but also its excellently preserved eggs, which was something entirely new in the history of dinosaur research.

Let us now return to the collecting in Shantung. Our discoveries in the Meng Yin valley spurred us on to new efforts. T'an, who had extensive and reliable knowledge of the geology of Shantung, had shown me large areas in the eastern part of the province, north of the well-known port of Tsingtao, under which there probably existed dinosaur formations. In the following year, 1923, T'an, accompanied by my collector Chang, journeyed to Eastern Shantung and made discoveries of great interest.[1] In our footsteps followed Dr. Zdansky, who, first at Ning Chia Kou, and later in Eastern Shantung, excavated with a

[1] H. C. T'an, " New Research on the Mesozoic and Early Tertiary Geology in Shantung ", *Bull. Geol. Survey of China*, No. 5, Part 2, 1923, pp. 95–135.

care and technical skill which in this respect placed him ahead of us all.

We will now recount the results of our collecting work in Shantung. We returned to the little village of Ning Chia Kou, where in December 1922 we made our first finds. It is in quite a small village, just on the border between the cultivated lands and the " bad lands ", that the dinosaurs are to be found. Small, irregular, winding ravines here separate the rounded hills, on the surface of which not a blade of grass could grow. The soil is everywhere loose, consisting of a crumbling gravel, originating in the weathered sandstone. In this curious formation, which came to be named the Meng-Yin series, we found in many spots mussels and shells which were identified and described by Dr. Grabau, and among which he recognized the mussels *Unio johanböhmi* and *Unio cf. menkii*, as well as the new forms described by him, *Mycetopus mengyinensis*, and also the additional new shells *Bithinia mengyinensis* and *Valvata suturalis*.[1] All these molluscs are freshwater species, and in this fact we find an indication that the Meng Yin formation was deposited in an inland lake, an assumption which is fully proved by Professor Wiman's examination of the dinosaur material.

The plant remains which quite commonly occur in the sandstone are unhappily so badly preserved that no conclusions can be drawn from them, though it appears probable that they are remains partly of growths in the lake in which the sandstone formation was deposited, and partly of the land flora which grew around the lake.

Of much greater interest are the fish remains which were found at Ning Chia Kou. These consist of aggregations of perfect examples of a *Lycoptera* species and also a number of crania of a highly remarkable form, *Synamia Zdanskyi*, which was named by Professor Stensiö.

We now come to the reptile discoveries, and must first mention the turtles found by me in December 1922 and subsequently by Dr. Zdansky.

Pre-eminent in scientific interest are the dinosaur discoveries at Ning Chia Kou. I have already related that the first find was

[1] A. W. Grabau, " Cretaceous Fossils from Shantung ", *Bull. Geol. Survey of China*, No. 5, Part 2, 1923, pp. 143–81.

made about 1913 by the German missionary R. Mertens, and that a block of sandstone with three dinosaur vertebrae, which were donated by Mr. Behagel to the Geological Survey in Peking, gave the initiative to our collecting campaign of 1922–3.

The dinosaur bones which were dug up by T'an and myself during a couple of days in 1922 were only of slight importance. But all the more epoch-making were the model excavations executed here by Dr. Zdansky in the following spring, which led to the despatch home of an exceptionally complete and fine material representing a new and extremely remarkable family of dinosaurs, which Professor Wiman has described under the name of *Helopodidae*, of the species *Helopus Zdanskyi*. In a popular account of these excavations Professor Wiman writes as follows : [1]

> The skeleton of the approximately 10-metre long saurian lay in quite hard sandstone. The extraction of the skeleton was effected, according to Dr. Zdansky's account, mainly as follows. First the superimposed rock had to be removed in order to ascertain in which direction the skeleton lay. The parts of the skeleton which were exposed in this manner were bandaged with strips of cloth dipped in gum. Just as the bandage dried, the neighbouring town was raided by a robber band, so that Dr. Zdansky and his workmen were obliged to retire behind its walls. When it was possible to resume work the robbers had, apparently out of curiosity, torn off the bandages. Some bits of bone fell away with the bandages in the process and were missing, but fortunately no serious damage was done. The skeleton lay on a slope and above it a deep channel was hewn. Then the part of the rock in which the skeleton lay was cut away and finally the whole was broken loose in large blocks which fitted each other. The various blocks were numbered and the contact surfaces were marked to show their connection, and a plan was drawn of the size and shape of the blocks. Then the blocks were slid down in large iron-bound crates and packed in straw. Here at home it took three or four persons about a year to hew the skeleton out of the rock. Some pieces of the skeleton had to be divided and joined together again.

If we add to Professor Wiman's picturesque description the fact that Dr. Zdansky was forced to effect the transport of these immense and heavy packing cases on carts over indifferent roads to the railway at Tai An, we shall realize to some extent the difficulties which this skilful expert so brilliantly surmounted.

[1] C. Wiman, *Extinct Animals*, 1929, pp. 24–5.

If Dr. Zdansky's field-work must in all justice be described as perfect, the same can be said of the preparation and scientific study of the Ning Chia Kou material, which gave rise to Professor Wiman's superb treatise " Die Kreide-Dinosaurier aus Shantung ", *Palaeontologia Sinica*, Ser. C, Vol. VI, fasc. 1, 1929.

We have already read how it took three or four persons a whole year in Professor Wiman's laboratory to dig out this mighty skeleton from the sandstone and to join up the various fragments. The most difficult work had to be done by Professor Wiman himself. His description of his method of reconstruction of the head is too technical to be repeated here, but it affords a picture of the insight and thoroughness with which this eminent palaeontologist works. After the material had been completely reconstructed, Wiman passed on to the scientific study and interpretation of the two *Helopus* skeletons, which compare favourably with the finest and completest specimens of dinosaurs in other museums.

In the beginning of this chapter I mentioned the discovery by the American expedition of *Protoceratops* eggs in Mongolia and referred to it as an event of the utmost pre-eminence in the dinosaur research of recent years. Now, when Professor Wiman's work is before me, I do not hesitate to say that his account of the *Helopus's* mode of living is an equally great achievement, the more remarkable since it affords a solution of a very complicated scientific problem.

The *Helopus Zdanskyi* was an animal about 10 metres in length, with a short body but very long neck and tail. The legs were quite close to each other, perpendicular and stump-like, resembling the legs of an elephant. The *Helopus* had very thick cartilages in the joints, so that the whole of the ends of the bones consisted of cartilage. In this respect it differentiates itself from the vertebrates living on land, but resembles the great water animals, such as the whale. The explanation of this circumstance is that land animals require a firm bone structure in order to carry their weight, whereas water animals are borne by the water and can therefore be satisfied with a skeleton which is only partially of bone. From this circumstance Professor Wiman draws the conclusion that the *Helopus*, moving in the manner of elephants on stumpy legs, progressed not on the land but in the water.

Once this circumstance has become clear a whole series of peculiar features in the structure of the animal can easily be explained.

The feet were so constructed that the hoofs, the soles of the feet, were much enlarged and expanded towards the sides, and to a much greater degree than in those modern animals whose feet show adaptations to prevent them from sinking into marshy or soft ground. Hippopotami, tapirs and swamp antelopes, which all live in swamps, have enlarged hoofs. The reindeer have broad hoofs, which prevent them from sinking into the loose snow, and camels have a different structure which prevents them from sinking into loose sand. Among elephant types, which all have a tendency to enlargement of the hoof, it is especially in the prehistoric form of mammoth that this adaptation is carried further than in any other modern animal, and it is just concerning the mammoth that we know that it lived on swampy tundras.

The enlargement of the hoof of the *Helopus* was so pronounced that it gave Wiman occasion to recall the artificial enlargement of the sole of the foot which man has devised for himself and his domestic animals for movement across swampy peat bogs. Such devices are known in Sweden as *trugor*. A special kind, which is also called a " water-shoe " and consists of rounded pieces of wood, is used by harvesters who move in the water on a loose and muddy bottom. Usually the *trugor* are made of pieces of willow branches laced together, and are used on swampy marshes.

Similarly horses easily learn to walk on *trugor*, and Wiman relates how he had seen horses with their packs going over marshy peat bogs with *trugor* on their feet.

He also describes the greatly enlarged hoof of the *Helopus* as a *trug*-foot or marsh-foot. The word *Helopus* itself means marsh-foot.

The spinal vertebrae of the *Helopus* have a very curious structure. They are filled with air spaces to as great an extent as in certain birds, and the same is true of the upper part of the pelvis. These pieces of the skeleton were therefore very light. The lower part of the pelvis, like the legs and feet, consists, on the other hand, of massive bony substance and was accordingly relatively heavy. The skeleton as a whole was therefore below average weight, and Wiman points out the analogy to divers, who wear leaden soles under the feet in order to be able to walk on the bottom.

The head of the *Helopus* is very small and of light construction, like the vertebrae. The nostrils, eyes and tympanum are placed high up on the upper part of the head. Wiman draws from this fact the following conclusion : the head was so constructed that only a very small part of it need be raised above the water level in order not only to breathe, but also to look around and listen. One can compare the head of the *Helopus* with the periscope of a submarine, but a periscope not only for the purpose of sight, but also of hearing, and especially of breathing.

The form and wear of the teeth, as well as their whole disposition, shows that they were intended for biting off parts of plants, as if with a nail clipper.

Wiman sums up his studies of the manner of living of this dinosaur as follows : the *Helopus* moved on large-soled feet and long legs on the bottom of lakes and fed on water plants. When it required air, it lifted its head on its long neck above the water level.

Fig. 16, which we have taken from Wiman's monograph, shows the most probable reconstruction of the whole of the skeleton material discovered in this manner. On the basis of this section drawing Mr. Sven Ekblom has drawn, under the direction of Professor Wiman, the scene shown in Plate 5, which gives a clear picture of that scientist's conception of the home and manner of living of this curious animal.

At Ning Chia Kou we also found traces of yet another kind of dinosaur. Among the bones which T'an collected in December 1922 there is an object which Wiman identified as belonging to a *Stegosaurus*, one of the most fantastic monsters of the dinosaur type. This little discovery at Ning Chia Kou represents the first trace of a Stegosaur in Asia.

We have now rendered an account of all the known fossils in the rock strata of Ning Chia Kou. All scientists who have studied these fossils are agreed that they belong to the Cretaceous system, which was here established for the first time in China

PLATE 5

Helopus Zdanskyi. Reconstruction, under the direction of Prof. C. Wiman, by Sven Ekblom

[*face page* 40

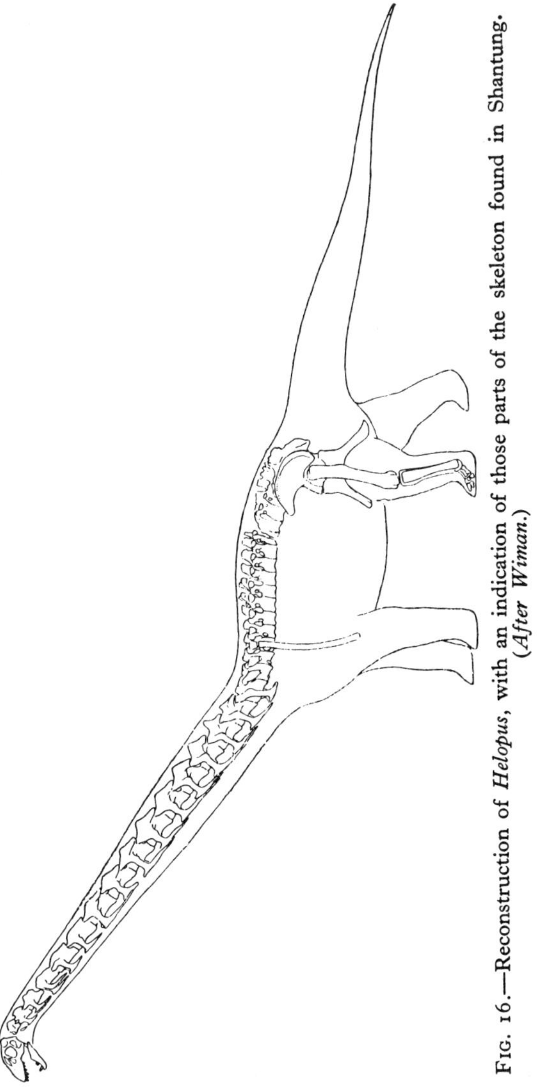

FIG. 16.—Reconstruction of *Helopus*, with an indication of those parts of the skeleton found in Shantung. (*After Wiman.*)

proper. This series of dinosaur-bearing deposits has been named, after the district, the Meng Yin series.

If we now turn to the districts in eastern Shantung explored by T'an, districts which in age correspond to the Meng Yin deposits, we encounter a whole series of formations, extending over Lai Yang, Chi Mo, Chiao, Chu Chêng and Chü districts, which may be briefly characterized as follows, beginning with the oldest.

The Lai Yang series consists of shales and sandstone of greatly varying colour. North-east and south of the town of Lai Yang numerous fossils were collected, some of which were of extremely great interest. The plants found here have been described by the Chinese geologist and palaeontologist T. C. Chow. According to his classification, most of the plant remains are twigs of conifers, though there also occur representatives of a couple of other plant groups.[1] Among the forms illustrated in Fig. 17 are *Brachyphyllum multiramosum*, *Sphenolepis arborescens* and *Palaeocyparis cf. flexuosa*, all conifers, whilst *Zamites* and *Thinnfeldia* are remote relations of the modern *Cycas*. *Baiera* is related to the *Gingko biloba* tree, referred to in the foregoing account.

The animal fossils in the thinly laminated shales in which the plants were found have been described by Professor Grabau, and it appears that they are of the very greatest interest. A couple of fishes of the *Lycoptera* family are remarkable in so far as they link up the Lai Yang deposits with the Meng Yin series, and still more with the fish-bearing deposits of Jehol in Northern China and Siberia, in all of which *Lycoptera* forms are abundant. Common to the deposits of Shantung and Siberia is also a crustacean, *Esteria middendorfi*.

Of great interest are the new insect forms described by Professor Grabau. To the groups of cockroaches belong the *Sinoblatta laiyangensis*, whilst the *Laiyangia paradoxiformis* cannot with certainty be classified with any known order of insects. All the more definite in type, on the other hand, is the beetle *Proteroscarabæus yeni*, which is the oldest known representative of the scarabaeus family. Larvae of dragon flies have been described by Grabau under the name of *Samarura gregaria*. Fig. 18 gives us an idea of these insects from Shantung, which

[1] T. C. Chow, " Some Younger Mesozoic Plants from Shantung ", *Bull. Geol. Survey of China*, No. 5, Part 2, 1923, pp. 136–41.

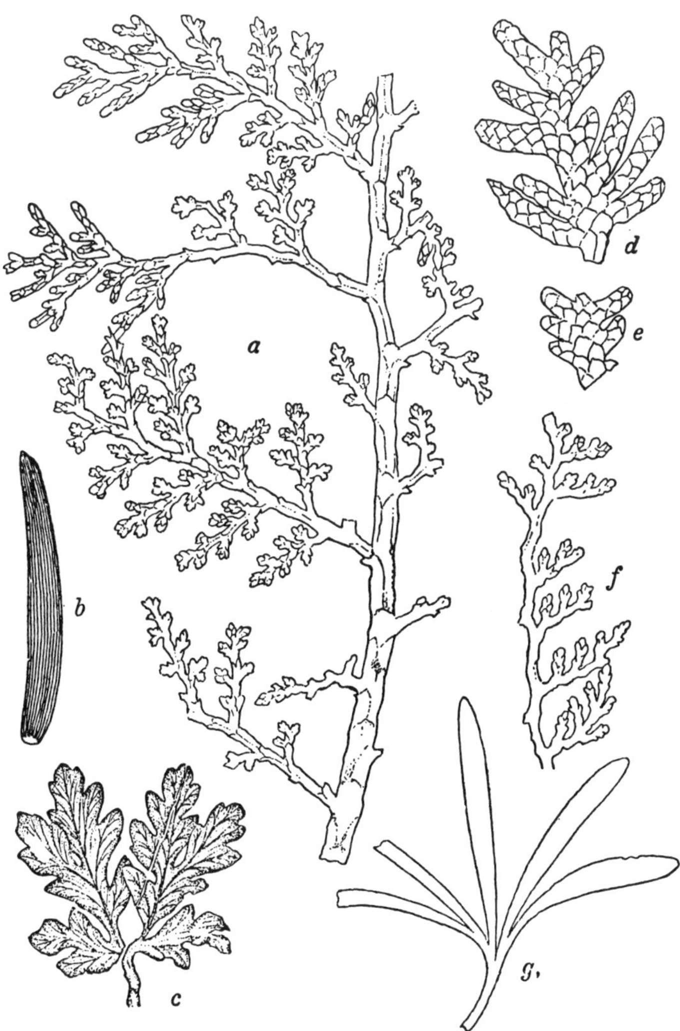

FIG. 17.—Plant fossils from the Cretaceous deposits at Lai Yang in Shantung. *a*, *Sphenolepis arborescens* (Chow); *b*, *Zamites sp.*; *c*, *Thinnfeldia sp.*; *d*, *e*, *Brachyphyllum multiramosum* (Chow); *f*, *Palaeocyparis cf. flexuosa* (Chow); *g*, *Baiera cf. australis* (M'Coy.)

are considered to belong to older stages of the Cretaceous age and are therefore rightly regarded as contemporaneous with the Meng Yin fauna.

The Chingshan formation is superimposed on the Lai Yang series and is regarded, like it, as belonging to the lower part of the Cretaceous formation and consequently as being also approximately contemporaneous with the Meng Yin deposits. In the lowest part of the Chingshan formation T'an discovered a freshwater mussel which Grabau describes as *Leptestis chingshanense*, and in a somewhat higher deposit T'an reports finds of remains of dinosaurs.

The Wangshih series of deposits, 2,000 metres thick, consisting for the most part of red clay, with lower strata of sand and conglomerate, is so extensive in Eastern Shantung that the great lowland areas in the Lai Yang and Chü Hsien valleys roughly coincide with the distribution of these deposits. From this series Grabau has designated a number of freshwater mussels of the *Cyrena* genus, as well as shells which possibly belong to the *Limnaea* and *Cyclophorus* genera.

This red clay, which is regarded as representing the later part of the Cretaceous age, afforded an abundant and important harvest of dinosaurs and quite a large turtle. According to Wiman's account these giant dinosaurs belong to widely different groups. The *sauropods*, immense, heavy, plant-eating dinosaurs with long necks and long tails, to which group also belongs our old friend from Ning Chia Kou, the *Helopus zdanskyi*, are represented by only a few fragments, vertebrae and a thigh bone, which must have belonged to a gigantic animal almost 20 metres long. Of the dinosaurs of prey, *Theropoda*, there are only a few vertebrae and a toe.

Of the order *Ornithopoda* there are probably two forms, but only one of them, the *Tanius sinensis*, is so completely represented that Wiman could give a descriptive survey of the animal and its manner of living. *Ornithopod* means bird-foot, a name given to this group of dinosaurs by reason of the resemblance of its hind foot to short, coarse birds' feet. Another name given to this animal by American palaeontologists is *duck-bills*, indicating the characteristic form of the head, the biological significance of which Wiman has explained in an illuminating way.

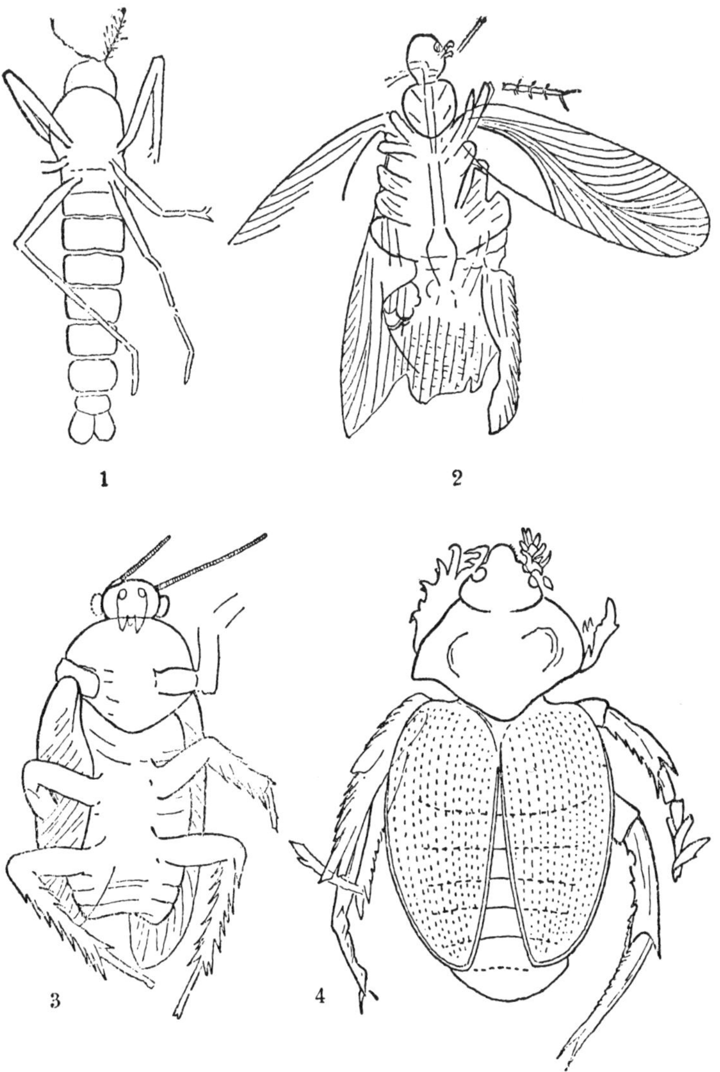

FIG. 18.—Insects from the Cretaceous formation at Lai Yang. 1, *Samarura gregaria* Grabau; 2, *Laiyangia paradoxiformis* Grabau; 3, *Sinoblatta laiyangensis* Grabau; 4, *Proteroscarabaeus yeni* Grabau.

Of *Tanius sinensis* there exists an originally almost perfect specimen from Chiang Chün Ting, a place about 6 miles south-west of the town of Lai Yang in Eastern Shantung. The specimen was discovered in April 1923 by T'an and was partially excavated by him. In October of the same year Zdansky, with extraordinary care, secured the remainder of the skeleton. The family name of the animal, *Tanius*, was selected by Professor Wiman in order to honour our friend and colleague H. C. T'an, who with such great success investigated the geology of Shantung. The type name *sinensis* means Chinese.

The *Tanius* was almost as large as the *Helopus*, that is to say, a medium-sized dinosaur. But the shape of the body was quite different. As will be remembered, the *Helopus* moved about on its four stumpy legs in much the same way as an elephant. The *Tanius*, on the other hand, walked only on its hind legs, which were long and powerful, whilst the front legs were short and slender and functioned as arms. The neck was not so prolonged as in the *Helopus*, but short, and carried a large head, reminding us in form of a horse's head. The tail was short and thick, and from the construction of the vertebrae we may conclude that it served as a support when sitting, exactly as in the case of the Kangaroo.

Like the *Helopus*, the *Tanius* was a water animal, as appears from the circumstance that here also the skeleton, especially the joint of the thigh bone with the pelvis, was not ossified and therefore not nearly strong enough to support the heavy body in the open air. Only constant habitation in water, lakes or rivers, is consistent with such a bone structure.

The *Tanius* was probably, to judge from this bone structure, able to swim, but for the most part, like the *Helopus*, it moved on the swampy bottom of lakes. This giant dinosaur also moved on a sort of *trug*-foot, though of a construction quite different from that of the *Helopus*. Whilst the *Helopus* tramped on the whole of the enlarged soles of the feet, the *Tanius* moved about on its three broad and flat toes.

Similarly in regard to the procuring and consumption of food the two dinosaur series of Shantung were in contrast with each other. The *Helopus* bit off with its teeth the plants which nourished it. Probably such food was ground up in a powerful muscular stomach with the help of grindstones of the kind which one finds in many animals which cannot chew. The *Tanius*, on the other hand, with its powerful head, had in each of the four half-jaws rows of closely sitting teeth, which together constituted large grinding surfaces. The teeth were rapidly worn out and were gradually renewed from a so-called tooth magazine of successively developing new teeth.

I have now related how we discovered and investigated the Shantung dinosaurs. It is pleasant to look back on this chapter of harmonious co-operation between Chinese and Swedish scientists. My friend T'an will assuredly remember with the same pleasure as I do the frosty but bright December days of 1922 when we made our first discovery at Ning Chia Kou. Then came the memorable year 1923 with co-operation between T'an and Zdansky. These two men complemented each other in a happy manner. T'an was a field-worker, a pioneer, who went in advance and found the right places, whilst Zdansky, the highly trained palaeontologist, was the incomparable technical expert, whose conscientiousness and master hand we have to thank for having been able to take back from Shantung two new dinosaur types, material which in completeness and scientific importance rivals the treasures of the great American museums.

And last, but not least, it was another master-hand which in Upsala arranged this precious material. Wiman's art of preparation is only exceeded by the simplicity, clearness and accuracy with which he interprets skeletons which, despite all his skill of preparation, are yet far from complete. With the delight which only complete confidence in a leader can give, we follow him over the shallow, sandy lakes of the Cretaceous age in Shantung. Conifers and ferns fringe the low shores, and other strangely formed plants shimmer at the bottom of the shallow water. Whole shoals of the graceful *Lycoptera* are in movement along the shores, where a turtle suns itself on a sandbank amidst empty mussel shells. But farther out at some fathoms depth the *Helopus* raises its little periscope head to the surface in order to breathe and blink at the light.

In the previous chapter I referred, when speaking of the ancient floras of Northern China, to the profound change which the plant and animal life of the earth underwent towards the end of the Cretaceous age. Ferns and conifers, Equisetales and Cycadophytes, which had hitherto set their stamp on the flora, were compelled to yield a good part of their predominance to a new and higher group of plants, flowering plants, which, especially in the form of tree-like representatives and leaf trees, in a short time covered the earth with plants of a new type. Whether it is an accidental coincidence in time or a profound causal connection we do not know, but during the same period of time in which the flora received new and remarkable additions, the dinosaurs vanished, as if they could not adapt themselves to their new surroundings, and into the vacant position as lords of the animal world there moved the mammals, previously living in modest retirement, but shortly to populate the earth with a new dynasty of giant animals.

According to the accepted geological scheme of time it was the Tertiary age, the new age in the history of the earth, which here began, and the first part of this age is called the Eocene, a name which we can somewhat freely translate as the dawn of the age of the mammals.

Among the many different phases of my collecting work it was granted to me to make a contribution to our knowledge of the Eocene mammals, but to tell this story I must revert to one of the first years of my labour in China.

In the spring of 1916 I had been sent to the mountainous districts of Southern Shansi to investigate the copper ores which were mined there as early as the T'ang dynasty and which had since repeatedly been the subject of experiment. I travelled together with Mr. Cheng, who was himself born in Southern Shansi and consequently knew the local conditions well. It was to be a journey of many and varied experiences, both pleasant and, sometimes, not so pleasant. We had wandered about in the valleys and lived alternately in country farms and small village temples. Then we arrived late at the district town of Wen Hsi, down on the plain. Out of alleged anxiety for our safety the magistrate practically made prisoners of us in his yamen, owing to certain rumours of bandits who were reported to have broken into a temple up in the mountains. In my book *The Dragon and the Foreign Devils* I have recounted how at last, early one morning, when the magistrate was asleep, we were compelled to escape from the yamen and to betake ourselves to the mountains again, where we soon discovered that it was stories of our own wanderings which had reached the magistrate in Wen Hsi in a distorted form and had been elaborated into reports of robber bands who had plundered a small mountain temple the very night we stayed there.

Well, after many and changing experiences we concluded our examination of the somewhat valueless copper ores and on June 16th, early in the morning, we were on the point of traversing the Yellow River with a little caravan of pack mules, just below the district town of Yuan Chü, in order to begin our return journey to Peking, through the province of Honan. At the spot where a ferry boat links up the two banks of the river, of which the northern one is in Shansi and the southern in Honan, the northern bank consists of a perpendicular cliff, about 10 metres high. True to my habits as a geologist, I used the few minutes required for putting the pack mules on the ferry in examining this cliff, which turned out to consist of loose marl beds covered by loess. The marl beds attracted my special interest, for I soon found that they were full of freshwater shells, amongst which an immense *Planorbis* was especially conspicuous. The collection of fossil-bearing pieces of marl which I first hastily gathered up I stuffed into a coffee pot and anything else I found handy, for the leader of the caravan had shouted that the pack mules were on board and that we must leave this tempting shore.

Later I succeeded, with the help of a Swedish friend, in having this little collection of shells sent, in the middle of the War, from Yuan Chü to Stockholm, where it was entrusted to our eminent mollusc expert, Dr. Nils Hj. Odhner, for examination. The conclusion to which he came was highly significant. His careful and, as subsequently appeared, accurate comparisons with similar discoveries in France and Germany revealed for the first time the occurrence of Eocene deposits in China. In reality this investigation had far-reaching practical importance, for it gave me the impulse to the whole study of the Tertiary and Pleistocene deposits of Northern China, which in due course led me into the field of archaeological research. I take this opportunity of expressing to my friend Odhner, who subsequently examined so many collections of molluscs from China, my hearty thanks for the inspiration which he gave me by determining the age of the Yuan Chü deposits.

I need scarcely say that, as soon as I heard of Odhner's surprising decision, I was full of eagerness to return to Yuan Chü and to examine further the deposits which we now knew to be China's first representatives of the oldest Tertiary. My zest had been increased by Wiman's observation in a letter to me that nothing could be of greater interest than the discovery in China of mammals of Eocene age. The opportunity for this tempting investigation came in the spring of 1921, when I spent the period between April 29th and May 13th in a reconnaissance of the Eocene field at Yuan Chü.

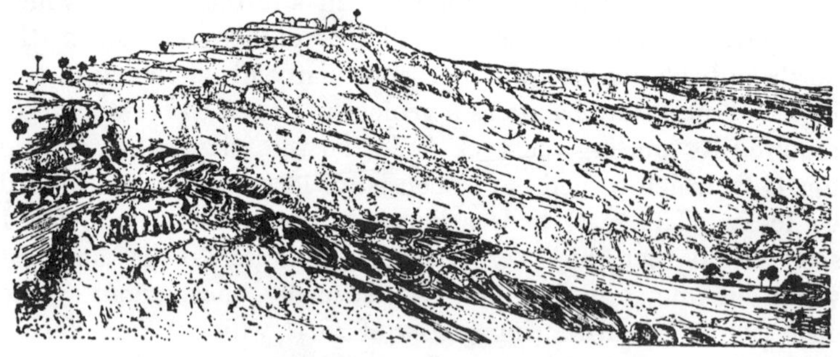

FIG. 19.—Tilted Eocene strata at Yuan Chü Hsien.

In the next chapter I shall return to this area, which was to play a fundamental part in the interpretation of the rock formations of Northern China. It is sufficient to remark here that I was able to confirm the existence at Yuan Chü of a series of Eocene strata at least 1,000 metres thick. The lower part of this formation consists of old gravel beds which are now compressed into conglomerate. In this lower series there are also thick beds of red-brown clay. In the upper part of the Eocene formation we find the same red-brown clay alternating with whitish sand, and in this series of clay and sand we encounter regular, 3–10 decimetre thick, beds of green or blue-green marl or marl-like limestone. It was in these beds of marl by the river shore that I made my first discovery of molluscs, in 1916, and in the same place I found, immediately on my return in 1921, two fine jaws of a mammal. In the early winter of 1921 Dr. Zdansky visited this Eocene field, on my suggestion, and made further discoveries of mammals, especially in a bank on the southern side of the river.

When, in December 1922, T'an and I examined the dinosaur deposits in the Meng Yin valley in Shantung, we found that the green-grey shaly sandstone of the Cretaceous system was overlaid by a formation, 600–1,100 metres thick, of a quite different type. It consists of red sand, clay and conglomerate with inlays of yellow and grey sandstone, marl and limestone. Here, as in Southern Shansi, we found the marl full of freshwater molluscs,

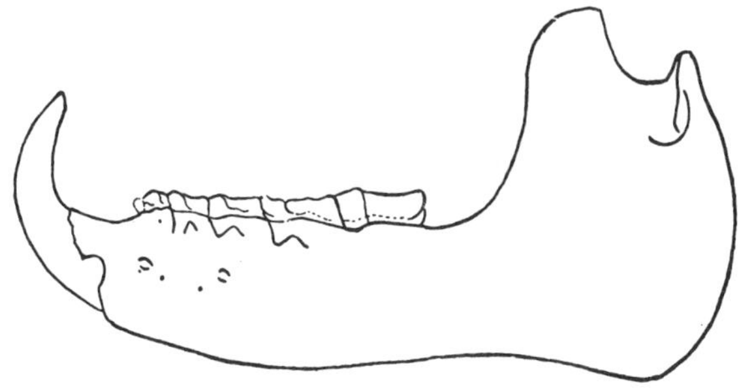

Fig. 20.—Lower jaw of *Amynodon sinensis* Zdansky, from Eocene deposits at Yuan Chü Hsien in Honan.

partly of the same kind as at Yuan Chü, and both in the whitish marl and in the sand we found numerous remains of reptiles and mammals. It thus became clear that there exists a thick and extensive Eocene formation in the valleys of Shantung also, where it is superimposed partly on the sandstones of the Cretaceous age, but in parts also on older rock strata.

The study of the Eocene formation in Southern Shansi and in Shantung gave me the clue to a number of observations which I had made long before, but could not understand.

On the station at Chang Sin Tien, a large railway station on the Peking-Hankow railway, 20 km. south-west of Peking, there are some fine cuttings, some metres in height, through deposits of gravel, sand and clay, the whole being predominantly red in colour. When I saw and measured these for the first time, I only knew of one similar formation, namely the late Tertiary Hipparion clay with intercalated conglomerate beds, of which I shall speak in my fifth chapter.

But there was one feature of these clay and gravel beds at

FIG. 21.—Professor Carl Wiman, who organized the study of the fossil vertebrate material from China and himself described the dinosaurs.

Chang Sin Tien which I could not harmonize with the Hipparion formation. Whereas the Hipparion beds, wherever we found them, are always in an undisturbed horizontal position, just as they were originally formed, the deposits at Chang Sin Tien dip quite steeply towards the north-east. In this respect they agree substantially with the Eocene formations in Shansi and Shantung, which have everywhere been moved out of their original position by the great movements in the body of the earth which occurred after the Eocene age. Since the Chang Sin Tien deposits agree even in appearance with the Eocene deposits, I expressed the surmise, as early as my treatise on *The Cenozoic of Northern China*, that we have to do with Eocene deposits at Chang Sin Tien also.

After I had come to this conclusion, I took out my diaries of journeys on the Peking-Hankow railway in the years 1916–20 and found a note that I had observed from the train at various places in Southern Chihli and Northern Honan as far as the Yellow River, patches of exposed red clay and gravel, as well as marl beds, all of which seem to show that along the line of the Peking-Hankow railway, from Peking to the Yellow River, we may expect the discovery of a great, though hitherto unexplored, Eocene field.

In 1930 Zdansky published his monograph on the older mammals of the Chinese old Tertiary.[1] As these numerous forms usually occur in a very fragmentary state, we must here content ourselves with illustrating, after Zdansky, a form belonging to the rhinoceros family, *Amynodon sinensis*, from Yuan Chü. A great deal of the material of this kind, as well as of many other forms, is taken from a section examined by Dr. Zdansky on the southern bank of the Yellow River, opposite Yuan Chü.

It is a very important result of Zdansky's treatment of the mammal material from Yuan Chü and Shantung that in both areas there are found early Tertiary faunas, probably from both the first stage (Eocene) and from the second (Oligocene).

[1] " Die altertiären Säugetiere China's nebst stratigraphischen Bemerkungen ", *Palaeontologia Sinica*, Ser. C, Vol. VI, Fasc. 2.

Fig. 22.—Dr. Wong Wen-hao, Chief of the National Geological Survey of China, a charming and wise little gentleman, author of several important treatises on mountain folding in the Pacific region.

CHAPTER FOUR

HOW THE MOUNTAINS CAME INTO BEING

We shall now wander together over the country in which we moved in our first three narratives, but as your guide I will endeavour to extract a new interest from it.

Hitherto we have regarded these old limestones, coal shales and sandstones as ancient deposits in the sea, or in lakes and rivers, and we have dwelt by preference upon those places in which these deposits speak to us, through the organic remains which they conceal: trilobites, molluscs and mussels, which lived in the ancient Chinese seas, Equisetales, ferns, cycads, conifers, and in later times leaf trees, which formed forests around the swamps in which China's abundant coal deposits were formed.

We have accompanied the geologists T'an, Dr. Zdansky and Professor Wiman over the waste "bad lands" of the Meng Yin valley in Shantung and seen the vertebrae of dinosaurs of the Cretaceous age lying in the light crumbling sandstone, half exposed by weathering. Finally, we have searched the marl beds of Yuan Chü and Hsin T'ai and the sands of the little streamlet ravine at Kuan Chang (the two latter in Shantung), and found there pieces of crocodile skin and teeth of the reptiles and mammals of the Eocene age.

But hitherto we have not noticed at all that these strata, which represent widely different ages, from the earliest and middle down to the beginning of modern times, scarcely ever remain in their original horizontal position, but slope, or dip, as the geologists call it, more or less steeply, in one place in one direction and in another perhaps in the absolutely opposite direction.

When we see a whole series of strata, as for example on the edge of the Kaiping coalfield, where the whole series, limestone, coal shale and sandstone, all incline 30 degrees towards the centre of the coal basin, we are compelled to stop a moment and consider the significance of this observation.

First of all we must be agreed that these strata, when they were formed, first the coal series and last the sandstone, were all horizontal. It is true that a violent stream may sometimes deposit gravel or sand on a sloping bank, but that is a rare exception. Similarly in the sea, on the steep outer side of a coral reef, fragments broken off by the surf may be deposited on a slope, but this also is an exceptional case. As a general rule we can safely say that regular strata such as those at Kaiping, which we can follow mile after mile along the edge of the coal basin, were deposited in a horizontal position in the sea, just as in the case of the Cambrian or Ordovician limestone, or in lakes or river deltas, as in the case of the coal series. When we make the acquaintance of the Belgian mining engineers at Kaiping, who have studied this coalfield for decades for purely practical reasons, we shall be able, with the help of their detailed maps, to ascertain that the Kaiping basin resembles an elongated trough running lengthwise, roughly east-north-east and west-south-west, with the strata falling more or less sharply towards the centre. On the northern edge of the field the strata in places are perpendicular or somewhat overhanging inwards. Away to the west, at Tangshan, the dislocation is so marked that the old Ordovician limestone is partially pushed in over the much younger coal series, but at the southern end of the field the strata incline gently towards the centre.

If we may trouble the reader, in order to understand properly the structure of the Kaiping basin, we would beg him to take a long and narrow book, preferably with leaves of different colours, and bend it up so that it assumes the form of a trough. If there is a black leaf in the book, we will assume that it represents the coal series lying between the older limestone and the younger sandstone. The reader will then, with the help of this home-made model, better understand the mining engineers when they tell him that the coal formations lie like a black leaf under the whole of the Kaiping field, but that in the middle of the basin they are perhaps at least 1,000 metres deep, so that the mining company must content itself with cutting in along the outer edges of the coalfield where, it is true, the coal seams rise steeply, but at so slight a depth that mining is economically possible, which is not true of the central and deepest part of the basin.

How does it come that the rock strata at Kaiping, with a combined thickness of more than 2,000 metres and with an area 31 km. long by 8 km. broad, have been so pressed down that they now form this immense elongated trough? There can only be one answer: a folding movement in the earth's crust. When this folding took place, and how long it took, we cannot determine from Kaiping alone, but it is certain that some mighty force at some time in the past pressed together this part of the earth's crust in much the same way as the little book with the black leaf was pressed between the hands of the reader.

There remain further lessons to be learnt from the mountain ridges on the northern edge of the Kaiping basin. The actual fringe of the coalfield here consists of an almost continuous limestone ridge, in the northern part of which we find thin layers of limestone containing Cambrian fossils, but these Cambrian beds are overlaid in the south by the massive Ordovician limestone. All these strata, as has been said, lie as if on their edges, and as we wander over the bare limestone rock we see how the strata point upwards into space. These ancient marine strata, which are there pushed up by some mighty unknown force, look like a tumbled ruin, of which the upper part has been torn away. (Cf. Fig. 4, p. 12.)

When we extend our inquiry to the neighbouring districts it becomes clear to us that in the hills of Kaiping we have to do with the ruins of a once much higher rock structure. At Luan Ho, for example, where the railway crosses the river, 45 km. east of Kaiping, we find hills with the same Cambrian strata and with the same fossils. The same observation may be made in many places in Northern China, where we find Cambrian and Ordovician limestones which often rise steeply, as in Kaiping, and which everywhere have the same appearance and certainly contain the same fossils. It is clear that during these stages of the antiquity of the world Northern China was a shallow sea in which was deposited lime mud which subsequently hardened to stone and enclosed the shells of the animals which then lived in it. Later these petrified marine deposits were pushed up and folded together with the remaining crust of the earth. Mountains were thus formed of material which had once been the sea bottom. But these mountain ridges were not permanent. The tooth of time gnawed at them and now they appear to us like ruins of what they once were. Mountains are formed and mountains are destroyed; these are the fluctuations in the history of the earth, as we glimpsed them in our wanderings in the Kaiping basin.

The folds at Kaiping have the shape of a trough, i.e. the rock strata are pressed down towards the interior of the earth. The opposite of the trough-like fold is the saddle fold, with an arch formation. In the mountain ranges the trough and saddle folds usually alternate, and north of the coalfield at Kaiping I found in 1916 the older rock strata, which in Kaiping are concealed in the interior of the earth's crust, pressed together in alternate trough and saddle, as appears in Fig. 23. In this section through a small part of the earth's crust we also see distinct marks of the destructive forces. The saddle folds are scooped out and partially destroyed, so that the very oldest part of the earth, the Archaean rock, becomes visible where once the saddle fold threw its bold arch.

When Dr. Ting and Dr. Wong, directors of the Geological

Survey of China, trained their first company of young field geologists, they quite naturally began with the immediate task of preparing a geological map of Hsi Shan or the Western Hills which rise up to the west of Peking and form a part of the semi-circular frame to the Peking plain, and of which the northern part is composed of the Nankou mountains.

Hsi Shan is a mountainous district with peaks rising up to 1,500 metres, intersected by steep and deep, sometimes canyon-like valleys, of which the most important is the Hun Ho canyon, of which I have already spoken in the first chapter (Plate 2). During their work in this district the Chinese geologists made the acquaintance not only of various folds (Fig. 24) but also of

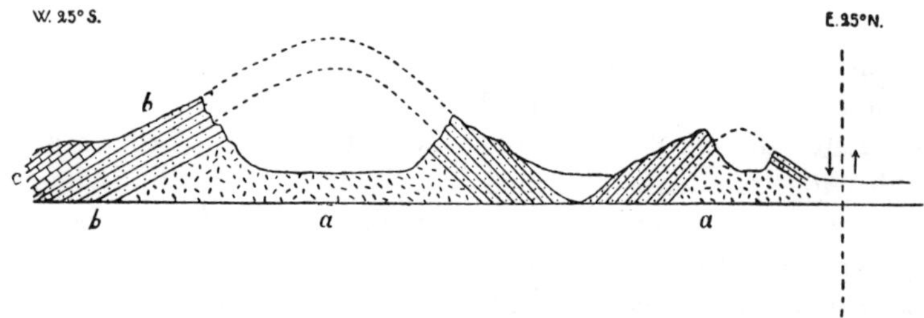

FIG. 23.—Section through a part of the mountains north of Kaiping. *a*, Archaean rocks ; *b*, Red Sinian sandstone ; *c*, Siliceous Sinian limestone.

another kind of subterranean activity, volcanic eruptions in various forms. Near Chou K'ou Tien, a village on the outskirts of the mountains, there is a granite area which furnishes much of the hewn granite employed as building stone in Peking. This little granite field was clearly at one time formed in the interior of the earth as a molten mass, which forced its way into the rock strata and slowly hardened under a cover of stratified rocks. This *laccolith* (the geological term for a molten mass which has hardened in the depths of the stratified rocks) was subsequently laid bare during the course of the geological ages by the destructive forces. The cover has now completely disappeared, and the granite itself weathers more quickly than the surrounding rocks, so that the former laccolith now reveals a low surface, surrounded by the more enduring stratified rocks ; sandstone, shale and limestone.

The coalfield at Chai T'ang, concerning which I made some remarks in connection with the Jurassic flora, lies deep in the Western Hills, 60 km. due west of Peking. The coal deposits belong, as will be remembered, to the early part of the Jurassic age, and the whole of the coal formation is greatly disturbed, not only by folding but also by the penetration of laccolithic masses of another volcanic rock, diabase. It is thus clear that the folding and the volcanic activity in Hsi Shan are later than the earliest Jurassic age. On the other hand we appear to be in the fortunate position of being able to give a *terminus ad quem* to these great mountain-forming events. The geologist Yih, who has surveyed

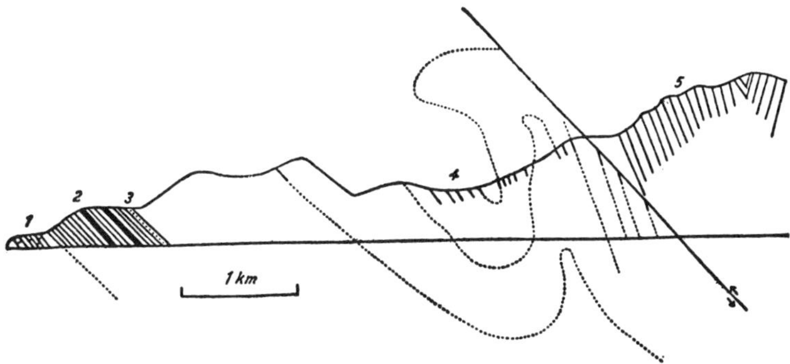

FIG. 24.—Section through the coalfield at Chang Kou Yü in the Peking Western Hills. 1, Ordovician limestone; 2, Carboniferous formation; 3, coal formation of Jurassic age. (*V. K. Ting and H. C. T'an.*)

his own field work and that of his colleagues in a valuable volume,[1] distinguishes a latest formation, which he calls the Tiaochishan series, which is identical with what T'an and I used to call tuff conglomerate, a formation consisting largely of the products of volcanic eruption, which is very extensive in Northern China, and which we regard as contemporary with the Meng Yin series of dinosaur deposits in Shantung, i.e. a deposit belonging to the first half of the Cretaceous age. The Tiaochishan formation shows fewer disturbances than the older formations, and it therefore seems probable that the mountain movements in Hsi Shan took place in the interval between the formation of the coal

[1] L. F. Yih, "The Geology of Hsi Shan or the Western Hills of Peking", *Memoirs of the Geol. Survey of China*, Ser. A, No. 1.

series at Chai T'ang, which is strongly influenced, and the deposit of the tuff conglomerate of the Tiaochishan series, which is almost undisturbed. The folding of the rocks and the volcanic action would thus have reached their zenith during the later Jurassic age, and for this period of mountain folding Dr. Wong has proposed the name Yen Shan folding, taken from a name of the mountains round Peking, which has been accepted by Chinese geographers. Dr. Wong has endeavoured to show, by an interesting analysis of the above facts, that the period of folding which he names after Yen Shan can be discerned in other places in China, Korea and Japan, and that parallel phenomena are also known in North America. He therefore considers the Yen Shan foldings as a characteristic feature of the whole of the Pacific Ocean, a pan-Pacific upheaval of the earth-crust of the first order.

Hitherto we have been engaged only with that kind of movement in the crust of the earth, folding, which originated in lateral pressure on the rocks. We shall now, however, make the acquaintance of another kind of movement in the crust, movements in a perpendicular direction. In this case, so-called block-faults, we are concerned with larger or smaller pieces of the crust of the earth which become detached from their surroundings along great fissures and have sunk into the depths, whilst leaving the flanking portions intact in their original position.

Let us now for a short time return to the first place we visited in the first chapter, the iron-ore field at Hsin Yao in the mountains north of Peking. We are now in the village of Hsin Yao and look out over this ore-bearing area. To the north, on the northern side of a river valley running east and west, we see a characteristic mountain silhouette of Yü T'ai Shan, with strata inclining about 25 degrees to the east. In the west, i.e. at the very bottom, we see the heavily weathered Archaean gneiss, upon which is imposed the red sandstone, which in turn is overlaid by shale containing the iron ore seam. Upon the ore-bearing series there follow several hundred metres of limestone, containing the fossil *Collenia* of which I spoke in the first chapter. In direct continuation, in a southerly direction, we can see the ore deposit like a blood-red band in the mountain cliffs east of Hsin Yao.

This ore zone is the great source of supply of ore, of which about 17 million tons of good quality are available for mining.

Quite near to the village of Hsin Yao we discover another area where the ore is on the surface, a deposit of no practical importance, but of great interest to the scientist.

The explanation of the re-emergence of the ore at this unexpected place is that a great fault line runs through the earth's crust from north to south between the two ore zones, and the western one belongs to a block which has sunk several hundred metres in relation to the great eastern one (Fig. 25).

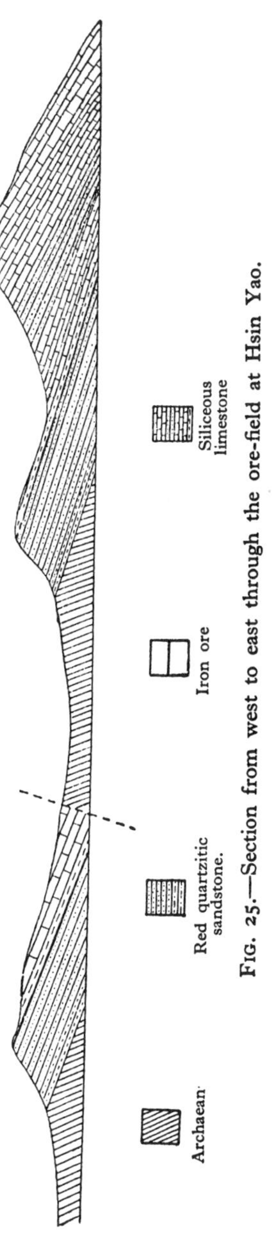

FIG. 25.—Section from west to east through the ore-field at Hsin Yao.

If we now transfer ourselves to Yen Tung Shan, the most westerly of the three ore-fields, and the one which I discovered in 1918, we shall find exactly similar conditions (Fig. 3, p. 6). Here, too, the ore is on the surface in two areas, separated from each other by a great line of cleavage, along which the northern block has sunk about 400 metres in relation to the southern.

At Yen Tung Shan we discovered a *terminus ad quem* for the age of the faulting. On the southern side of the limestone ridge which borders the field to the south there lie almost horizontal beds of tuff conglomerate, presumably of Cretaceous age, on the steeply rising limestone, and it therefore seems clear that the rock movements here are older than the

Cretaceous age. We are thus tempted to assume a connection between these great dislocations and the Yen Shan folds somewhat farther south. Moreover, it is possible that actual folding movements entered into the processes which moulded the lines of the Yen Tung Shan field, for in the said limestone ridge in the most southerly part of the field we find everywhere a fanlike lifting of the strata until they become perpendicular, or even overhanging. This structure is common in the districts of folds, but can scarcely be consistent with faults alone.

It seems probable that the great ore zone which we have traced from Hsin Yao in the east to beyond Yen Tung Shan in the west over a stretch of 82 km., and which everywhere shows the same rock structure, is a geographical border line of the first order. It lies on the dividing line between the Mongolian plateau and the Chinese mountain country and seems to be the line of division between these two in every respect so different areas.

Let us now pass on to Southern Shansi, to Yuan Chü on the Yellow River, the district where, with the assistance of Dr. Odhner, we first observed the existence of Eocene formations in China.

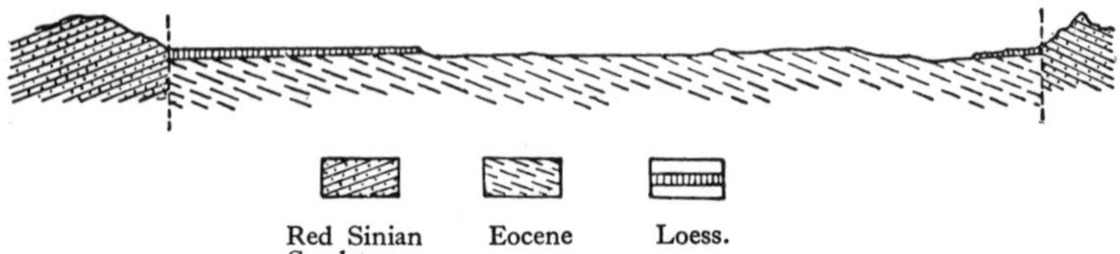

FIG. 26.—North-Southern section through the Eocene area of Yuan Chü.

The loose, easily destroyed Eocene beds form a comparatively low-lying landscape of small hills, which are encompassed on all sides by higher land consisting of much older strata of rocks. Fig. 26 shows an imaginary section from north to south through the Eocene field at Yuan Chü. The Eocene strata dip to the south-east. On all sides the Eocene field is surrounded by higher land consisting of older rocks, in the north and south the Sinian red sandstone (approximately the same formation as the sandstone which underlies the ore deposits in the Hsüan-Lung field, cf. Chapter I). In the west the Eocene frame consists of Ordovician limestone and Permian coal strata, and in the east of the younger Permian *Gigantopteris* series.

In few places in China does the fault topography appear to the eye of the geologist more splendidly than here. So also the immense scale of the vertical movements is easy to assay. Beneath the Eocene formation, which is at least a thousand metres thick, we should certainly, if we could penetrate into the depths, find the same limestone strata as up in the high mountain ranges away on the south side of the river, and under the limestone the red sandstone which constitutes the southern foothills nearest the river. As the sandstone and limestone formations together are at least 1,000 metres thick, there must be a difference of level of about 2,000 metres from the highest limestone peak in the south to the same limestone stratum deep down below the Eocene covering in the sunken area. This difference of level of about 2,000 metres is thus an approximate value, or rather a minimum figure, for the vertical subsidence of the earth's crust into this sunken area.

We find similar movements of the earth's crust in the mountain country in Shantung, with the difference that the depth of the subsidence was about double and the movements in the strata were of a very complex nature.

The whole of the earth's crust is here split into elongated ribs running north-west and south-east. Each rib has subsided differently, most in the south-west and least in the north-east margin. The geologist T'an, who has a very thorough knowledge of the geology of these tracts, has estimated the whole series of strata, from the Archaean rock at the bottom up to the Eocene, which is the youngest formation, at a total of 4,330 metres, in accordance with the following table:

Eocene	900 metres
Dinosaur formation (Cretaceous)	800 ,,
Red sandstone (Trias)	700 ,,
Permo-Carboniferous coal series	250 ,,
Ordovician limestone	850 ,,
Cambrian strata	780 ,,
Pre-cambrian limestone	50 ,,
Total thickness of sediment series	4,330 metres

From this composition T'an has drawn the conclusion that the vertical movement in these long obliquely sunken areas is at least 4 kilometres.

Geological research has shown the existence in other parts of the mountain country of Shantung of great fault lines along which the movements have also been horizontal and amount to much greater figures than the one just given.

In all probability a further geological survey of Northern China will show great lines of cleavage in the crust of the earth where, with our present knowledge, we can only guess at their existence. Thus it is extremely probable that the boundary between the Peking plain and the semi-circular mountain frame which encompasses it is made up of one or more such fault lines, and it is worthy of note that in one or two places hot springs exist just where we suspect these lines to be.

Far up in the extreme north-west corner of China Proper, in the province of Kansu, I found another region of great block faults. Especially the Kuei Te valley, with its steep canyon, fully 1,000 metres deep, shows in several places the contrast between remnants of old crystalline rocks and areas of depression filled with the loose, many-coloured, but predominantly red, Tertiary clays. So also we find the phenomena of folding in certain places in clay strata of the Kuei Te basin, as, for example, near the village Ashgona on the western bank of the Yellow River, below the town of Kuei Te. But in this case the folding was probably only a subordinate phenomenon caused by the great faults.

I obtained a very interesting insight into the rock movements in this district by the Hsi Ning River, a little below the town of the same name. Fig. 27 shows a mountain, in the stratification of which we can clearly see that the oldest rock strata dip most steeply, whereas each succeeding later formation lies a little flatter, but with the slight inclination always in the same direction as the steep gradient of the underlying formations. In this case it is clear that the movement of the rocks continued for long periods of time in the same direction, with the consequence that the oldest strata show the total of the turning over of the rocks in the various successive ages.

In Eastern Kansu there exists a mountain zone running north

and south, known as Liu Pan Shan, but of which the correct name is Lung Shan. This mountain range is made up of sharp folds, including the latest sandstones and shales of the Cretaceous and Tertiary ages. This Dragon Mountain, as it may be called in translation, is unique in the whole of Northern China in so far as its highest peaks consist of the loose, extremely crumbly, grey-green shale of the Cretaceous age. On the surface of these ridges the rock weathers so rapidly, and the resulting gravel is washed away by the summer rains at such a speed, that the slopes are quite bare and have no protective vegetation.

When one looks at this curious landscape, one is irresistibly seized by the feeling that one is witnessing the progress of forma-

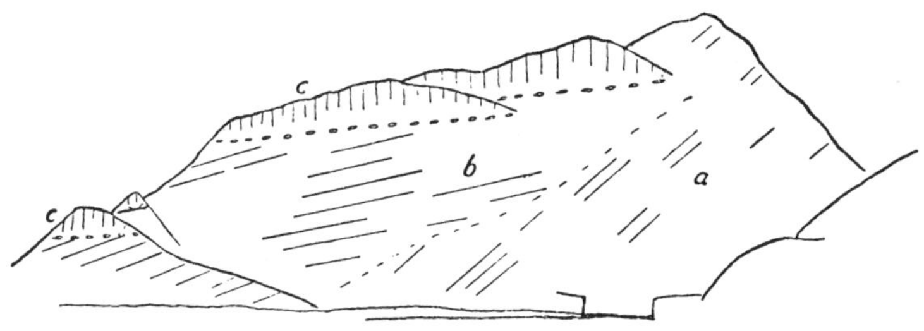

FIG. 27.—Mountain section at Hsi Ning Ho showing steeply inclined deposits of old crystalline rock. *a*, less steeply inclined red Tertiary deposits; *b*, superimposed on them a slightly inclined cap of loess, with gravel deposits at its base, *c*.

tion of a mountain range, that the rock movements are proceeding under one's eyes with such an intensity that the easily destroyed ridges have not yet had time to be obliterated.

We find remarkable support for this view in the circumstance that this precise district is the most important of the earthquake areas of China. On December 16th, 1920, this zone was devastated by an extremely violent earthquake. Late that winter evening the frozen earth was so terribly shaken that masses of loess were set in motion and flowed like immense rivers of soil for stretches of miles long, destroying whole villages and fundamentally transforming the face of the land. When, more than two years later, I travelled through the earthquake district, the traces of the desolation were still overwhelming. Villages with hundreds of inhabitants had been swallowed up by the moving masses of earth, city walls had crumpled up into heaps of bricks, tombstones had fallen down or broken in two. In places we could not ride, but had to walk, cautiously leading our horses between the black gaping fissures in the ground.

It is tempting to associate the violence of the frequent earthquakes in this part of China with the later, not to say present-day, rock movements of which Lung Shan affords an example.

Hitherto in this chapter we have interested ourselves almost exclusively in the mountain-forming forces, side pressure forcing up the rock strata into saddle folds or thrusting them into the depths in the form of trough-like folds, as also the vertical movements which cause whole masses of rock to sink into the depths.

But we have seen how all the mountains of Northern China still in process of formation, are, with the exception of the Dragon Mountain in Kansu, ruins of former higher and bolder mountain forms. We may with justice, therefore, ask for the name of the forces which effected this destruction of the ancient mountains.

One thing is clear immediately, namely that, in contrast to the mountain-forming forces which have their seat in the interior of the earth, the destructive forces are to be sought on the surface of the earth itself.

Let us for a short time return to the granite laccolith at Chou K'ou Tien, near Peking. We have already related how this mass of granite is now only the base of a high-arched structure covered by stratified masses of rock which have been torn away and destroyed. If we look at the steep sides of the low granite hills we shall obtain an idea of the manner of this destruction. Everywhere on the granite surface we see distinct channels, which have arisen from the spooling and excavation of rain water. These are what German geologists call " Regenrillen ".

These " Regenrillen " at Chou K'ou Tien show in miniature the same power of running water to excavate and destroy as the canyon of the Hun River reveals to us on a gigantic scale. As early as Chapter One I described how this immense steep and narrow valley was formed. It is very ancient in origin, belonging to a time so remote that the mountain forms were quite different from what they are now. The Huai Lai plain, over which the river takes its broad and shallow course until it cuts through the limestone mountains, has sunk down, but the river has obstinately remained in its old bed, which it has cut into the limestone, deeper and deeper in proportion as the limestone rock, carried by the mountain-forming forces, rose above the surrounding country.

It is not only by their deeply channelled canyons that the rivers of Northern China speak to us of the work which running water does in the disintegration and final destruction of mountains. The copious mud carried by the rivers tells us a similar story. The rivers of Northern China are famous for their silt, and especially the Yellow River, which derives its name from the yellow earth, is as thick as a thin gruel. When the mighty river flows out of the valley bordering the provinces of Honan and Shansi into the great plain, it broadens its bed, divides up and changes its course. The bed of the river rises year by year owing to the silt, of which the coarser elements have come to rest. In this way the bed has been raised through the centuries, until, during a rainy summer, high water bursts the dams and the vast, muddy masses of water seek a new bed, carrying destruction with them. It is owing to these mysterious and catastrophic changes in the Yellow River that it has earned the fatal name " China's sorrow ".

But only a small part of the copious mud sediment of the Yellow River is due to the action of the river on the solid rock. Most of it is washed out from the thick strata of fine, yellow-grey dust, the so-called loess, which covers large parts of Northern China to a thickness of as much as 100 metres. In a later narrative we shall have occasion to make closer acquaintance with this unique loess-formation, and it is sufficient in this connection to relate how the great German explorer and geologist, Ferdinand von Richthofen, correctly interpreted the origin of the loess covering as an eolian deposit of dust carried by the wind, which came to rest in suitable places like an immense carpet, which in the provinces of Kansu, Shensi, Shansi and Honan to a large extent conceals the bedrock. We thus see that the wind has also been a mighty force in the transformation of the surface of the earth, and we can properly sum up our observations by saying that weathering, running water and the wind are the agents which have most powerfully contributed to the creation of the landscapes of Northern China.

But I have already shown in my account of the great earthquake of 1920 that the mountain-forming forces in the interior of the earth can also set the outer strata in movement, as was the case with the great streams of earth which were set in motion owing to the quaking of the rocks, and which considerably changed the surface of the land in a large portion of the province of Kansu. We thus find that the internal mountain-forming forces and the external destructive forces frequently work in intimate association. In reality we must, in the interests of truth, correct the simplified picture of the course of events which, for pedagogic reasons, I have given above. It is not quite correct to say that the interior mountain-forming forces first raised up mighty chains of folds or a fault-block out of the plains, and

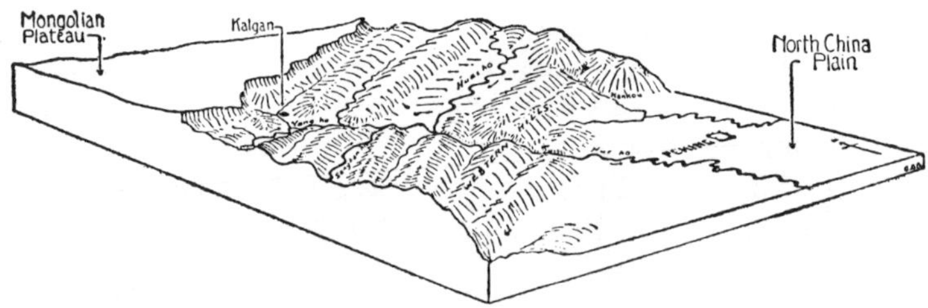

FIG. 28.—Model showing the mountains between the Peking plain and the Mongolian plateau. Notice especially the valley of the Hun River. (*After Barbour.*)

then that afterwards, when the work was completed, the destructive forces began to eat away the mountains and finally to lay them in ruins.

The interplay of forces is much more complex and is ever changing. As soon as a mountain fold appears in the crust of the earth, as the result of lateral pressure, in long and low arches over the ancient plain of horizontal marine strata or continental sediments, the rivers immediately begin to adapt their courses by carving out valleys through the fold, and mountain peaks are modelled freely in proportion as the fissures and canyons are cut deeper.

But on the other hand, if the destructive and levelling forces are to continue their work until, after incredibly long periods of time, they have achieved their final purpose, which the geologists call " peneplain ", an almost completely horizontal surface carved out of the mountain folds and fault-blocks, it will happen sooner or later that the crust of the earth, which in this area has long lain quiet and inactive, will again begin to move, so that new folds, new volcanoes, and new faults will appear.

From this slow, but ever-changing and highly complex interplay of creative and levelling forces arise the varied, though nevertheless strictly law-abiding forms of the crust of the earth which delight the traveller and lover of nature and which often force upon the scientist years of patient work before he succeeds in interpreting one single curious fold or a strange furrow in the wrinkled face of gigantic mother earth.

FIG. 29.—Dragon design on a tile from a grave of the Han dynasty.

CHAPTER FIVE

DRAGONS AND DRAGON-BONE MINES

To the popular imagination of the West the dragon was predominantly an evil power which was fought and defeated by some of the principal heroic figures of antique mythology and legend, such as Apollo when killing the dragon Python, Heracles who slew the Hydra of Lernaea, Perseus who cut off the heads of the Gorgon Medusa, and Cadmos who performed the fateful sowing of the teeth of a dragon slain by him.

Similar conceptions are found in Germanic heroic saga, as in the stories of Sigurd Fafnirsbane and Beowulf.

In the Psalter and the Book of Revelation the dragon is mentioned as a spirit of darkness, and in the symbolism of the mediaeval church it appears as the image of evil powers, the devil or Antichrist, and again we witness its defeat by the champions of light, such as the Archangel Michael and St. George.

In the sagas of the East the dragon predominantly represents a force well disposed towards mankind, and has even become the symbol for the perfect man, the Son of Heaven, the Emperor.

Two of the earlier emperors were actually sons of dragons.[1] The Emperor Yao, a legendary figure of the proto-historical period, came into the world by the visit of a red dragon to his mother. On the back of the dragon was an inscription reading, "Thou shalt enjoy the protection of Heaven." Darkness and

[1] For information concerning dragons in Chinese literature I have drawn on M. W. de Visser's work, "The Dragon in China and Japan," *Verhandelingen der Kon. Akademie von Wetenschappen te Amsterdam*, 1913. Some notes have also been taken from Hayes, *The Chinese Dragon*, Shanghai, 1922.

storm enveloped the two, and fourteen months after this meeting Yao was born.

A similar story is told of Kao Ti (who ruled from 206–195 B.C.), founder of the Han dynasty. T'ai Kung, his father, saw that one day his wife received a visit from a dragon whilst she was asleep by the side of a lake during a storm.

The woman dreamed that she was embraced by a god and later gave birth to Kao Ti. Of this emperor, who came into the world in such a remarkable manner, it is further related that he was much addicted to wine and that he was always guarded by a dragon when he was drunk.

The dragon was associated in many ways with the imperial dignity. When the emperors fell into vicious ways of life the dragon appeared under circumstances which constituted a warning to the monarch who was so forgetful of his duties.

When Shih Huang Ti (246–210 B.C.), the great emperor who founded the Ts'in dynasty, had the dragon god slain with poisoned arrows, the monarch fell ill and died within seven days.

The dragon and the imperial dignity were identified so far that the emperor was named " The real dragon ". The emperor's throne, purposely decorated with pictures of dragons, was called the " dragons' throne ", his robes were richly ornamented with embroidered dragons. Of special importance as an indication of rank was the lapel of the coat, with a dragon embroidered in gold and silver thread on black silk. This emblem might only be worn by the emperor, the imperial princes and the prime minister.

The emblem of the imperial standard was also a dragon.

It was not only the emperors who were associated with dragons. The births and lives of other great men were also characterized by the appearance of a dragon. The night when Confucius (551 B.C.) was born two azure-coloured dragons descended from heaven to his mother's home. She saw them in her sleep and the same night she bore the child who was later to be the great teacher.

Even the small peasant finds his patron in the dragon, in so far as Lung Wang, the dragon king, rules over the sea, the rivers and the rain. Every place of any importance in China has its Lung Wang Miao, a temple for the worship of the giver of rain, and during periods of prolonged drought processions are held and offerings are made to induce the mighty one to grant to the thirsting country the greatest of all gifts—rain.

The fifth day of the fifth month of the Chinese year is devoted to the worship of the dragon king. It should be noted that this festival, the dragon boat festival, coincides with the beginning of the summer rainy season. It has derived its name from the races which are then held between dragon boats, long vessels, propelled by numerous oarsmen, with a carved dragon as figure-head.

De Groot, the great expert on Chinese religious life, considers that these regattas are a case of imitative magic, in which the competing dragon boats are intended to represent the conflicts of dragons, which in the Chinese conception are always followed by violent rain.

The dragon appears in Chinese history in association with the very earliest civilized monuments. Among the objects found in the capital of the Yin dynasty (about 1100 B.C.), the modern An Yang in Honan, there have been found ivory carvings which are supposed to represent dragons' heads, and the character Lung (dragon) is found among the archaic characters inscribed on plates of bone and tortoise shell.

In the *Yi King* (" The Book of Change "), a work probably produced shortly after the oracle bones (about 1000 B.C.), we find numerous references which point on the one hand to the dragon as a bringer of rain and on the other to its connection with the birth of great men.

In the graves of the Han period and the succeeding " six dynasties " in China and Korea there have been found numerous and sometimes very fine dragon images, which as a rule represent the dragon as a long fabulous animal with four legs and a long tail.

In the art of the T'ang and Sung ages we find the dragon types almost fully developed in the form in which they survive in modern art. Space does not permit us to attempt the alluring, but certainly difficult, task of ascertaining the origin of the multiform dragons in Chinese art. Rostovtzeff has expressed the surmise that the dragon as an artistic motif is not of Chinese origin, but has been borrowed, via Iran, from the Babylonian-Assyrian civilization.[1] On the other hand it is worthy of mention that on an urn of the Hsin Tien period in Kansu (probably of the second millennium B.C.) we find a snake-like animal with forelegs and horns, a form which may evidently be a prototpye of the more elaborate dragon of historical times.

It is by no means improbable that crocodiles, the alligator of the Yangtse district, *Alligator sinensis*, and the crocodile of Southern China have played a fundamental rôle in the development of the early type of dragon.

The usual modern dragon type has, however, characteristics which are borrowed from quite different animal species, especially the stag horns, the head, which has certain resemblances to the lion, and the claws, which have been borrowed from beasts, or, even better, birds, of prey. An examination of the dragon of Chinese art on the same lines as are followed in the study of the animal forms of natural history would probably show that there are in existence not only several species but also several genera or even families of the Chinese dragon. In certain divergent forms of this composite monster I have thought I could recognize such features as the long filaments of the mouth of *Silurus*, the curious body of the *Hippocampus* and the arms of the cuttle-fish.

It seems quite natural that such a popular mythical figure as the dragon should be surrounded by a host of legends, and there are indeed extraordinarily remarkable things related about it.

In the summer, which is China's wet season, the dragon dwells in the clouds, and when these fabulous animals quarrel with each other up in the skies there are clouds, thunder and the longed-for rain. If, on the other hand, the dragon feels thirsty, it sucks up the water of the ocean into the skies and thus reveals itself to man in the form of pillars of water, or waterspouts, which are sucked up by strong local whirlwinds.

In the autumn, when the rain ceases, the dragons descend from the skies to visit their palaces on the bottom of seas and

[1] *Iranians and Greeks in South Russia*, 1922, p. 198.

lakes. It is their ascent to the clouds at the spring equinox and their return to the ocean in the autumn which cause the violent equinoctial disturbances of the atmosphere.

The dragon loves three things above all others: bamboo, arsenic and swallows. The fine lattice of the bamboo appeals to his eye. When nobody is in sight the dragon loves to lie in the bamboo groves and listen to the soughing of the wind in the leaves above him.

Arsenic is the dragon's favourite food; he grows fat on it. The food which he prefers to all others is, however, the meat of the swallow. Woe to the man who attempts to pass over water in a boat after having eaten roast swallow. It will give him a peculiar and pleasant aroma, which the dragon will detect from the depths of the water. The man in the boat will be followed by one of the animals, which will blow up a storm. The boat will capsize and the unhappy occupant will become an easy sacrifice to the lord of the waters. Usually the dragon does not eat human flesh, but under these circumstances he must be regarded as having sufficient excuse.

Dragon's blood is a costly liquid and rubies are made of petrified drops of it. Even dragon's saliva has a high value, as it is the most aromatic of all perfumes. "Dragon's body incense" was formerly sent as a tribute to the emperor.

So powerful is this creature, which watches over the emperor's well-being and sends the life-giving rain to the peasants, that even 10,000 years after death it can bring blessings to the sons of Han.

In Chinese apothecaries' shops may be purchased two substances originating in the dragon: Lung Ku (dragon's bone) and Lung Ya (dragon's teeth), which stand in high esteem for their healing power.

In the pharmacological works which Chinese literature has produced since the third century A.D., and right through the centuries, there is much information concerning dragon's bone and its medicinal use.

The places of discovery are given as certain districts in Shansi and Ssŭch'uan, information which has been largely confirmed by our own investigations.

Lei Hiao (A.D. 420–77) gives the following, in parts very amusing, description of these remarkable objects:

> Dragons' bones from Yen Chou, Tsang Chou and Tai Yen are the best. Those which are narrow with broad veins are from female dragons; those which are coarse, with narrow veins, are from the opposite sex. Those showing five colours are best; the white and yellow are medium quality and the black ones are worst. As a rule it may be said that those in which the veins are longitudinal are impure, and those collected by women are useless.

Regarding the relation between dragons and dragons' bones there exists a difference of opinion among ancient authors, in so far as some of them consider that the bones are remains of dead dragons, whilst others insist that the dragon changes not only its skin, but also its bones.

Concerning the preparation of the bone for medicinal purposes the above-mentioned author Lei Hiao gives the following directions:

> To use dragon's bone first boil some aromatic herbs. Wash the bone twice in the hot water, then reduce it to powder and place it in bags of thin stuff. Take two young swallows and, after removing their entrails, stuff the bags into the swallows and hang them over a spring. After one night take the bags out of the swallows, remove the powder and mix it with a preparation for strengthening the kidneys. The effect of such a medicine is as if it were divine.

In later times the procedure seems to have been considerably simplified, for an author of the Sung period writes that the bone should lie in spirit overnight, then be dried over a fire and then powdered.

A modern apothecary told me that the bone should merely be pulverized and the powder taken in tea.

According to the ancient pharmacopoeia many diseases may be cured by dragon's bone: dysentery, gall-stones, fevers and convulsions in children at the breast, internal swellings, paralysis, women's diseases, malaria, etc. Dragon's teeth are also highly esteemed as medicine, and according to the oldest medical work, written by the mythological emperor Sheng Nung, dragons' teeth drive out the following afflictions: spasms, epilepsy and madness and the twelve kinds of convulsions in children.

According to another author dragons' teeth have the quality

of appeasing unrest of the heart and calming the soul. According to a third they cure headache, melancholy, fever, madness and attacks by demons. All the authorities are agreed on one point, that dragons' teeth are an effective remedy for liver diseases.

Even though notes relating to the true nature of the Chinese " dragon bones " are to be found dispersed in the older scientific literature, it was owing to a German scientist that at the turn of the century we first obtained detailed knowledge of this interesting object.

A German naturalist, K. A. Haberer, went to China in 1899 to explore the interior of the country, but owing to the disturbances and the hostility to foreigners which marked that period, the " Boxer " period, he was forced to restrict his activities to the Treaty Ports.

He purchased from apothecaries' shops in Shanghai, Ningpo, Ichang and Peking a number of dragon bones and dragons' teeth, and this abundant material was examined and described by Professor Max Schlosser of Munich in a treatise entitled " Die fossilen Säugethiere Chinas ".[1]

The very title of Schlosser's treatise indicates the conclusions at which he arrived concerning the " dragon bones ". The veil of mysticism over these objects was removed by the exhaustive and perfected investigations of the learned Munich palaeontologist, while at the same time these once so mysterious objects gained greatly in scientific interest. It appeared that the dragons' bones had no connection whatever with any kind of reptile, but were on the contrary fossil remains of mammals which lived on the Chinese steppes and beside the rivers during the Tertiary and Pleistocene ages.

Schlosser distinguished in the material collected by Haberer no less than about 90 mammal forms, divided into widely differing groups. The apes were represented by only a single tooth, which was possibly human. Among the beasts of prey Schlosser described several kinds, among which were bears, hyenas and the remarkable sabre-toothed *Machairodus*. Of the elephants there were the *Stegodon*, the *Mastodon* and the *Elephas* ; among

[1] *Abhandl. der Königl. bayerischen Akad. der Wissenschaften*, Band 22, Abteil. 1, 1903.

the rhinoceri the *Aceratherium* and the *Rhinoceros*; of equine animals the three-toed *Hipparion* and *Equus*, also a *Hippopotamus*, several kinds of the genus *Sus*, a new type of camel, *Paracamelus*, giraffes and various stags and antelopes.

Schlosser's monograph constitutes a giant stride forward in the investigation of the ancient animal life of China. It is evident, however, that material acquired by purchase in apothecaries' shops and consisting of broken bones, pieces of jaws and in many cases isolated teeth, cannot afford a complete picture of the appearance and relationship of the ancient animals. A still greater defect in this material is that it was not known at all where these dragon bones came from. For obvious reasons the merchants would not disclose the names or the situations of the places in which they made their finds. The few and hesitating local indications to be found in Schlosser's book tell us, with our present knowledge, nothing, and are even in parts definitely misleading.

Such was the state of knowledge of China's fossil mammals when we resolved in 1917 in the Geological Survey in Peking to attempt to find the places where dragons' bones are obtained from the Tertiary deposits.

Our first step was to send out to the mission stations of China, and to foreigners who might be expected to be willing to help us, a circular in which we reported Schlosser's investigations and asked for help and guidance in our search for dragon-bone sites.

Among the first to reply to our appeal was Father Fl. De Preter, of the Belgian Catholic Mission at Sungshutsweize in Eastern Mongolia, and the Rev. A. Bertram Lewis of the Protestant China Inland Mission at Hotsin in the southern part of the province of Shansi.

Pre-eminent among those who assisted us, however, were the Swedish missionaries in Central Honan.

When, in the late autumn of 1918, I visited this district, the missionary Richard Andersson showed me at Honanfu a Rhinoceros skull, and I had an opportunity on November 26th of examining the place in the loess deposits south-east of Honanfu where it was stated to have been found.

When, some days later, I came to Hsin An, west of Honanfu, on the railway to Kuanyintang, I found in one of the women missionaries at that place, Miss Maria Pettersson, the best support for my work.

In my book *The Dragon and the Foreign Devils* I have recounted my first meeting with Maria Pettersson in the spring of 1917, and my personal impressions of this devoted worker's service to her mission. I have also described the excursion which I made in her company on November 29th, 1918, in a north-north-westerly direction from the little town of Hsin An, where the station is situated.

Having expressed to Maria Pettersson my warmest thanks for that day, which was a turning-point in my scientific work in the East, I can now confine myself to a description of the district in which we made our discoveries of Tertiary mammals.

The district north of Hsin An is hilly, with heights rising from 40 to 70 metres above the bottoms of the valleys. The bed rock consists of steeply inclined strata of red sandstone and shale belonging to the great sediment formation of which the Palaeozoic coal formation is the most important element.

These strata are only visible in a few places in the bottom of the valleys north of Hsin An. Elsewhere the solid bedrock is covered by beds of red variegated clay with inlays partly of tuffaceous limestone and partly of river gravel. In the smaller valleys are found accumulations of Huang Tu, so characteristic of Northern China, the yellow earth or loess, to use a term originating in Germany. This loess deposit is much later than the red or multi-coloured clays and corresponds in time, as we shall see more closely in chapter seven, to the Ice age.

It was in the red clay that, thanks to Miss Pettersson's co-operation, we succeeded in finding our first fossils. The place where the discovery was made is called Shang Yin Kou, and lies 9 km. from the town of Hsin An. The site of the fossils is on the eastern side of a small valley, in the cultivated fields. The fossil bones were found in the red clay in a space 5 metres long by 2 metres high. Here we found a closely packed accumulation of leg bones, skulls, etc., of a number of animal forms. It was the first opportunity offered to me and my Chinese collectors to obtain possession ourselves, in a well-stocked site, of these "dragons' teeth", which had hitherto been surrounded in so much mystery, and the lure of the discovery was heightened because we now for the first time held in our hands complete jaws of rhinoceri, hyenas, etc., whereas hitherto we had only been able to acquire isolated teeth, or at best pieces of a jaw, from medicine dealers.

We devoted two of the first days of December to collecting at Shang Yin Kou. We wandered in the early morning along the 6-mile road from Hsin An to the little clay hill, and returned in the evening with a procession of coolies, each carrying two baskets full of lumps of clay containing the fossil bones. There was certainly much of the lure and excitement of novelty in these days of work at Shang Yin Kou. We knew that we had stripped from the dragon a good deal of his mystery, and I could foresee with certainty that my friend Professor Wiman in Upsala would be pleasantly surprised when he came to study these discoveries in his museum.

After we had concluded the preliminary examination of Shang Yin Kou we continued along the railway to the west to Mien Chih Hsien, where we found most zealous help at the Swedish Mission Station from the missionary Malte Ringberg. North of the town of Mien Chih we made several discoveries of mammal remains in a somewhat later red Tertiary clay.

Even though these discoveries in Central Honan increased in a very high degree our belief in the possibility of making rich discoveries of mammal faunas, it was not yet clear that we had to do here only with objects of secondary importance and that the major discoveries were to be made elsewhere. At these places in Honan " dragon bones " were only collected occasionally, and exclusively for local use. It was evident that the medicine market of the whole of China was supplied with its needs of dragon's bone from some other place.

Inquiries at an apothecary's shop in Peking pointed to a market in Chichou in Southern Chihli, south of Paotingfu, as the place where large quantities of medicines, including dragons' bones, were purveyed and where there was a prospect of obtaining further information concerning the great sources of supply.

With the gracious assistance of the Director of the Geological Survey, Dr. V. K. Ting, one of its younger geologists, Mr. Li, was placed at my disposal. Mr. Li had even before the above-mentioned journey to Honan visited Chichou in May 1918 and had there received information which pointed to a remote and very inaccessible place of the name of Pao Te Hsien, far up in the north-west of Shansi on the Yellow River.

It was only in the summer of 1919 that I had an opportunity to send two of my collectors, Yao and Chang, to Pao Te Hsien, but this reconnaissance bore no fruit, since they arrived at an unsuitable season. Later on I sent Chang alone. He succeeded beyond all expectations and brought back to Peking large collections, which in respect of completeness and excellent state of preservation of the skeletons far surpassed the material collected by me in Honan.

It became clear from the collections made by Chang that in the district of Pao Te Hsien we had made the acquaintance of one of the most important regions that exists for mammals of the later Tertiary period. Our activities had now grown so much in importance that it seemed desirable to entrust the systematic exploitation of the Pao Te Hsien discovery to a real expert. I therefore addressed myself to Professor Wiman, who persuaded a young Austrian palaeontologist named Dr. Otto Zdansky to journey to China for two years in order to co-operate with me in the excavation and scientific treatment of these fossil remains of mammals.

During a stay of some months at Pao Te Hsien, Zdansky carried out an exhaustive model investigation of the site of the dragons' bones and of the curious industry to which these deposits had given rise. From his treatise " Fundorte der Hipparion-Fauna um Pao Te Hsien " I take the following data.[1]

The district most prolific in dragons' bones is situated 13 km. north-east of the town of Pao Te, around the village of Chi Chia Kou. The landscape here, as north of Hsin An in Honan, consists of a plateau intersected by valleys, though the valleys here have more the character of narrow ravines. The bedrock beneath the later strata consists of the productive Palaeozoic coal series, from which coal is extracted in many places for local use. Farthest to the north-north-west there lies immediately over the coal-bearing formation a series of strata of at most 25–30 metres thickness, consisting of gravel beds, green-yellow or green-white deposits of marl or marly limestone and fine

[1] *Bulletin of the Geological Survey of China*, No. 5, 1923.

yellow sand. In these strata we found some remains of a rhinoceros, an animal belonging to the horse family, fragments of fishes and freshwater molluscs. Zdansky named this series of strata the Lu Tzŭ Kou series, after the name of a village situated in this part of the country.

The Lu Tzŭ Kou series is covered by the same red clay as we encountered in the Hsin An district of Honan. Where the Lu Tzŭ Kou series is missing, the red clay lies direct on the coal formation. The clay, which contains embedded banks of gravel, is about 65 metres thick. Somewhat above the centre, i.e. about 25 metres above the base of the clay formation, we found in several places nests of mammal bones which gave rise to the curious mining industry which stimulated our interest in this place.

For at least 60–70 years back, and probably longer, dragons' bones have been extracted at Chi Chia Kou by a special kind of mining. Wherever an accumulation of bones was discernible in the clay walls of the ravines a sort of gallery was dug, somewhat less than 1 metre in height and breadth. When the supply of bones was exhausted, the digging was continued haphazard in the hope of finding a new stock in a few days' time. In this way during the course of decades a whole network of narrow winding galleries has been formed, many of them over 100 metres in length, and many industrious bone seekers still carry on their work with their simple tools deep into the interior of the clay. The principal implement in the process is a very simple pick-axe. In addition they use, after the fossil-bearing lumps of clay have been brought into the open, a small axe in order to cut away the bone from the clay and in order to hack out the teeth from the jaws and skulls, as these command a higher price. The blocks of clay are conveyed from the mine galleries on small wooden trolleys running on four solid wooden wheels. The length of the trolley is 1·3 metres, its breadth 60 cm. and its height 35 cm. The trolley is hauled by a man on all fours by a rope running from one shoulder between his legs to the trolley.

During work in the galleries light is supplied by simple lamps burning vegetable oil of local manufacture.

Work in the galleries is performed preferably during the cold seasons. The work is purely seasonal, alternating with summer agriculture.

In the spring the buyers of the large druggist firms arrive at Chi Chia Kou and the bones are sold for 6 small copper coins per Chinese pound, whilst the much more valuable teeth fetch 6–8 large copper coins per pound.

Workmen in these mines have a very good idea of the real nature of the skulls which they bring to light. The resemblance of a *Hipparion* skull to that of a horse is sufficiently striking for the nature of the animal to be approximately clear to them. The large beasts of prey are the Lao Hu (tiger) and the small ones the wolf or a similar species. On the spot, therefore, it is fairly well known that, at any rate in part, there is no question of dragons, but only of ancient mammals. But the teeth are struck out of the skulls and the sick Chinaman who buys from the chemist in his native town, let us say, a rhinoceros tooth, is assuredly convinced that he is enjoying the help of his revered patron, the dragon.

When Dr. Zdansky and my Chinese collectors were at work at Chi Chia Kou they did everything possible to remain on a friendly footing with the workers in the mines. They induced them to make special efforts to excavate the skulls intact, and such complete specimens were paid for at a higher rate than that offered by the druggists' buyers. In this way Zdansky succeeded in amassing an immense collection, which in completeness and perfection of preservation probably surpasses even the famous collection of fossil mammals of the same period from Pikermi and Samos.

In 1922 Zdansky collected mammal fossils at Ching Yang Fu in eastern Kansu. One of his discoveries was high up in a perpendicular clay wall (Fig. 30*a*). When he had succeeded in hewing out from this steep wall an immense block of clay filled with skeleton parts, he rigged up a tackle by means of which he succeeded in lowering the colossal block (Fig. 30*b*). Finally we see ten men carrying the block out of the ravine (Fig. 30*c*).

The very large collection of mammal fossils was sent from Peking to Upsala for treatment by Professor Wiman.

All who are interested in the successful prosecution of this great piece of scientific research have reason to admire the resolution, insight and unique endurance with which Professor

FIG. 30.—*a*, *b*, *c*. Zdansky's three sketches. For explanation see the text.

Wiman first completed the preparation of this vast material and then distributed it among a number of skilled collaborators for study and description.

The preparation of the Chinese fossil material was conducted in Upsala during the years 1918–28 under especially unfavourable local conditions, but, in spite of this difficulty, rapidly and well.

It would be out of place in this popular account to enumerate the long series of frequently unknown mammal forms in the *Hipparion* fauna. As illustrative examples we shall dwell instead on a few of the commonest and most interesting forms.

Let us begin with Torsten Ringström's monograph on the rhinoceri, which appeared in 1924.[1]

Of horned rhinoceri Ringström describes three widely different kinds.

Dicerorhinus orientalis (Schlosser) possessed two horns, of which the stronger one was far forward on the nose and the other just in front of the eyes.

Diceratherium palaeosinense Ringström, on the other hand, had two small horns pairwise on the sides of the nose bone.

Most interesting of all the rhinoceros discoveries and perhaps the most significant novelty which China's *Hipparion* strata furnished to palaeontological science is the curious form which Ringström described under the name *Sinotherium lagrelii.* Both the family and the species were new to science. The former name indicates that it was China which contributed this gift to science. The type name is given in honour of Dr. Axel Lagrelius, the great benefactor of our work in China, who not only rendered possible our collecting activities but also found the means to defray the costly work of preparation.

The *Sinotherium* is a gigantic member of the rhinoceros group, but otherwise shows little relationship to the majority of its forms. The most characteristic feature of the animal is that the enamel of the molars is folded in a manner which reminds us of the equally gigantic *Elasmotherium*, two species of which are found in soil of the steppes of Southern Russia. There is no doubt that the *Sinotherium* and *Elasmotherium* are closely

[1] " Nashörner der Hipparion-Fauna Nord Chinas ", *Palaeontologia Sinica*, Ser. C, Vol. 1, Fasc. 4, Peking, 1924.

related, even though there is a great difference in age. The *Elasmotherium* belongs to the latest geological age, the Pleistocene, but the *Sinotherium* belongs to the transition from the Miocene to the Pliocene. The *Sinotherium* is the largest of these forms, and there is much to indicate that the whole type had reached its zenith as early as the age of the *Hipparion* fauna. The Pleistocene *Elasmotherium* makes rather the impression of overspecialized degeneration.

Commonest of all the rhinoceros forms in the abundant material from Pao Te Hsien are species of the *Chilotherium*. A reconstruction of this type executed by the artist Sven Ekblom, under the guidance of Professor Wiman, is to be found in Fig. 31, for which the *Chilotherium anderssoni* has served as the principal model. We see that we are here concerned with a type in which both sexes lack horns and in which the legs are shortened, so that the shape of the body reminds us rather of a hippopotamus than a rhinoceros. The arrangement of the teeth suggests that the animal lived on hard grass containing silica, and it is possible that the extremely fine lines to be observed on the inside of the lower teeth are the marks of this rough food.

In this place we can only mention that in the *Hipparion* fauna there are numerous deer, which have been described by Dr. Zdansky,[1] as well as some antelopes and elephants, which have not yet been described. As regards the three-toed horses of the *Hipparion* family which were described by Dr. Ivar Sefve,[2] we would only mention that side by side with the long familiar form *Hipparion richthofeni* Koken a number of new forms have been described. An English woman palaeontologist, Helga Sharpe Pearson, has described the pigs of the *Hipparion* fauna, of which the most important, by reason of its curious nose, bears the difficult name *Chleuastochaerus stehlini* (Schlosser). The family name is new to science and the learned authoress informs us that this peculiar name comes from the Greek χλευαρω, which means " disguise oneself by making ugly grimaces ".

In 1927 another of Professor Wiman's students, Dr. Birger

[1] " Fossile Hirsche Chinas ", *Palaeontologia Sinica*, Ser. C, Vol. 2, Fasc. 3, 1925.

[2] " Die Hipparionen Nord-Chinas ", *Palaeontologia Sinica*, Ser. C, Vol. 4, Fasc. 2, 1927.

FIG. 31.—A Chilotherium family. Reconstruction by the artist Sven Ekblom under the guidance of Professor Wiman.

Bohlin, subsequently famous for his excavations at Chou K'ou Tien and his participation in Sven Hedin's central Asian expedition, published a richly illustrated monograph on the giraffes of the *Hipparion* fauna.[1] We cannot in this place give a report on these relatives of the giraffes of the South African steppes and of the okapi of the primeval African forests, but we would emphasize

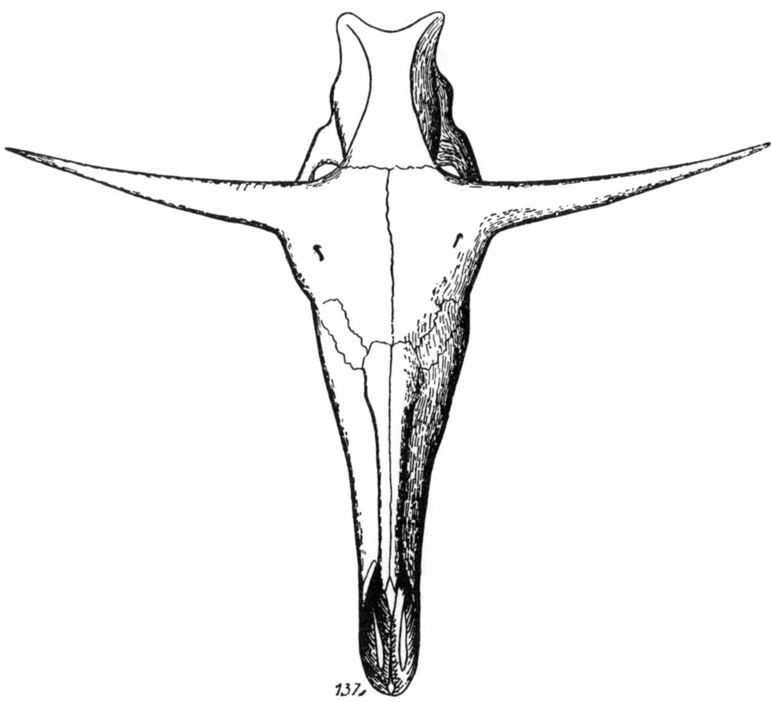

FIG. 32.—*Samotherium sinense*. Reconstruction of male skull. (*After Bohlin*.)

that the frequency of giraffes in the *Hipparion* fauna is one of the grounds for the assumption that the big game of Africa, and especially of the steppes, is a modern survival of the abundant animal life, the *Hipparion* fauna, which during the transition from the Miocene to the Pliocene age existed in a broad belt running across Southern Europe and Central Asia.

[1] " Die Familie Giraffidae ", *Palaeontologia Sinica*, Ser. C, Vol. 4, Fasc. 1.

Professor Wiman, together with the artist Ekblom, has been so exceedingly kind as to reconstruct one of these giraffes, the *Samotherium sinense*, described by Bohlin (Plate 6). In the background we see a pair of these animals grazing among the branches of the *Hipparion*-steppe trees. In the foreground one of the numerous large cats has attacked a *Samotherium*, but has fatally miscalculated its powers of defence.

This picture, which shows two widely differing types of mammals of the *Hipparion* steppes, induces us to mention the splendid monograph on the beasts of prey of the *Hipparion* fauna which the collector of the whole material, Dr. Zdansky, published in 1924.[1]

Beasts of prey constitute to a certain extent the finest material in the collection of the abundant and splendidly preserved skeletons of the *Hipparion* age. Whoever beholds in Professor Wiman's fine new museum in Upsala the monster beasts from the *Hipparion* clay of China will scarcely imagine that these complete and gleaming skulls of beasts of prey are about a million years old.

In the composition of the scene in Plate 6, Professor Wiman probably had in mind a new genus of cat, *Metailurus*, of two types, the *M. major* and *M. minor* (Fig. 33) which were described by Zdansky in the work just cited.

In addition there are to be found in the *Hipparion* fauna three kinds of the terrifying group of sabre-toothed tigers. These three forms are *Machairodus palanderi* (Fig. 34), *M. tingii* and *M. maximiliani*. All these were unknown species and in Zdansky's description the naming shows that he regarded these forms as special treasures, to which he assigned three men, each of the highest repute in his own field of work. The *M. palanderi* has taken its name from Louis Palander of Vega, the first chairman of the Swedish China Research Committee, *M. tingii* is a name given in honour of Dr. V. K. Ting, the creator of the China Geological Survey and the founder of the great " Palaeontologia Sinica " series, *M. Maximiliani* recalls Professor Maximilian Schlosser of Munich, who in 1904 published the first great monograph on China's *Hipparion* fauna. As a final specimen of the abundant

[1] " Jungtertiäre Carnivoren Chinas ", *Palaeontologia Sinica*, Ser. C, Vol. 2, Fasc. 1.

Plate 6

Samotherium sinense from the Hipparion strata at Pao Te Hsien. Reconstruction, under the direction of Prof. C. Wiman, by Sven Ekblom

[*face page* 88

Hipparion fauna I should also mention that we likewise found a number of tortoises as well as the pelvis of an ostrich.

Before we leave the *Hipparion* age it remains to endeavour to resolve the question how the immense hordes of varied big game lived, died and became embedded in the red clay.

The sediments indicate that large parts of Northern China were grass steppes with a dry but warm climate. The nature

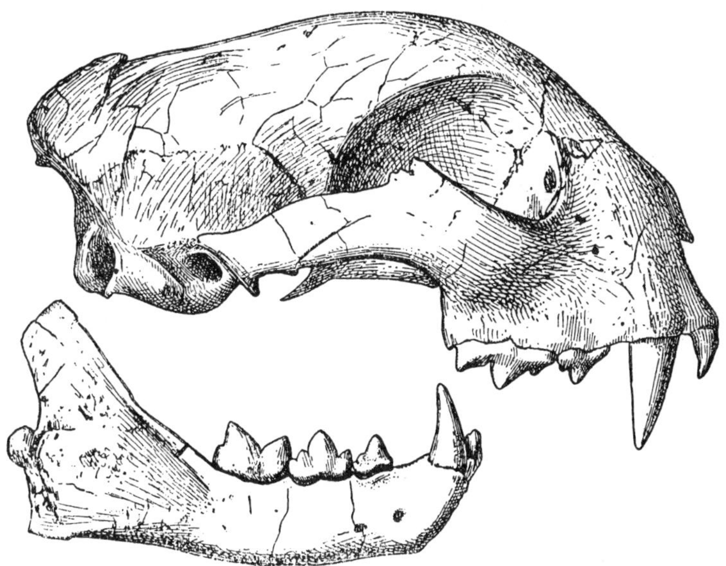

FIG. 33.—Skull of *Metailurus minor*. (*After Zdansky*.)

of the fauna points in the same direction, even though there were, especially in Central Shansi, also tracts with abundant forest vegetation.

We must therefore suppose that the *Hipparion* fauna lived on grassy steppes, with here and there park-like patches of wood, very much like the South African steppes. In this steppe country was formed, under the influence of the warm climate, the red clay, with its high percentage of iron oxide, in which the bones lie embedded.

We must, however, pay heed to yet another circumstance, namely that the red clay is in most cases entirely devoid of fossils,

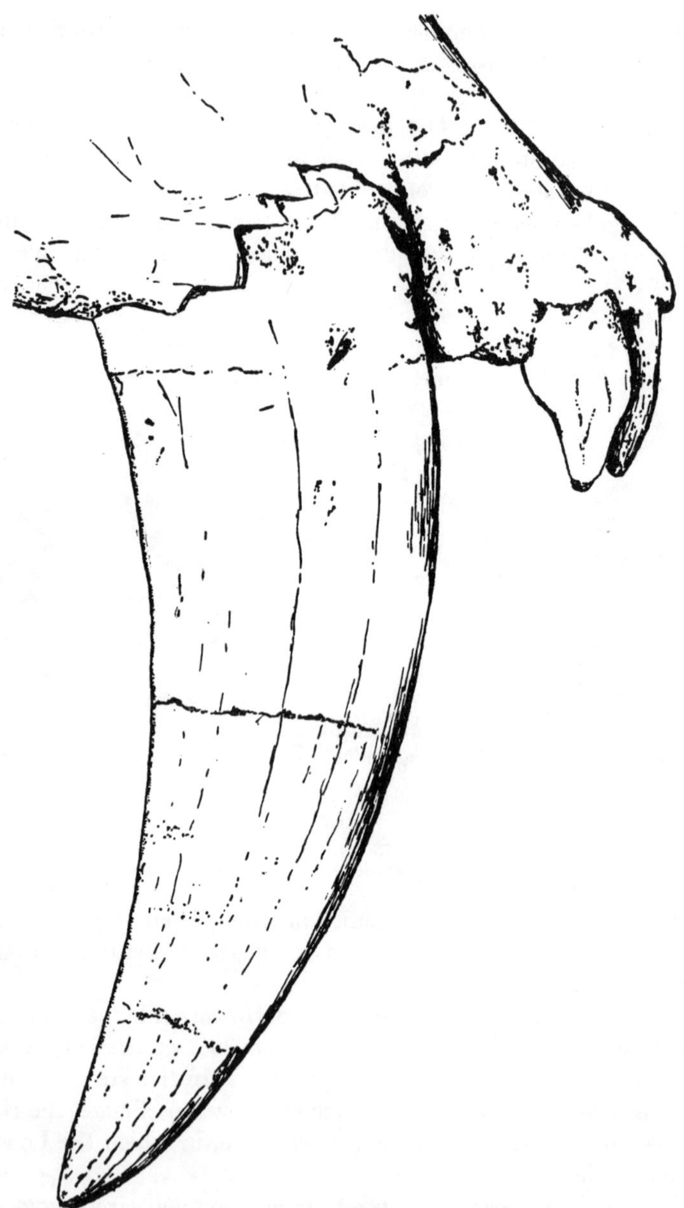

FIG. 34.—Snout of sabre-toothed tiger, *Machairodus palanderi*, with the terrible knife tooth, in natural size.

and that only in a few places are mammal remains found in it. But where such a discovery is made it happens in many cases that in a space of a few square yards one finds an accumulation of bones which never belong to the same skeleton, but are chaotically piled up together. Not least significant is the fact that several widely different hoofed animals and beasts of prey are packed together anyhow. This fact struck me particularly during the excavation of the first copious *Hipparion* discovery at Shang Yin Kou in Honan, and Dr. Zdansky found similar accumulations of fossils on the great site of medicine bones at Pao Te Hsien. At Shang Yin Kou I also observed, in close association with the bones, beds of gravel, certainly deposited by running water.

From these observations we are able to reconstruct the following explanation of these accumulations of bones.

Under normal conditions the animals of the *Hipparion* fauna were eaten up by beasts of prey or died natural deaths out in the steppes. In both cases the bones remained on the surface and soon decayed, so that nothing remained of them. But occasionally there occurred natural upheavals which disturbed the uniform life of the steppes. Violent cloudbursts converted the clay steppes in a few hours into a treacherous morass. Whole hordes of terrified animals of widely different types were drowned and washed together, often perhaps only after the floating corpses had decayed and fallen to pieces, with the clay and gravel, in a chaotic mass of bones.

Other kinds of natural catastrophes are also conceivable. The brilliant palaeontologist, Professor Abel of Vienna, has drawn attention to the fact that drought may have produced a similar result. If the steppe were set on fire by a flash of lightning, all sorts of frightened animals would be driven by the wall of fire towards the rivers. When the wild flight reached the precipitous banks masses of animals would be forced down in the clayey river beds.

If these conclusions are well founded, we must regard each *Hipparion* accumulation as a mass grave concealing the sacrifices of some catastrophe of the steppes. Were these heaps of bones refuse near the lairs of beasts of prey, we should scarcely find so often the remains of tigers beside the animals which were ordinarily the prey of this great bloodthirsty feline species.

When in 1923 I published my comprehensive account of the Tertiary and Pleistocene deposits of Northern China,[1] I ventured the surmise that there exists in Northern China between the early Pliocene *Hipparion* clays and the Pleistocene loess formations a transition series of clay-like sediment, which in certain places is quite like the red *Hipparion* clay and in others more like an unusually red loess. I thought therefore that during the later Pliocene period the character of the sedimentation had successively changed from the red *Hipparion* clay to the grey-yellow loess soil and I suggested that these later Pliocene clays are remarkable, among other things, for a genuine horse, *Equus*.

In the same work I pointed out that the problem of these transition stages from *Hipparion* clay to loess would be further elucidated when our fossil material had been fully described under Professor Wiman's direction.

This expectation has been fulfilled. It is now clear that there exists an extensive series of late Pliocene age. The site at Lan Kou in Mien Chih Hsien, Honan, which I considered *Hipparion* clay, now proves to be late Pliocene and is characterized, among other things, by an extremely curious horse form, which Sefve has described under the name *Proboscidipparion sinense*, an animal provided with a snout resembling that of a tapir. In the same place there occurs a stag, new both in genus and species, *Epirusa Hitzheimeri*.

Most remarkable among the late Pliocene discoveries is a complete skeleton of a camel, *Paracamelus gigas* Schlosser, which was found at Yang Shao Tsun, a discovery made quite near to Lan Kou, a place which has won great renown as the first known prehistoric dwelling-place in Northern China, and discovered by us in 1921 (cf. Chapter X).

Since 1923, when I completed my researches in the geology of Northern China, our knowledge of the late Pliocene deposits has made great progress.

In 1924 E. Licent and G. B. Barbour found in the San Kan

[1] " Essays on the Cenozoic of Northern China ", *Memoirs of the Geol. Survey of China*, Ser. A, No. 3.

Ho, a tributary of the Hun River, an extraordinarily rich collection of fossils in a lake deposit, together with a most magnificent late Pliocene fauna, which has been called, after the place of its discovery, the Ni Ho Wan fauna. According to the investigations conducted by Teilhard de Chardin, this abundant mammal fauna is probably roughly contemporaneous with the rich deposits of freshwater mussels which were first found by Dr. V. K. Ting in 1918 at San Men in the Yellow River between Shansi and Honan. This series of deposits is now differentiated as a special stage of formation under the name of *Sanmenian* and ascribed, together with the Ni Ho Wan deposits, to the latest Pliocene. The San Men deposits in the valley of the Yellow River are here described in Chapter VII in connection with the yellow earth, or loess, which covers them.

The Chou K'ou Tien fauna, which has become world famous owing to the " Peking Man " (cf. next chapter), is regarded as somewhat later than the Ni Ho Wan formation and consequently as belonging to the earliest section of the Pleistocene age.

Fig. 35.—Dr. Otto Zdansky, now Professor at the University of Cairo, who with extraordinary skill excavated our most important vertebrate fossils and who later described large parts of this vast material.

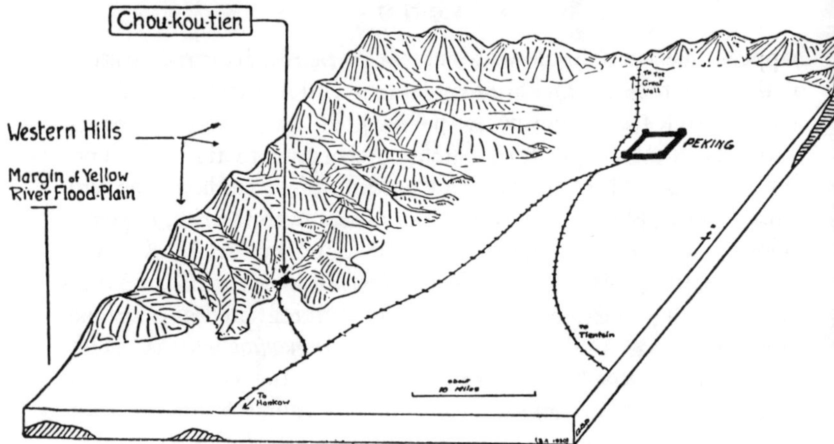

FIG. 36.—Block diagram showing the situation of Chou K'ou Tien. (*After Professor George B. Barbour.*)

CHAPTER SIX

THE PEKING MAN

WHEN I sit and muse on the history of the development of animal life as it is reflected in the long series of fossil-bearing strata of the geological formations, I am struck by a comparison with the modern film drama.

As it were endlessly, the long, sharply illuminated film unrolls itself in the darkness of the theatre. The pictures change, often with sudden turns from wide vistas and crowds of minor players to near views with only a couple of stars on the stage. From a small beginning the drama develops, the plot becomes more complicated and more and more characters are drawn into the action until the tense culmination of the finale is reached.

Layer after layer of fossil-bearing strata follow each other in endless numbers, just like the pictures in a film. Just as the film lies rolled up and lifeless until it is set in motion and until the beams of the electric arc-lamp project it, so also the fossil remains lie silent and unintelligible in the beds of rocks until scientific research illumines them with its penetrating searchlight. But the resemblance goes much further : certain strata are filled only with the commonest forms of fossil research, perhaps one single common form in endless numbers, whilst it sometimes happens that a single blow of hammer or pick will reveal a rarity of the first order, capable of awakening interest far beyond the narrow circles of scientific journals.

We have sat for a time watching the geological film. The first figures to appear, the *Collenia* nodules, deep down in the Sinian deposits, were quite obscure; then, scene after scene followed, a mass of supernumeraries: trilobites, brachiopods, mussels and corals. The forms of ancient plant life, *Cordaites* and *Gigantopteris*, *Gingko* and *Sequoia* formed a setting before which our great modern producers would stand abashed. The Cretaceous system presents us with a mythical drama of giants and trolls such as *Helopus*, *Tanius* and the isolated *Stegosaurian* tooth, which is a charming subject for a detective drama of prehistoric research.

But it is only when we reach the first mammals in the Eocene deposits of the Yellow River and in Shantung that the intensity of the performance is increased and we are completely captured when the white screen reveals the splendid pictures from the *Hipparion* steppes.

The approach of our own species is heralded by another riddle, the *Pliopithecus* tooth in the lake deposits at Ertemte, possibly a near relative to our own forefathers.[1] And finally there appears on the scene the Douglas Fairbanks of the prehistoric drama, the Peking Man.

One day in February 1918 I met in Peking J. McGregor Gibb, professor of chemistry at the mission university which at that time bore the somewhat pretentious title of Peking University. He knew that I was interested in fossils and consequently he told me that he had just been out at Chou K'ou Tien, about 50 km. south-west of Peking, a place which I have already described on a couple of occasions during my story.

He had there heard of a place called "Chicken Bone Hill", Chi Ku Shan. It was so called because red clay had been found there full of the bones of birds. Professor Gibb had himself visited the place and had brought back to Peking various frag-

[1] *Pliopithecus* is an extinct Tertiary relative of the gibbon, which is regarded as close to the original form of man. The discovery here referred to was made by me in 1920 in a Pliocene lake deposit at Ertemte in Southern Mongolia.

ments of the bone-bearing clay. He was kind enough to show me these fragments. They consisted of the characteristic red clay which fills up the cavities in the limestone in many places in the district of Chou K'ou Tien, but the remarkable thing about this particular clay was that it was full of small bones, most of them hollow and evidently belonging to birds.

Gibb's description was so alluring that I visited the spot on the 22nd–23rd March in the same year.

Chou K'ou Tien's primary distinction is the numerous limestone quarries in the Ordovician limestone, and the bones are to be found in the middle of such an old quarry. The bone-bearing clay rises like a detached pillar from the bottom of the quarry. Its total height is 5·5 metres. It is clear that the clay at one time filled a cavity in the limestone and that the limestone burners had carefully preserved this mass of clay, which thus gradually changed its character from being a filling of a cavity to that of a detached pillar.

We may ask ourselves why the workmen so carefully avoided this clay deposit, of which they could easily have got rid. The explanation is perhaps to be found in a story told to us while we were there collecting bones :

" Once upon a time, more than a hundred years ago, there was a cave here in which lived foxes, which devoured all the chickens in the neighbourhood. In the course of time some of these foxes were transformed into evil spirits. One man tried to kill the foxes, but the evil spirits drove him mad."

It seems not improbable that the superstition associated with this bone deposit protected it from disturbance.

During our visit we only broke off a small portion of the middle of the pillar and found the bones of a couple of species of rodents, as well as of one smaller and one larger beast of prey, but especially numerous bones of birds.

We were much pleased with our discovery, which was the first of fossil bones. But the bones were small, and belonged, as it seemed, to common and possibly still surviving forms. It also seemed probable that the age of the deposit was not great. When, later on in the same autumn, we made the great *Hipparion* discoveries in Honan, our interest in Chicken Bone Hill entirely vanished.

Landscape at Chou K'ou Tien

[*face page 96*

But when Dr. Zdansky came out to China in the early summer of 1921 in order to assist me in the excavation of the *Hipparion* deposits, we agreed that he should first of all journey to Chou K'ou Tien and excavate on Chicken Bone Hill in order to obtain some knowledge of conditions in Chinese country districts.

Just at that time there arrived in Peking the famous mammal palaeontologist, Dr. Walter Granger, from the American Museum of Natural History in New York, in order to take up his duties as Chief Palaeontologist in Dr. Roy Chapman Andrews' great expedition to Mongolia.

Dr. Granger and I agreed to visit Chou K'ou Tien in order to see Dr. Zdansky, and to give Dr. Granger some idea of working conditions in China, whilst at the same time Dr. Granger very kindly offered to acquaint us with the extraordinarily developed technique of excavations which had been one of the factors in the phenomenal progress of the American vertebrate palaeontologists.

Zdansky had taken up his headquarters in the same little village temple in which I had lived in 1918. Dr. Granger and I installed ourselves with Zdansky and went with him to Chicken Bone Hill, where we pointed out some of the small bones. Whilst we were sitting at our work a man of the neighbourhood came and looked at us.

" There's no use staying here any longer. Not far from here there is a place where you can collect much larger and better dragons' bones," said he.

Knowing well that in the matter of search for dragons' bones in China we must never neglect any clue, I immediately began to question the man. His information seemed so reliable that after a few minutes we packed up our kit and followed him in a northerly direction over the limestone hills. It appeared that the new discovery also lay in an abandoned quarry 150 metres west of, and at a higher level than, the railway station at Chou K'ou Tien. In an almost perpendicular wall of limestone, about 10 metres high, which faced north, the man showed us a filled-up fissure in the limestone consisting of pieces of limestone and fragments of bones of larger animals, the whole bound together by sintered limestone. We had not searched for many minutes before we found the jaw of a pig, which showed that we were in the presence of a discovery with much greater possibilities than Chicken Bone Hill. That evening we went home with rosy dreams of great discoveries.

Granger sat that evening and pondered over a toothless jaw which he had found and which I guessed to belong to a stag. The learned palaeontologist would assuredly have laughed at me if he had not been such a far-sighted and kindly man, for this remarkable lower jaw showed such a marked thickening that it was almost circular in section and consequently far from the type of a normal stag's jaw. Now it so happened that in the late autumn of 1918 I had found in red clay on the Huai Lai plain north of Peking well-preserved jaws with the teeth intact, which convinced me that I had to do with a stag with an extreme development of the mysterious phenomenon of bone thickening which the learned call hyperostosis.

The following day broke in brilliant sunshine and we wandered along the straight road from our temple to Lao Niu Kou, as the new place of discovery is called, and which will one day become one of the most sacred places of pilgrimage for investigations into the history of the human race.

The day's harvest exceeded all expectations. Not only did we find the jaws, with all the teeth intact, of the hyperostotic animal and were able to confirm that it really was a stag. Rhinoceros teeth, the jaws of a hyena and pieces of jawbone belonging to the bear genus were also some of the finds of the day. When we raised our glasses at the beginning of dinner, our happy trio was able to drink to a certain discovery. Dr. Granger had during the course of the day instructed Dr. Zdansky and myself in the excellent American bandaging system and we now decided to leave the completion of our new discovery to Dr. Zdansky, who probably had weeks of work in front of him on this spot. The next day it poured with rain and Granger and I, who were to take train back to Peking, were helplessly flooded in, for the little stream which flows out into the Chou K'ou Tien valley, and which during the preceding days had been an insignificant purling rill, was now a wild foaming mountain stream which nobody dared to cross so long as the cloudbursts continued to hurl new masses of water into the valleys.

We drank grog and told stories of almost every part of the world and tried to guess what Zdansky would find during his

Sinanthropus site at Chou K'ou Tien. The man on the extreme left is Dr. Zdansky. Dr. Walter Granger is standing in the lower centre

further excavations at Lao Niu Kou. Then came the evening of the third day and when the sun rose on the fourth day Granger and I prepared for our return home. But right opposite the station we had to strip almost naked and wade across the stream, which had carried away the footbridge and which rose breast high, even though the turbulence of the day before had subsided considerably.

Thus ends the history of the discovery of the Chou K'ou Tien deposit.

Dr. Zdansky remained several weeks at Lao Niu Kou and continued his digging. He has published the results of his work in an essay " Über ein Säugerknochenlager in Chou K'ou Tien " (*Bulletin of the Geological Survey of China*, No. 5, pp. 83–9, 1923). Zdansky's investigations clearly proved that the Lao Niu Kou find fills a cavity in the Ordovician limestone, and that consequently it is essentially of the same kind as the Chicken Bone Hill, only of much greater dimensions. The perpendicular filling in which we made the first discovery and which is visible on the left-hand side, lower down, on Plate 8, is rather a root-like branch of the larger cavity, which is seen in the middle of the section (p. 114).

I give below Dr. Zdansky's measurements, from which it appears that the large central part of the cave was clearly stratified and consisted primarily of clay and clayey sand as well as breccia and yellowish sandstone.

The succession of strata from the top to the bottom is as follows :

SECTION A

8. Breccia of angular sandstone fragments, unstratified. Binding material sandy limestone. Contains land molluscs and pieces of bone.
7. 80 cm. bright red clayey sand with sandstone inlays. Land molluscs.
6. 33 cm. brown clay, slightly banded.
5. 21 cm. dark brown, banded fat clay.
4. 6·5 cm. light yellow clay.
3. 4·5 cm. black-brown fat clay. Bones and occasionally much corroded teeth. Contains flakes of quartz.
2. 15 cm. light yellow sandy clay with numerous bone remains. Contains angular pieces of quartz.
1. Yellow sandstone of unknown thickness. Contains numerous bone remains, bits of limestone and of travertine.

SECTION B

9. Like A 8.
8. 80 cm. red stratified sand.
7. 16 cm. clay deposit, yellow at the bottom.
6. 15 cm. red sandstone.
5. 30 cm. red banded, partially hardened sand.
4. 6 cm. light yellow clay.
3. Like A 3.
2. 17 cm. light yellow sandy clay with numerous bone remains. Contains flakes of quartz.
1. Like A 1.

On studying these descriptions of the two sections the reader will observe that in both cases deposits 2 and 3 contain angular

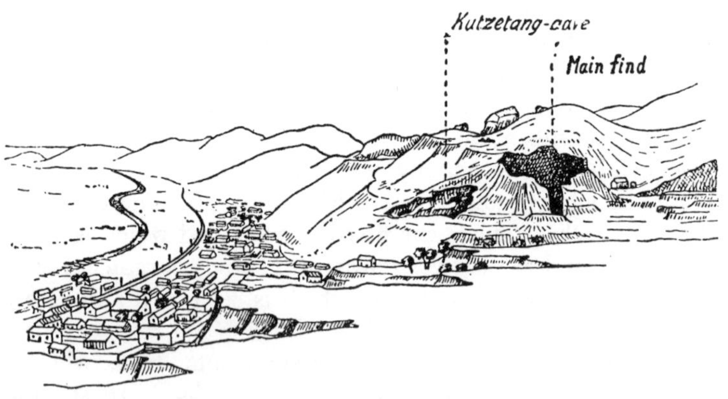

FIG. 37.—The Chou K'ou Tien cave, seen from the north-east. (*After Barbour.*)

pieces of quartz. During my visit to Chou K'ou Tien in order to follow the progress of Zdansky's work I was especially interested in these pieces of quartz, which had often such sharp edges that they might very well have been used as cutting tools.

I also observed that the limestone beside the cave is streaked with narrow veins of quartz, which are cleft in such a manner that it is quite conceivable that the edged pieces of quartz in deposits 2 and 3 simply fell down from the roof.

This is perhaps the most probable, or at any rate the least sensational, interpretation of the occurrence of the flakes of quartz. But, if we begin to reflect on the origin of the human species we are inevitably forced to the conclusion that the very earliest and extremely simple implements *were not prepared* by the

" Hominid ", but were picked up and selected from the bits of wood and stone which came his way.

In accordance with this compelling conclusion it seemed entirely reasonable that if a hominid had lived in or near the Chou K'ou Tien cave, he would have made use of these flakes of quartz, in order, for example, to cut up the animals which he had succeeded in killing.

This was the train of thought which led me on one of my visits to Zdansky to knock on the wall of the cave deposits and say :

" I have a feeling that there lie here the remains of one of our ancestors and it is only a question of your finding him. Take your time and stick to it till the cave is emptied, if need be."

The Chou K'ou Tien deposits were more difficult than we at first supposed, and Zdansky concluded his excavations in the late summer of 1921, when he had reached a stage when it would have been dangerous, without large scaffoldings, to dig farther into the now overhanging wall of the cave deposits.

But I could never forget the thought of hominid remains in this cave, and thus it happened that Zdansky, at my request, returned to Chou K'ou Tien for further excavations in the summer of 1923. We shall soon come to the result of his search for the expected hominid remains, but we must first survey the other discoveries of bones which were made in the cave deposit. On the whole the fossil bones of the Chou K'ou Tien cave are rather badly preserved. Whole skulls are scarcely ever to be found and still less complete skeletons. It thus appears as if these animals had been completely broken up, possibly by some beast of prey, and that the bone remains had been exposed to soaking, with the result that only those parts with the greatest powers of resistance, such as teeth and jaws, had been preserved. Zdansky has described the whole of the material found in a volume : " Die Säugetiere der Quartärfauna von Chou K'ou Tien ", *Palaeontologia Sinica*, Ser. C, Vol. 5, Fasc. 4, 1928. With the exception of less important forms such as smaller insect eaters and rodents, I have, in the present instance, derived from this work the following list of species :

Scaptochirus primitivus, n., mole.
Erinaceus sp., hedgehog.
Trogontherium cfr. cuvieri, beaver.
Ochotona sp., hare.

Canis cfr. dingo, dog.
Ursus arctos, bear.
Ursus angustidens n., bear.
Hyaena sinensis.
Machairodus sp., sabre-toothed tiger.
Felis acutidens n., cat of the size of a lion.
Felis, 2 smaller species.
Rhinoceros 2 sp., rhinoceros.
Equus sp., horse.
Sys lydekkeri n., pig.
Pseudaxis grayi n var., deer.
Cervus canadiensis mongoliae, deer.
Bibos geron, buffalo type.
Cynopithecid, ape.

Among these forms we find a small number of dogs (*Canis cfr. dingo*), bears (*Ursus arctos*) and deer which are nearly related to modern animal forms, or, as regards *Pseudaxis grayi*, with deer found in the Northern Chinese loess formation, which we regard as belonging to the middle part of the Pleistocene age.

Two forms, *Bibos geron* and *Hyaena sinensis* are known partly from the fauna of the loess formation and partly from Wan Hsien in Ssŭch'uan, where Granger investigated a fauna including the elephant *Stegodon* and other mammals which are regarded as belonging to the latest Pliocene period. It should be noted that *Hyaena sinensis* does not resemble the modern hyaena. The mole, *Scaptochirus primitivus*, and the pig, *Sus lydekkeri*, have also no close relations in the modern fauna, and the horse represented in the Chou K'ou Tien cave is also of an ancient type, just as the sabre-toothed tiger belongs to an extinct type of beast of prey common in the late Tertiary and Pleistocene ages.

On the whole the Chou K'ou Tien fauna reveals many features which indicate that it is not younger than the earliest part of the Pleistocene age.

In the next two chapters we shall make the acquaintance of the curious loess formation and the animal remains which are found in it. We encounter there a fauna belonging to the middle Pleistocene period and consequently later than the cave fauna of Chou K'ou Tien.

For the present we must content ourselves with the fact that all the scholars who have been engaged on the problem regard it as probable that the Chou K'ou Tien deposits belong to the earliest Pleistocene.

When the Crown Prince and Crown Princess of Sweden set out in May 1926 on their journey round the world via North

America and the countries of the Far East, they invited Dr. Lagrelius and me to meet them in Peking and to me was entrusted the special mission of arranging the archaeological and art studies of the Crown Prince in China. I then conceived the idea of trying to arrange, among other things, a scientific meeting in Peking at which some of the scholars living there might communicate something of the results they had achieved. In order to offer my own contribution to this reception for the royal archaeologist I wrote to Professor Wiman before my departure for the East and asked him to send some notes on the important Chinese mammal material which was just then being described at his institute in Upsala. Thanks to the instant willingness which always made co-operation with Wiman so pleasant, I received shortly after my arrival in Peking a report on what was at the moment achieved in his research. Thus he gave an account of the dinosaur *Helopus*, which was perhaps our most valuable discovery, and of the peculiar giraffes of the *Hipparion* deposits, as well as of the snouted horse, *Proboscidipparion*. But what was to me personally of much the greatest interest was a communication from Zdansky that in working on the Chou K'ou Tien material he had found a molar and a pre-molar of a creature resembling a human being, which he designated merely *Homo sp?* He had dug out the molar himself and identified it at Chou K'ou Tien as belonging to an anthropoid ape. The pre-molar he had discovered only while cleaning the material in Upsala.

So the hominid expected by me was found.

On October 22nd the scientific meeting was held in the auditorium of the Medical High School in Peking. After the President of the Geological Society, Dr. Wong Wen-hao, had welcomed the royal guests, the Crown Prince in reply recalled the thousand-year-old traditions of archaeological research in China. The first address was given by a famous political reformer and author, Liang Chi Chao, who also spoke of archaeological research in China. The next speaker was Professor Teilhard de Chardin, who described Father Licent's and his own great discovery of the early Stone-age man in the Ordos desert (cf. Chapter VIII). The last contribution to the programme of the evening was reserved for me, and I reported, on behalf of Professor Wiman, the latest results of the great palaeontological work done in Upsala. When, finally, I showed in a lantern picture the hominid teeth discovered by Zdansky, I suggested that this in itself extremely incomplete discovery might come to be the most important result of the whole of our Swedish work in China. I further explained that we had no plan to follow up this result by further investigations, but that we would gladly see a large-scale examination of the Chou K'ou Tien cave organized by the Geological Survey of China, in co-operation with Dr. Black, as representative of the Peking Union Medical College, and with the Rockefeller Foundation.

I now remember with pleasure that the far-reaching importance of this announcement was fully appreciated by the leading scientists of China, such as Dr. Ting, Dr. Wong, Dr. Black and Dr. Grabau. Dr. Black worked up Wiman's pictures and text in a short notice on the discovery, which was published in *Nature* in November 1926. My proposal to continue work in the field found active support on all sides and the three institutions which together organized the new undertaking showed so much confidence in us Swedes as to invite Professor Wiman, through Dr. Black and myself, to engage one of his students to conduct the new campaign of excavation at Chou K'ou Tien. Dr. Grabau, who invents such excellent scientific terminology, immediately named the new discovery *The Peking Man*, and it it was under this name that this hominid discovery became known throughout the world.

During the first days, nay months, after the communiqué of October 22nd, a shadow of doubt fell upon the hominid discovery at Chou K'ou Tien. The two French scholars, Licent and Teilhard, were present at the reception in the Peking auditorium, and two days later Teilhard wrote a little note to me, of which I take the liberty of reproducing the brief contents.

Dear Dr. Andersson,

I have reflected much on the photographs which you so kindly showed me and I feel that it would not be right, and still less friendly, to conceal from you what I think of them.

As a matter of fact I am not fully convinced of their supposed human character. Even the rootless assumed pre-molar, which at first sight seemed most convincing, may be one of the last molars of some carnivore, and the same is true of the other tooth, unless the roots are distinctly four in number.

Even if, as I hope, it can never be proved that the Chou K'ou Tien teeth belong to a beast of prey, I fear that it can never be absolutely demonstrated that they are human. It is necessary to be very cautious, since their nature is undetermined.

I have not seen the specimens, however, and since I place great reliance on Zdansky's palaeontological experience I hope most intensely that my criticism will prove unfounded. I have only wished to be absolutely frank with you.

Sincerely yours,
P. TEILHARD.

I need scarcely point out that the French scientist, who is one of the most far-seeing and most delightful men I have ever met, expressed this warning in a spirit of candour and warm friendship, with the sole purpose of checking a too optimistic faith and one which might prove erroneous. I knew only too well that this learned palaeontologist had good reasons for his hesitation, since certain teeth of beasts of prey may, when worn to a certain extent, easily be confused with human teeth. My only reply to this criticism was that I had complete confidence in Zdansky's critical acumen, the more so as he had conducted extensive investigations into the fossil carnivores of China and should thus be proof against the danger suggested by Teilhard.

One evening during these months of anxiety there was an amusing intermezzo. Some time after the October reception and its little sequel there visited Peking the famous French mineralogist and secretary of the French Academy of Sciences, Professor Alfred Lacroix. Everyone of importance in Peking and Tientsin in the domain of natural science had assembled in a Chinese restaurant in Peking in order to celebrate the distinguished visitor. Teilhard and Licent were present and of course the inexhaustible and delightful Grabau. Spirits ran high towards the end of dinner and pointed remarks flew like arrows across the table. Then I was struck by a full bull's eye :

" Well, Dr. Andersson," Grabau exclaimed to me, " how are things just now with the Peking man ? Is it a man or a carnivore ? "

I felt that the ground was rocking beneath my feet and that both the Peking man and I myself would be ridiculed if I could not return the compliment promptly. Then an idea struck me.

"My dear Dr. Grabau, the latest news from the Chou K'ou Tien field is that our old friend is neither a man nor a carnivore but rather something half-way between the two. It is a *lady*."

And from that time for months afterwards the discovery changed its name to the "Peking Lady".

Dr. Birger Bohlin, one of Wiman's disciples, who had won his spurs by an especially fine investigation of the giraffes of the *Hipparion* clay, had undertaken to journey to China in order to direct the new excavations at Chou K'ou Tien.

This enterprise was placed in the hands of Dr. Ting, as Honorary Director. The excavations were made under the auspices of the Geological Survey and the whole of the material was to be the property of that institution. Eventual discoveries of hominidae were to be studied and described by Dr. Black at the anatomical institute of the Medical High School. The Rockefeller Foundation financed practically the whole of the enterprise. The official direction on the spot was entrusted to the geologist C. Li, who was also responsible for the geological and topographical observations.

Work at Chou K'ou Tien began on April 16th, 1927, and continued until October 18th. As a newcomer to China, Dr. Bohlin experienced to the full the disturbed political conditions of that country. War was raging between Chang Tso Lin and Yen Hsi Shan, and the thunder of the guns was heard for a long time at Chou K'ou Tien. Divisions of troops came and went and occasionally thoughtless youthful soldiers came swinging along with hand grenades to the cave where Bohlin worked. The disturbances round about, however, affected the young Swede very little and work proceeded as usual, though the air buzzed with stories of the movements of troops and attacks of bandits.

The cavity in which the bones had been deposited was now to a large extent laid bare, and it appeared that the cave deposits extended east and west for a distance of about 50 metres, with a breadth north and south of more than 16 metres. The thickness of the deposits varied between 11 and 17 metres, but only a part of it was richly fossil-bearing.

Both the geologist Li and Dr. Bohlin have left brief accounts of this period of their work, during which 3,000 cubic metres of cave deposits were hewn and examined.[1] In this manner the shape of the cave became well known. Both the above-mentioned scientists appear to agree that the cave is a cleft in the limestone which has possibly been widened by the erosive activity of water.

On October 16th, only three days before work for the year ceased, Dr. Bohlin found a hominid tooth, which he conveyed to Peking under very disturbed conditions and delivered to Dr.

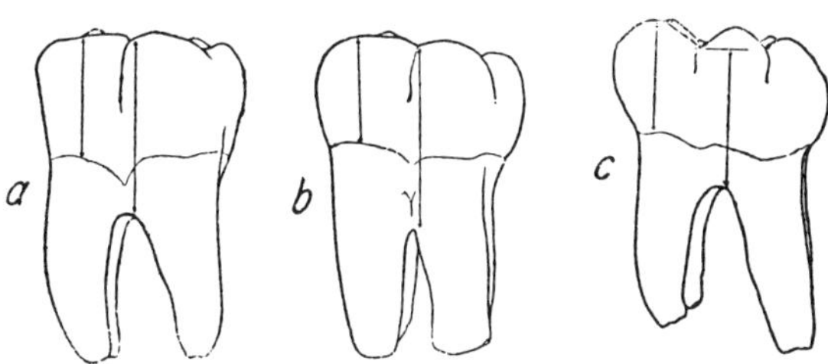

FIG. 38—Foremost molar in the left half of lower jaw of *a*, ten-year-old Chinese child ; *b*, *Sinanthropus* ; *c*, young chimpanzee. (*After Black.*)

Black, who in a letter to me dated October 29th, 1927, makes the following handsome recognition of the manner in which Bohlin had accomplished his mission :

> Bohlin is a splendid and enthusiastic fellow who refused to allow local difficulties and military crises to affect his work. . . .
>
> On October 19th at half-past six in the evening Bohlin came to my institution in field dress, covered with dust but beaming with pleasure. He had finished the season's work despite the war, and on October 16th he had discovered the tooth. He was himself on the spot when it was taken out of the deposits. Certainly I was overjoyed ! Bohlin came to me before he told his wife that he was in Peking. He is indeed a man after my own heart and I hope you will tell Wiman how much I value his assistance in procuring Bohlin for our work in China. . . .
>
> Bohlin is quite certain that he will find more of *Homo pekinensis* when he begins to sift in the laboratory the material he takes home.

This third tooth has been very thoroughly described by Dr. Black in " The Lower Molar Hominid Tooth from the Chou K'ou Tien Deposit ", *Palaeontologia Sinica*, Ser. D, Vol. 7, Fasc. 1, 1927. The tooth in question is somewhat worn and

[1] *Bull. of the Geol. Soc. of China*, Vol. VI, Nos. 3–4, 1927.

is probably the first of the series on the left side of the lower jaw. This extraordinarily well-preserved and complete tooth has been carefully compared on the one hand with corresponding human teeth and on the other hand with those of the chimpanzee, and it appears that it is more primitive than the former and more specialized than the latter. Dr. Black regards it as certain that in this case also we are dealing with the same species of animal as that which first became known by the two teeth found by Zdansky. The hominid character of this creature was placed beyond all doubt by the new discovery and Black therefore set up a new hominid genus *Sinanthropus*, with the species name of *pekinensis*.

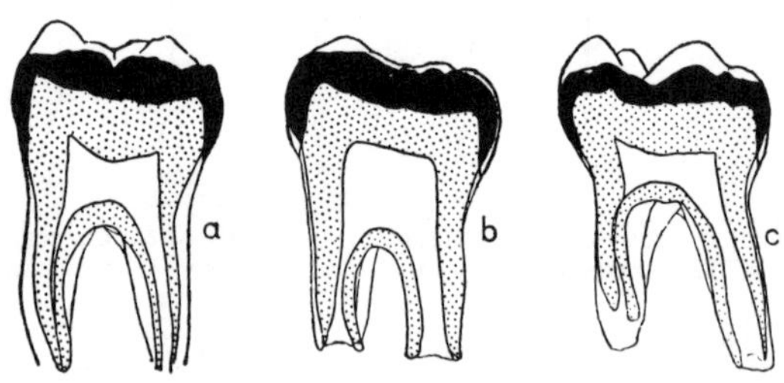

FIG. 39.—Section of the foremost molar in the left half of the lower jaw of *a*, ten-year-old Chinese child ; *b*, *Sinanthropus* ; *c*, chimpanzee. (*After Black.*)

The existence of the Peking Man was hereby fully proved and he was given a scientific name in accordance with the rules of the science.

In the following year, 1928, the excavations at Chou K'ou Tien were resumed, and Dr. Bohlin was assisted this time by W. C. Pei and Dr. C. C. Young, a young palaeontologist who had described the rodents collected by us in China.

This fourth period of work was crowned with much greater success than Dr. Black and his collaborators ever dared to dream of. The new material has been known up to the present only by Black's brief preliminary notice : " Preliminary Note on Additional *Sinanthropus* Material discovered in Chou K'ou Tien during 1928 " (*Bull. of the Geol. Soc. of China*, 1929).[1]

[1] Dr. Bohlin also gave some interesting details in a letter of August 28th, 1928.

In the north-eastern corner of the cave there was found, about 10 metres above the deposit in which the tooth had been found in the preceding year, a whole nest of *Sinanthropus* remains. In addition, further discoveries were made on the former site, partly in the cave and partly during the treatment of the material in Peking. More than a score of teeth, of different ages and degrees of wear, as well as parts of skulls of both young and adult individuals, were found. The skulls, however, were embedded for the most part in hard sintered limestone and could therefore not be more closely examined.

The most important of the finds illustrated and described in Black's essay are two fragments of jaws, one belonging to a young

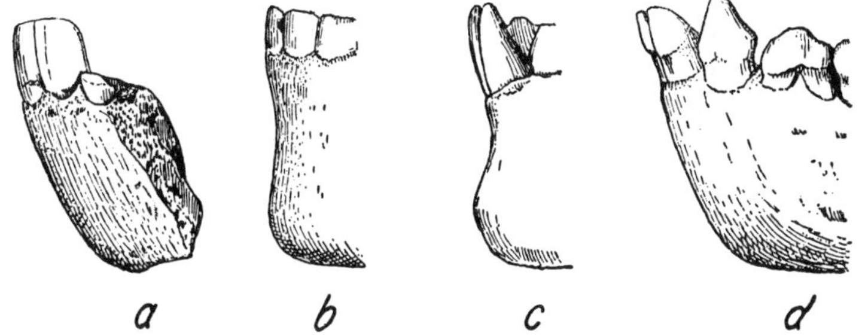

FIG. 40.—Front portion of lower jaw of *a*, *Sinanthropus* ; *b*, a child of the latest Stone-age in China; *c*, a modern Chinese child ; *d*, a young chimpanzee. (*After Black.*)

and the other to an adult individual. The comparisons which Black drew between these old Pleistocene jawbones and modern Chinese children and a young chimpanzee in the former case and an adult Northern Chinaman and a full-grown orang-outang in the latter, show clearly the position of *Sinanthropus* as being intermediate between modern man and the man-like apes. Especially significant is it that *Sinanthropus*, like the anthropoids (chimpanzee, orang-outang, etc.), lacks the projecting chin which is characteristic of man. Even as regards the structure of incisors and canine teeth the Chou K'ou Tien form shows some anthropoid features. On the whole, however, the arrangement of the teeth is quite like that of man. Black also considers that the *Sinanthropus* corresponds very closely with modern man in size of brain.

I have probably tried the reader's patience too long already by repeatedly using the term *hominid* without giving any explanation of its meaning.

Within the great order of apes we meet a long series of widely differing forms, from the stooping Lemuroidea up to man and his nearest relations, the man-like apes. Among laymen there exists an incorrect conception of the relationship of man to the modern anthropoids, in so far as it is thought, either with satisfaction or with horror, that modern science seeks to establish a direct relationship between man and the anthropoids. This is entirely wrong, in so far as both the modern man-like apes and man himself are highly specialized descendants of a common, but long-extinct and still undiscovered, original form belonging to the Tertiary period.

Highest in the varied group of anthropoids is the *Hominidae* family, which has one single living representative—modern man, *Homo sapiens*. In addition to a number of named forms of minor importance, prehistoric research has acquainted us with a long extinct human type, the *Homo neanderthalensis*, who lived during the middle Pleistocene age and represented the early Palaeolithic civilization. The Neanderthal man is represented by a considerable number of skeletons found in Western and Central Europe and is therefore a well-known human race.

When we pass further back in time the hominid material becomes very scarce.

In 1891–2 there were found at Trinil in Java the famous skeletal parts which were described by the discoverer, Dr. Eugen Dubois, under the name of *Pithecanthropus erectus*, the erect ape-man. At another place, about 40 km. from Trinil, Dubois had found in the deposits, together with the same early Pleistocene fauna of elephants, rhinoceri, tapirs, hyaenas, etc., a fragment of a lower jaw which he thought belonged to *Pithecanthropus*. Large-scale attempts have since been made to obtain more material from this extremely important site, but the sole further result has been one tooth from Trinil. All the above discoveries in Java were made in early Pleistocene alluvial deposits.

In 1908 there was found in the river sand at Heidelberg in Germany an extremely well preserved lower jaw of a hominid, which has been named *Palaeanthropus heidelbergensis*. In this jaw also the chin projection is lacking, but the arrangement of the teeth is singularly like that of a man.

Yet another hominid should be noted, namely *Eoanthropus dawsoni*, which was found by Sir Charles Dawson in 1911–12 in the river sand at Piltdown in Sussex, in Southern England. In this case we have to deal with some fragments of a cranium, a piece of the lower jaw, with two worn molars as well as a canine tooth and a couple of nose bones. The opinion of scholars is divided as to the connection between the cranium, which is man-like, and the lower jaw, which is very like that of a chimpanzee.

All these three forms—the *Pithecanthropus* from Java, the *Palaeanthropus* from Germany and the *Eoanthropus* from England—are of about the same age and represent the little we knew, until the Chou K'ou Tien discovery, of hominids older than the well-known *Homo neanderthalensis*. The scarcity of earlier hominid material made even the first discovery at Chou K'ou Tien a sensational occurrence. But Chou K'ou Tien is a place of a kind which raises very special hopes.

All the other discoveries of hominids earlier than the Neanderthal man were made, as we have seen, in widespread alluvial deposits, in which hominid remains can be expected only sporadically. And it is also true that later attempts to find additional material at Trinil, Heidelberg and Piltdown have met with little or no success.

The discovery at Chou K'ou Tien is of quite a different kind; it is a cave deposit of very limited extent. Owing to the frequency and the fragmentary character of the bones one can scarcely avoid the conclusion that some great beast of prey—or *Sinanthropus*—had its abode near the entrance to the cave and that the refuse was washed down into the depths. Consequently a deposit of this kind offers much better possibilities of further discoveries than do places like Heidelberg or Piltdown.

On December 9th, 1927, I gave an address to the Swedish Anthropological and Geographical Society on "The Hominid Discoveries at Peking and the Investigations of the Origin of Man".

At that time I had access only to Zdansky's discovery, but on the basis of the nature of his discovery I expressed the following views concerning the possibility of new ones.

"As regards the possibility of renewed discoveries of hominids at Chou K'ou Tien, I would like to express the following view: to look for remains of hominids in alluvial deposits is like looking for a lost pin in Hyde Park, but to look for them in a cave deposit of the same period may be likened to looking for a pin which has been lost in the reading-room of the Royal Library. The latter is by no means easy, but it is less hopeless than looking for it in a park."

The discoveries of Bohlin, which have been described by Dr. Black, fully justify my optimism and I do not hesitate here to express the belief that as yet we are only at the beginning of a period of great discoveries in Northern China of primeval relations of our own species. The extensive limestone areas offer in many places the same favourable conditions as at Chou K'ou Tien, and at one place in Eastern Shansi my collector Chang found a place of the same kind as Chou K'ou Tien, even though in this case the bones were much corroded.

Money, endurance, and a good flair are the three things which will produce new treasures.

This is the point which I had reached at the turn of the year 1929–30, when I finished my chapter on the Peking Man. Little did I imagine that the closing month of the old year had brought to us the greatest of all discoveries from the Chou K'ou Tien cave, a treasure which has already become one of the most important relics in natural history research.

Before I refer to the account by the discoverer, the geologist W. C. Pei, of his great find, I must devote a few words to a description of the Chou K'ou Tien site submitted for publication by Teilhard de Chardin and C. C. Young to the Geological Society of Peking.[1]

During Zdansky's excavations in 1921 and 1923 only a small part of the upper and outer portions of the cave deposits was examined. But during the great campaign which was begun in 1927, on my initiative, with the support of the Rockefeller Foundation, the field organizers, C. Li, B. Bohlin, C. C. Young and W. C. Pei, excavated during the years 1927–9, in a total of

[1] "Preliminary Report on the Chou K'ou Tien Fossiliferous Deposit", *Bull. of the Geol. Soc. of China*, Vol. VIII, No. 3.

64 working weeks, 8,800 cubic metres of the bone-bearing deposit, and brought back to Peking 1,485 cases of their collections.

In this way a large part of the old cave was exhausted and towards the end of 1929 a very clear conspectus of the site had been obtained. Inside and in the depths considerable portions of the bone deposits still remained to be investigated.

In studying the section in Fig. 41 it should be noted that the shape of the cave, which was practically unknown to us pioneers, is now clear. A good deal of the floor and sides is distinctly shown in the illustration. To the right stretches down a cleft still only partially explored. The roof is missing, but we can see from the illustration that there once was a roof, though towards the end of the formation of the bone deposit it fell in and dropped into the cave. Higher up we see large blocks of limestone, of which the inclination still corresponds to some extent to that of the solid limestone rock, even though the inclination of the blocks is, as would be expected, as a rule somewhat more flat. There cannot be any doubt that these immense blocks of limestone are parts of the caved-in roof which formerly constituted the upper limit of the cave.

The section shows us that the sediment, which has here been examined with the utmost care, has a total thickness, from the top of the large chamber to the bottom of the narrow cleft, of not less than 35 metres.

The whole cave deposit contains, from bottom to top, a uniform fauna and thus belongs to the same geological age. But, as is to be expected from the changes in the sediment, the fossils are quite unequally distributed in the various deposits, some of which contain copious remains of the large mammals, whilst a thick sand deposit yielded at most a few teeth and jaws of rodents and other small animals.

The first hominid discoveries were made in 1927[1] at the point marked (SA).

At the point (SB) was found in 1928 a quantity of *Sinanthropus* material.

The lower cleft is of great importance, since it was there that

[1] Probably Zdansky also found his *Homo sp.* teeth in approximately the same spot.

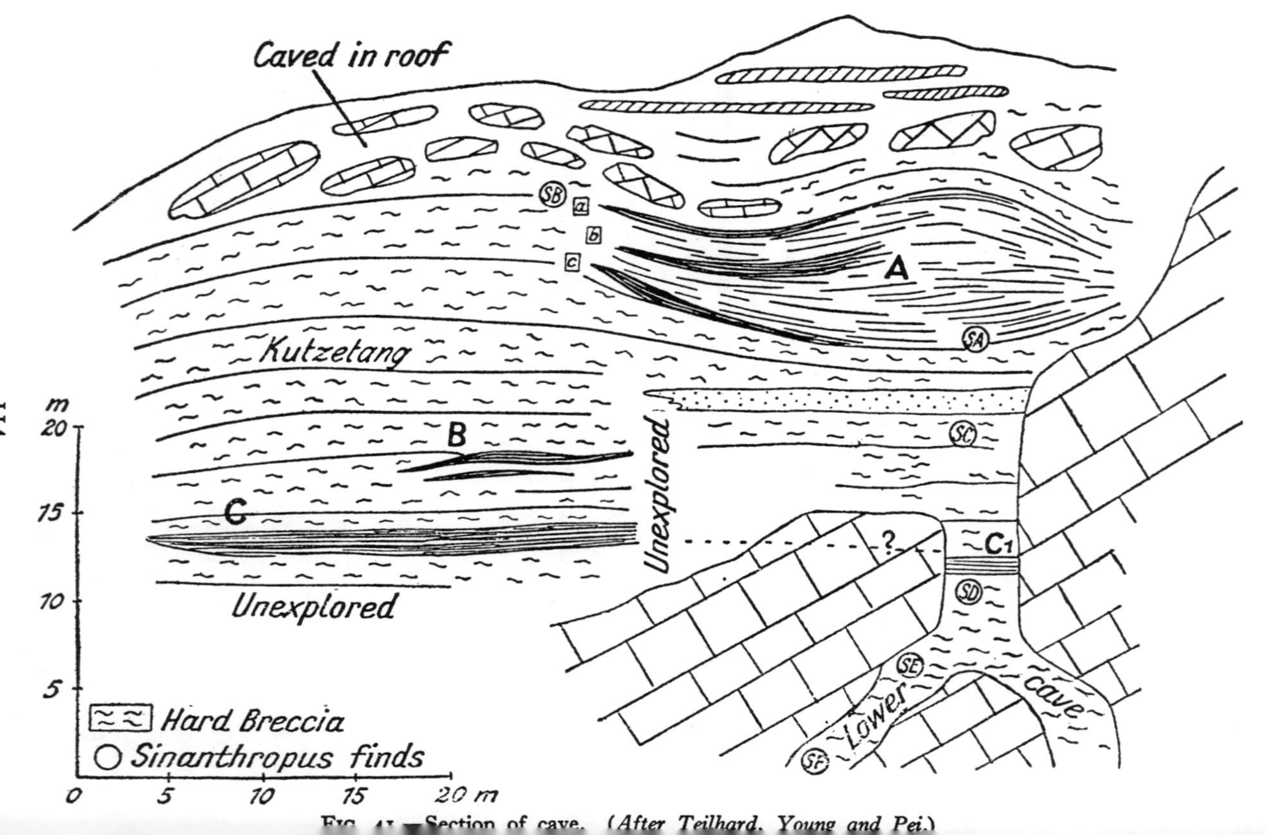

Fig. 41.—Section of cave. (After Teilhard, Young and Pei.)

six *Sinanthropus* (SC) teeth were discovered as well as five teeth and a fragmentary skull (SD).

This cleft extends downwards to what is called the " lower cave ", where one of the most important discoveries, the most complete *Sinanthropus* skull, was made (SE).

In addition to the abundant and epoch-making material of the Peking Man which was brought to light in 1927–9, our knowledge of the varied cave fauna has been enlarged far beyond that which we obtained from Zdansky's monograph.

It is of especial importance that in the lower chamber of the cave better and more complete material was discovered of mammals which had previously only been known from fragmentary specimens. Thus, for example, there were found an elephant's tusk and skulls of buffaloes, deer, pigs, etc. In the lower cleft complete skulls of hyaenas were found, as well as horns of the stag with the thickened jaws which is now called *Euryceros*.

Thanks to the profounder knowledge of the mammal fauna of Northern China which Teilhard had obtained, not least by his work on the abundant Ni Ho Wan fauna, Li and Young were able in their report to establish more certain data for the Chou K'ou Tien deposits. The most archaic forms of the Ni Ho Wan fauna, such as the large *Hipparion* species and *Chalicotherium*, were never found at Chou K'ou Tien, and similarly in other respects the cave deposits at Chou K'ou Tien bear a somewhat later stamp than the lake deposits at Ni Ho Wan. For this reason the two authors designate Ni Ho Wan as late Plicoene, but Chou K'ou Tien as very early Pleistocene (see table at the end of the book).

Mr. W. C. Pei, who during the autumn of 1929 conducted operations at Chou K'ou Tien, has published a report on the discovery of the *Sinanthropus* skull which is most attractive in its modesty and thoroughness (SE).[1]

When the rainy season was over, the search for bones was resumed on September 26th and was concentrated on the bottom cleft. Towards the end of November, when Pei had reached a depth of 22·6 metres below datum level, he struck two open holes at the southern end of the cleft. Into one of them, which

[1] " An Account of the Discovery of an Adult *Sinanthropus* in the Chou K'ou Tien ", *Bull. of the Geol. Soc. of China*, Vol. VIII, No. 3.

he calls cave 2, he could only penetrate by means of a rope. Into cave 1, on the other hand, he could penetrate horizontally, and on December 1st he began to dig out the sediment in that cave. The following day at four o'clock in the afternoon he found an almost complete *Sinanthropus* cranium. It was partially embedded in loose sand and only to a small extent in travertine, for which reason it was possible to detach it without difficulty.

> On the morning of December 3rd I sent a note to Dr. Wong and Dr. Young containing details of my discovery, and at the same time I telegraphed to Dr. Black.
>
> The skull, situated in a large block of travertine, was first wrapped in a covering of Chinese cotton paper and then in a thick covering of coarse cloth impregnated with flour paste. The weather was so cold that these wrappings had not dried in our comparatively warm rooms even after three days, but on the night of the fifth day I thoroughly dried the block with the help of three chafing dishes. On the morning of the seventh day I left Chou K'ou Tien with the *Sinanthropus* skull and deposited it undamaged at midday at the Cenozoic laboratory.

The travertine enclosing the skull was very hard, and Black was therefore engaged for four months in extremely careful preparatory work before it could be completely laid bare. Happily the sutures between the cranial bones were open, and since the bones were cracked in places, he was able to remove the pieces and to join together all the parietal bones, frontal bones, neck and temple bones. In this manner the inner impression of the skull preserved in the travertine was reserved for future examination and the bones of the cranium could be studied from every point of view before they were joined together into a complete cranium by a final process of preparation (cf. Fig. 42).

In addition to his preliminary reports, Dr. Davidson Black has published a large and beautifully illustrated monograph on this epoch-making discovery, entitled " On an Adolescent Skull of *Sinanthropus pekinensis* " (*Palaeontologia Sinica*, Ser. D, Vol. 7, Fasc. 2, Peiping (Peking), 1931).

During the course of 1932 the major part of another skull from the material brought to Peking was prepared, and was designated " Locus D ", to distinguish it from the first discovery, which is named " Locus E skull ", after the place where it was

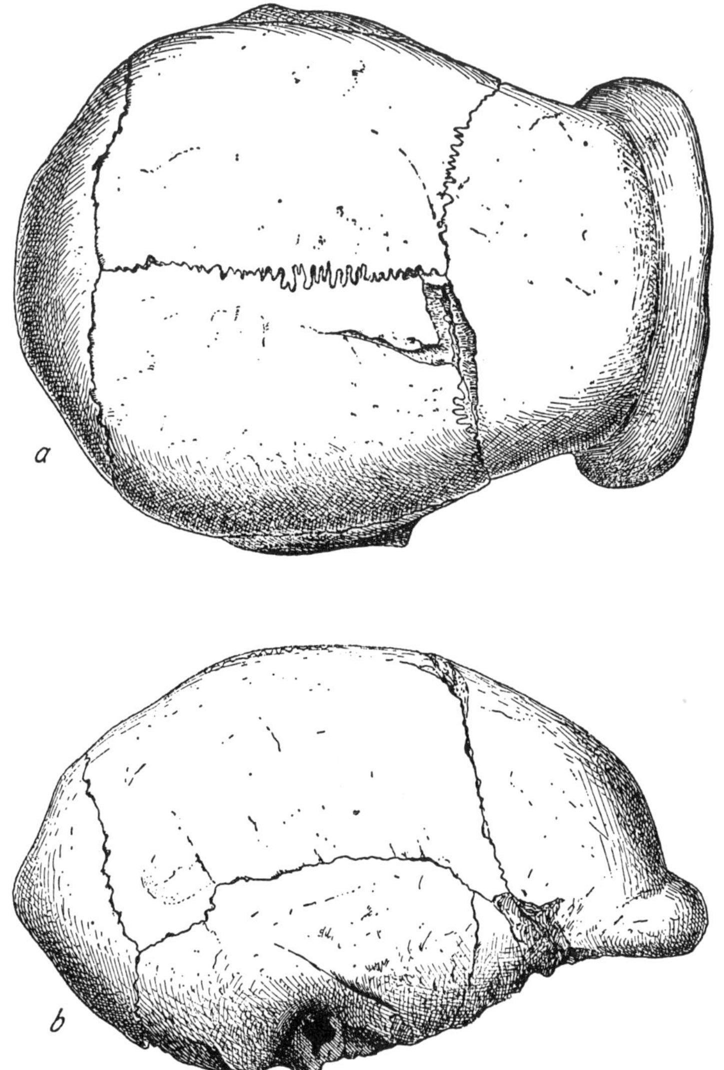

FIG. 42.—*Sinanthropus* skull (SE); *a*, seen from above; *b*, seen from the right side.

discovered. Apart from these two crania, which are the best preserved, there were two fragmentary skulls in the 1928 material, one of which was that of a child.

Primarily as a result of the fact that the sutures of the cranium bones are open in the locus E skull, Black has concluded that its owner died between childhood and adolescence. The sex is not definitely determined, but is probably male.

The locus D skull belongs to a young, but full-grown individual, possibly a woman.

The examination of these two *Sinanthropus* crania has enormously extended our knowledge of the earliest history of man. In respect of the massive thickness of the cranial bones the Peking Man reminds us most of the extremely thick-skulled *Eoanthropus* of Southern England. But in many other characteristics, as, for example, the thick eyebrow arches and the low forehead, the *Sinanthropus* is so closely related to the *Pithecanthropus* of Java that it has sometimes been asked whether the new Chinese species should not rather be connected with Dubois' genus *Pithecanthropus*. Black's extremely exhaustive comparison between these two original hominidae has nevertheless disclosed a contradiction in principle between them. Whereas *Pithecanthropus* is a highly specialized, not to say in certain respects degenerate type, *Sinanthropus* is a remarkable combination of highly original and purely modern features. Black sums up its characteristics by saying that *Sinanthropus* is a generalized and progressive type, closely related to the original type of hominidae which was the prototype not only of the Neanderthal man and the South-African fossil human races, but also of the modern *Homo sapiens*.

Already a whole literature of commentary on this epoch-making find has grown up. The distinguished London professor of anatomy, Elliot Smith, Davidson Black's teacher, travelled to Peking in 1931 in order to study the discovery *in situ* and described it in a lecture, " The Significance of the Peking Man " (The Henderson Trust Lectures, Edinburgh, 1931). In all essentials his interpretation of the material agrees with that of Black. " In several respects the Peking Man differs from *Pithecanthropus* and resembles *Eoanthropus*, though the differences from the latter are still more striking. It occupies a position intermediate between the two, but it is more primitive and more generalized than either of them."

Sir Arthur Keith, who in a series of comprehensive works had already surveyed the development of our knowledge of the

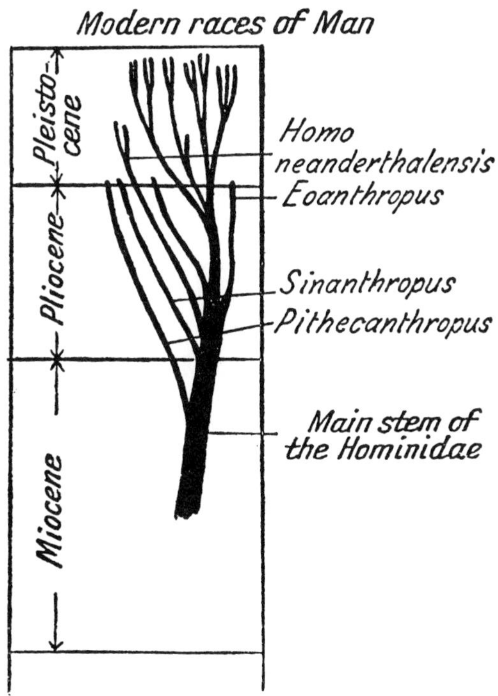

FIG. 43.—The genealogical tree of the Hominidae. (*After Keith.*)

earliest history of man, published last year a new work, *New Discoveries Relating to the Antiquity of Man*, in which he devotes three chapters to the Peking Man.

In *Sinanthropus* we find a curious mingling of characteristics. Most people connect it with *Pithecanthropus*; others would have us think of the European Neanderthal type; others again reveal the relationship to modern man. In order to explain this blending of various features we must assume that in the course of the development of man *Sinanthropus* derives from the genealogical tree near the two points where the forefathers of the Java man and the Neanderthal man separated from the branch leading to modern man" (cf. Fig. 43).

W. C. Pei, the sedulous and successful foreman at Chou K'ou Tien, published at the beginning of 1932 an exceedingly interesting essay, which, with kind recollection of my pioneering work, he opens with the following words : [1]

> As early as ten years ago Dr. J. G. Andersson, when he made this locality known to the scientific world, drew attention to the occurrence in the fossil-bearing deposits of Chou K'ou Tien of fragments of quartz which might possibly be regarded as traces of a being resembling man.
>
> Five years passed before proof of the correctness of Andersson's supposition came to light in the first discoveries of the remains of hominidae in the Chou K'ou Tien deposits. Ever since we began, in 1927, to excavate in this cave we have found time after time such quartz fragments (some of them reminiscent of real implements), but it was only in 1931 that we found *in situ* stone implements which were actually formed by human hands.

Pei first gives a very detailed and clear description of the partly open cave, Ku Tzŭ Tang, which bounded on the east the main site and which was now found to constitute a part of it. Without entering into Pei's extremely important, but perhaps somewhat technical local description, we reproduce one of his sections (Fig. 44), which shows that parts of skeletons of *Sinanthropus* were dug out together with stone implements, and that consequently there can be no doubt of their connection. Together with implements and remains of *Sinanthropus* there were also found some other mammals of the

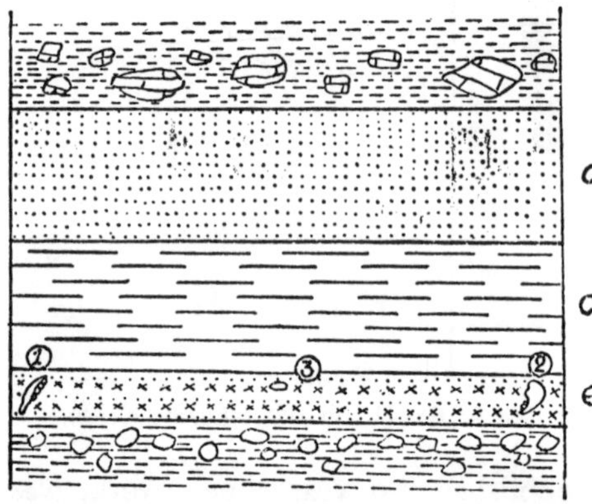

Fig. 44.—Section through one of the layers (*e*) containing skeletal remains of *Sinanthropus* together with stone implements. (1) and (2) jaws of *Sinanthropus*; (3) fragments of skull. (*After Pei.*)

[1] " Notice of the Discovery of Quartz and other Stone Artifacts in the Lower Pleistocene Hominid-bearing Sediments of the Chou K'ou Tien Cave Deposit ", *Bull. of the Geol. Soc. of China*, Vol. XI, No. 2, pp. 109–39.

cave fauna, the deer, *Pseudaxis* and *Euryceros*, as well as the large horses, *Equus sanmeniensis* Teilhard et Piveteau.

From one deposit there were collected no less than 2,000 quartz fragments and about 10 stones of a kind not native to the cave, fine green sandstone, green shale, quartzite of various colours, 3 limonite concretions and two pieces of flint which were found to fit together. Only a very few of these stone fragments show indisputable signs of having been worked upon, and of these we here illustrate one, after Pei (Fig. 45).

In connection with Pei's most sensational discovery the most eminent expert on the stone technique of the early Stone age,

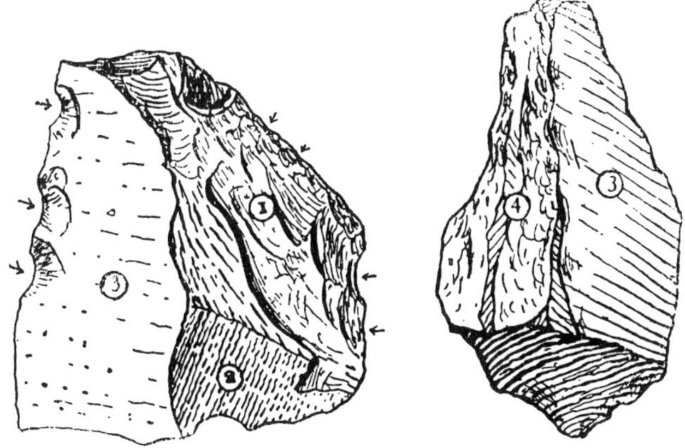

FIG. 45.—Stone implement from the deposits in the Chou K'ou Tien cave.

the Abbé Breuil of Paris, was invited to visit Peking and Chou K'ou Tien. During his visit to the East in the autumn of 1931 Breuil fully accepted Pei's view that these objects were indisputably artifacts, and the French scholar considers that some of the horn and bone objects also show traces of having been used as implements.[1]

These finds are still comparatively little known, and we must await the thorough examination of them, which will certainly be undertaken by the energetic scientists in Peking.

[1] Breuil, " Le feu et l'industrie lithique et osseuse à Chou K'ou Tien ", *Bull. of the Geol. Soc. of China*, Vol. XI, No 2, pp. 147–54

Both Pei, in the above-mentioned report, and Dr. Black[1] and the Abbé Breuil refer to traces among the discoveries made in 1931 of charred wood and burnt bone as showing that *Sinanthropus* had also turned fire to his use.

It is already established that the discoveries in the Chou K'ou Tien deposits have revolutionized the whole theory of the earliest history of mankind.

The earlier finds of pre-Neanderthal hominidae in Java, in Southern England and near Heidelberg seem poor to us now beside the spate of new and fundamental discoveries which, since 1926, have been made in this wonderful cave deposit near Peking: a number of teeth, several jaws, two complete and several

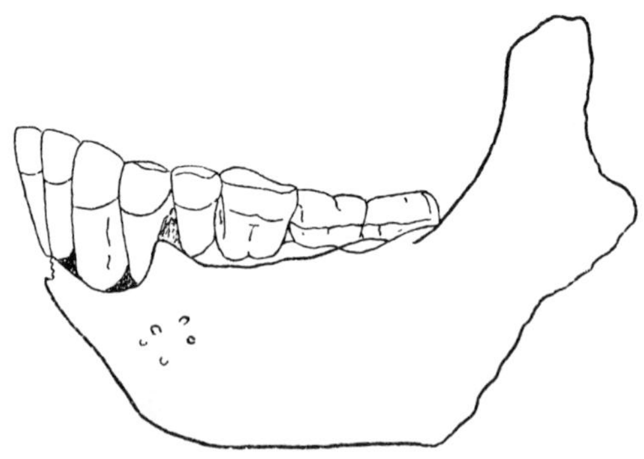

FIG. 46.—Lower jaw of *Sinanthropus*. (*After Black.*)

fragmentary skulls of the actual *Sinanthropus*, a number of implements formed by him and traces of the fires with which he roasted his bag of large mammals. And in addition the cave deposit is dotted with tens of thousands of more or less fragmentary bone remains of the for the most part extinct animals which this early Chinaman hunted.

In anticipation of the new information which is certainly to be expected from this gold mine of anthropological research at Chou K'ou Tien I can for the present lay down my pen. As one who first came to hear of this place by a stroke of luck and who during the first years sustained his belief in the possibility

[1] Black, "Evidences of the Use of Fire by Sinanthropus", *Bull. of the Geol. Soc. of China*, Vol. XI, No. 2, pp. 107–8.

of finding a hominid, I should like most cordially to wish success to those who in 1926, by my suggestion, undertook to continue the work and made of it such a brilliant scientific success. My thoughts turn in the first place to the two directors of the National Geological Survey of China, Dr. V. K. Ting and Dr. Wong Wen-hao, whose friendship, organizing ability and foresight I was able to test during many years of co-operation. Next I think of my charming friend, Professor Davidson Black, who with such incomparable technical skill prepared the priceless cranium material and described it with a learning and a conscientiousness which fully justify his privilege of acquainting the scientific world with the most precious material which has ever come into the hands of an anthropologist. I am also happy to find among those who supported the work at Chou K'ou Tien the amiable French palaeontologist Teilhard de Chardin, whose further great contributions to the investigation of China's earliest history are described in Chapters V and VIII.

I am also especially anxious to convey my heartiest good wishes to the two young scholars, C. C. Young and W. C. Pei, who directed the excavations during recent years and of whom the latter during 1930 and 1931 not only made some of the most important anthropological discoveries, but also described his field observations and his stone implements in an expert and comprehensive manner. Just when this chapter was ready for press I received from my friends in Peking two very important communications relating to the progress of the investigations at Chou K'ou Tien.

One of them was composed by Teilhard de Chardin and W. C. Pei: "The Lithic Industry of the *Sinanthropus* Deposits in Choukoutien" (*Bull. of the Geol. Soc. of China*, Vol. XI, No. 4, 1932).

This essay originated in the desire to take up a position with regard to certain objections and questions which had been raised by scientists in other countries after the quartz fragments and pieces of other species of rocks from the Chou K'ou Tien deposits had been interpreted (see above) as implements found and used by *Sinanthropus*.

Nobody nowadays doubts that these broken stones really are artifacts. The reservations relate to two other points.

The suggestion is made that in the Chou K'ou Tien cave there exist on the one hand an older deposit containing the old Pleistocene fauna, including the *Sinanthropus*, and on the other hand a later deposit to which the artifacts belong. This suggestion is definitely repelled by the circumstances of the discovery, which were made clear by Pei in his 1931 report and which we now again emphasize. The remains of the *Sinanthropus* and the artifacts occur together, not only on one level, but in several parts of this cave deposit, which throughout contains one and the same old Pleistocene fauna.

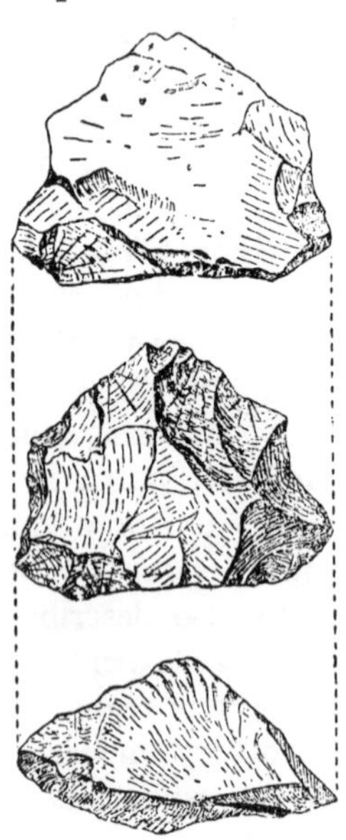

FIG. 47.—Stone implement from the Chou K'ou Tien cave. (*After Teilhard and Pei.*)

The second objection is that there lived not one, but two, hominidae at the same time in the Chou K'ou Tien cave, of which the more advanced one, possibly a real man, may have made the implements and hunted not only the other mammals but also the *Sinanthropus*. Of this attempted explanation no more need be said than that it is extremely far-fetched and improbable. All the indications show that the *Sinanthropus* lived in the cave for long periods and left behind not only his stone implements but also thick deposits of ashes.

Teilhard and Pei have published a description, supported by many good illustrations, of the implements found, among which there have now been found rare examples made from limestone and a flint-like rock. The artifacts are less differentiated than those even of the oldest cultures in France, but the authors are still of the opinion that *Sinanthropus* and his implements are to be regarded as early representatives of the oldest Palaeolithic culture cycle.

It should be added that the two authors make very interesting observations on the rôle which *Sinanthropus* played in the Chou K'ou Tien cave. In the lowest deposits of the " lower cave " remains of bears and hyaenas predominate, and it therefore seems probable that these beasts of prey were at first masters of the cave. But higher up we encounter at three levels thick deposits containing artifacts and fragments of bone, which are probably to a large extent remains of the meals of the *Sinanthropus*.

It is of especial interest that Teilhard and Pei confirm an observation made by the foremost expert on Palaeolithic sites, the Abbé Breuil, that the seven metres thick " sand " in which we all dug is nothing else but a deposit of ash soaked during geological ages and that it therefore speaks eloquently of the long duration of the abode of the *Sinanthropus* in the cave.

It was in fact in this " sand " deposit that, during the first days of 1921, I observed the flakes of quartz which during all those years sustained my faith in a hominid, a faith which has now at last triumphed.

In the same bulletin in which Teilhard and Pei published the report above referred to, Black published an essay " Skeletal Remains of *Sinanthropus* other than Skull Parts ".

It has long been a mystery to those interested in the subject that so many parts of the skull of *Sinanthropus* have been found and practically nothing of the remainder of the skeleton. The same is true to a certain extent of the other mammals, but the Abbé Breuil thought it proper to pose the question whether *Sinanthropus* had the same customs as certain modern savage races, among whom it happens that the head is severed from the body and interred separately.

In any case Black now reports that some unimportant parts of skeletons have been found which do not belong to the skull. They are a collar-bone and an *os lunatum* from the wrist of a *Sinanthropus*, which latter, together with the *os lunatum* of *Homo sapiens*, is unlike the same bone of full-grown specimens of the modern anthropoid apes. It thus appears as if this maker of coarsely hewn stone implements had a hand not essentially different from our own.

We now come to the greatest surprise of Black's essay. He describes in conclusion four end phalanges which in all probability belonged to the foot of a *Sinanthropus* and of which one in particular is believed to be the top joint of the big toe.

These phalanges are so different from those of the human toe that Black found himself constrained to describe them as abnormal. It seems strange, however, that all the toes found should deviate from the normal, and Black consequently concludes his essay with the suggestion that possibly the foot of the *Sinanthropus* deviated more from that of modern man than did the hand.

As the human foot is a specially characteristic development of the anthropoid foot for the purpose of the equally characteristic rapid upright movement, this suggestion is of special interest. But we must not forget concerning the structure of the *Sinanthropus* foot that the available material is infinitesimally small and that we must therefore await more plentiful discoveries before we can draw any conclusions whatever. In this connection it is of interest that according to the introductory words of Black's last communication only a small part of the immense deposits of Chou K'ou Tien has as yet been excavated.

The consistent tendency has hitherto been for the deposits to yield more and more material the deeper the excavations have been conducted. Let us therefore hope for still more illuminating discoveries in the as yet unexplored parts of the Chou K'ou Tien deposits.

FIG. 48.—Dr. Davidson Black at Chou K'ou Tien.

FIG. 49.—The loess basin at Hsin Yao in the mountainous region north of Peiping. In the background are visible hills which contain the iron ore deposits. The valley in the centre is occupied by the loess formation, with its dark, gaping ravines.

CHAPTER SEVEN

THE YELLOW EARTH

THE tillers of the soil have in all ages and amongst all peoples been closely bound to the earth.

Sweden's hard and stony till, the poor sandy heaths of North Germany, the black earth of Southern Russia, are some of the cultivated lands which are intimately bound up with the agricultural population. But nowhere else in the world is the bond between the soil and the peasant population so close and so varied as in Northern China.

The supreme hold of the yellow earth upon the people and their lives is due to its unique topographical rôle. Where the yellow earth prevails, it rules over the land and the waters, and even over the air, which is filled with its fine dust with every storm that blows.

Huang T'u, the yellow earth, is the name given by the Chinese to the dust-fine soil which rules over Northern China. Western science has taught us to call it loess, because in the Rhineland a similar soil has been thus named.

The stranger visiting the great loess regions of Northern China is struck most of all by the great depth, or thickness as the geologist prefers to call it, of the loess soil. Early explorers, like Richthofen, imagined that the thickness of the loess might in some cases amount to 400 metres or more, but I have been able to show that this assumption was due to the fact that Richthofen did not know of the Tertiary, loess-like *Hipparion* clay and the probably late Pliocene clays which lie below the genuine loess and are often so like it that I also, though the problem was clear to me, frequently could not decide where the real loess finished in the downward direction and where the clays began. It is my personal experience that in eastern China (Shansi and Honan) the loess deposits have scarcely been observed to a greater thickness than 50–60 metres, whereas the thickness in Shensi and Kansu sometimes amounts to over 100 metres. In this case I beg the reader to study Fig. 50, which shows a thickness of loess of 130 metres, a figure which, however, must for certain reasons not be regarded as perfectly accurate.

The most striking thing about the Northern Chinese loess formation is its particularly fantastic topography. The vignette at the head of this chapter gives a very good idea of it. Broadly speaking, the loess deposits in this case form a cover which fills up the valleys and above which the mountain ridges rise in much the same way as our own mountains stick up in winter out of the cover of snow. Indeed, this comparison with a snow-covered landscape is in reality very significant, for according to Richthofen's now generally accepted theory of the formation of the loess it is, like snow, an Eolian sediment, i.e. it has been transported by the wind and laid to rest where the velocity of the wind is least and where the configuration of the ground offers shelter and protection.

But we now come to a description of the process, later than the formation of the loess deposits, which has imparted to the modern landscape its picturesque, puzzling, and to the inexperienced traveller, positively bewildering character. The once unbroken cover of loess has been disintegrated and intersected by rain-water, so that an excursion in the loess region becomes a wonderful experience, in which the wanderer often stops short with surprise and even trembling before perpendicular drops of 30 metres or more. Or he may meet thin, fantastic pillars of the yellow earth, or he will glimpse bits of landscape through natural tunnels or arches which remain standing for some time while the washing away of the loess proceeds. As we see from the illustrations, the loess ravines are gulleys with almost perpendicular walls and are so narrow that not infrequently the depth is greater than the breadth. If we follow such a gulley to its innermost part we shall find to our surprise in most cases that it has its full depth from the beginning. It will soon become clear to the acute observer that these ravines were not formed by water running on the surface. During the great summer rains, it is true, the water rushes in cascades from the fields down into the depths, but the essential process of erosion is of quite a different kind.

In order to understand the manner of formation of the loess ravines we must examine the yellow earth a little more closely. The typical Huang T'u is a greyish yellow dust which does not as a rule show any stratification, but shows, on the other hand, a remarkable capacity for adhering to perpendicular cliffs. This fine,

FIG. 50.—Section through the Ching Ho valley, Eastern Kansu. *c*, loess; *b*, gravel; *a*, schistous rocks belonging to the Carboniferous system.

porous earth easily lets through the water which falls upon its surface. Consequently only a part of the summer rains drain off its surface. For a large part of the rainfall it acts like a sponge, or, perhaps better, like a gigantic filter, through which the water sinks to the bedrock of the loess deposits, consisting of gravel, Tertiary clay or solid rock. The lower part of the loess soil in this way often becomes saturated with water and assumes a consistency like that of a thin porridge or gruel. This bottom layer then slowly begins to move and slides down any slope, and in proportion as the saturated bottom slides away towards the open valley, the superimposed, relatively dry mass of loess sinks down perpendicularly. This vertical movement may be studied everywhere in the ravines, in which one sees large and small blocks of the old vegetation-covered surface in all sorts of more or less inclined positions half-way or more down to the bottom of the ravine. Only when we have clearly understood this curious process of erosion, which occurs, not on the surface, but, on the contrary, by the flow of the basic portion of the loess, shall we be able to understand the remarkable and extremely fantastic topography of the loess landscape: the narrow ravines with their perpendicular walls and uniform depth right to their source, the detached islands and castle-like pillars, and, not least, the frail vaults and arches.

I have already given a preliminary sketch of the explanation of the origin of the loess formation which has found the widest acceptance, namely Richthofen's Eolian theory, according to which the loess is a deposit left in its present position principally by the agency of the winds.

If we seek to penetrate further into this alluring but difficult problem, we shall first agree that there exist in general three groups of forces which might have deposited the peculiar soil which now lies like an immense carpet over large parts of Northern China. The three alternative lines of interpretation are: the inland ice of the Ice age, running water, possibly in combination with great lake basins and, finally, the winds.

It is extremely easy to dispose of the first suggested explanation. Ice can never directly produce such a deposit as loess. It is true that loess appears in Europe on the outer margin of the ancient ice cover under such conditions that loess material in no small quantities was derived from the moraines, which contained abundant dust. But this is a resifting of inland ice deposits which is only conceivable in those districts where during the Pleistocene period the inland ice eroded the bedrock. In Northern China we have as little evidence as in Mongolia of a Pleistocene ice cover. On the contrary, everything indicates that the climate in those parts during the Pleistocene period was too dry to permit of the existence of an ice cover. The ice theory may therefore be promptly dismissed as quite improbable.

Had the loess been deposited in water, we should find freshwater molluscs and mussels, but the mollusc shells which are most commonly found in the typical loess deposits are mostly *Helicidae* and other land molluscs, i.e. forms which directly contradict the theory of deposit by water. The striking absence in the loess formation of stratification, which characterizes any genuine water deposits, is also definite evidence against the lacustrine theory.[1]

If we examine carefully a loess basin, such, for example, as that at the iron-ore field of Hsin Yao (cf. the vignette at the beginning of the chapter) we shall certainly find close to the mountain-side certain signs of stratification, consisting in the fact that this border zone shows an oft-repeated alternation of loess and gravel layers, which consist of stones from the nearest mountain-slopes and which have clearly been washed down from them. But out in the middle of the loess basin one finds very seldom even the thinnest of gravel beds. Here we find as a rule only the homogeneous, unstratified, fine loess soil.

If we now survey as a whole the observations which have just been made—the fine dust, constituting the loess, its lack of stratification and its wealth of land molluscs and lack of fresh-water molluscs—we are compelled to abandon the theory of deposit in water and we are irresistibly led back to Richthofen's Eolian theory: during a period when a steppe climate prevailed in Northern China masses of dust were conveyed over these areas,[2] and everywhere, especially in valleys and basins, where the power of the wind was abated, the wind-borne dust sank to earth and grew during the course of centuries into a cover of several tens of metres thickness, a cover which in many places completely obscured the original contours of the land.

With this explanation it is easy to account for the gravel rims by the mountain-sides as having been washed down from the

[1] Even Richthofen distinguished besides the typical loess a so-called " lake loess " which he assumed to have been deposited in inland lake basins. Similar observations were made by Teilhard and Licent on the southern edge of the Ordos desert, where they found a sandy loess containing freshwater molluscs, which they take to have been deposited in a lake basin approximately contemporary with the genuine Eolian loess (cf. Chapter VIII).

[2] Richthofen assumed that the material of the loess deposits came from the desert areas of Central Asia. This is probably in the main correct, but it is possible that local deposits in China itself also contributed to the loess formation. The Tertiary clays which in many places underlie the loess, but which in others were still exposed to the erosion of the wind during a large part of the loess period, are in composition and consistency so like loess that they may very well be conceived as having made a considerable contribution to the loess formation.

slopes during the rare, but violent, floods of rain which are characteristic of the steppe climate.

That large parts of Northern China were an undrained grass steppe during the period of loess formation I can prove directly by my investigations on the Yellow River. I have had occasion to navigate or otherwise follow this mighty and peculiar river for long stretches, from its emergence from the Tibetan highlands right down to the point at the Peking-Hankow railway bridge where it flows into the great Northern Chinese alluvial plain. Almost everywhere along this stretch of 2,000 km. the river is surrounded by loess formations, which in many places form high, almost perpendicular banks. From the two banks of the river these face each other in such a manner that there cannot be the least doubt that at one time the loess deposit constituted one great

FIG. 51.—Section across the course of the Yellow River at Shan Pai Wan in Kansu. *c*, loess; *b*, gravel; *a*, red sandstone.

whole in the form of a gently undulating grass steppe, even where the mighty river now rolls along with its yellow waters of muddy loess soil.

Therefore the Yellow River and its tributaries did not flow at the time when the loess was deposited. Over Northern China there extended an undulating grass land, a landscape probably similar to that of the steppes of Southern Mongolia to-day.

The vision of the great steppes of Northern China during the loess period became real to me one day in 1923 when on the march to Kansu. Just in the district from which Fig. 51 is drawn I stood on the edge of the loess deposits and looked down on the mighty river. I then saw how the river had cut its way down by erosion, not only through the loess cover and its foundation of gravel and conglomerate, but also through a good piece of the ancient red sandstone which is the bedrock of this district. It was a picture of a tremendous process of erosion, later than the loess formation, which I saw revealed here in the perpendicular banks.

Then I walked back about 10 yards on to the loess plateau.

The river had suddenly vanished, the two opposite precipices merged into each other and the picture of the ancient unbroken loess plateau stood clearly before me.

Fortunately the position is such that we can give another, direct and tangible proof that loess is an ancient steppe deposit.

In 1898 the American zoologist Eastman described the very remarkable discovery of a large fossil bird's egg which was found in Northern China, not far from Kalgan. The fossil was identified with a similar egg which had been found long before, about 1857, near the town of Cherson in Southern Russia, which was described by the Russian scientist Brandt as the egg of an extinct ostrich, named *Struthiolithus chersonensis*.[1]

Further discoveries of the *Struthiolithus* in Northern China occurred during the course of years, and in 1923 I was able in my *Essays on the Cenozoic of Northern China*, pp. 53–71, to report no less than 18 finds of *Struthiolithus chersonensis* in the provinces of Shantung, Chihli, Shansi and Honan, all in Northern China.

It appeared during the course of my studies that these eggs had long been known to the Chinese, for in the collection of the Emperor Ch'ien Lung in the Art Museum of Peking there is such an egg. But still more remarkable is the fact that in the spring of 1922 we found in the prehistoric site at Yang Shao Tsun in Honan numerous pieces of the shell of the *Struthiolithus* under such conditions that there can scarcely be any doubt that the people of the latest Stone-age had found one of these large birds' eggs and wondered at it in the same way as does the Honan peasant to-day when he finds a " dragon's egg " in his fields or, as once happened, floating on the Yellow River.

It was first fully established by my investigations in Honan in 1921 that the *Struthiolithus* eggs originated from loess soil. Especially decisive were observations in the village of Kou Yü Kou in the Mien Chih district. I was led to this place by the circumstance that an antique dealer in the town of Mien Chih sold me fragments of an egg which, according to his report, came from the village of Kou Yü Kou. Some days later I

[1] " On Remains of *Struthiolithus chersonensis* from Northern China ", *Bulletin of the Museum of Comparative Zoology*, Harvard College, Vol. XXXII, No. 7.

visited the place and entered into conversation with the peasant who had found it. He conducted me to a cave which he had excavated as a store room in 1917. This cave lies almost side by side with his dwelling, which is similarly a cave hewn out of the loess wall. Two eggs had been seen whilst digging out the cave. One, which was intact when discovered, lay in the middle of the space now occupied by the cave, at a depth of 4 metres below the surface. The man had struck a hole in the shell when he dug it out. This was the egg which I had bought in Mien Chih.

FIG. 52.—*Struthiolithus* egg from the loess formation in Honan. The size is shown by comparison with a match-box of ordinary size.

The peasant had observed fragments of another egg in the wall of the cave. Several still remained entirely untouched in the loess wall, and in this manner I obtained the long-cherished opportunity of personally digging out a *Struthiolithus* egg in a place certainly untouched. The pieces of shell were situated 1 metre inside the opening of the cave and 5 metres below the surface of the ground, in absolutely typical loess, together with numerous land molluscs. Thus we found here in typical loess soil the two fossil groups, ostrich eggs and land molluscs, which support with special force Richthofen's theory that loess is a wind deposit.

There is one feature of these egg discoveries which still further strengthens the Eolian theory. In no less than 8, or possibly 9, of the 18 discoveries there were found in each case 2 (and in one case 4) eggs together, and with few exceptions the eggs were embedded intact. All this indicates that they had lain out in the steppes—probably just as the mother bird had left them—and that these specimens have been preserved until our day just because in some heavy loess storm they were completely covered over by the driven dust. Only the Eolian theory can explain why so many of these thin and brittle eggshells have been found quite uninjured.

The form and structure of the *Struthiolithus* shell show that Brandt, who first described one of these eggs, was quite right in his interpretation of them as belonging to an ostrich. This Asiatic fossil ostrich was, to judge by its egg, certainly considerably larger than the *Struthio camelus*, the modern African ostrich. The mean length of the *Struthiolithus* egg of Northern China is 179 mm., as against 162 mm. of the *Struthio camelus*.

Remains of mammals are very rare in loess, and bones or teeth only occur occasionally and singly. Thus one cannot dig systematically for bones in well stocked sites, as is the case in the *Hipparion* clay.

Sometimes, however, I came across remains of elephants in Honan, and the most important find, bits of a skull, was made under circumstances so peculiar that there is ground for repeating the account which I wrote down shortly after the event and which in my manuscript I entitled " The History of an Old Woman and an Elephant ".

During my journey by boat on the Yellow River in the spring of 1921 I arrived in the afternoon of May 18th at a little village, Ching Kou, in the Kung Hsien district of Honan. The village lies in one of the numerous ravines which cut deep into the yellow earth (loess) and which run into the Yellow River. My collectors went inland to reconnoitre, whilst I occupied myself on board with labelling, packing and writing of notes.

From a previous journey I knew that this district was rich in remains of fossil elephants.

This wealth showed itself also on this occasion. Early in the evening the cook brought in a couple of fine pieces of an elephant tusk, and a little later Yao arrived with a similar find.

Early the following morning some of the villagers brought down to the boat a large piece of an elephant's skull, with large parts of one, or probably two, molars.

Somewhat later others arrived with an almost perfect lower jaw in two halves, of which one was broken in two by carelessness just as it was being placed before us. There then followed some hot bargaining. We began by offering 3 dollars and the men demanded 200. After more than an hour's bargaining we finally obtained the lower jaw for 20 dollars.

Scarcely was this hard bargain concluded when another company arrived with a big basket full of large and small pieces of skull. This material was less acceptable than the lower jaw, as it was badly broken, but since it was a question of collecting as complete a specimen as possible, I was anxious to obtain these fragments. Here again there was much chaffering and we were obliged to invoke the assistance of the alderman before we succeeded in obtaining the parcel for 7 dollars.

As soon as we had finished this long-winded business I was anxious to try the site of the discoveries myself. It was now lunch-time, so we ate a hasty meal and set out.

Our road led for 3 km. through the deep and narrow ravine which runs up in a southerly direction through the loess plateau from the village of Ching Kou (" Kou " means " ravine ")

Rumours of the business we had done had evidently spread afar, for our road was flanked by hosts of people studying our appearance and behaviour.

When, with a constantly growing following, we reached the neighbourhood of the site, we were met by the real owners of the ground on which the discoveries had been made, and we gradually obtained a lot of interesting information. It appears that of the various groups of collectors who had sold to us portions of the find, none represented the owner of the soil, but all had successively plundered the site.

The knowledge of a great find of " dragons' bones " in the locality was clearly shared by many, and some parties of freebooters had forestalled the owner in exploiting the spot, since there was a " foreign devil " down in the valley who was willing to pay big money for dragons' bones. In order fully to understand the situation the following circumstances must be borne in mind. The incident occurred at the end of one of the most severe famine periods in the modern history of China. Three wheat harvests in succession had failed. Now a new and especially fine harvest was almost ready for gathering in. Indeed, the harvesting had already begun in some places.

The site was located high up on the very steep, extremely narrow, cultivated, terraced strips of the side of the ravine. Access to the upper cultivated terraces of the slopes was had from the top of the plateau, and to climb to them from below was an acrobatic feat. Everywhere the wheat was trampled down by the unfortunate traffic which had passed over it the whole of the morning. Although I had dismissed all superfluous members of our all too large company, we could not help continuing this destruction.

At last we reached the site of the discovery itself, a small, recently excavated hole in the wall of loess, about 30 metres above the bottom of the ravine and 15 metres below the edge of the plateau. It was immediately clear that everything of value had already been removed. Only three small bone fragments were still visible in the walls of the cavity.

As, however, it was evidently in our interests to dig these out also, I commissioned Yao to obtain from the owner permission to do so. Yao offered 3 dollars, which was good pay considering that there was nothing else left in the place. The man, however, was confused and hesitating. It was impossible to obtain any decision from him. I offered to pay more if we should find anything of real value. But we could still come to no agreement. I then proposed that we should make a trial excavation and pay according to results.

The excavations, however insignificant they may have been, were yet in some respects illuminating. They showed that the bones lay scattered in the loess and that stone-hard concretions, " loess-puppchen ", had grown solid with the bones. It was thus due not only to the carelessness of the peasants in excavating that the material was brought to me in such fragmentary forms.

Just as I sat digging peacefully in the cavity and the men were standing round in friendly conversation, I heard a shrill and angry woman's voice. Quite right, behind the men stood an old woman who shrieked and clamoured as loud as she could. It was the aged mother of the owner, and her clamorous complaints related to the trampled wheat.

I had long since learnt that in China everything can be put right except hysterical old women. I realized that the situation was very serious, so I asked Yao to propitiate the old lady.

Yao could talk quite charmingly when he really did his best, but this was of no avail, for the old woman worked herself up into an even greater frenzy. Finally she climbed up resolutely into the cavity, in this way preventing all further excavation work. It was undoubtedly most amusingly done and was a genuine sample of the famous passive resistance of the Chinese.

I opened my parasol and held it over the old woman, an action which gave rise to some merriment, but did not materially alter the situation.

I knew there was *one* infallible means of driving out a Chinese peasant woman, so I made preparations to take a photograph of the spot, as I wished in any case to have one.

I was right; the camera had the desired effect: the old lady got up from the hole and crept behind the back of her son. Apparently my counter-move had succeeded, but it was perhaps far from well conceived. Perhaps I had offended the old lady and her followers by my photographing. Anyhow Yao advised me to retire, "because otherwise we soon have big trouble". I hastily surveyed the situation. We were about 30 persons on a very narrow terrace, apart from the fact that the slopes above and opposite were lined with people, perhaps a couple of hundred of them.

On the assumption that we came to blows, somebody, either we or the others, would certainly be tumbled over the cliffs, to say nothing of the projectiles in the form of blocks of loess which might be expected from above. Our means of defence consisted of a pickaxe, some large knives and a Browning, with 16 cartridges. The Chinese were for the moment more or less unarmed but in an overwhelming majority. The decisive consideration was that

Fig. 53.—The old woman and the elephant, both invisible.

any kind of turmoil would most unfavourably affect our future work in this district.

I followed Yao's advice and we retired to the boat without being in any way molested by the numerous spectators.

I sincerely hope that until the day of her death the old lady may, as a slight compensation for the damage to her trampled wheat, enjoy great honour as one who cast out a foreign devil.

Our fossil elephants from China have not yet been described, and I cannot therefore give the definitive name of the elephant form of the Chinese loess. In any case it is not the mammoth, as was earlier assumed in certain quarters, but a species identical with, or standing near to, the Indian *Elephas namadicus* Falc. et Cautley.

Apart from a number of isolated and less important finds we may further mention the woolly-haired rhinoceros, *Rhinoceros tichorhinus* Cuv., as well as two hyaenas, *Hyaena sinensis* Owen, and *H. ultima* Matsumoto, found in the loess. The woolly rhinoceros is of great interest, as it is a characteristic fossil of the middle Pleistocene in Europe and thus gives us some indication that the period of formation of the Chinese loess corresponded fairly closely with the Ice age of Europe. If this determination of age is correct, North China had a steppe climate while Europe was submerged under the great covering of ice of the Pleistocene age.

On the other hand our investigations have shown that below the loess there are strata of gravel and sand, evidently deposited by running water, which in places contain fresh-water mussels of great interest.

The first discoveries of this kind were made by the first Director of the Geological Survey, Dr. V. K. Ting, in 1918, in the bed of the Yellow River, beside the famous San Men rapids on the boundary between Honan and Shansi. In the sand stratum beneath the loess he found a number of large fresh-water shells which were ascribed by Dr. Wm. H. Dall in Washington to the genera *Quadrula* and *Cuneopsis*.

Another find was made by me in 1921, a little farther down the course of the Yellow River, at the village of Ho Ti Tsun in the Yuan Chü district of Shansi. The local conditions are

The San Men formation on the Yellow River, Yuan Chü Hsien

shown in Plate 9. The series of strata, beginning from the lowest, is:

A. A hardened bed of coarse gravel of Eocene age. The stratum dips 30 degrees to the south-west . . 17 metres.
B. Coarse gravel of Pleistocene age, horizontally superimposed on the Eocene strata . . . . 25 metres.
C. Gravel and coarse sand interstratified. In this tightly packed mass were found numerous fresh-water mussels, many of them very large. Many of the large shells stood on edge, almost in a vertical position . . 2 metres.
D. Alternate strata of loess and gravel . . about 20 metres.

The mussels collected by me in bed C have been carefully described by our eminent mollusc expert Dr. Nils Hj. Odhner, in a work "Shells from the San Men Series", *Palaeontologia Sinica*, Ser. B, Vol. 6, Fasc. 1. Odhner cites the following kinds of fresh-water mussels:

Solenaia carinata.
Anodonta woodiana.
Cristaria herculea.
Hyriopsis descendens n.
Lepidodesma ponderosa n.
Nodularia douglasiae.
Cuneopsis maximus n.
Lamprotula antiqua n.
Lamprotula antiqua undulata n.
Corbicula fluminea.

Most of these mussels have their nearest modern relatives in Southern China, the climate of which is much more rainy than the district in which I found the fossils. Dr. Odhner also considers that mussels of the San Men series indicate that they lived in a damp and warm climate.

The banks of the Yellow River on the boundary between Honan and Shansi thus bring to our knowledge two climatically opposite Pleistocene formations [1]; the fresh-water beds of mussels belonging to the oldest Pleistocene, which point to a damp and warm climate, probably the same as that of the Yangtse valley

[1] Since the above was written, in 1928, we have acquired further knowledge of the lake deposits at Ni Ho Wan in the mountain districts north-west of Peking. Here the San Men series of fresh-water mussels occurs together with a very abundant and excellently preserved mammal fauna which has been described by Teilhard de Chardin and Jean Piveteau ("Les Mammifères Fossiles de Nihowan", *Annales de Paléontologie*, T. XIX, 1930).

These writers consider the Ni Ho Wan fauna to belong to the very latest Pliocene (see table at end of book). Teilhard now also includes the Chou K'ou Tien fauna (oldest Pleistocene) in the San Men series, which thus represents the transition from Pliocene to Pleistocene.

in modern times, and reposing on these river deposits, the mighty loess formation, of which the structure and absence of stratification, together with the presence of land molluscs and the discovery of ostrich eggs, all point to a relatively dry steppe climate during which no river flowed through this area. The presence of the woolly rhinoceros, which in Europe and Siberia belonged to the icy tundra, shows that the climate of the loess age was quite cold.

Huang T'u, the yellow soil, and Huang Ho, the Yellow River! Listen to the two names, so like in sound! And indeed they are closely related. Just as the yellow soil covers the whole of Northern China under its immense carpet, so the mighty river with its many tributaries rules over the same land, from its sources in icy Tibet to its mouth on a desolate strand of the Yellow Sea. Both river and sea take their names from the yellow soil, which tinges everything: earth, river, sea and sky.

The Yellow River and the yellow soil symbolize two opposite, even intensely hostile natural forces: the spirit of water and the spirit of air.

At the beginning of the Pleistocene age, the period of formation of the San Men deposits, the spirit of water appears to have ruled alone, for everywhere we find its remains under the loess formation in the form of beds of sand and gravel formed by running water.

But there followed a new age, when the spirit of air ruled unchallenged. The rivers became more feeble with every year that passed. Soon they were even unable to carry their waters out to the ocean and finally they dried up entirely. The wind-swept dust filled the empty river channels, and the whole of Northern China became an undulating steppe, to which every storm brought new beds of dust between the knolls of the steppe.

Great and terrible was the victory of the spirit of the air; but it was not of long duration.

Again the summer clouds were charged with rain, again the streams grew into rivers, which again reached the ocean.

The carpet over the land woven by the spirit of air was of fragile texture, and the purling water merrily carved its way deep into the loose yellow soil. It was a splendid act of vengeance.

Soon the level carpet was torn and disintegrated into rags and tatters.

But the spirit of air did not give up the fight. Principally in the spring, when every part of the country sighed for rain, it rose up for a new attack. The storm raged over mountain and vale ; masses of dust were torn up from the interior of Asia ; the day was darkened and the clouds lay low in eerie blue-grey over the dusty earth, whilst the sun peeped through like a faint light in the clouds.

The very destruction of the mighty work of the spirit of air became a curse to the rivers. The fine loose soil filled the river, so that it no longer carried water, but a nauseous yellow-grey gruel, and its course became shallow, shifting and capricious. When the river reached the great coastal plain, its bed rose rapidly owing to the quantities of mud which here sank to rest, and with a summer torrent it overflowed and broke out into a new course. In this way the river came to change its course on the plain, now to the south, now far to the north.

During this constant struggle between the two forces of nature the Northern Chinese power developed. We know from the great discoveries of French scientists in the Ordos desert (cf. next chapter) that the man of the Old Stone age lived there already at the beginning of the formation of loess. Then we lose the thread, but we pick it up again during the Yang Shao age, the latest Stone age, four to five thousand years ago. The country at Yang Shao Tsun was then quite different from now. The loess plain was still intact, where to-day we find a network of deep ravines.

But the great river and its thousands of tributaries continue their work of destruction into historical times. Like a turbid and dangerous current runs the story of " China's sorrow ", Huang Ho, through the annals of the land, from the days of great Yü, the water engineer who tamed the river monster and became emperor by his superhuman hydrotechnical feats.

Stretches of roads sank into the depths and houses slipped away when the hand of the ravines stretched its fingers farther and farther across the land. And when during the summer floods the river twisted convulsively out on the great coastal plain whole provinces were sometimes obliterated.

But water was not only a dreaded destroyer. All the wealth of the country flourished and bore fruit when the fructifying rain fell on the fertile yellow soil. Rather rain in excess, rather new ravines and floods than the deadly drought which might hang year after year over the bare dusty fields, until the exhausted people sat powerless on their heels and waited for death.

During this ceaselessly shifting struggle between the Yellow Soil and the Yellow River, between rain and drought, between abundant crops and famine, there developed those elements of character which make the Chinese the world's best agriculturalists :

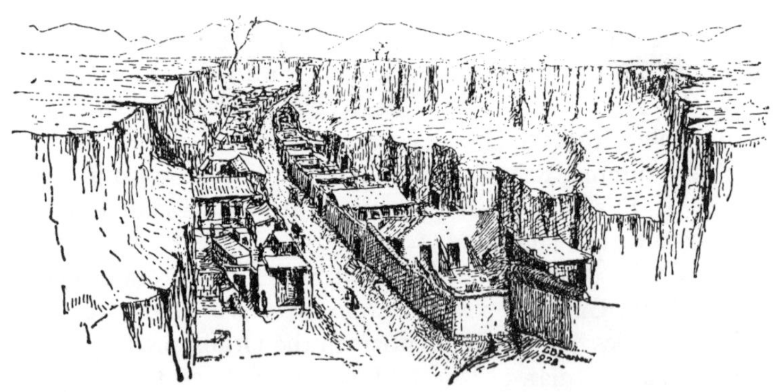

Fig. 54.—The loess village of Su Chia Chiao, near Kalgan. (*After a drawing by Professor George B. Barbour.*)

industry and thrift, the ability to enlist every source of help, and the endurance to begin patiently afresh when destruction seemed well-nigh inevitable.

Thus ran my thoughts on May 17th, 1921, when I stood in Erh Liang Kou in Honan on the flat banks of the Yellow River and looked at one of my men digging out of the old steep banks the remains of a grave of the Han dynasty (about the time of Christ's birth) (Plate 10). On that day I had gone to look in the gravel under the loess formation for mammal remains and I then quite unexpectedly found at the foot of the bank some pieces of the large decorated tiles with which the Han people built their graves. An agile coolie clambered up the cliff and soon brought down to us all that remained of the old grave, one whole and several large broken tiles. When the grave was pre-

Loess Terraces at Erh Liang Kou, Honan

[*face page* 144

pared nearly 2,000 years ago, the country certainly looked very different. Later on the river flowed southwards and cut away the greater part of the grave. Now it has shifted north again, and a low level strand lies between the flowing water and the abandoned river cliff.

Fig. 55.—Father Emile Licent, the great collector and founder of the Huang Ho-Pai Ho Museum.

CHAPTER EIGHT

PLEISTOCENE MAN IN THE ORDOS DESERT

Of all the missionary societies which have been active in China the Society of Jesus deserves the place of honour in respect of the promotion of scientific research.

Many are the scientific *magna opera* which the Catholic missionaries, and especially the Jesuits, have accomplished.

During the last period of the Ming dynasty and under the first Manchu Emperors it was Jesuits like Adam Schall and Ferdinand Verbiest, astronomers of the Imperial Court at Peking, who constructed six of the famous instruments in the Peking observatory.

Closely connected with this astronomical work is the great cartographic atlas which was executed during the years 1708–18 by the order of the Emperor K'ang Hsi under the direction of Father Tartoux, whose collaborators, except the Augustinian monk Father Bonjour, were all Jesuits. In certain districts of the interior of China the Jesuit maps are still the best available.

Father du Halde, who, curiously enough, never visited China, published in 1735 a great geographical work in four folio volumes based on the information of twenty-seven Jesuit missionaries.

During the last century there was established at Zikawei, outside Shanghai, a remarkable centre for the scientific work of the Jesuits in China. In the forefront is the observatory, blessed by all navigators in Chinese waters because of its typhoon warnings.

The Zikawei Museum has published a work in six volumes on the fauna and flora of China, and another series of great importance, published by the Fathers of Zikawei, is the *Variétés Sinologiques*, some fifty volumes describing the religion, history, geography and social conditions of China.

A Catholic, belonging to the Lazarists, who has been especially meritorious in the investigation of China's flora and fauna is the Abbé Armand David, who during three expeditions, 1862–74, in China, Southern Mongolia and Eastern Tibet, collected a large amount of material and who, among other things, was the discoverer of the remarkable stag, *Elaphurus davidianus*, which in his day existed in the imperial hunting preserve in Peking and has found its last refuge nowadays in the park of the Duke of Bedford in England.

In our days the French padres have resumed this scientific work in Northern China in a manner which fully upholds the proud tradition created by the Jesuit fathers at the end of the Ming period and the transition to the Manchu dynasty.

In 1914 Father Emile Licent began the collecting activity which he described ten years later in an all too substantial work, *Ten Years' Investigations in the District of the Yellow River*. During that decade he had traversed Northern China in many directions and made large collections of the modern fauna and flora.

In 1920 he found in Eastern Kansu (Ching Yang Fu) rich deposits of the *Hipparion* fauna and improvised his partially quite successful methods of preserving this material. By the removal of deposits of loess which covered the *Hipparion* clay he found at the base of the loess formation some pieces of quartz which seemed to have been worked by the human hand, and the idea of the possibility of finding traces of Man of the Old Stone age was thus born in him.

Two Catholic fathers, Mostaert and de Wilde, had, prompted by the Mongolian Wansjock, informed Father Licent that there existed at Sjara Osso Gol, at the southern edge of the Ordos desert, another abundant site of bones. When, in 1922, Licent examined it, he found the conditions so promising that he invited the co-operation of the professor of palaeontology of the Institut Catholique in Paris, P. Teilhard de Chardin, a scientist of international repute, who, by many years of study at the natural history museum in Paris, and especially by a critical revision of the famous Eocene mammals of Northern France, had received a superb training. It was this enthusiastic palaeontologist who became Licent's scientific collaborator.

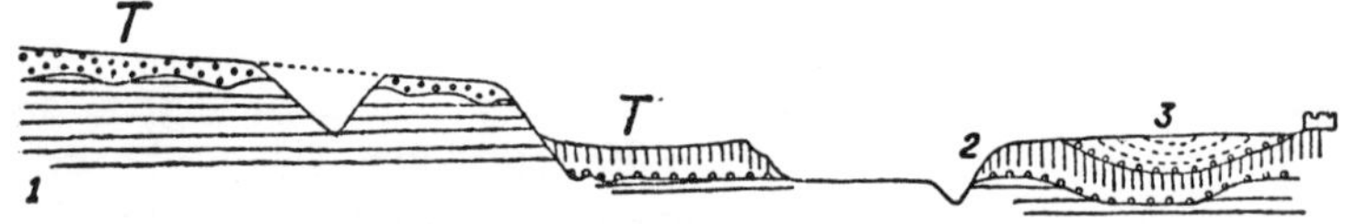

FIG. 56.—Section through the Choei Tong Keou basin. 1, Tertiary clay; 2, loess with gravel deposits below; 3, fresh-water deposits above the loess; T, terraces. (*After Teilhard and Licent.*)

West of the Ordos desert there lies on the left bank of the Yellow River an important town of the name of Ning Hsia Fu, and opposite it, on the right bank, close to the Great Wall, a little place called Hung Cheng. About 12 km. farther east, and likewise close to the Great Wall, Licent had observed at Choei Tong Keou (Shui Tung Kou) interesting sections through the loose deposits, and here the first great discovery was made.

Within the loess formation, which is here partly covered by a later river deposit, there was found, under at least 12 metres of typical loess deposit, over a stretch of 20 metres, a dwelling place of the Old Stone age. The culture stratum, which was 0·5 metres thick, contained masses of coarsely hewn stone implements, as well as fragments rejected in the making of the implements (the total yield was no less than 300 kg. of stone fragments worked by the human hand). Together with the implements were found bits of charcoal from the camp fires of the Stone-age people and also remains of their meals in the shape of bits of bone of the

Mongolian desert wild ass, *Equus hemionus*, and, more rarely, rhinoceros, hyaena, antelope and cattle, as well as bits of egg-shell belonging to the now extinct giant ostrich of the loess period.

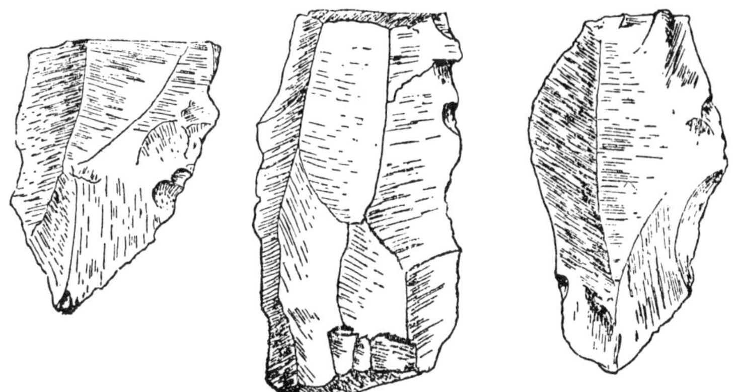

Fig. 57.—Stone implements from Choei Tong Keou, presented to the Museum of Far Eastern Antiquities by Licent and Teilhard.

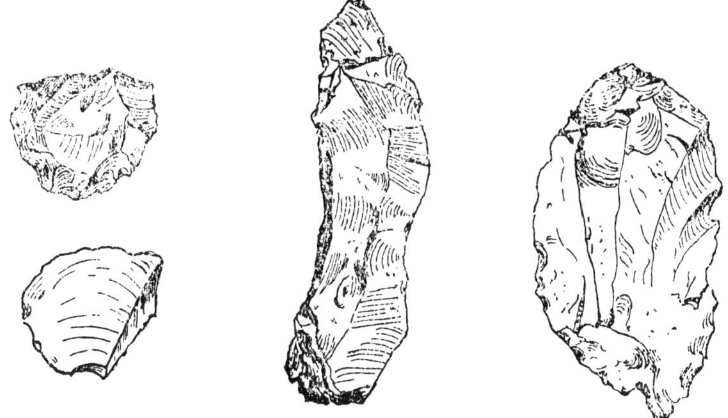

Fig. 58.—Stone implements from Choei Tong Keou, presented to the Museum of Far Eastern Antiquities by Licent and Teilhard.

The stone implements, as well as raw materials and chippings of their manufacture, which were found in large quantities in this ancient dwelling, were for the most part made on the spot, to judge from the fact that the material had in most cases been taken from the rubble in the gravel deposits which in this place lie under the loess. It is thus the same red quartzite and siliceous limestone, found both in the stone implements and in the gravel beds, which served the people of the Old Stone age. Many of these scrapers, blades and drills, etc., are of considerable size, in exceptional cases as much as 17 cm. in length.

During my visit in 1927 to Father Licent's fine museum in Tientsin, where some of these collections are preserved, the two Fathers were so very kind as to donate to the Museum of Far Eastern Antiquities twenty implements from Choei Tong Keou, and the illustrations 57 and 58 are selected from this material.

The site here described is certainly by far the richest, but by no means the only one, at Choei Tong Keou. At several other places similar finds were made in the loess formation and the

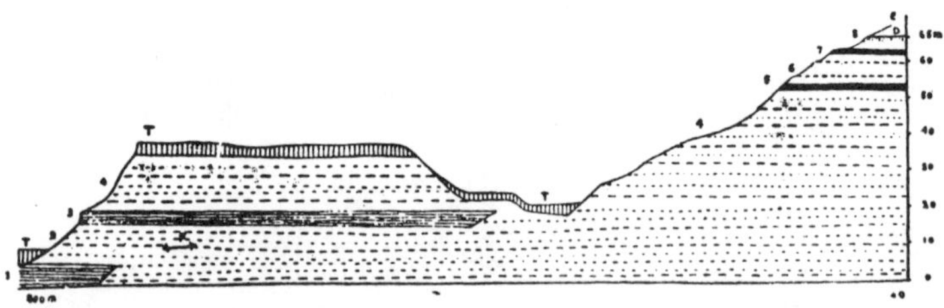

FIG. 59. Section at Sjara Osso Gol. (*After Teilhard and Licent.*)

discoverers of these primeval traces of human beings summarized their observations thus : " in the whole Choei Tong Keou basin the loess contains numerous traces of an absolutely homogeneous Palaeolithic industry, left by a population which appears to have inhabited the district during the whole period of formation of the loess."

Right in the middle of the southern border of the Ordos desert, near Sjara Osso Gol, a desert river which runs eastwards into the Yellow River, the two scientists discovered a Pleistocene fauna, both enormously rich in species and well preserved, and in combination with it implements made by human beings contemporary with the Pleistocene animals.

Fig. 59 gives a section of the conditions existing in this place. The whole of the Pleistocene series of deposits consists of layers of sand with inlays of sandy clay, containing the shells of fresh-water molluscs (*Planorbis*, *Bythinia*). This series of deposits is interpreted by Teilhard and Licent as contemporary with the genuine Chinese loess, but as deposited in a basin in which dune formations alternated with genuine lake deposits.

In these Pleistocene deposits was found a fauna much richer in species than one is accustomed to find in the typical loess, and this abundant animal life was clearly made possible by the copious supply of water, and consequently of pasture, to which the clay deposits with their numerous fresh-water molluscs bear witness.

It was, of course, the same favourable natural conditions—access to water and the availability of big game—which caused the traces of Pleistocene man to be so abundant in this place. On the whole it appears as if the southern fringe of Ordos was an oasis in the great loess steppe, which was little less than a desert.

The imposing list of the Sjara Osso Gol fauna is as follows :

Elephas cf. namadicus. The same form of elephant as constitutes one of the genuine loess fossils.

Rhinoceros tichorinus Cuv., the woolly rhinoceros.

Equus hemionus Pallas, the Mongolian wild ass.

E. cf. prjewalskyi Poliakof, the wild horse of Central Asia.

Sus scrofa L., the wild boar.

Camelus knoblochi Brandt, a species of camel, first described from the Pleistocene of Russia.

Cervus elaphus L., red deer.

C. Mongoliae Gaudry.

C. megaceros Hart. var. mongoliae.

Gazella prjewalskyi Büchner.

G. subgutturosa Guldenst.

Spirocerus kiakhtensis (Pavlov). This genus, established by Boule and Teilhard de Chardin, represents an extinct East Asiatic form of antelope, found in the trans-Baikal region, Altai, Ordos and Northern China.

Ovis ammon Pallas, a form of Central Asia's big horned sheep.

Bubalus wansjocki Boule and Teilhard, a species of buffalo named after the Mongolian Wansjock, who first discovered the bone deposit at Sjara Osso Gol.

Bos primigenius, aurochs.

Canis lupus L., wolf.
Hyaena spelaea, hyaena.
Meles taxus Bodd., badger.

In addition to these major mammals there are in the Sjara Osso Gol fauna a number of smaller forms, insect-eaters and rodents, as well as birds, among which the most interesting is the Asiatic fossil ostrich (*Struthiolithus*).

Boule and Teilhard de Chardin, who described this beautiful and extremely interesting fauna, have shown that it consists of the following three elements :

1. Extinct forms characteristic of the Pleistocene age, *Elephas cf. namadicus*, *Rhinoceros tichorinus*, *Camelus knoblochi*, *Cervus megaceros var. mongoliae*, *Spirocerus kiakhtensis*, *Bos primigenius*, *Bubalus wansjocki*, *Hyaena spelaea*, *Struthio sp.*

2. Forms still surviving which have disappeared from the Ordos district : *Equus hemionus*, *Cervus elaphus*, *Ovis ammon*, *Sus sp.*

3. Forms still surviving in Ordos ; antelopes, wolves, insect-eaters and rodents.

In the lower part of the section of Sjara Osso Gol, marked by the letter F in Fig. 59, there were found numerous traces of human beings, but the stone implements here were consistently very small, veritable microliths, to use the terminology of the archaeologists (Fig. 60). The explanation of the use by human beings at this point of these small and light implements is not far to seek, for here there is a complete absence of raw material in the shape of rubble, which existed in such abundance at Choei Tong Keou, and which there gave rise to a profuse development of, in some cases very large, stone implements. The difference between the finds at Choei Tong Keou and Sjara Osso Gol is simply to be attributed to the abundant raw material in the former case and the absence of raw material in the latter. There is probably no considerable difference of age between the two places, since in Choei Tong Keou there are also a number of microliths, even though they are there less important in comparison with the larger implements.

An interesting discovery at Sjara Osso Gol was a fine little carved bone object (Fig. 61).

The stone implements of the Ordos desert remind us very much of the well-known discoveries in Western Europe, especially in France. In type most of these implements are connected most closely with the cultural epoch which is known in Europe as Mousterian, which terminates the earlier part of the Old Stone

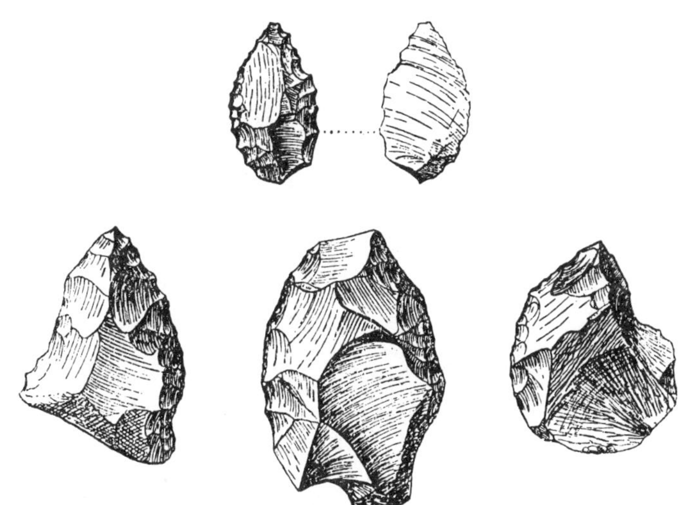

Fig. 60.—Stone implements from Sjara Osso Gol. (*After Teilhard and Licent.*)

age. But there are also numerous resemblances to the next succeeding period, the Aurignacian. Exceptionally, we find even objects which in their perfection remind us of the still later culture which the French call the Magdalenian. In view of our limited knowledge of the Old Stone age in Eastern Asia it may be too early, however, to enter into detailed comparisons, and we must content ourselves for the present with the suggestion that the Ordos discoveries most resemble in type the Mousterian Aurignacian civilizations in Western Europe, that is, the middle of the Old Stone age.

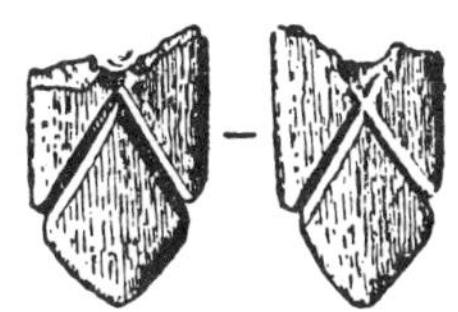

Fig. 61.—Bone object from Sjara Osso Gol. (*After Teilhard and Licent.*)

Although the two French scientists discovered thousands of stone implements, they failed, in spite of all their searching, to discover *in situ* remains of skeletons of Old Stone-age man. The only discovery of this kind was a tooth, which was found on the surface of the soil of the modern

Sjara Osso Gol and which, in view of its state of preservation, is supposed to belong to the Palaeolithic age.

In *L'Anthropologie*, 1925, Licent and Teilhard de Chardin described their epoch-making discovery in the Ordos desert in an essay entitled " Le Paléolithique de la Chine ". Under the same title there was published in 1928 a large and magnificently

FIG. 62.—Professor Pierre Teilhard de Chardin, the eminent French palaeontologist, who, together with Father Licent, discovered the traces of Old Stone-age man in the Ordos desert.

illustrated monograph as Mémoire 4 of the Institut de Paléontologie Humaine in Paris. In the writing of this inspiring monograph there collaborated, in addition to the two discoverers, the director of the institution, M. Boule, and the famous expert on the Old Stone age, the Abbé H. Breuil.

The supposed Palaeolithic tooth has been described in an essay by Licent, Teilhard de Chardin and Davidson Black : " On a presumably Pleistocene Tooth from the Sjara Osso Gol " (*Bull. of the Geol. Soc. of China*, Vol. V).

In the summer of 1928 Teilhard undertook, in conjunction with the Chinese geologist C. C. Young, a journey through the great loess districts of Shensi and Shansi, and succeeded in finding occasional traces of Palaeolithic man in the valley of the Yellow River, between these two provinces. These discoveries are described by the two scientists in an essay published by the National Geological Survey of China, *Geological Memoirs*, Ser. A, No. 8.

The discovery by the two French scientists of traces of Palaeolithic man in the Ordos desert was in every respect an exemplary and especially brilliant scientific achievement, not only because the stone implements all indisputably belong to the Palaeolithic types, but also because, and this is the most important fact, the discovery was made in a series of deposits which evidently belong to the lower portion of the loess formation. What is more, in combination with the Palaeolithic implements, and partially in the form of remains of meals, there were found enormous masses of mammal bones, as well as shells of the Pleistocene ostrich, all belonging to an extinct fauna which we know very well as contemporary with Man of the Old Stone age in Europe. The triumph of this epoch-making discovery can with equal justice be attributed to Licent's enthusiasm and initiative and to Teilhard's perfected and exact scientific method.

FIG. 63.—The ancient Pao Te surface with the superimposed beds of gravel, 200 metres above the present bottom of the Chai T'ang valley. In the foreground later erosion valleys.

CHAPTER NINE

THE FACE OF THE EARTH GIANT

It is a wonderful spring in the mountains. The storm raises such masses of fine dust that I can almost believe myself transplanted to the age when the wind laid the thick soft carpet of yellow earth on the dusty steppes.

In the afternoon all vision is obscured, so that I am compelled to pack up my drawing board and carry it down the stony path into the valley. The dust clouds come in gusts and spread over the grey fields a stream of shifting soil.

Bells sound in the dusty darkness and from the clouds of dust there appears a rugged herd of cows, goats and sheep, which two cowboys drive home from their pastures. Thus in earliest history must the boys of the steppes have driven through the dust clouds the small flocks of half-tame cattle which their parents had captured from the great wild hordes of the plain.

Capriciously, as it comes roaring down the valley, the storm sinks to rest. The next morning, I return to the scene of my labours under a cloudless sky, and I obtain a wide open view over the whole of the undulating country, with its thousands of flowering apricot trees.

Just as the clouds of dust give way to a breathless day, so on this beautiful morning the varied elements in the history of these valleys are linked together in an intelligible picture.

On the southern side of the principal valley of Chai T'ang there stand out on the extreme ridge of the plateau two towers, familiar to every visitor to this valley. From these towers we obtain an open view both over the highest mountain ridges at

1,500 metres above sea level and over the bottoms of the valleys, which are only some 200 metres above it. We are ourselves at a height of about 400 metres.

The landscape to the south of us consists of low hills and is difficult to survey, but when, after an hour's exploration, we succeeded in obtaining a proper orientation, we observed one feature which was extremely illuminating for our studies. Here and there we observed that the highest hills consisted of a gravel formation which covers the bedrock. The frequently large rubble in these beds of gravel does not, curiously enough, originate in the loose sandstone or shale which here constitutes the rock formation, but in the green and violet, hard, shale-like rocks of the high mountain chains to the extreme south.

The plateau on which we stand is completely cut off by deep valleys from this mountainous terrain in the south, and it slopes steeply down 150 metres to the valley at Chai T'ang. All this shows us that the ancient gravel beds are to be referred to a period long since vanished, when the Chai T'ang valley was broad and almost 200 metres higher than at present. The intersected plateau on which we stand was then a part of the bottom of the valley, which to the south merged by easy gradients into the slopes of the high mountain plateaus.

This ancient mature topography was transformed and revived when the rivers began to cut deeper into the rocks and, during the course of ages, carved out narrow ravines, often with perpendicular sides and with a valley bottom 200 metres below the old, broad valley bottom. Let us glance at Plate 12, which shows the main valley of the Hun river about 10 km. east of Chai T'ang. High up among the banks of clouds we see the remains of the gentle slopes of the old valley, but we also see in the foreground the almost perpendicular cliffs of the more recent canyon valley.

We are now familiar with two stages in the physiography of this mountainous district. The former, the mature, broad valley landscape, is called the Pao Te stage. The latter, characterized by the carving out of the canyon, is called the Fen Ho stage, both names being taken from places in the province of Shansi where these phenomena were first studied.

Now we are back again in the Chai T'ang valley and proceed

along the intersected plateau, on which we began our studies, to the north-west corner, from which we have an interesting view into the deepest parts of the valley, both to the west and north. Just below us a tributary valley, Ma Lan, runs into the main valley from the south-west. Almost the whole of the Ma Lan valley consists of a remarkable terrace formation. Let us look at Plate 11, taken from the western side, just where it joins the main valley. The picture shows not only the extraordinarily fine terrace formation, which occupies almost the whole of the valley bottom, but also, on the other side of the Ma Lan valley, the broken plateau landscape which we have already described, and in the farthest background the highest mountain peaks dominating the whole landscape.

The great terrace lobe of the Ma Lan valley is a unique formation. On both sides it is flanked by small vales, but the whole of the centre portion of the valley consists of this dominating tongue, with sharp cliffs round about and with a surface which at first sight seems almost horizontal, but which on closer examination is found to rise gradually towards the upper parts of the valley. This slow and regular rise of the Ma Lan terrace is admirably shown in the picture by the dark stone walls, which enclose the cultivated fields, and rise upwards like broad, low steps from the valley entrance.

If we now descend into the valley and examine the cliffs of the Ma Lan terrace, we shall find that the terrace consists of comparatively fine gravel with a yellowish loess-like cement and intercalations of loess soil.

Here and there in the Chai T'ang valley, especially on the northern side, we find deposits of loess lying like enormous drifts, heaped up wherever the rock formation affords a little protection from the wind. It was, indeed, in the Chai T'ang valley that we were first enabled to demonstrate the connection in time between the Ma Lan terraces and the loess deposits. During the dry period of the loess deposits there occurred, it is true, occasional torrential rains which washed down the weathered gravel from the mountain sides and mixed it with thin layers of the Eolian loess, then in the process of formation. But the work of the running water was only occasional and transitory. After a few hours of rain the stream of water was

The Ma Lan Valley at Chai T'ang

[*face page* 158

exhausted and the mixture of loess and gravel accumulated in thicker and thicker beds. In this way the gravel beds of the Ma Lan age (the Loess age) were formed in the old canyon valley.

But conditions changed once again. The rainfall became more copious and more enduring. The rivers again began to flow down to the sea and cut their channels deeper and deeper in the old valley deposits. This is the erosion which we see in the form of the small side valleys flanking the Ma Lan terrace, and we see the same valley formation at P'an Chiao (Figs. 64 and 66), in which erosion has not only washed away a part of the terrace formations of the Ma Lan age, but has also cut a channel, 10 metres deep, into the solid rock. We have called this latest stage the P'an Chiao stage, after the valley of that name to the east of Chai T'ang.

We are thus able to distinguish four stages in the valley formation of the Chai T'ang district. The oldest is the Pao Te period of the old broad valley, the floor of which is characterized by the intersected plateau (Fig. 63). This surface is approximately contemporary with the *Hipparion* clay which was deposited on this mature land surface. The Pao Te stage thus belongs geologically to the end of the Miocene age.

Thereupon followed a period of intense river action during which the valleys were deepened into narrow canyon valleys. This is the Fen Ho stage (Plate 12) which, at a guess, we may place at the end of the Pliocene age and the transition to the Pleistocene age.

The middle period of the Pleistocene age, the ice age of our parts of the world, was in Eastern Asia a dry period during which the Eolian loess was formed and the canyon valleys were partly filled with gravel beds of the Ma Lan type.

Last, and quite near to our own age, probably corresponding to the New Stone age, came the P'an Chiao stage, with renewed river erosion (Figs. 64 and 66).

This study of the development of the landscape of the western hills beyond Peking was of fundamental importance to us, and it appeared later that the same large cycle of development was to be found almost everywhere in Northern China. In a district somewhat north of Chai T'ang Professor George B. Barbour

Fig. 64.—The P'an Chiao valley with terrace formations of the Ma Lan age which have become broken by erosion during the P'an Chiao age, which has even reached into the solid rock.

The Hun River Canyon

[*face page* 160

later made detailed investigations which he has incorporated in his splendid work *The Geology of the Kalgan Area*, Peking, 1929.

By way of comparison I will here only adduce my own observations on the T'ao River in Kansu, a southern tributary of the Yellow River, and flowing into it a little above the provincial town of Lanchow. The middle course of the T'ao River, where we made our richest archaeological discoveries in 1924, is a broad, open valley, the floor of which resembles a well planted and generously watered garden. On both sides of the broad, level valley bottom there rises steeply a terrace landscape, the edge of which is about 50 metres above the bottom of the valley (Plate 25). There can be little doubt that this imposing terrace formation in the T'ao valley (Fig. 65, *b*) may be compared with the Ma Lan terrace at Chai T'ang, with the difference only that the terrace formation in the T'ao valley is much more magnificent.

FIG. 65.—Section through the T'ao valley in Kansu.

Four hundred metres above the bottom of the T'ao valley we find an ancient plateau, intersected by erosion, which in all essentials reminds us of the broken plateau landscape at Chai T'ang. The only essential difference is that in this case also the landscape of Kansu is formed on a much larger scale.

In order to make the comparison complete, we would add that canyon valleys similar to those we have seen in the Hun River in the western hills of Peking are also to be found in Kansu (the upper course of the T'ao River, the Hsi Ning River). We find these canyon formations in their most interesting and beautiful form in the wild river terrain which the Yellow River forms below Lanchow, where we can distinguish the old cliff canyon which was formed as early as the Fen Ho stage, and the later renewal in the form of an almost perpendicular cliff channel, probably formed as late as the P'an Chiao stage, i.e. the New Stone age.

We have thus been able to trace right through Northern China, from the Peking plain to the borders of Tibet, the same superb rhythm of the soft, undulating landscape of the Pao Te age, the vigorous canyon formation of the Fen Ho age, the valley deposits of the Ma Lan age, and, finally, the renewed, vertical river erosion of the P'an Chiao age.

Fig. 66.—The P'an Chiao valley with Ma Lan terraces and later erosion during the P'an Chiao stage.

Fig. 67.—During the excavation at Yang Shao Tsun. From left to right: P. L. Yuan, Andersson, old Wang, the father of the village, and the evangelist Wang.

CHAPTER TEN

WE DISCOVER THE FIRST PREHISTORIC VILLAGE

When a number of Stone-age implements were discovered in China at the beginning of this century they were regarded by the learned men of China and by foreign sinologists as belonging to barbarous races living in these areas before the Chinese, or eventually on the outskirts of the Chinese Empire during early historical periods.

This belief was connected with the prevalent view of Chinese literati that the Chinese had known the use of the metals from the beginning of Chinese civilization, and it was indirectly supported by the fact that the first considerable finds of stone implements and prehistoric ceramics were made by the Japanese scholar Torii in Manchuria and Eastern Mongolia, that is to say, districts which demonstrably were inhabited until comparatively late periods by barbarians. Our own first discoveries were made in Northern Chihli (Hopei), likewise still a barbarian area when the genuine Chinese civilization was first moulded in the region which now constitutes the boundary territory between Shansi, Shensi and Honan.

In the autumn of 1920 I had sent my collector Liu Chang-shan to the district west of Loyang in Honan, where, two years earlier, we had made the discoveries in the Hsin An and Mien Chih districts of fossil vertebrates which we have described in Chapter V.

Liu's principal mission was to collect more of the Tertiary remains of vertebrates, but I had also asked him to keep his eyes open for the possibility of Stone-age discoveries.

Imagine my surprise and delight when on his return in December to Peking Liu unpacked a collection of several hundred axes, knives and other objects of stone, many of them exceptionally fine and well-preserved. The collection was the more remarkable as Liu related that he had purchased everything from the inhabitants of a single village, Yang Shao Tsun, where the peasants had collected the coveted objects in their fields.

There could scarcely be any doubt that we had here hit upon a Stone-age site, and I was naturally eager to investigate conditions on the spot.

The following year I had an opportunity for new studies in Honan, and on April 18th I wandered from the town of Mien Chih along the 6-mile road northwards to Yang Shao Tsun with the purpose of discovering the site from which Liu's abundant find of Stone-age implements had been derived.[1]

About 1 km. south of the village of Yang Shao Tsun I had to traverse a very great ravine, a real miniature canyon, which was subsequently a very notable feature of our topographical survey of the district. When I had reached the northern side of the ravine I saw in the side of a gulley a very interesting section. At the bottom the red Tertiary clay was exposed and it is with a distinct contact overlaid by a peculiar loose soil, full of ashes and containing fragments of pottery. It seemed not improbable that this might be the deposit from which the Stone-age implements had been derived. After some minutes' search I found at the very bottom of the deposit a small piece of fine red ware with black painting on a beautifully polished surface. At that time I knew nothing of the fine ceramics with black painting on a red ground which were found by Pumpelly's

[1] In *Ymer*, 1923, I incorrectly gave on page 210 the date of my arrival in Yang Shao Tsun as the 21st April.

expeditions of 1903 and 1904 at Anau in Russian Turkestan, and equally little of similar polychrome vessels of the late Neolithic and Aeneolithic finds in South-eastern Europe, and it therefore seemed to me inconceivable that such clay vessels could be found together with stone implements.

Somewhat dejected I felt that I had followed a track which would only lead me astray, and I thought it safer to return to my geological-palaeontological research. I was at that time especially interested in the large eggs of prehistoric ostriches, of which several specimens had come into my hands, but of which the geological age was not yet clear.

I now returned, on April 19th, to the study of this problem and succeeded in personally excavating one of these eggs from a genuine loess deposit, so that the question of the age of the Asiatic ostrich was finally settled (cf. Chapter VII).

Meanwhile, I lay in the evenings and reflected on the Yang Shao Tsun riddle. I had by accident taken up my quarters just in that village. For a few pence the boys of the village constantly gave me new stone axes which they had found in the fields, and I myself made similar finds. On the other hand almost everywhere in the walls of the ravine south of the village I could see thick deposits of the same ashy soil in which I had found the fine painted fragment of a bowl on the first day.

I decided to devote a whole day to a search in these ravine walls in order to clear up the question of the relation between the stone implements and the painted ceramics. After a few hours' search I extracted from the untouched ashy soil a fine example of the stone adze which I shall describe in greater detail in Chapter XII under the name of *pen*. During the course of the day I made other interesting discoveries, and it soon became clear that we here had to do with a deposit of unusual magnitude, rich in artifacts, especially fragments of pots, including the fine, polished, polychrome ware to which I have referred above.

This time I could not undertake any detailed investigation of the new dwelling places. I had not the necessary official support for such a comprehensive task, and I had, moreover, on this occasion, important geologica land palaeontological work awaiting me.

On my return to Peking I had the great good fortune to find in the library of the Geological Survey the three splendid volumes in which the discoveries of the Pumpelly expedition in Anau in Russian Turkestan were described. I found in them coloured illustrations of fragments of vessels with paintings which reminded me very much of the fragments which I had found at Yang Shao Tsun. These discoveries are referred by Hubert Schmidt to a very early Metal age, and it therefore seems not unreasonable that such ware should occur in China in a cultural association of a late Neolithic character.

In the autumn of the same year I was accorded permission by the Government to undertake larger scale excavations at Yang Shao Tsun, and most effective support was given to this undertaking not only by my colleagues of the Geological Survey and the Ministry of Agriculture, but also, through their mediation,

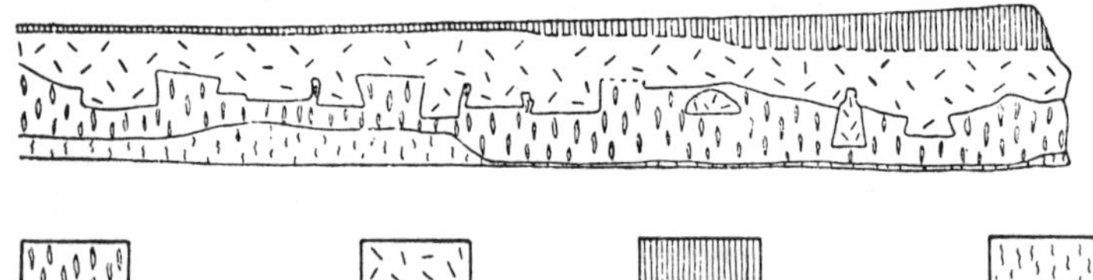

Fig. 68.—Wall profile of the site of the central portion of the Yang Shao dwel lings.

by the provincial governments of Honan, and by Mr. Yeh, subprefect of Mien Chih. Accompanied by my Chinese assistants I arrived at Yang Shao Tsun on October 27th, and our excavations continued until December 1st.

During the whole of this period I was assisted by Mr. P. L. Yuan, geologist to the Geological Survey in Peking. Mr. Yuan not only carried out the topographical survey of the whole area of the discoveries, but he also conducted all negotiations with the local inhabitants and the district authorities. It was thanks to his wise and tactful behaviour that work proceeded without any kind of disturbance.

Dr. Zdansky, my palaeontological collaborator, who was visiting the district for the purpose of collecting fossils, participated for a time with great interest in our archaeological work and carried out with extraordinary care the excavation of a number of graves which we found in the southern part of the site.

PLATE 13

Yang Shao Tsun: view from the most northerly part of the modern village

[*face page* 166

For some days we had the pleasure of co-operating with Dr. Davidson Black, who in most important respects assisted in the investigation of the burial ground, which, as we have said, was excavated by Dr. Zdansky.

During the first period I was also assisted by Miss Elsa Rosenius, who subsequently became my wife, and who devoted herself more especially to the modern village and took a number of successful photographs of folk life.

All my five private collaborators, Yao, Liu, Chang, Chen and Pai, participated in this work, and many a fine discovery was due to their zeal and care.

Before I proceed to a description of the prehistoric dwellings it may be appropriate by way of orientation to give an account of the topographical conditions and to make some observations upon the modern village.

Mien Chih Hsien, the district in which Yang Shao Tsun is situated, lies beside the great and ancient highway between Loyang in the east and Sianfu in the west, the two foci of the dynastic and cultural life of the Chou and Han dynasties. The open situation of the place beside the chief artery of the early historical periods is a circumstance deserving of notice.

The town of Mien Chih, which is one of the stations on the Lunghai railway, lies in an east-west valley, from which the land north and south rises by gradually sloping plateaux, consisting of red Tertiary clay, covered by loess. These plateaus are intersected by numerous ravines, about 30–50 metres deep, running into the Mien Chih valley.

In the blue distance to the south rises a mountain wall belonging to the great Tsin Ling Shan range, and similarly to the north we find mountainous country which separates the Mien Chih valley from the deeply cut, cliff-bound channel of the Yellow River far away to the north. In that direction we see the first limestone hills about 3 km. north of our destination, the village of Yang Shao Tsun.

If one walks northwards from Mien Chih towards Yang Shao Tsun, one sees on both sides of the road the deep ravines which run southwards into the Mien Chih valley. In the walls of these ravines one obtains a glimpse of the structure of the Tertiary and Pleistocene strata, below, the red clay of Pliocene age and, above these clay beds, the yellow loess soil. It was in these ravines that, during our previous visit, we made a number of discoveries which essentially revealed the later geological history of this district—in the red clay a hitherto unknown horse, *Proboscidipparion*, and in the loess Asia's extinct ostrich, *Struthiolithus*.

If the district is thus rich in geological relics it is not less so in respect of the early historical periods. At a glance one will often find here burial urns and bronzes of the Han dynasty, and from one tomb of this period in a neighbouring village north of Yang Shao Tsun we brought home no less than twenty-four clay vessels and one bronze dish. The architectural monuments of later times are visible on the limestone hills to the north, where a temple and two ancient fortifications testify at once to peaceful contemplation and dangerous times of unrest.

The traditional ancestor worship of the people is visible in the beautifully carved monuments to local celebrities which flank the road and give an impression of piety and sanctity to the fertile, well-cultivated countryside. One may therefore with justice say that it would be difficult to imagine a setting richer in early monuments, in the widest sense, for the imposing prehistoric remains which we will now more closely examine. On the other hand the discovery of this great site of Stone-age dwellings will link up in time the more remote geological discoveries with historical periods as the oldest monument, so far as we at present know, of human activity in these parts.

The modern village of Yang Shao Tsun lies in the narrow apex between the inmost parts of two ravines, Hsi Kou and Tung Kou. The central part of the village is situated on top of the loess plateau and consists of detached brick houses, but both by Tung Kou and on the edge of Hsi Kou there are houses of a quite different type, loess caves dug into the side of the ravine. A very small part of the village, in a sense a small village to itself, lies far down to the south, east of Tung Kou. Some abandoned caves on the peninsula, which was formed by the confluence of Tung Kou and Hsi Kou, show that some dwellings, Hsi Tzŭ Kou, once existed here beside a small temple.

Life in this small agricultural community moves in the uniform regular rhythm of century-old custom. Life is still very simple

Loess dwellings at Yang Shao Tsun

[*face page* 168

and existence is hard. Interest is therefore centred in material things and the maintenance of life directs activity predominantly to the cultivation of the fertile loess soil.

The most fatally incalculable factor of the seasons is the rainfall. Since reckless felling has destroyed the last remnants of the primeval forests which, by the evidence of the Stone-age deposits, once covered the land, the treeless loess plain has become exceptionally sensitive to changes in the rainfall. If the normally light rainfall fails, there is no reserve of moisture in the plateau, which is drained by innumerable ravines. If on the other hand the summer rains come with the violence of a cloudburst, as not infrequently happens, the ravines are widened with catastrophic rapidity. New miniature ravines are formed in a single night of rain, houses are threatened and roads are diverted. Most feared is a drought, which is synonymous with starvation.

Quite naturally many of the domestic utensils of these peasants bear the stamp of antiquity. The more we become familiar with these simple implements, the clearer it becomes that many of them go back to prototypes of prehistoric times. The whole of this alluring problem deserves a chapter to itself (Chapter XII). But most of the life of the modern Honan peasant points to degeneration, and these simple beings have no idea that the pieces of vessels in the walls of their ravines speak of a prehistoric ceramic art which nowhere flourished more profusely than during the Yang Shao civilization, and which in the history of China was not succeeded by a similar artistic renaissance until the Sung dynasty.

The prehistoric cultural deposits at Yang Shao Tsun lie to the south of the modern village, on the detached piece of the loess plateau which is enclosed between Tung Kou and Hsi Kou, the two great ravines. On the whole, therefore, the ravines constitute a frame round it. But there exists a small area of cultural deposits outside this frame, just where the road to Mien Chih leaves the confluence of the ravines, near a small village named Tung Tzŭ Kou.

On the other hand, directly south of the modern village, there are considerable barren areas. But within the southern half—

or more—of the island between the ravines almost every square yard reveals cultural deposits varying between 1 and 5 metres thick, with an average of about 3 metres. In a north-south direction the length of the inhabited area is more than 600 metres, with a breadth from east to west of about 500 metres.

Yang Shao Tsun is not only our first prehistoric discovery in China, but also perhaps the greatest. The Chu Chia Chai site in Kansu, which is approximately comparable in age, covers a somewhat larger area, but the cultural deposits are more sporadic and not so thick.

Similarly in comparison with other parts of the world Yang Shao Tsun is a prehistoric area of considerable size, as the following comparisons will show.

The Danish kitchen middens have become famous not only because of the interesting remains of an early Neolithic civilization which they contain, but also because of their enormous dimensions. They are 100–300 metres long and 3–6 metres broad, with a thickness varying from 1 to 3 metres.

The Kurgans in Russian Turkestan, which became better known by Pumpelly's expedition, are rounded or elliptic hillocks consisting of the refuse of prehistoric dwelling places. The length of the northern Anau Kurgan is 100 metres. The height of these refuse heaps is very great, 10–15 metres, but this becomes less surprising when we learn that it represents a series of successive civilizations from Neolithic (or at any rate Aeneolithic) age to the Iron age.

The Yang Shao site represents one single period of civilization, probably of short duration, to judge by the circumstance that the same artifacts are found everywhere in the deposits. When we remember, from the information just given, that the site had a length of more than 600 metres, with a breadth of 480 metres and cultural deposits with a thickness, on the average, of 3 metres, full of fragments of clay vessels and other remains of human activity, it is clear that the ancient Yang Shao village must have been of considerable extent and have had a considerable population.

I have already described how within its area the larger part of the surface consists of 1–5 metre thick cultural deposits. This soil, " ash soil " as we called it, is, owing to its loose con-

Ravine landscape: Yang Shao Tsun

[*face page* 170

sistency and consequent lightness, its grey colour, and wealth of ceramic fragments, easily distinguished from the untouched natural sediments beneath it, Tertiary clay and loess, and the line of contact is in many, even in most, cases sharp as if cut by a knife.

Easy as it is to delimit the ashy soil from its substratum, it is just as difficult, sometimes impossible, to determine to what extent the cultural deposit, especially in its upper part, is affected by later influence. As is well known, all modern Chinese agriculture is based on the laying out of the soil in long and narrow horizontal terraces, separated by vertical earth- or stone-faced walls. In the construction of these cultivated terraces there naturally occurs a considerable shifting of masses of earth, with a consequent mixing of soils originally belonging to different strata. In certain places the cultural deposit exhibits a kind of primary stratification. Evidently the detritus from the probably still inhabited Neolithic village was transported by the floods and left in the immediate vicinity of the dwelling place, sometimes in depressions in the middle of the village. In such cases we have in the stratification a sure indication that these parts of the cultural deposits are undisturbed. But in most cases the deposit is little, if at all, stratified, and it is difficult to determine whether a particular portion of it has been disturbed or not. On one occasion I encountered at a considerable depth, in a section of ashy soil which betrayed no signs of having been disturbed, a piece of glazed ware which cannot be older than Sung. This case is a warning in excavation, and in subsequent discussion of a discovery, to proceed with the utmost caution. In many cases I have been able in taking my measurements to distinguish an upper " redeposited cultural soil " from the intact lower deposit, but I was never able to achieve absolute certainty.

At the bottom of the cultural deposit we often note a peculiarity which is admirably illustrated by Fig. 68 (p. 166), which shows a small portion of my large road section. The cultural deposit descends, with sharply defined, acute-angled pockets, into the substratum of Tertiary red clay. These pockets are 1·9–2·8 metres in diameter, circular in form and their present depth varies between 0·5 and 1·9 metres.

These pockets cannot be graves, because no remains of human skeletons have been found in them. They are filled with the ashy soil, sometimes more than usually porous, and with a large proportion of ash. The pieces of pots and other artifacts found in the pockets are usually very fragmentary.

Another conceivable explanation is that the pockets are the bottoms of cabins in which the inhabitants of the prehistoric village lived. Such have been found in Europe in dwellings of the same age.

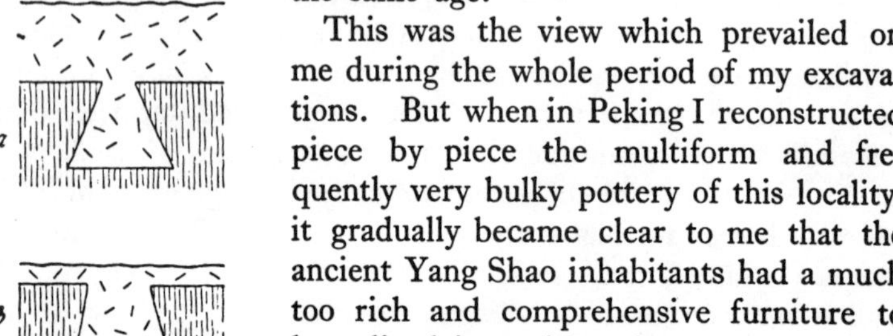

FIG. 69. — Kellergruben. *a*, Yang Shao Tsun; *b*, *c*, Achenheim in Alsace. (*After Forrer.*)

This was the view which prevailed on me during the whole period of my excavations. But when in Peking I reconstructed piece by piece the multiform and frequently very bulky pottery of this locality, it gradually became clear to me that the ancient Yang Shao inhabitants had a much too rich and comprehensive furniture to have lived in such confined cabins.

The most probable parallel to these pockets which I can find in the West are the *Kellergruben* of Neolithic dwellings at Achenheim and Stutzheim in Alsace, described by Forrer.[1] I reprint in Fig. 69 Kellergruben B and P at Achenheim, as well as one of the Yang Shao pockets. These figures are all drawn to the same scale and the resemblance is striking, even with regard to the truncated conical section of the cavities.

Forrer interprets his Kellergruben as underground storerooms, but it appears from his description that there probably existed forms intermediate between " Kellergruben " and " Wohngruben ".

We also know, from quite different parts of the world, of similar vertical pockets dug into the earth and intended as storerooms. My friend Dr. Davidson Black has been so kind as to

[1] Forrer, *Reallexikon der prähistorischen, klassischen und frühhistorischen Altertümer*, articles on Achenheim, Kellergruben, Stutzheim, Wohngruben.

The cultural deposit at Yang Shao Tsun

[*face page* 172

draw my attention to an essay, of especial importance in this connection, by E. A. Hooton, " Indian Village Site and Cemetery near Madisonville, Ohio," papers of Peabody Museum of American Archaeology and Ethnology, Harvard University, 1920, in which, under the name of " cache-pits ", there are illustrated pockets identical with those in Honan and Alsace.

The site in Madisonville belongs to the earliest historical period of North America. According to Willoughby, who worked up the material and surveyed the results, the site was inhabited by an Indian tribe " immediately before the first contact of the Indians with Europeans, but the site was still inhabited in the protohistoric period when the inhabitants were in a position to obtain a few objects of European iron, brass and copper, together with some glass beads, an exchange which was effected either directly with early missionaries and traders or indirectly with their Indian neighbours ".

The cache-pits of Ohioare thus, judged by our Asiatic standards, almost completely modern, and the striking resemblance to our discovery at Yang Shao Tsun only indicates a parallelism of similar conditions of life, or possibly—a somewhat far-fetched alternative—an obstinate retention of a custom which the Mongolian ancestors of the Indians brought with them to America from their Asiatic home.

These American cache-pits were filled with leaf mould, sand, ashes, etc., in distinctly varying layers, and it is interesting to note that the only cache-pit which I carefully examined in Yang Shao Tsun also showed a distinct stratification of a 5–15 cm. thick yellow substratum, with abundant plant impressions, and above it, up to 60 cm., a clear alternation between light ash strata and dark layers with abundant pieces of charcoal.

In the cache-pits of Ohio, as in Honan, artifacts abounded : fragments of ceramics and implements of stone and bone, etc.

Concerning the use of these cache-pits Hooton gives such a picturesque and instructive account that it deserves to be reproduced :

> In the opinion of the author the cache-pits were used for the storing of seed and other goods. During the harvest the maize was placed in a number of such store pits, which were situated near the dwelling of the family. Perhaps they were even within the cabin,

> or connected with it. During the winter one pit after another was emptied and the empty ones became refuse rooms into which were thrown ashes, remnants of meals and other household refuse. When the contents of a pit show stratification it is due to the fact that the pit was filled at successive intervals: when it is not stratified it is probable that it was completely filled at once.

Direct proof that the cache-pits were used for the purpose stated is to be found in the fact that in two cases seed has been found in them.

Within the Madisonville area were found numerous graves, but they had no connection with the cache-pits, except in rare cases where for the sake of convenience an abandoned cache-pit was used for the interment of a corpse.

It remains to mention one more feature of the topography of the Yang Shao Tsun dwelling-place, namely the deep cavities, filled with ashes, which we found in two places.

One of them we found in a narrow ridge between two branch ravines of Tung Kou (Fig. 70). When we found this "well", as I shall continue to call it, the wall facing south-west was opened up by ravine erosion, so that it is uncertain how high its edge had been on this side. The greatest observed height of the wall of the well was 5·4 metres, and it seemed most probable that it must have had this dimension all round. At its greatest the diameter was 1·85 metres, but at the bottom only 0·97 and 1·09 metres.

The well was very carefully excavated by Dr. Zdansky, who observed that in the upper part the filling consisted of ash-like unstratified earth, but that the lowest, 2·7 metres, showed excellent horizontal stratification, with alternating bands of gravel, a few centimetres thick, as well as sand and clay and here and there larger stones. Pieces of vessels occurred throughout, though in the lower part mostly in the beds of gravel.

In a branch ravine of Hsi Kou we encountered a similar "well" of no less than 7 metres depth. During the excavations we made an observation of very special interest. In the ashy earth which filled the well we found an empty space, no less than 1·3 metres long and with a regular, straight section of 12 by 34 cm. This cavity, which was vertical, can scarcely be anything else than the negative of a wooden beam which was embedded when the well was filled with ashes. In addition to the large cavity described above we also encountered two horizontal cavities of smaller dimensions.

I regard it as probable that these deep wells served an entirely different purpose from the Kellergruben. There would scarcely be any point in digging store-rooms of such a depth as 6–7 metres, and in addition the vertical contour of the wells is quite different from the conical expansion at the base of the Kellergruben.

FIG. 70.—" Well " during excavation.

gruben. It seems almost inevitable that we should look for another interpretation of these wells and nothing could be more natural than to regard them as wells from which the people of the Stone age satisfied their need of water.

But doubtless our assumption will at first sight appear incompatible with the circumstance that the wells are situated high above the water level and are thus now perpetually dry. We obtain an idea of the present-day water level in the ravines from the natural springs which flow at four points within this ravine district and all of which lie in the bottom of the ravines, about 40 metres below the plateau.

In order to explain this apparent contradiction between the old wells and the present-day water level, we must take into

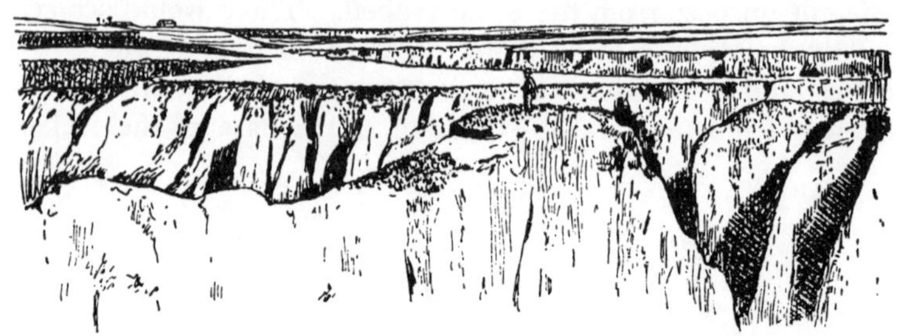

FIG. 71.—Ravine topography, Yang Shao Tsun. My assistant Mr. Yuan is standing on a small ridge between two ravines. Immediately below him is a small patch of cultural soil. The picture shows clearly how the ravine topography is later than the Stone-age village, the deposits of which have been dismembered and partly destroyed by erosion.

consideration other topographical features of the site, which I described in the geographical journal *Ymer* in 1923, from which I quote the following:

> The Yang Shao site, as has been said, lies in a setting of two ravines, which have been cut to a depth of 40–50 metres into the plateau of Tertiary clay and Pleistocene loess. At first it seemed to me probable that this site had been selected because nature here offered protection on all sides, with the exception of a very narrow isthmus which connects the site on the north with the plain outside the ravines. I therefore at first regarded the ravines as the primary phenomenon and the village as a settlement conditioned by the ravines. But as early as my first visit in the spring of 1921 I had observed a section which pointed to an entirely different and much more astonishing conclusion. During the detailed examination of the autumn of the same year I had an opportunity of completely proving the correctness of this new view.

In many cases the cultural deposits extend to the edge of the ravine and in certain places one sees isolated pillars consisting mainly of clay or loess, but with a thin cap of cultural earth. This, however, only shows that a certain amount of erosion has taken place since the dwelling site was abandoned and that locally parts of the once connected cultural deposits have been completely encircled by this erosion.

But in the southern part of the field of discovery we find circumstances which speak a much clearer language. The unstratified cultural soil is replaced here by deposits laid down in water, finely stratified sand and gravel, repeatedly alternating, of a thickness of 6 metres. In these stratified deposits we found numerous artifacts, fragments of pottery of the kind characteristic of the inhabited site, and even occasionally such a brittle thing as a fine sewing needle of bone.

FIG. 72.—Erosion topography from the southernmost part of the dwelling site.

As appears from Fig. 72 and the section in Fig. 73, these artifact-bearing stratified deposits form fantastically shaped, castle-like excrescences, thanks to the erosion which has cut away ravines of 40 metres' depth all round them.

The conclusion which must be drawn from these observations suddenly becomes clear and inevitable: at the time when the artifact-bearing sand and gravel deposits were formed, the present ravines did not exist, but a water-course flowed approximately at the level of the plateau (Figs. 72 and 73). Far from being, as at a later stage, vertically erosive, this age was marked by accumulation, as appears from the thickness of 6 metres of the artifact-bearing deposits left in running water. We cannot definitely decide whether, and to what extent, these deposits were formed whilst the prehistoric village was inhabited, or only somewhat later. But this does not in the least affect our extremely important conclusion that the ravines did not exist at the time of the Yang Shao civilization, but that on the contrary the village was built on the unbroken plain, which was here watered by a water-course running in a very shallow valley.

The great ravine system, two branches of which enclose our field of discovery at Yang Shao Tsun, continues in a southerly direction for 8 km., until it joins the main valley at the town of Mien Chih, 5 km. south of Yang Shao Tsun. I observed in the main ravine conditions very similar to those described above. In the middle of the ravine there still remains an island protected from erosion, the greater and lower part of which consists of loess with a covering of stratified deposits, and in these latter I found some pieces of easily recognizable Yang Shao pottery. The conclusions drawn above concerning Yang Shao Tsun thus apply equally to this place.

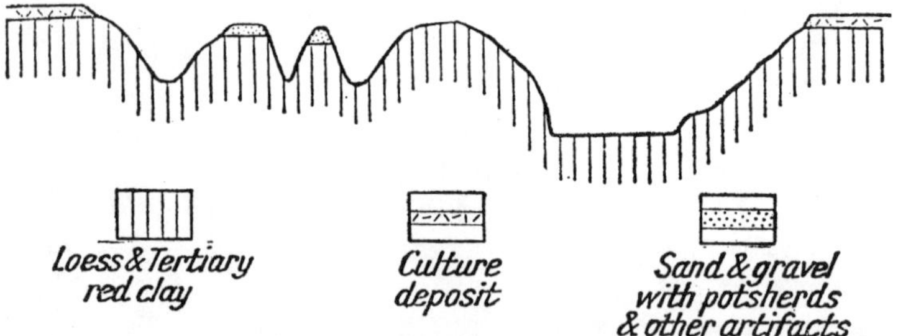

FIG. 73.—Section through the southern part of the Yang Shao site, showing how erosion has intersected the cultural deposit and the deposits made by the water-course which at one time flowed on the surface of the unbroken plateau.

In another ravine system, 6 km. west of Yang Shao Tsun, we find another formerly inhabited place, which has not yet been properly surveyed, Pu Chao Chai, which yielded important discoveries of the Yang Shao type. Here also the cultural deposits are untouched and broken up by the ravines, so that frequently collecting has to be done on very steep cliffs.

This ravine topography round Yang Shao Tsun is not especially limited to this district. On the contrary the territory of Northern China, with its loess and Tertiary clay, is characterized by this breaking up of a once connected surface into thousands of lobes, separated by precipitous, narrow ravines. The sharp V-form of these erosion valleys shows that they are quite recent (Plate 18), and in places one can see directly how the work of disintegration is still proceeding. Our present material is still too local and too small to justify the assumption that the whole of this ravine topography was everywhere cut out after the Yang Shao period, i.e. in historical time. But even with the few facts which are already available we are quite justified in saying that the people of Yang Shao in Honan lived in a much more connected plain and that a great deal of the erosion indicated by the innumerable ravines has taken place during the last 4,000 years.

The elucidation of this fundamental fact furnishes a new perspective of the civilization of Northern China and also of its political history.

The secret of the catastrophic action of the Huang Ho and other northern Chinese rivers is their abnormally heavy sediment, by reason of which they quickly raise their beds, until, during a rainy period, they break through the banks at a weak point and take a new course.

One factor in the explanation of this copious sediment is the covering of loess, which provides the greater part of the mud which sweeps forward in the bed of the Huang Ho. But so long as it was supposed that the erosion, which demonstrably occurred in the loess territory, was distributed over a good part of the period from the deposit of the loess, i.e. over the later Pleistocene period, the terrible ravages of the Yellow River remained a mystery. When, on the other hand, we now learn that the work of erosion was to a large extent completed during the last 4,000 years, we must, after having made a guess at the dizzy figure of cubic volume which has been spooled away, rather wonder that the river, with all its breaking of banks and mysterious shiftings, should yet have been able to carry away all the material which at one time filled the ravines.

All this is only one side of the process. Let us now see what erosion does within the ravines. In places the ravines occupy 10 per cent, and locally more, of the total area, and this ravine area is almost entirely useless. The bottom of the valley is too narrow for cultivation. This is a serious national loss in a country where every square foot of fertile land is cultivated.

But the ravine erosion has devastating effects in other directions. This will be seen most clearly by a glance at Fig. 74, which shows the water level at Yang Shao Tsun at the time of the ancient village and at the present day. When the ancient inhabitants of Yang Shao lived and had their being here, the water was just below the surface of the plain; nowadays it is 40 metres deeper, in the bottom of the ravines.

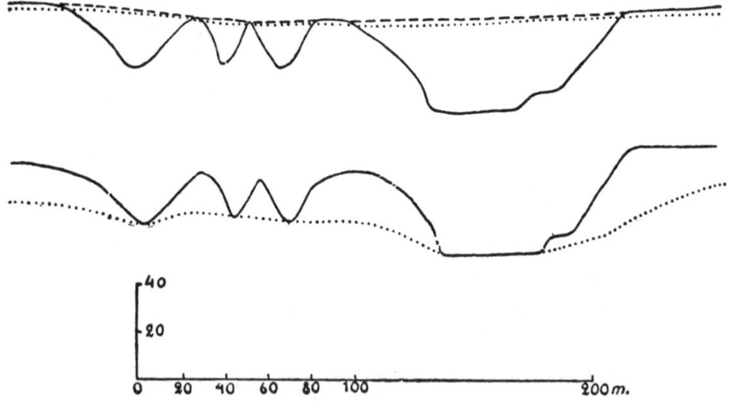

FIG. 74.—Diagram showing the fall of the water level from the Stone age to the present day.

In our account of the topography of the Yang Shao site it still remains to say a few words concerning the graves discovered there. Occasional skeletons were found in certain places, partly by the road which passes in a north and south direction through the site, close to the eastern ravine, and partly in the abandoned cave dwellings of Hsi Tzŭ Kou, far away in the South at the confluence of the ravines. A real cemetery was found near the eastern ravine a short distance north-east of the little village situated there. In this spot Dr. Zdansky dug up 17 more or less complete skeletons, together with, on the whole, very sparse remains. The skeletons lay on their backs in a horizontal position with the head in most cases turned to the south-east, though in some cases to the south-west.

During our extensive excavations in Yang Shao Tsun we collected a very large number of artifacts in stone, bone and clay.

First among the stone implements we should describe the symmetrical, frequently very thick, greenstone axes (Fig. 75).

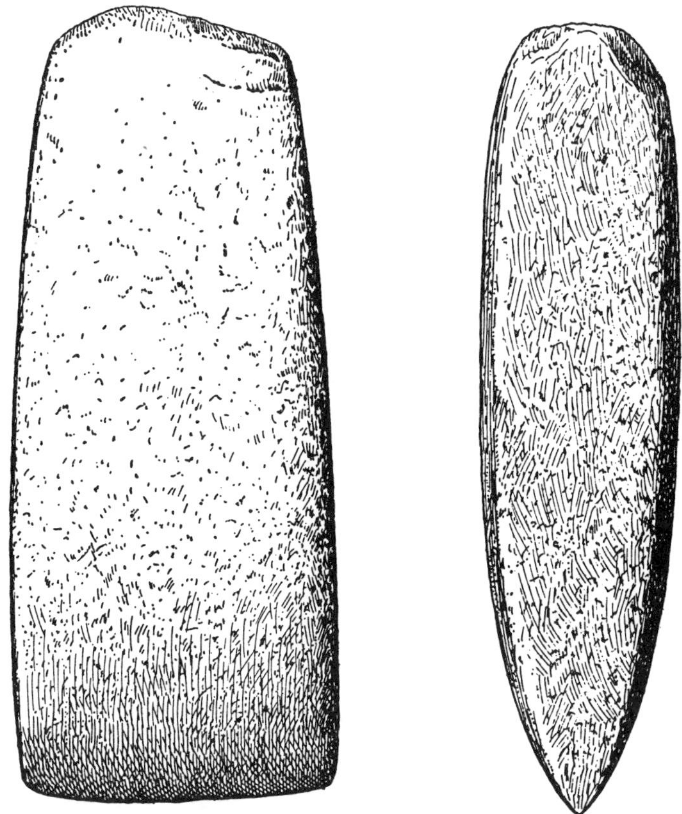

FIG. 75.—Greenstone axe from Yang Shao Tsun.

They show no hole for the shaft and were thus probably secured in a hole in the shaft itself.

In addition to these straight axes, the edge of which was parallel with the shaft, we also found all sizes of asymmetric axes or chisels, the latter being the right name for the small specimens of this type. The large asymmetric stone implements, on the other hand, certainly had shafts and thus deserve the name of adze, concerning which we refer to Fig. 76 and the text of Chapter XII, where we have sought to show that this stone adze is the prototype of the asymmetric, socketed celts of the Bronze age and of the modern Chinese carpenter's socketed iron celt.

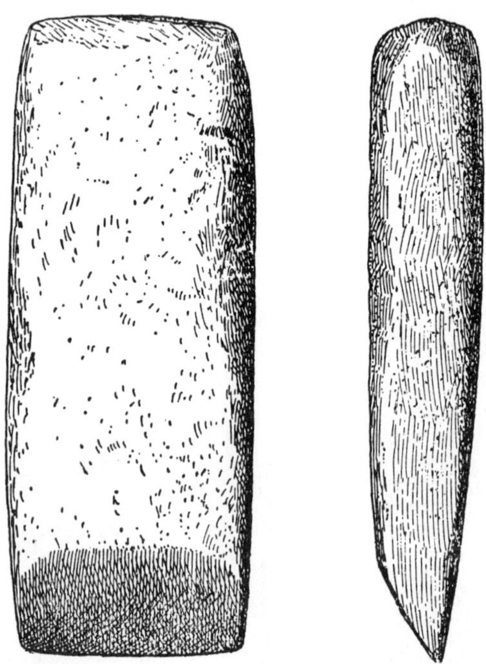

FIG. 76.—The asymmetric adze of stone, Yang Shao Tsun.

Rare, though functionally very important, are the large hoes of limestone, which probably had no shafts, but were held directly in the hand during use.

Arrow points (Fig. 77*a–b*) were usually made of some schistous rock, less frequently of bone or mussel shell.

Spinning whorls (Fig. 77*d*) and rings (77*e*), of which the larger ones were probably bracelets, were made either of stone or clay, which was burnt.

Awls and needles were made of bone (Fig. 77*c*).

Pottery constitutes by far the most important section of the artifacts, both because fragments of vessels are extremely abundant in the deposits, and also because the clay vessels are extraordinarily

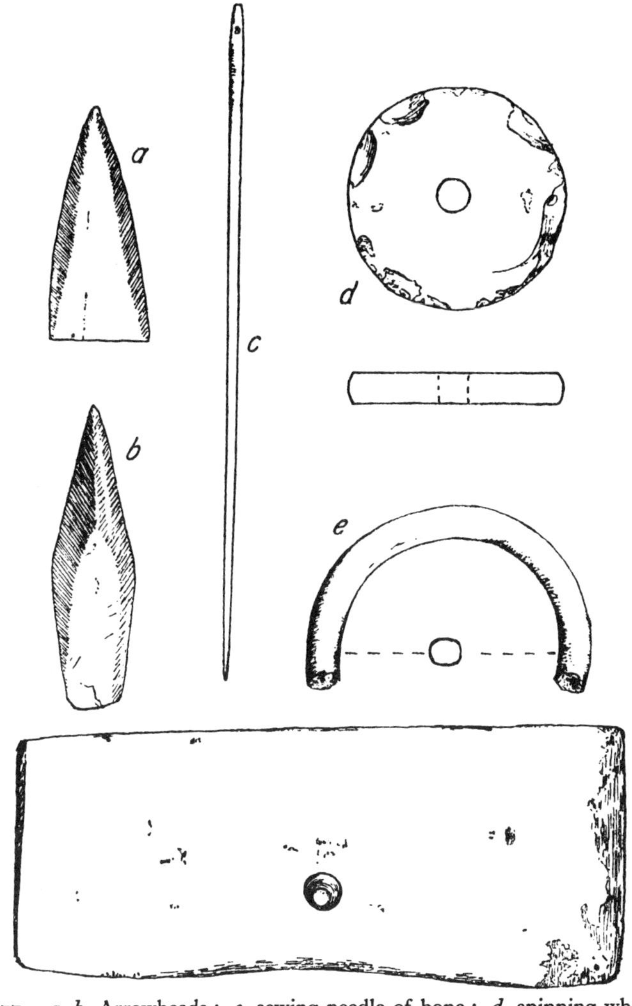

FIG. 77.—*a*, *b*, Arrowheads ; *c*, sewing needle of bone ; *d*, spinning whorl of stone ; *e*, bracelet of clay ; *f*, stone knife.

varied in form, very characteristic and, especially as regards the painted, high-class ware without an equal in the Stone-age civilizations.

Among the unpainted vessels, which are made of a comparatively coarse grey or grey-brown material, there are a number of shapes, such as dishes, bowls and, more rarely, cylindrical cups. Very common also are urns, as a rule with a low and wide opening. Two other groups of vessels are also of great importance, namely the pointed, often very large, urns and tripods, two ceramic types of which a detailed account is given in Chapter XII.

Beyond comparison the most surprising feature of the Yang Shao Tsun site is the painted pottery, which has awakened the keenest interest among the archaeologists and historians of the West because of its striking resemblance, not to say kinship, to the painted pottery in common use in Eastern Europe and the near East during the transition from the Stone age to the Copper age.

In the account of the painted ceramics of the Yang Shao civilization I have also had regard to certain Yang Shao dwelling places in Eastern Honan, in the Ho Yin district, where painted pottery has been developed with especial splendour.

This painted pottery from the dwellings of the Yang Shao period in Honan consists mostly of bowls with a plain edge, and jars. The material is very fine and even, the vessels have thin walls and are carefully shaped, the surface is well smoothed and not infrequently shows a high degree of polish. This fine polished surface was probably achieved by laying on what the English call " slip ", a fine covering of extremely finely ground clay, if necessary mixed with a pigment. On this polished slip the design was then painted.

The designs are horizontal, more or less broad, borders of straight or wavy lines, triangles with concave sides, dots frequently connected by lines, also a lattice of two systems of intersecting straight lines, etc. The commonest pigment is black on a frequently warm sealing wax red ground. But sometimes the material and surface are grey, with the pattern painted in red. In addition there occurs, exceptionally, white, combined with black and red.

My first publication on the Yang Shao civilization was an essay in the *Bulletin of the Geological Survey of China*, 1923,

FIG. 78.—Comparison between painted ceramics from Honan and Anau.

"An Early Chinese Culture". In it I compared the painted Yang Shao ceramics in the first place with painted fragments from the sites at Anau in Russian Turkestan, where the Pumpelly expedition in 1903 and 1904 excavated painted pottery of the Copper age which offers points of comparison with that of Honan.

Since my travels in Kansu, in 1923–4, made us acquainted with the splendid pottery of this phase of the Yang Shao age (Chapters XVII–XXI) it has become clear that the east-Asiatic painted

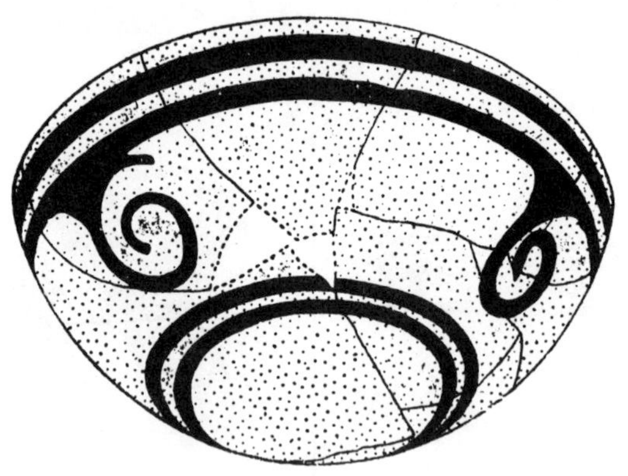

FIG. 79.—Painted bowl from Chin Wang Chai in Ho Yin Hsien, Honan.

ceramics of the latest Stone age are still more reminiscent of the painted ceramics of Southern Russia of the Stone-Copper age (Tripolje ceramics).

Before we leave the question of the Yang Shao Tsun ceramics we should mention that in one coarse, thick fragment we observed numerous imprints of plants which, as will appear from a description in the final chapter by G. Edman and E. Söderberg, have been shown to be husks of rice (*Oryza sativa L.*), which was thus cultivated at Yang Shao Tsun by the people of the late Stone age.

This extremely important discovery, for which we have to thank the acumen and erudition of the above-mentioned botanists, harmonizes perfectly with the account given above of the geographical changes at Yang Shao Tsun during the last 4,000 years.

At the present day the cultivation of rice in the ravine area would be impossible. At the time of the ancient Yang Shao village, when the district was a connected plateau with streams coursing through shallow channels, the conditions for rice cultivation were considerably more favourable.

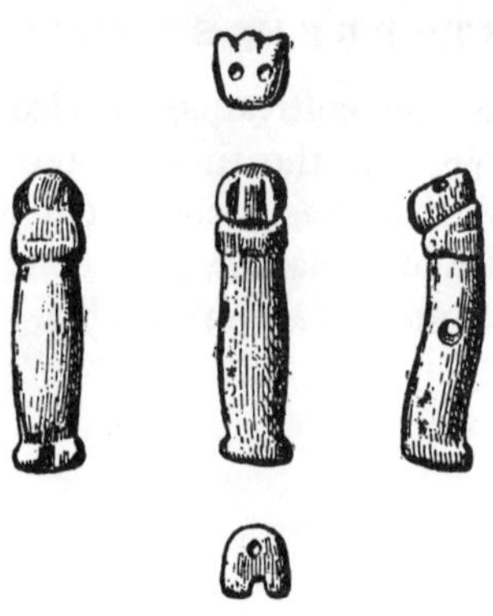

FIG. 80.—Figurine of marble. Sha Kuo T'un cave.

CHAPTER ELEVEN

A CANNIBALISTIC SANCTUARY[1]

IN the summer of 1921 I was ordered by the Ministry of Agriculture in Peking to make an official expedition to South-western Manchuria, the narrow strip of coast which juts out between Mongolia and the sea towards the Great Wall by Shanhaikuan.

My orders related to two things—firstly to investigate the geological conditions round about Hulutao, a projected harbour on the Yellow Sea, and secondly to assess the coal resources in a couple of coalfields in that neighbourhood.

When I had finished my work at Hulutao, I moved, on June 10th, to Sha Kuo T'un, the terminus of a small branch-line of the Peking-Mukden line. The main line proceeds along the coastal plain, but from the Nu Erh Ho station the above-mentioned branch-line runs up to the Ta Yao Kou coalmine which I was to investigate. The mine in question is owned by Japanese, and the Japanese manager invited me to stay with him. I had, however, brought tents for myself and my men and preferred to pitch my camp on the square in front of the station at Nu Erh Ho—which proved to be very advantageous to me in a way I could not have foreseen at the start.

As usual I brought with me two of my trained collectors, Yao and Pai. Besides them, the head of the American expedition to

[1] J. G. Andersson, " The Cave Deposit at Sha Kuo T'un in Fengtien ", *Palaeontologia Sinica*, Ser. D, Vol. 1, Fasc. 1, Peking, 1923.

Mongolia, Dr. Roy Chapman Andrews, had sent me a young Chinese, James Wong, who was to be a guide and interpreter to Andrews' palaeontologist, Dr. Walter Granger, who was just then expected in Peking. The intention was that Wong should see a little of our methods of locating sites and of excavating them.

The mountains south-east of Sha Kuo T'un consist of a pre-Cambrian siliceous limestone, and it therefore seemed to me possible that we might find caves containing interesting prehistoric finds. I therefore sent Mr. Wong with my men, Yao and Pai, to examine the caves which the inhabitants of the neighbourhood had shown to us.

Such a limestone cave was found about 1,200 metres south-east of the railway station, and from this cave Wong and Pai brought back the bones of some smaller mammals—probably badger—and bats, of the kind that are common in Northern China. Mr. Wong said that these bones had been found near the surface of the earth which filled the greater part of the cave. I pointed out to him the desirability of excavating down to the rock bottom of the cave, as the most interesting finds could only be expected at some depth.

In order to investigate the Nan P'iao coalfield, of which the Ta Yao Kou mine was only a small part, I left our camp for a few days. On my return on June 14th Wong showed me some very interesting prehistoric finds that had been made in the deeper deposits of the cave, and I realized at once that we had here to do with a prehistoric cave deposit of profound interest.

The following day we began together a systematic excavation of the cave. Unfortunately, however, Mr. Wong soon fell ill and had to return to Peking, whilst I stayed on until July 8th, when the whole cave had been emptied of its contents. As we had found lots of human bones during the excavation under circumstances that demanded the assistance of a trained anatomist, I wired to my friend, Dr. Davidson Black, professor of anatomy at the Peking Union Medical College. He arrived at Sha Kuo T'un on June 22nd and co-operated with skill and acumen in the latter part of the excavations.

Fig. 81 shows a longitudinal section of the Sha Kuo T'un cave as it looked before excavation. Apart from the inmost, very narrow portion, the cave has a length of 6 metres. The rocky roof of the cave, as seen in the longitudinal section, is nearly horizontal, with the exception of a rise over the inmost part.

The cave was at the time of our arrival for the most part filled with earth, consisting of a grey, finely powdered sand, with a large proportion of lime and small grains of quartz. When this earth was removed, as the excavation proceeded, it appeared that the bottom sloped towards the entrance. This earth filled the greater part of the cave, so that the free space above it was not more than a metre in height.

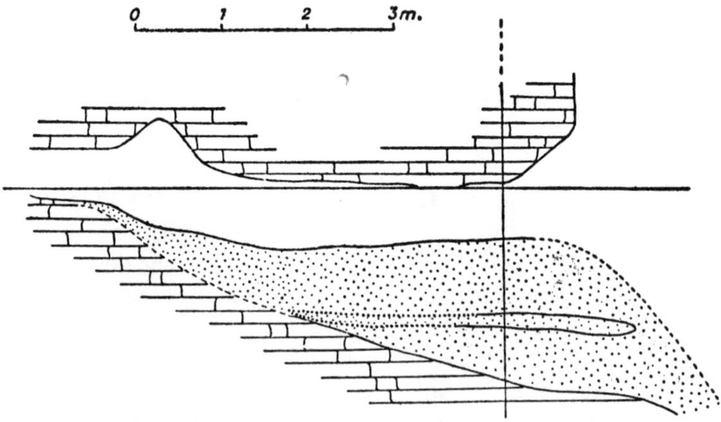

FIG. 81.—Longitudinal section of the cave. The horizontal line in the roof of the cave is the base measurement line; the perpendicular line shows the position of the cross-section in Fig. 82.

I arranged the measuring of the cave in a very simple way. A string was stretched very close to the roof from the innermost part of the cave to the mouth of the cave, and this base line, which was marked in metres and decimetres, was left during the whole excavation, so that every measurement, whether horizontal or vertical, could, as the excavation proceeded, be taken from this base line in the roof.

I have already mentioned that the earth which for the most part filled the cave was a finely powdered, grey sand. This filling was, however, not quite homogeneous. Deposit 2 was so filled with human bones that we called it BBB (Big Bone Bed) and the outer part of this deposit was so rich in charcoal that

Sha Kuo T'un cave

[*face page* 190

it was almost black. Higher up in the series of deposits there were two thin bands, 3 and 5, which were full of bits of charcoal and were therefore quite black.

When I examined the sample 2 of the white-yellow finely powdered sand of the lowest deposit 1, which I had brought back, I observed small fragments of charcoal, a fact of a certain importance, as it proves that man was active in this neighbourhood as early as the formation of the bottom deposit in the cave. This is proved still more clearly by the discovery of a few frag-

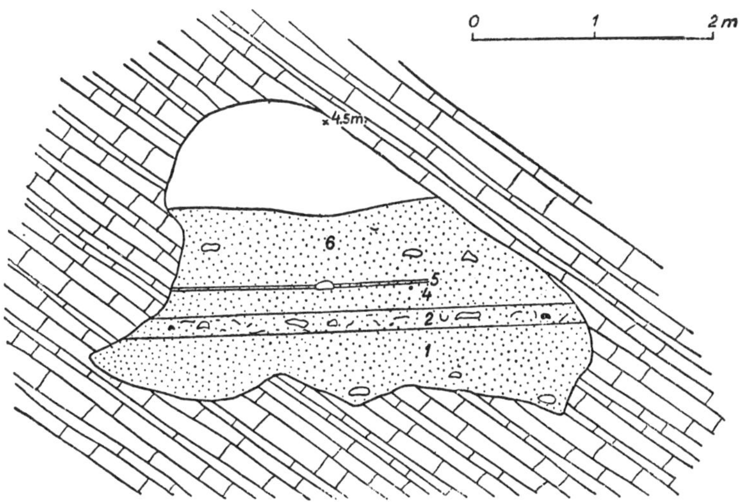

FIG. 82.—Cross-section through the cave.

ments of ceramics. Among them we specially noted that no less than three fragments of painted vessels were found in the bottom deposit, whilst in the upper deposits we only found a single fragment of this painted ware.

The largest number, not only of human bones, but also of fragments of ceramics and objects made of stone and bone, was found in deposit 2, or the Big Bone Bed. A few objects were also found in the upper layers (3–6), but it is quite evident that human activity in this cave existed predominantly during the period of formation of layer 2.

Of quite modern origin are a couple of copper coins which

were found right on the surface of the cave deposits. These are a Hsiang Fu Yuan Pao (祥符元寶), A.D. 1008–16, thus belonging to the Northern Sung dynasty, and a Ta Ting T'ung

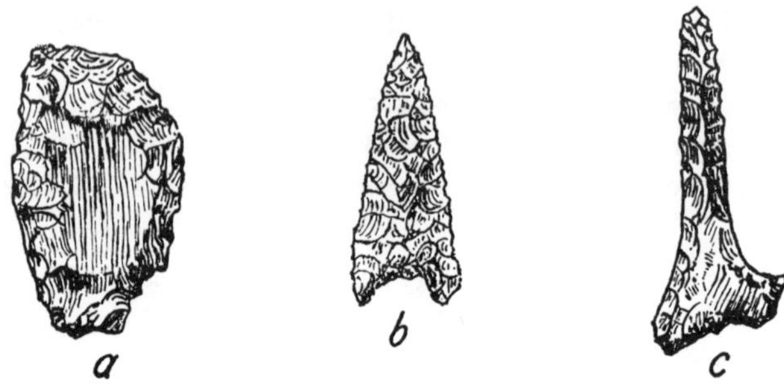

FIG. 83.—*a*, Scraper ; *c*, drill and *b*, arrowhead ; of chalcedony.

Pao (大定通寶), A.D. 1101–89, a coin belonging to the Chin dynasty. Copper coins of these types were in use till quite recently, and it is quite probable that they were left there by some recent visitor.

FIG. 84.—Polished stone axe.

Let us now examine the harvest we gathered in the Sha Kuo T'un cave. We first note some objects hewn from flint-like rocks ; partly from the impure chert which is found in the limestone of the neighbourhood and which is, however, not suitable for making stone implements ; partly and most important of all, of chalcedony, which fills out the cavities in the basic lava rocks, which occur quite frequently at some distance from Sha Kuo T'un. This last-mentioned stone lends itself to the making of the most delicate of stone implements, such as arrowheads, etc.

The objects seen in Fig. 83 were all made of chalcedony, and each of them is well made of its kind. Fig. 83*a* is a scraper, which reminds us very much of similar implements of the Old

Sha Kuo T'un cave, near view

[*face page* 192

Stone age in Europe ; Fig. 83*c* is a drill and Fig. 83*b* is an arrow-head of a most elegant shape.

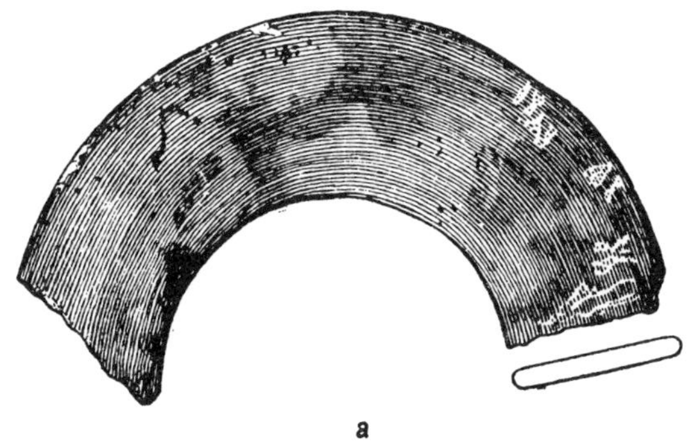

a

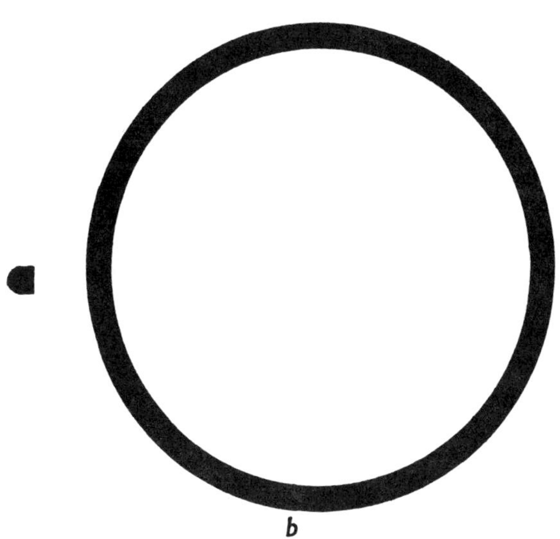

b

FIG. 85.—*a*, Fragment of marble ring ; *b*, reconstruction of thin marble ring. (Natural size.)

Of polished stone implements we have only four small axes, of which Fig. 84 illustrates a good specimen in natural size. Worth noticing is the fact that some of these axes are so small that we might almost doubt whether they were used as real implements. We shall return to this question later on.

We will now consider a number of stone rings of very different shapes, but all very thin in section. Fig. 85*a* is a comparatively broad ring seen from the side, and these rings remind us of the jade rings which Chinese archaeologists call *yüan*. There are also very thin marble rings, as, for instance, the fragment of which Fig. 85*b* is a reconstruction. We cannot help wondering both at the skill with which these brittle objects have been formed and at the uses of an object which could so easily be broken with the least carelessness of handling.

Whilst speaking of these marble rings we would also for a moment refer to a very remarkable and important group of finds, i.e. a couple of hundred fragments or, at best, complete examples, of extremely thin rings cut out of mussel shell, probably fresh-water mussels of the group Unionidae. Fig. 86 shows an example of these mussel rings which, even more than the stone rings, awaken our astonishment by their graceful form and extreme fragility. In thickness these mussel rings are only 1·5 mm., the breadth varies between 5 and 8 mm., and against these minute measurements we must set an exterior diameter of 57–105 mm.

FIG. 86.—Fragment of a mussel ring.

Amongst stone objects we must also mention a number of beads, of which at least the greatest number are carved out of marble. These beads are partly short and cylindrically rounded and partly tube-like. In connection with these beads we will also glance at about twenty globular buttons, in most cases cut out of marble. It strikes one that these buttons are very small (diameter only 4·5–11 mm.), and it seems probable that a people who used such small and neatly made buttons must have worn clothes made of fine material and of highly developed shape.

When Professor Black cleaned human bones from Sha Kuo T'un at his institution in Peking, he discovered in the earth adhering to the bones an object of the greatest interest and absolutely unique among all our prehistoric finds in China. It is a small sculpture of an animal, made of hard, whitish yellow marble (see the vignette to this chapter). It seems more probable that this figurine depicts a mammal, probably a cat, whose forelegs are only suggested by thickening, whilst the hind-legs are better represented. The object is pierced in the middle, evidently in order to be worn on a string.

Some bone objects are also to be found in the harvest from this cave. The most interesting is a sewing needle which was found stuck in a tube-like bone, the humerus of a fox. The cavity is so deep that there is room in it for the whole of the needle, and it does not seem improbable that this tubular bone was used as a sheath to protect the brittle needle.

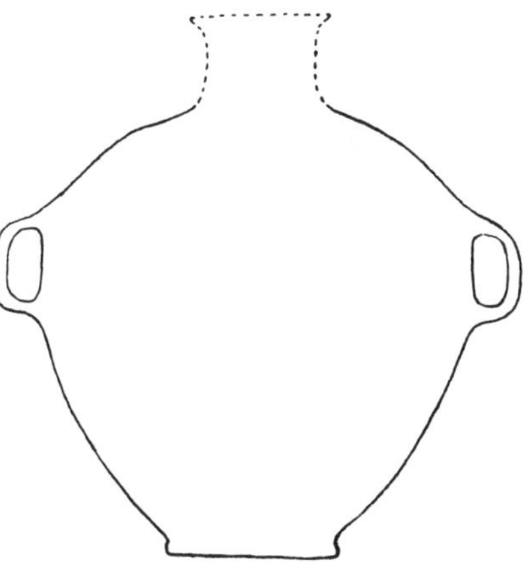

FIG. 87.—Outline of a jar with narrow neck (¼ natural size).

The remains of clay vessels are all very fragmentary —either isolated fragments or collections of pieces which we have been able to piece together in a reconstruction of the vessel. Amongst the former we must specially mention four pieces of fine ware with a brick-red surface and black painted pattern. We have already pointed out the remarkable fact that three of these pieces—and these the best—were found in the bottom deposits, otherwise so poor in finds. These painted ceramic potsherds are extremely characteristic, and I recognized at once in them the ceramic type that we first learnt to know in the large dwelling-site at Yang Shao Tsun. We might with good reason interpret the discovery of these painted potsherds in the Sha Kuo T'un cave in such a way as to regard the cave deposit, or at least its bottom stratum, as being contemporary with the above-mentioned site of major finds in Honan.

Some groups of potsherds which fitted together were found in the outer part of the cave. Several circumstances, amongst others the rich accumulation of bits of charcoal in the exterior part of deposit 2, the Big Bone Bed, point to the fact that the fireplace was situated in that part of the cave, and it does not seem improbable that at least in one case a piece of rock, loosened from the roof by the heat of the fire, had fallen down and broken one of the clay vessels standing by the fire.

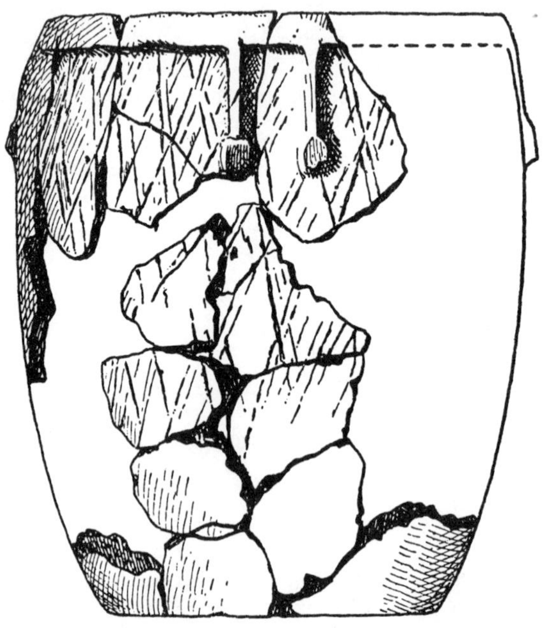

FIG. 88.—Cylindrical vessel with pendulum decoration (⅓ natural size).

Fig. 88 is a nearly cylindrical vessel, 162 mm. in height and in many respects of great interest. This vessel also has on the outside two systems of imprinted string lines crossing each other, but in addition to this it shows a decoration which we have never found anywhere else during our studies of the prehistoric ceramics of China. This consists of pendulum-shaped ridges, which stretch down perpendicularly from the brim about 30 to 39 mm. The " pendulums " are placed in ones or twos, and it seems probable that there were two opposite pairs and two opposite single pendulums.

Fig. 87 shows the largest vessel which we have been able

to reconstruct. From many small pieces we have managed to reconstruct the whole vessel, except the evidently narrow neck. Although we do not know exactly the form of this important part of the vessel, it is evident that we have here a type of which the form reminds us of the richly painted, large, narrow-necked burial urns from the Pan Shan graves of Kansu (see Chapter XX).

When—after having examined all the discoveries from the Sha Kuo T'un cave—we now endeavour to interpret this site, we must take into consideration some strange circumstances which, though they make the solution of the question much more difficult, nevertheless render the whole enigma ever so much more alluring.

On the whole it does not seem possible to suggest more than the following three alternative interpretations of the discoveries made in this cave:

(*a*) That the cave was a burial site, to which the large number of human bones seems to point.

(*b*) That the cave was a dwelling site for a group of people who were cannibals, or

(*c*) That it was the scene of a cult in which rites, including human sacrifices, were performed.

The first hypothesis, that we have here to do with a burial place, we must abandon, because of the fragmentary nature of the human bones and of the fact that they lie chaotically mixed up. Professor Black has, by his final examination of the material, established that we have in this little cave the remains of no less than 45 human individuals of both sexes and varying in age from small children to the very aged. In the " Big Bone Bed " the bone fragments were often heaped up in an extremely fragmentary state and in apparently hopeless confusion. Professor Black's description of the only fairly complete skull found among the masses of pieces and fragments is typical of this confusion. In the earth that filled this skull Professor Black found during his careful cleaning of the bones the following somewhat heterogeneous objects: several small stone beads, bits of charred wood, a tooth and several bones of a small rodent, human bones, i.e. a pelvis, four pieces of ribs, the lower part of a humerus, bits of two vertebrae, several splinters of long bones, bits of a shoulder blade, a piece of a breastbone, a piece of a finger and several small pieces of a cranium.[1]

To this description of the human bones it should be added that Professor Black has been able to prove that the breaking of the human bones at least in some, and probably in many, cases had taken place whilst the bones were fresh and whilst the soft parts were still attached to them. This leads us to the second possibility: that the cave had been inhabited by a small group of cannibals. Many of the hollow bones are splintered in such a way as to lead one to suppose that efforts had been made to extract the marrow from them, but on the other hand many of the extremity bones were quite unharmed—and it does not seem to fit in well with decent cannibal economy to leave them in this condition.

There is also another circumstance which does not properly accord with the hypothesis that this cave was inhabited by men who remained cannibals so long as supplies permitted. In the Big Bone Bed we certainly also found some bones of animals, but they were decidedly in the minority compared with the overwhelming mass of human bones. This seems to indicate a state "too good to be true", as the English have it, because it can scarcely have been possible that even the most progressive-minded cannibal could have found such a surfeit of his favourite food.

Another hypothesis supposes that a family group inhabiting the cave was attacked and killed and was possibly the occasion of a cannibal feast. This would explain the chaotic heaping up of the fragments of human bones.

As against this hypothesis, we are confronted with the inescapable fact that as many as forty-five individuals could never have found room in this little cave at one time, not even if they had been refugees, and it would have been still less possible for the persons in that small space to handle, break up and mix the bones of so many human bodies. Not infrequently the bones are partly blackened by fire, and we find, for example, pieces of the abovementioned cranium which are quite calcinated by great heat on one side, and in the middle only blackened, whilst on the other

[1] Davidson Black, "The Human Skeletal Remains from the Sha Kuo T'un Cave Deposit", *Palaeontologia Sinica*, Ser. D., Vol. 1, Fasc. 3, p. 3, Peking, 1925.

side they are not touched at all by fire. On the whole I think we receive the impression that the formation of this bone bed took some time and that the dismemberment of the human bodies took place on successive occasions.

This forces us to consider whether the cave should not be interpreted as the home of a cult in which religious rites were performed involving human sacrifices as a principal element. This interpretation agrees excellently with all the facts already mentioned in this discussion, and it is the only one that can explain certain peculiarities of the prehistoric finds in this cave. First of all, then, I would refer to the extremely numerous rings made of mussel shell; these cannot plausibly be regarded as ornaments intended for permanent use. They are far too fragile for that—but if we consider them as symbols to be used in cult ceremonies they are much easier to understand. It seems very probable that they were used as substitutes for the expensive stone rings which are also found in the cave. In that case there would be much the same relation between the stone and mussel-shell rings as between the "sycee" of silver paper and the paper "cash" which is nowadays used at Chinese funerals instead of the genuine silver "sycee" and the copper coins which they imitate.

To this group of supposed cult objects I should also like to add the four small stone axes, which are too small to be used as real implements or weapons. Such small stone axes were also found, but only rarely, in the large dwelling-site near Yang Shao Tsun in Honan, where small stone chisels and large, heavy axes and adzes show us the implements which were used by the people of that period.

Fig. 89.—Showing the forms of development of the written character " Ko "; *a–d*, archaic forms from inscriptions on bronze vessels and bronze weapons, all undoubted pictographs of the Chinese dagger axe; *e–f* transition forms to modern written character *g*.

CHAPTER TWELVE

ANCIENT IMPLEMENTS AND VESSELS

In the midst of our modern life we still retain innumerable inheritances from times long past, remnants of ancient customs and habits which are in many cases unnoticed by the layman, but which to the eyes of the specialist reveal the incredible tenacity with which the past sometimes survives under altered conditions.

A hardy group of ancient survivals is to be found, for example, in certain place-names. In Sweden names ending in -vi (place of sacrifice) take us straight back to heathen days, and when we meet such well-known place-names as Frövi, Torsvi and Odinsvi, the old cult places acquire a personal emphasis. It is probable that a group of other place-names, such as those in -hem, -vin, -sta and -inge take their origin in prehistoric times.

Pioneers in the field of folklore have familiarized us with a number of present-day customs, or customs common until quite recently, of which the origin is to be found either deep down in the early history of our own people or still more remotely in the prehistoric wealth of sagas, tales, popular beliefs and magic which seems to be common to a great part of the human race.

Christmas itself, the great central festival of Christianity, has been shown by modern research to be a Christian adaptation and embellishment of the pagan midwinter festival. Numerous habits and customs, especially in connection with our agriculture, derive from a fecundity magic, of which the origin goes back to the dawn of agriculture.

But it is not only our place-names and our folklore which are saturated with prehistoric memories. Until quite recently, when modern industrialism annihilated the older crafts, our household goods, our wooden sculptures and iron work were full of patterns as old as the roots of the language.

When a people so receptive of modern ideas as the Swedes still retain such a rich inheritance from ancient times, we may safely conclude that still greater treasures of the past will be found among a people such as the Chinese, who are still so primitive and so comparatively little affected by modern influences. For those who love the prehistoric features in the life of a people it is certainly a depressing fact that the modern storm now rages over the Chinese countryside. The missionaries, with their new arts of healing, the British and American Tobacco Company, which has taught the Chinese to smoke cigarettes, and the bands of soldiers who return home from the civil wars with new impressions—all these have contributed to make the Chinese peasant feel the first breath of American cosmopolitanism. But all the same the Chinese peasant population of the countryside, and indeed also the poor in the towns, are to this day a comparatively untouched and primitive race.

Whilst Chinese scholars have studied every side of their literary inheritance with immense energy and piety, they have rather neglected the evidence of the material side of life. In the simple household utensils and the implements of the poorer Chinese we find a material which speaks to us with convincing force and clarity of the early history of Chinese culture.

I should now like to show the reader some examples of this rich treasure.[1] The two Japanese scholars, R. and K. Torii, in

[1] I have already published a great part of the contents of this report in a more strictly scientific form in my paper " An Early Chinese Culture ", *Bull. Geol. Survey of China*, No. 5, 1923, and in " Arkeologiska Studier i Kina ", *Ymer*, 1923. Some new features are, however, here given for the first time, as, for example, the connection between the crescent-shaped knife of the Stone age and the iron scythe with which the Chinese of to-day performs his harvest work. The distaff and textile art, the arrowheads, and the mention of the pointed-bottomed vessels in the earliest writings, for which important contributions I must thank Professor Karlgren, are also new contributions now put forward here for the first time.

many respects broke new ground in research into East-Asiatic antiquity in two treatises published in 1914 and 1915 in the *Journal of the College of Science*, Tokio Imperial University. Amongst other things they gave us our knowledge of the characteristic rectangular or crescent-shaped stone knives, which are an important element of the furniture of the South Manchurian and East Mongolian prehistoric sites. Later on I found these stone knives again in almost all the prehistoric and early historical excavation sites which I have examined in China. Exquisite examples of the same type of implement are also to be found in the splendid work, edited by Hamada, *P'i-Tzu-Wo, Prehistoric sites by the river Pi-liu-ho, South Manchuria*, which is the first volume of the ambitiously conceived series, "Archaeologia Orientalis", which promises to open up a new epoch in the study of East Asiatic pre-history.

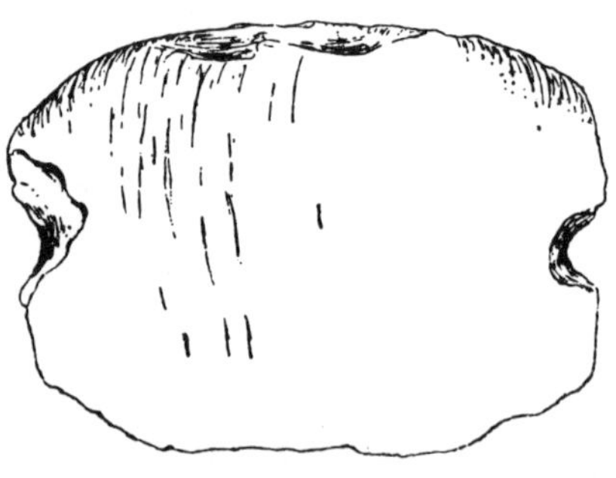

FIG. 90.—Stone knife formed from a flake broken out of a large pebble. The back is thickened, the sides provided with two incisions for securing a string (2/3 natural size.)

When, in 1923, I described the stone knives I had found in Northern China, I had not yet had my attention directed to the earliest type of these implements (Fig. 90), of which I now possess a rich material from Honan, but most of all from Kansu. Most frequently the knife is shaped from a flake, broken off a large greenstone pebble. This flake has by chipping been given such a shape that it acquires a thick rounded back with two incisions on the sides, which almost certainly served to hold the string by which the knife was carried. In its original form this knife had thus different sides, since one shows the even surface of the pebble and the other the uneven surface produced by breaking off the flake from the pebble. In our collection there are also a few knives of this type which are polished on both sides and which thus form a transition to the more perfect, crescent-shaped and rectangular knives which I have described in my earlier publications.

The knives which are polished on both sides are made of shale, sandstone or even of so soft a material as the shells of large fresh-water mussels. It also not infrequently happened that the people of the Yang Shao period chose suitable pieces of broken clay vessels and ground them into knives.

These knives vary considerably in form. A small number are crescent-shaped, the greater number are rectangular. There is, moreover, in a place in Kansu, Lo Han T'ang, in the Kuei Te valley, on the frontier of Tibet, a local form of knife with the sides swung out like wings, which are decorated with scores on the edge that is swung out.

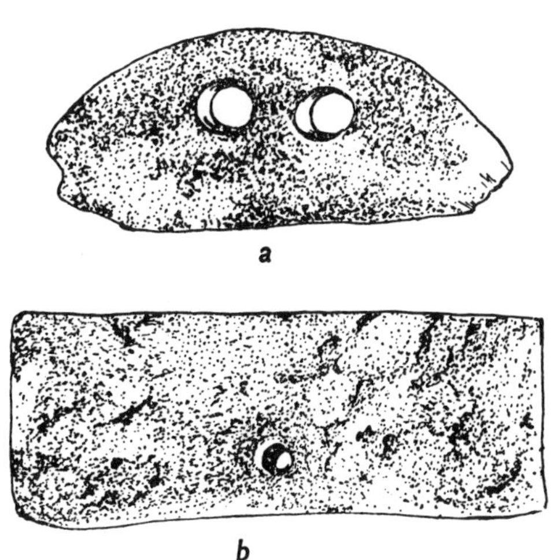

FIG. 91.—*a*, crescent-shaped, and *b*, rectangular polished stone knife.

In most cases the rectangular and crescent-shaped knives are provided with one or two holes. It is a remarkable fact that these holes are very often placed near the edge. In very worn examples the edge has worn down so much that it is close to the perforations.

Similar stone knives have also been found in Japanese prehistoric dwelling-sites. Fig. 92 shows a beautiful Japanese stone knife which was presented in 1926 by Prince Oyama to the Swedish Crown Prince, who presented it to the Museum of Far Eastern Antiquities.

Torii has drawn attention to the fact that similar crescent-shaped stone knives have been found in old dwelling sites within the territory of the North Asiatic Chukchi as well as amongst the North American Eskimos. Knives of the same type, but now made of iron, are still in use amongst these two Arctic peoples.

In the beginning of 1920 I found that this type had survived in the same way among the Northern Chinese population. In the northern part of the province of Chihli (Hopei), where kaoliang (*Andropogon sorghum*) is generally cultivated, they use a crescent-shaped, rectangular or trapezoidal iron implement to cut off the ears of the kaoliang. This iron knife is provided with two holes, just in the same way as the Manchurian crescent-shaped stone

FIG. 92.—Japanese stone knife from Prince Oyama's collection.

knives. The back of the iron knife is provided with a covering of stuff or leather, attached to the iron knife by a string which passes through the two holes. This leather handle also has a loop for the thumb, as is shown in Fig. 94.

There can be no doubt that these modern iron knives are the descendants of the crescent-shaped and rectangular stone knives, which, for their part, since they occur among the arctic peoples, both in Asia and America, must be regarded as a prehistoric inheritance from the still undivided Mongolian race, i.e. are older than the period when a Mongolian tribe crossed the Behring Strait and settled in America.

As soon as I had my attention drawn to the connection between the prehistoric stone knives and the modern iron harvest knives, I began to collect all sorts of modern Chinese knives and scythes, and during this work of collecting I have gradually come to the opinion that the majority of these modern implements are descendants of the late Neolithic ones.

One of these modern implements is of a particularly amusing kind.

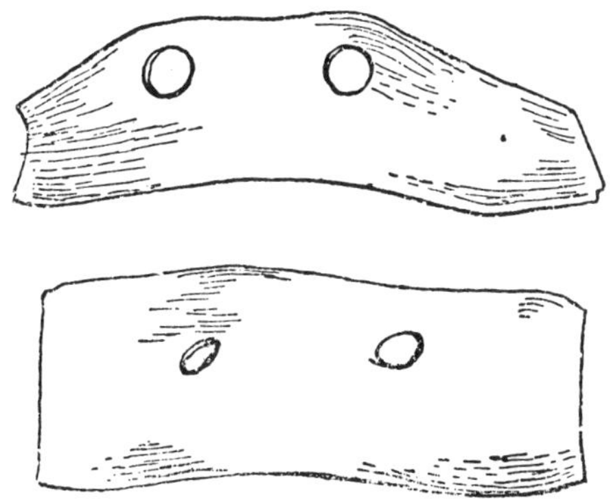

FIG. 93.—*a*, crescent-shaped, and *b*, rectangular modern iron knife.

Everyone who has visited Peking has certainly noticed a striking feature in its picturesque street life, i.e. the different kinds of itinerant traders who try to attract attention with the aid of different kinds of musical instruments. The cloth dealer swings a miniature drum, with wooden handle and two little balls attached to it by short strings; the lemonade dealer makes a noise with two brass bowls, the barber strikes a gigantic tuning fork, etc.

The knife-grinder, who walks through the streets with his grindstone, uses one of two instruments, either a trumpet or a strange implement consisting of four elongated rectangular iron plaques, each perforated in the upper edge by two holes through which runs a string securing the iron plaques loosely together to a wooden handle.

FIG. 94.—Iron knife with leather covering on the back and a loop for the thumb.

When this instrument (Fig. 95) is set in rhythmic motion a peculiar metallic sound is produced.

In order to explain the origin of this instrument we must for a moment return to the rectangular kaoliang knife and especially note that among its many forms there is one of exceptional length and of a slightly trapezoidal form. Starting from this knife it is not difficult to give a genetic explanation of the knife-grinder's rattle as consisting from the beginning of four long trapezoidal knives, each perforated with two holes, which were tied together with a string in order to form a resonant instrument. This idea occurred to me one day as I drove past a knife-grinder who was walking in the street, playing his instrument. I jumped out of my rickshaw in order to examine the instrument more carefully and found to my great joy that each one of the iron plaques had the lower edge ground down. They are real knives, though they are never intended for use as such. The man who carries the instrument does not know why he has given an edge to each plaque. His only explanation is that such is the ancient custom; and this old custom is without doubt one of many examples of the hardy survival of features which have lost their original meaning and purpose. Once upon a time a clever knife-grinder had the brilliant idea of fastening together four knife blades so that they formed a rattle, a really striking announcement to the customers that the knife-grinder had arrived. A biologist would express the relationship between the kaoliang knife and the musical instrument of the knife-grinder by saying that the former is a solitary type, whilst the latter is a colony consisting of four individuals, that have assumed a new function, whilst retaining the sharp edge as a persistent, rudimentary character.

FIG. 95.—Knife-grinder's rattle.

The most important harvest implement of the Chinese peasant is a scythe, which is represented in different parts of the country by different provincial types. One form (Fig. 96*a*) which I noticed in Anhui, takes exactly the form of the crescent-shaped knife, only with the addition of a small thin protuberance in one corner, which is turned round the wooden handle.

I have repeatedly seen in the frontier country between Northern China and Inner Mongolia a type of very great interest to our present study. I have thus examples from the Lung Kuan and the Hsüan Hua districts. Another I bought above Kalgan (Fig.

96*b*) from a man who was on his way to harvest work in Mongolia, and out on the Mongolian steppes I acquired at Chaggan Obo a somewhat different variety. This harvest knife has a long straight blade, which is perforated at the broad end by a rather large hole. The same end is further drawn to a thin, bent spindle. The wooden handle is S-shaped and rather long. The upper end of the handle is cleft, sometimes even to a third of its length. By means of an iron pin the blade is fastened to the handle, so that it moves on the pin and can, when not in use, be folded against the handle in such a way that the sharp edge is protected.

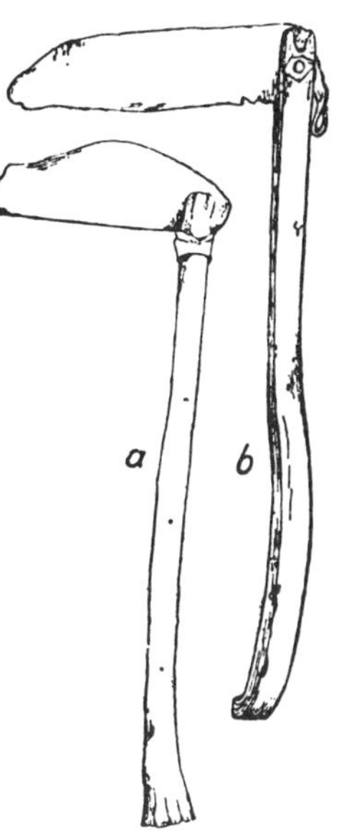

FIG. 96.— Knives, *a*, from Anhui ; *b*, from the Kalgan district (⅛ natural size).

As early as 1920, when I began to collect these iron scythes, I played with the idea of discovering whether these modern implements were not also descendants of the prehistoric stone knives. But there was a big gap in my series between the handleless prototype on the one hand and the present-day iron scythe with a handle on the other. The years, however, passed in a constant study of this unsolved problem, and one fine day missing links in the chain came to me of their own accord. In 1927, I saw in Peking, partly in the museum and partly in General Munthe's collection, some rather large stone knives (Fig. 97), which, according to information received, came from the famous excavation site An Yang in Northern Honan, whence the inscribed bones and magnificent ivory carvings come (Yin dynasty). Assuming that the information concerning the place of discovery is correct, these stone knives should belong to a period about 1000 B.C., an age which we archaeologists call China's Bronze age. On the whole these knives remind us rather of the prehistoric crescent-shaped knives, but one of the ends is cut off aslant. We obtained the explanation of this form in 1929, when our highly esteemed collector, O. Karlbeck, sent us the remarkable object which is depicted in Fig. 98. It is a bronze knife, the form of which strongly reminds us of the stone knife in Fig. 97, because it is pointed at one end, and blunt at the other and without perforation. Fortunately this remarkable example shows clearly how it has been inserted into a wooden handle, approximately in the same way as the above-mentioned blades from the Mongolian frontier area.

This bronze knife gives us an idea how the large stone knives from An Yang had been furnished with handles, and with this important specimen in our hands we can safely say that the long-sought link between the late Neolithic stone knives without handles and the modern iron scythe with handle has been found.

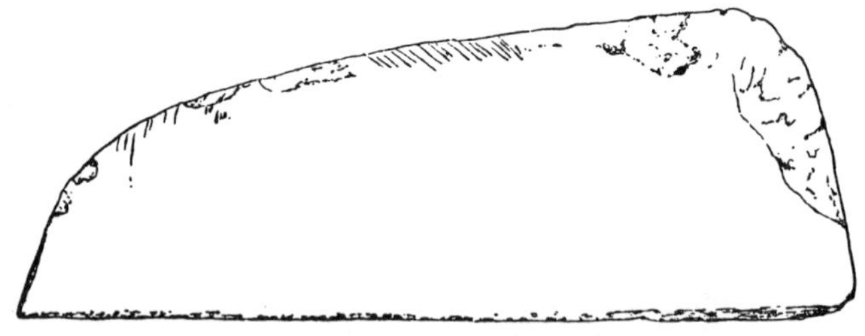

FIG. 97.—Stone knife, probably from An Yang (½ natural size).

Our account of the evolution of these implements would be misleading in a very important point if we did not here remind the reader that metal scythes were common in the cultures of the Near East (Egypt, Mesopotamia) during periods which may possibly coincide with the Yang Shao period in China. It is thus more than possible that cultural influences from the West were responsible for the advance in culture which gave to the Chinese a wooden handle for their harvest knife. On the other hand we must point out that the handleless crescent-shaped and rectangular knife blades which play such an immensely important rôle in prehistoric China are not known at all in the Near East or in Europe, where crescent-shaped flint saws are the only, and very uncertain, parallels to the stone knives of Eastern Asia.

But just as these knife blades were unknown to the prehistoric peoples of the West, so also they seem to have been equally widespread among all the Mongolian races. In Baron

Erland Nordenskiöld's rich collections from prehistoric South America in the Gothenburg Museum I have seen stone knives which remind me very much of the rectangular knife-blades of Eastern Asia. It is thus possible that this stone knife was such an early possession of the Mongolian peoples that it accompanied them when, during the New Stone age, a section of this populous human tribe found its way across the Behring Strait and gave to America its first population.

Stone knives form the largest group of prehistoric implements which have survived till the present day. Nowadays they are made of iron, and their descendants have developed into a whole family, in which the different individuals are widely differentiated from each other.

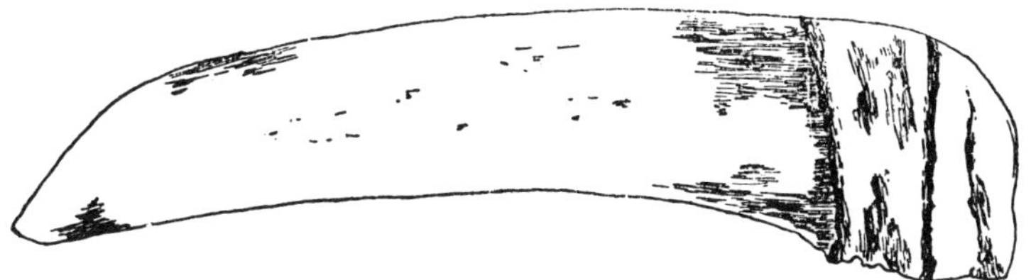

FIG. 98.—Bronze scythe with clear marks of the shaft (½ natural size).

If we now begin to examine the collections of implements of Chinese craftsmen, we shall find a good many other types, whose origin we can trace back to a very remote past.

Especially do we find such examples among Chinese carpenters and joiners, whose drill is a variant of the arc-drill, found among several present-day primitive peoples, which has been hypothetically traced by Sollas [1] as far back as the late Palaeolithic Magdalenian civilization.

Another very important implement, which is frequently used by carpenters and woodworkers in Hupei and Honan, and probably in many other parts of China also, is called *pen*, an adze, generally of considerable size, but also found in a smaller type. The iron part of the pen is, to use an archaeological term, a socketed axe, a metal edge provided with a socket, which is intended to hold the wooden handle. These metal-saving implements were developed during the period when metal was rare

[1] Sollas, *Ancient Hunters*, p. 464.

and costly. They were in general use over large parts of Eurasia during the Bronze age, and were represented by numerous, sometimes very tastefully shaped, varieties. We ought, however, to point out that axes with shaft holes, both in bronze and stone, existed before the socketed axes of bronze. Nowadays, when the supplies of metal are more ample, the socketed axe has to a large extent been supplanted by axes whose characteristic is that the whole of the head of the axe is of metal, and has a hole for the wooden handle. Socketed axes made of iron are probably not of infrequent occurrence nowadays. I cannot offer a complete survey of this interesting question, but some data may be given here. Lord Avebury states in *Prehistoric Times* that socketed axes of iron are used in Siberia and in certain parts of Africa (on page 29 of his book there is an illustration of a socketed axe used by the Kalmucks). A. R. Colquhoun gives an illustration of two types of socketed axes used by the Shan tribe in southwest China.[1]

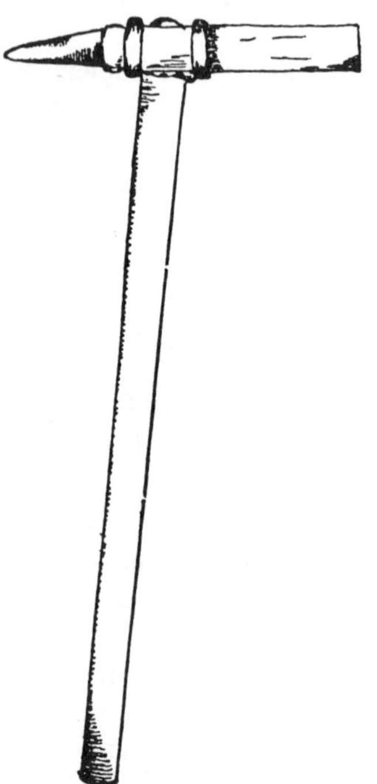

FIG. 99.—Chinese lumberman's pen ($\frac{1}{10}$ natural size).

For those who know the extremely conservative character of the Chinese and their low standard of living, in which a bit of metal represents considerable value, it seems really quite natural that the socketed axe should survive as a form of implement still in use, and we much admire the cleverness with which the Chinese, by means of the thickened wooden head, have imparted the necessary head weight to the axe.

That socketed axes were common even during the Bronze age of China—as also during the earlier Iron age, when bronze was

[1] Colquhoun, *Amongst the Shans*, 1885, p. 298.

still in general use—is shown by the numerous types of bronze axes which are found in the Chinese tombs. As a rule they are very plain compared with the magnificent types which we know from the Bronze age of the Scandinavian North.

Amongst the Chinese socketed bronze celts there is one type (Fig. 100, 2a–c) which bears such a striking resemblance to the modern iron " pen " (Fig. 100, 3a–c) that there can be no doubt that they have a common origin. The resemblance is complete,

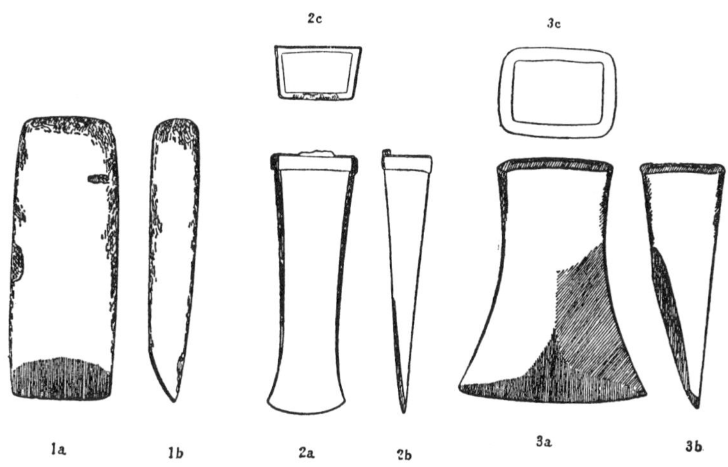

Fig. 100.—Illustrations showing the assumed connection between the asymmetric stone adze (1a and b), the bronze adze (2a–c) and the modern iron adze (3a–c) (½ natural size).

except that the bronze celt is more slender and more elongated, which was probably due to the fact that it was not an agricultural implement but rather a weapon or a votive object.

Montelius has among his typological series described the complicated but unbroken sequence of evolutionary steps between the simple Neolithic stone celt and the gracefully shaped and richly decorated axes of the Bronze age.

We do not yet possess such a complete typological series for China, but I think I am justified in drawing attention to a type of stone celt (Fig. 100, 1a and b) which, to judge by its form, may possibly be the prototype of the Chinese socketed celts.

Before we begin to study this stone celt, it is necessary to draw attention to a difference which seems to exist between the socketed celts of the West and those which are in use in China. The majority of European socketed celts were evidently true *axes*, i.e. the edge was parallel with the shaft. The Chinese pen on the other hand is what the English call an adze, with the edge transverse to the handle. This is also the case with the above-mentioned bronze celt, as is evident from its asymmetric profile and its trapezoidal cross section. We might also add that the majority of Chinese bronze celts are adzes. Consequently with regard to the socketed celts there has been a preference for axes in countries of the West and an equally pronounced predilection for adzes in China.

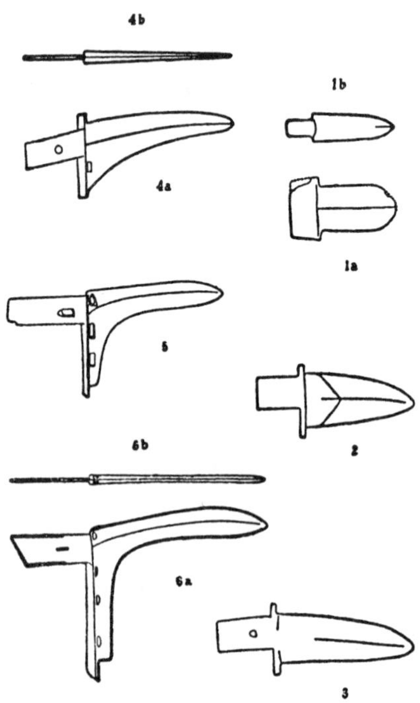

FIG. 101.—Development of the Chinese dagger axe, Ko. Fig. 1a–b of stone, 2–6 of copper and bronze.

Together with numerous stone axes of other varying forms we find in China very frequently an asymmetric, often slightly bent, chisel-shaped stone implement, which was probably a genuine stone adze (Fig. 100, 1a and b). The pronounced preference for adzes which we have seen expressed both in the asymmetric stone chisels and in the bronze and iron pen, has led me to suppose that the asymmetric stone chisel is possibly the prototype of the socketed adzes of bronze and iron. This is at most a working hypothesis, which will be verified or refuted by future examination.

Let us now proceed to examine a Chinese weapon, which is no longer in use, but which was a favourite weapon during the

Bronze age and the early Iron age. We ought perhaps first to regard it from a Chinese point of view, as it were, and then discuss its origin and its possible relation to similar types of weapons in the Western countries.

The object in question is called by the Chinese " ko " and ordinary handbooks describe it as a sort of halberd. The fundamental problem in the interpretation of this weapon is the question what sort of handle it had.

Fig. 101 shows the evolution of this Chinese dagger axe from a prototype in stone, a short and clumsy type, to the elegant, final stage, which is shown by Fig. 101, 6a–b. There can scarcely be any doubt that these two extreme links in the long series have been provided with handles in the same way as is shown in Fig. 102. For the purpose of fastening the wooden shaft, the example in Fig. 101, 1, is provided with two bosses, and these bosses are very evident even in the earlier metal stages 2 and 3. At stage 4 there is a hole added for binding, and these holes increase in numbers in the later stages, 5 and 6.

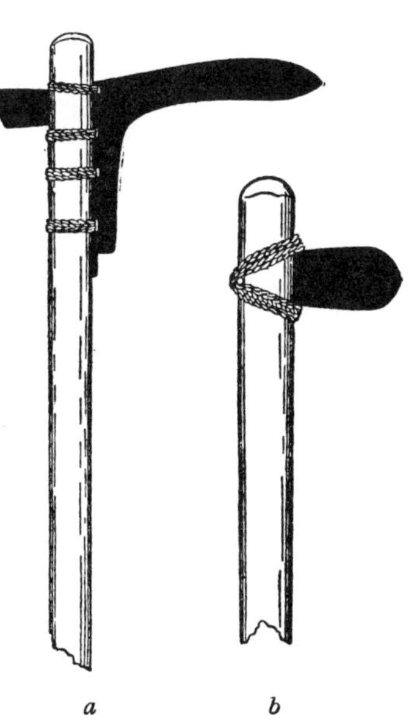

FIG. 102.—Method of attachment for *a*, stone ko ; and *b*, bronze ko.

That the interpretation we have given here of the manner of attaching the handle to the " ko " weapon is correct, is proved conclusively by the evolution of the Chinese written character Ko (Fig. 89, p. 200). In its modern form *g* this character is a conventional calligraphic product which has grown out of many intermediate stages (*e* and *f*), but which in its original shape (*a–d*) is a faithful image of the metal blade with its wooden handle.

We have in the Museum of Far Eastern Antiquities a very

rich collection of Chinese arrowheads of widely separated ages from the Stone age until modern times.

I acquired some modern arrows in September 1920 during the walking tour through the Western Hills near Peking in company with Mr. and Mrs. Richert, which I have described in the first chapter of this book. We had passed through the narrow rocky gorges of the Hun River to Ching Pai K'ou, when we emerged

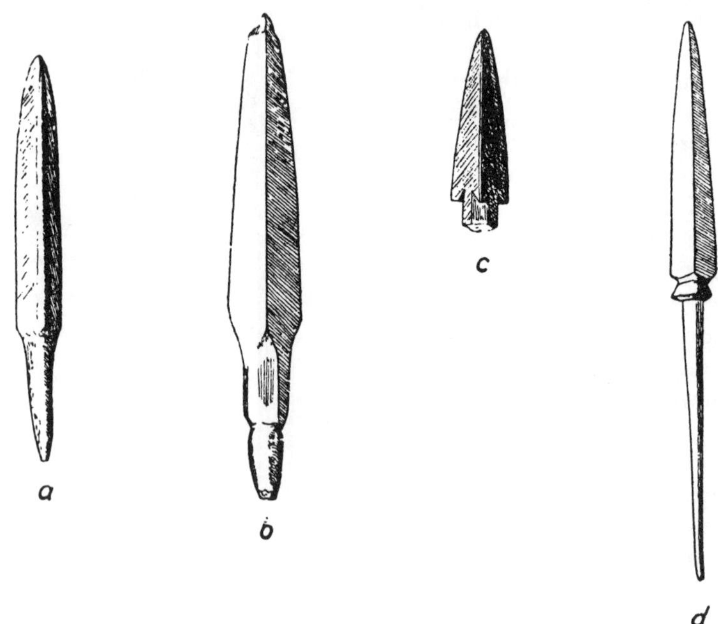

FIG. 103.—Triangular arrowheads : *a*, of bone ; *b*, of stone, both of the Yang Shao age ; *c*, of bronze, early Iron age ; and *d*, modern arrowhead of iron.

into a broader valley. Here at the opening of the narrow rocky gorge there are two watch-towers belonging to the defence system of the Great Wall. Probably the last Manchu garrison had forgotten a part of their arsenal, for I bought in Ching Pai K'ou a large collection of arrows, which, they told me, came from these watch-towers.

Other collections were acquired in Peking. Many of our most beautiful old arrowheads we owe to O. Karlbeck, especially his exquisite collections from the Huai-Ho valley.

A very large collection of arrowheads from the centuries round about the birth of Christ came to us from the Larsson collections from the Ordos desert. Our excavations in Honan yielded very rich material from prehistoric times, whilst the sites in Kansu, otherwise so extremely rich, are strikingly deficient in arrowheads.

When we now survey this collection, numbering several thousand specimens, we shall find a large number of different types. In this great variety we soon distinguish a triangular arrowhead, of which we possess some examples in iron, a great many in bronze, and a not inconsiderable number in stone and bone, the latter coming from the excavations at the Yang Shao dwelling-site in Honan. We thus have here a type of arrowhead which runs with remarkable tenacity through the whole development of Chinese culture from the Yang Shao period to our own day. To me it is not so much the tenacity of the type that seems to be of importance. The form of these arrowheads strikes me as foreign to the stone raw material and seems to me to point to a fully developed metal technique. If this surmise is correct, we are confronted in our study of these arrowheads with a conclusion of far-reaching consequence. The civilizations of the Near East and Eastern Europe (Tripolje), which, by their painted ceramics remind us most of the Yang Shao culture, are rather to be referred to the Copper age than to the latter part of the New Stone age. There seem to be many reasons for believing that at least in the Near East copper was in use at the time when the Yang Shao culture flourished in China. Certainly this Northern Chinese cultural epoch, with its complete absence of metals, makes, locally considered, a purely Neolithic impression, but it is perhaps permissible to reason that the triangular arrowhead of which we are speaking may have been evolved in the Near East, where metal was already in use, and that the type migrated thence faster than the art of producing metals, so that the Yang Shao people made out of stone a type which had originally developed in the service of a civilization familiar with the use of metals. If this chain of reasoning were unassailable we might be able to fit the Yang Shao culture into the whole chain of Eurasian cultural evolution in a much more positive way. I wish to add, however, that that great expert on the cultures of the Stone age, Professor O. Menghin, expressed the opinion, when he viewed our collection of arrowheads in 1931, that triangular arrowheads of the above-mentioned type most certainly occur even in indubitably Stone age cultures.

Another field of the material culture of the Chinese in which prehistoric features have survived amongst the country population, is that of the textile crafts.

In the Museum of Far Eastern Antiquities we have arranged a textile exhibition which is probably unique of its kind. In the first place we have exhibited the silk rags and pieces of patterned woollen material of the third century A.D. which Sven Hedin brought home from the desert town of Loulan.

In indirect ways we have succeeded in acquiring textiles from much older periods. Thus we have a dagger axe from An Yang in Northern Honan, a splendid weapon with incrustations in turquoise on the part behind the hole for the handle. This example of the Chinese dagger axe is about 3,000 years old. Perhaps more interesting than the weapon itself are the traces of a stuff which covers it almost entirely. Probably the weapon had, before it was placed in the tomb from which it had probably come, been wrapped up in a piece of material, which has been preserved because carbonate of copper penetrated into the stuff and replaced it—with the fortunate result that the structure of the textile has been preserved in beautiful green malachite.

We have in our collections several other Chinese bronze objects, knives, mirrors, etc., covered by such textile remains transformed into carbonate of copper, but the dagger axe from An Yang nevertheless takes the place of honour, both by its great age and by its exquisite state of preservation.

In other ways we have been able to go back yet another couple of thousand years, with the result that we have been able to arrange an exhibition of textile remains from the Yang Shao dwelling sites. A very great part of the coarse unpainted ceramics in these dwelling sites shows a surface which is evidently the result of the vessel having been formed with a mat or piece of stuff as a foundation. We have collected a number of the finest cloth impressions and, with the kind help of Professor Stensiö, we have made positives of them, which have since been photographed. The result of these positives has been, so to speak,

Man spinning with a distaff. Hsi Ning Ho, Kansu

to resurrect weavings of the Yang Shao period, which had mouldered into dust 5,000 years ago.

Whilst working on the Tibetan frontier it sometimes happened that I met little shepherd boys dressed only in a very coarse and ragged shirt. For a few cents I obtained the owner's permission to cut off a small piece of the humble garments, and a few of these bits of shirts are now on view in our exhibition of textiles as material for comparison with the weavings of the Yang Shao period.

In yet another way I succeeded, in the field of the textile crafts, in connecting the present day with the beginnings of Chinese culture in the Yang Shao dwelling-sites. During our excavations we often found spinning whorls of burnt clay and stone (Fig. 77*d*). In Honan and in Kansu I saw the people spin with distaffs of which the whorls were quite like those of the Yang Shao period. One day on my way up to the town of Hsi Ning I photographed a man who stood spinning (Plate 19). (Behind him we see, by the way, one of those strange rafts made of inflated sheepskins, on which the people there cross the turbulent and shallow rivers.)

In this case I proceeded like the modern hunters of big game: first you photograph the tiger and then you shoot it. I had scarcely photographed the man who was spinning, when I bought the distaff of him. It is now on view in our museum, by the side of his photograph. This distaff has a whorl of stone (and I have several other such whorls on modern distaffs) which in no way differs from the stone whorls which we found in the Yang Shao dwelling-sites.

During my journey through the province of Kansu in the summer of 1923, I one day had a strange experience. On the other side of P'ing Liang we arrived in the district that was destroyed by the great earthquake in December 1920. The easily moved loess strata had slipped down the slope like a heavily moving porridge. Whole villages had been swallowed up by the moving masses of earth, and everywhere gaping cracks in the earth bore witness to the violence of the catastrophe. Sometimes we had to lead our horses through the network of earthquake cracks. We had reached a high point in the hilly country.

When we had passed over a ridge I stopped for a moment, fascinated by a, to me, most significant spectacle. In a little valley among the hills lay a small farm which had quite escaped annihilation, and this farm, with its watch-tower in the corner, fascinated me particularly, because it was built on the pattern which was in use 2,000 years ago, to judge by the models of houses which we find in the tombs of the Han dynasty.

This time I was fortunate enough to have my camera handy. But that was not the case on my return from Hsi Ning to Lanchow. Just as I was walking over the plain near the Hsi Ning River, I caught sight—near some houses, but standing quite apart on the flat ground—of an oven of exactly the same type as the ovens of which one finds models in the Han tombs. This

Fig. 104.—Peasant farm in Kansu, reminiscent of the models in the Han graves.

was an oven still in daily use, and we had here, as in the case of the farm up in the mountain valley, an example of a 2,000-year-old survival of very characteristic constructive types. This time I had with me a coolie, who carried my instruments, including my camera. He was far ahead of me and I had to resign myself to the hope that I should find another isolated oven. But I had no such luck.

During our excavations at Yang Shao Tsun, and still more at the Pu Chao Chai site close by, we found strange bluntly pointed bases of some grey ware, with the outside covered with a basket pattern. We never found any even approximately complete vessel of this type, and it was only after long experimenting that the extremely skilful technician of the Lund museum, A. Gräns, succeeded in reconstructing from our fragments a couple of vessels of this type (Plate 20, Fig. *c*).

At Chin Wang Chai in the Ho Yin district, east of Yang Shao Tsun, on the southern bank of the Yellow River, my Chinese servants, Yao and Pai, collected a lot of magnificent fragments of painted Yang Shao vessels. Together with these there were also thin-walled fragments of a brick-red ware without any painting, but with a cord or textile pattern. Pai had, by much careful work, managed to collect all the bits of the lower parts of a vessel which in many respects is the most remarkable within this group. It was extremely thin and had a delicate textile pattern over the whole of the surface. Thanks to this reconstruction we learned that we had here to do with a vessel with a pointed bottom and two perpendicular handles on the broadest part of the vessel. At that time we knew nothing more about the mouth than that we had found a good number of narrow, thick-walled pieces of a mouth of rather strange form, but of exactly the same material as the fragments with the pointed bottom and the textile pattern. To some of these pieces there were still attached bits of the walls of the vessel, with the same textile or cord patterns as on the vessel reconstructed by Pai. From this we could conclude that the pointed bottoms and the narrow mouths belonged together. Pai's reconstruction already pointed to the fact that there had been a broader shoulder above the waist of the vessel, and this was fully proved by the skilful reconstruction made by Gräns (Plate 20, Fig. *b*). We are here concerned with one of the largest, and in many respects most remarkable, clay vessels among our prehistoric finds : a vessel with a sharply pointed bottom, with a height of 960 mm. and a thickness of the wall of only 5 mm. How such brittle vessels could have been used is an enigma to me, but on the other hand it is very probable, in the first place, that they were used as water-jars, and further that their strange shape betrays that they are probably copies of water-bags made of sheepskin or some similar animal skin. These slender vessels, with their pointed bottoms, present a good many still unsolved problems : how were they carried, with their handles so far down on the lower part, and how were they kept ?—in holes in the ground or in specially constructed racks ?

Even these vessels with pointed bottoms have survived to our day. One day in May 1921 during a boat trip on the Yellow River on the frontier between the provinces of Honan and Shansi,

I caught sight of a small vessel with a pointed bottom which hung fastened to the mast and which contained oil (Fig. 105, *c*).

When once my interest in these vessels with pointed bottoms had been aroused, I noticed that in Peking people sold lemonade in glass bottles with pointed bottoms (Fig. 105, *a*). In this case I do not pretend that it is necessarily a survival from olden days. The pointed bottom of the lemonade bottle may be explained by the fact that some cunning business man realized that the customer must finish the contents at one time if the bottle had

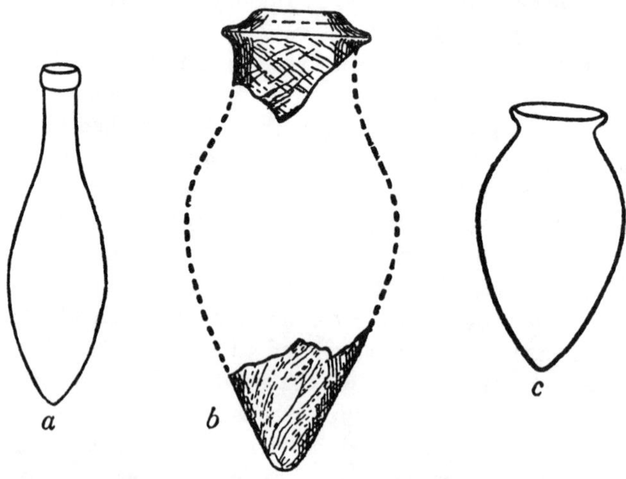

FIG. 105.—Pointed-bottom vessels: *a*, modern lemonade glass bottle; *b*, clay vessel from the Yang Shao dwelling site; *c*, modern clay vessel found on a boat on the Yellow River.

this shape, and must buy a new bottle next time he became thirsty.

The reader will perhaps recollect that when we described the vessels with pointed bottoms we began with a type of the Yang Shao period with a wide bottom and made of grey ware (Plate 20, Fig. *a*). It is possible, not to say probable, that this type gives us the explanation of one of the most wonderful vessels of Chinese ceramic art, the Li-tripod, with bulged, hollow legs. If we compare the pointed vessel with the Li-tripod (Plate 21, Fig. *a*) it certainly seems probable that the tripod has been created by joining together three vessels with pointed bottoms with a com-

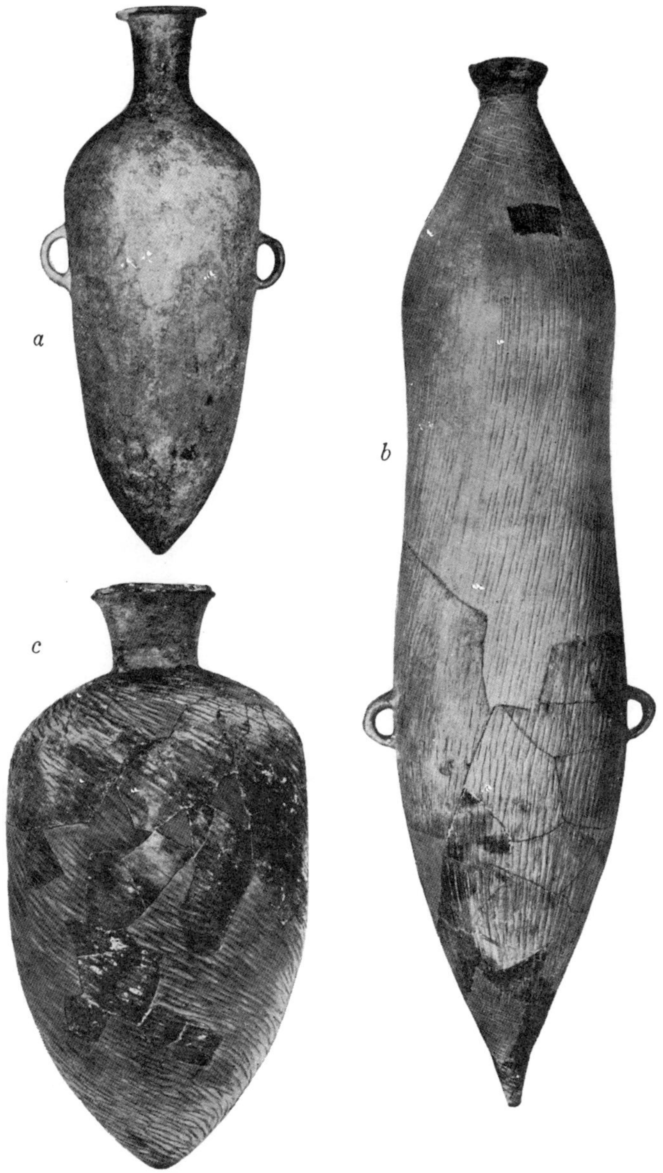

Pointed bottom vessels. Yang Shao civilization

mon collar. It must always have been a standing problem for the ancient families at Yang Shao Tsun to place their pointed vessels so that they would not fall over. The man who discovered the idea of joining three vessels into one solved that difficulty for all time. But at the same time he made a still greater discovery. When it was a question of using the clay vessels as cooking utensils the low conductive power of the pottery must always have presented a difficulty. This inconvenience was to a great extent overcome by the new construction, which made it possible to cook in the legs and to put fuel between them. If to this we add the fact that the surface was enlarged by being made rough through the carpet pattern, we may with some justice say that the discoverer of the Li-tripod would have deserved

FIG. 106.—Archaic characters for vessels with pointed bottom, from inscriptions upon oracle bones (end of second millennium B.C.) and bronzes (first millennium B.C.). (*After Karlgren.*)

a Nobel prize in physics if he had not lived 5,000 years too early for such a distinction.

The Li-tripod is, with its complicated and fantastic form, perhaps more than anything else among the household utensils of the Chinese, a symbol of their whole cultural development. We meet it in numerous forms as early as the Yang Shao deposits. Indeed, I think we may say that the type then reached its highest point of development. But it survives through the ages. In the older Bronze age it assumed a significant form, as the legs were then formed like a cow's udders, and thus evidently belong to the fertility magic of agriculture, which seems to be such a strong motive in the Chinese Bronze age.

In the finds from Chên Fan the Li-tripod culminates in gigantic pieces, so large that a young antelope might have been cooked in one leg, a goose in another and the vegetables in the third.

In the Yang Shao dwelling-sites at Honan we made acquaintance with an interesting variety of the Li-tripod. It has in its mouth a broad turned-in brim, which forms a sort of platform on which evidently another vessel was placed. We had no need to speculate as to what this upper vessel was like, because we found in the same excavation site an almost cylindrical vessel slightly contracted at the base with large filter holes in the bottom. Since at least one specimen of this type of vessel was covered on the bottom with a thick layer of " fur ", the problem was at once clear : here we had the vessel that was placed on the Li-tripod, and the whole was an exquisite steaming apparatus of the Stone age. In the tripod steam was produced, which rose through the perforations of the upper vessel and converted the vegetables placed in the sieve-like vessel into well-cooked dishes.

This type of two-storied vessel survived in the Chinese Bronze age. It is called by the Chinese antiquaries Hsien, and the old sources testify that this double vessel was used for steaming, even though it subsequently became a sacred temple or burial vessel.

There is, however, among the Yang Shao ceramics yet another type of tripod, i.e. the Ting-tripod, which in its simplest form is a large hemispherical bowl on three cylindrical legs (Plate 21, Fig. *b*). In all probability this is a very early invention in human history, which was made in two stages. First of all a clay vessel was placed over three stones and then the stones were replaced by lumps of clay.

The Ting-tripod also survives through the ages until the present day. The small brass tripods which one buys for a few cents in the temple markets in Peking, and which are used as ashcups, almost exactly resemble the clay tripods of the Kansu graves of the earlier Bronze age.

In reaching this tripod type with its bowl-shaped body and thin solid legs, we encounter one of the great commonplaces of mankind. Such a simple discovery did not require the fertile brain of the Chinese. The three-legged iron cooking vessels of our old Swedish peasant huts were of the same universal type as we find among widely separated peoples.

But the wonderful Li-tripod is the peculiar possession of the Chinese alone ; the fact that it flourished in the Yang Shao civiliza-

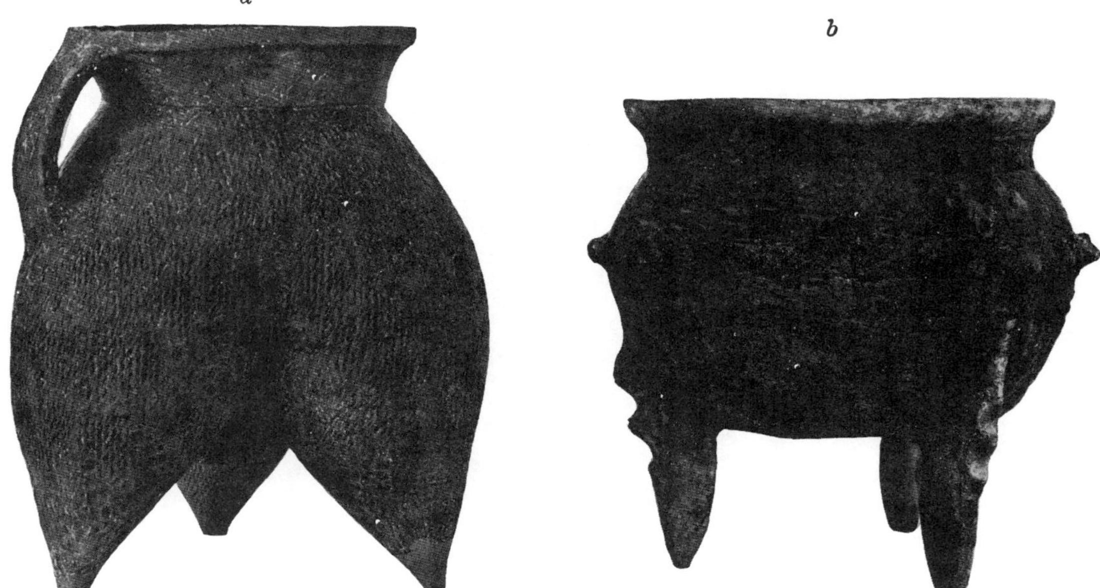

a *b*

Tripods. Yang Shao civilization

[*face page* 222

tion gives us some idea of the perfection and refinement which the Chinese race even in prehistoric times were able to impart to their material life.

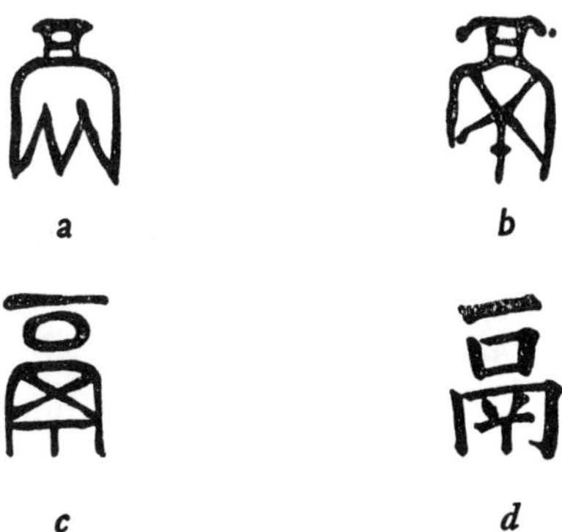

FIG. 107.—Development of written character li, *a*, an archaic form, a pictograph of the Li-tripod; *b*, *c*, transition forms to *d*, the modern character.

FIG. 108.—Camp on the northern banks of Kokonor.

CHAPTER THIRTEEN

WE FOLLOW THE YANG SHAO PEOPLE TO KOKONOR

IT was my intention that my journey in Shantung in the month of December 1921, when we discovered the dinosaur formations, should be my last in Eastern China.

We had now completed the excavation of the *Hipparion* fauna, and my palaeontological collaborator, Dr. Otto Zdansky, had undertaken to continue the work in Shantung, as well as the excavation of the cave at Chou K'ou Tien, near Peking.

Our archaeological work in Eastern China had also come to an end. It was evident to me, of course, that generations of archaeologists would be fully occupied with the prehistoric dwelling sites of eastern China before the latter were fully examined. But the whole of my archaeological work was of a pioneering character, and by the end of 1922 I had obtained such immense collections from Honan, that it scarcely seemed necessary to continue any field-work until the material already collected had been investigated and described.

On the other hand, I was tempted by another great field enterprise before I shut myself up for long and detailed laboratory work. The painted ceramics which we found at Yang Shao Tsun and other dwelling-sites in Honan resembled so strikingly the prehistoric ceramics of Anau in Russian Turkestan and the Tripolje ceramics of Southern Russia, that it was very tempting to seek a connection between these different discoveries extending right across the interior of Asia. On the assumption that the prehistoric migrations of the peoples had brought these painted ceramics from Eastern Europe to China it is not difficult to calculate approximately the point at which this migration encountered the valley of the Yellow River. Everything seems to indicate that the " pass " between Tien Shan and the Altai mountains was the route by which the tides of migration surged eastwards into the Mongolian basin. In that region the movements of the peoples probably avoided the central and almost sterile desert regions and followed the grassy steppes which surround the desert. Under these circumstances a migration route to the south-east passed along the foot of the Nan Shan mountains, just in the same way as the great route to Central Asia is to be found there at the present day. A migration, or, to express ourselves more cautiously, an exchange of cultures, which was effected along the Nan Shan mountains over the pastures of the mountain slopes, should cross the Yellow River approximately at Lanchow, the capital of the modern province of Kansu.

This was the working hypothesis upon which was based my journey to Kansu in the spring of 1923.

The traveller who wishes to penetrate from the eastern provinces to the most north-westerly corner of China proper may choose one of two routes : the northerly route by rail, via Kalgan, to the west, to Paoto, and then along the Yellow River to Ninghsia and Lanchow ; the other from Honan, of which at the time of my departure Kuanyintang was the western railway terminus. From this point one travels by cart through Western Honan to Tung Kuan, the frontier fortress of the province of Shensi, and then on to Sianfu, Pingliang, and Lanchow. This route traverses the greatest loess areas of China, the provinces of Shensi and Kansu. It was just these loess plateaus which enticed me, for my experiences in Honan had led me to the belief that the Yang Shao civilization was bound up with the loess regions.

In actual fact I had knowledge at the outset of a prehistoric dwelling on the route which we were to follow. When my collector Chang accompanied Dr. Zdansky in 1922 to Ching Yang Fu in eastern Kansu to look for *Hipparion* finds, he had found, 6 km. east of Sianfu, the ancient capital of Shensi, a prehistoric dwelling-site, in many respects resembling those which we had previously investigated in Honan.

When we approached Sianfu we seized the opportunity of examining, as rapidly as possible, this site, which is on the margin of a loess plateau, with an open view over a river valley leading down to the Wei River. Our finds in this locality were quite insignificant, but everything seemed to indicate that there were here no painted ceramics, exactly as in the case of the fruitful discoveries in the dwellings at Pu Chao Chai, some miles west of Yang Shao Tsun. It is a minor peculiarity of Shih Li P'o (which means simply " the village situated 10 li from the town ") that all the small awls, which are otherwise usually made of bone, were here made of stone.

Whilst we were slowly conveyed in our heavy carts along the great main road which leads from Sianfu across country to Lanchow, we were constantly on the look-out for fragments of vessels in the walls of the loess ravines. But all that we found belonged to historical times. We arrived on June 21st at Lanchow without having seen, beyond Sianfu, a single trace of prehistoric remains.

My next objective was the Blue Lake, Kokonor, the great salt lake in North-Western Tibet, not far from the Yellow River. I wished to study nature around this great inland lake and seek for traces of prehistoric men along its shores.

The entrance gate to Kokonor from Chinese territory is the town of Hsi Ning on the river of the same name. In order to reach it from Lanchow one can choose either of two routes, either the great main road, on which one can travel by cart, or the smaller road along the slopes of the river valley, which offers many adventures. I chose the latter, because I expected that the deeply eroded river valleys would afford good opportunities for studying the geological structure of the country. This expectation was fulfilled beyond my wildest hopes.

The river landscape between Lanchow and Hsi Ning is very varied and picturesque. At first one follows the southern bank of the Yellow River, then crosses to the northern bank, just where the Hsi Ning Ho runs into the Yellow River, and then follows the Hsi Ning Ho upstream. This river trip was full of amusing episodes. A German explorer, Filchner, has described one point, the Tiger Cliff, as simply dangerous to life to pass. I arrived at Hsi Ning without noticing any special danger and found that at low water I could quite comfortably walk round the foot of this dangerous cliff. On the return journey we took the fairly broad ledge which winds round the top portion of the cliff, and there too I was confirmed in my view that Filchner's description was in many respects unnecessarily sensational.

Much more romantic was the long series of caves which we found dug in the almost perpendicular walls of the variegated and ever-changing clay mountains which for long stretches flank the road to Hsi Ning. During the last Mohammedan rising, about forty years ago, the terrified Chinese peasants dug out these caves and transported thither their families and movable property. These caves, to which they had to lower themselves by ropes, or climb up by frail ladders, could be defended by a mere handful of men, and here some of the Chinese held out until relief troops arrived from the coast and the fortune of war turned to a campaign of extermination against the Mohammedans.

About 12 miles below Hsi Ning we passed " The Temple of the White Horse ", Pai Ma Ssŭ, a small, picturesque temple on the cliffs situated in the centre of the perpendicular face of a red clay mountain. A little higher up we wandered from the left side of the river to the right side, over a wooden bridge of a peculiar and ingenious construction.

We were only 6 kilometres from Hsi Ning when the great event happened. At the beginning of our journey, down in Honan, I had promised 50 to 100 dollars to the first man who made a prehistoric discovery. Until this point we had found nothing from the time we left Shih Li P'o, 10 li before Sianfu. Here we found another lucky Shih Li P'o, with the distance reckoned this time from Hsi Ning. The discovery was made by my cook, Chuang, a wide-awake fellow, who saw some fragments of vessels and promptly jumped off his horse. Soon we were all busy searching the wall of the roadside ravine, and it was not long before one of us drew forth a painted fragment from the ashes of this cultural deposit. It was the greatest event of the whole of our outward journey. By his discovery Chuang had in a trice shifted the boundary of the Yang Shao civilization from Honan to the neighbourhood of the Tibetan frontier.

We rode first to Hsi Ning and reported to the local authorities. Then we returned to Shih Li P'o and excavated for a week. We then found, in addition to stone and bone implements and coarsely painted vessels, numerous fragments of typical Yang Shao ware, as well as fragments of very large, thick-walled vessels painted with vigorous patterns. This latter group is probably somewhat later than the other discoveries.

On July 21st we had for the moment finished with the Hsi Ning district and broke up to proceed to the west to our immediate objective, the little town of Tangar. Tangar is the last Chinese outpost towards Tibetan territory, and we there completed our purchases and engaged a Chinaman called Li as our Tibetan interpreter. On July 25th we left Tangar and followed the course of the Hsi Ning Ho. By evening we had reached the last Chinese settlements and pitched our tents between some mountain knolls on pure Tibetan territory. The next day we crossed a low pass which led to the Kokonor basin, and here we pitched our tents beside a little stream which ran down to the immense sand-dunes which fringe the eastern part of Kokonor.

The weather, which had been misty and showery, cleared up towards evening, and at sunset we obtained our first view of the overwhelmingly beautiful Blue Lake, whose clear salt water seemed incredibly deep blue as it lay embedded in the fresh green slopes, the blinding yellow sand-dunes, and the dark mountains.

On July 28th we left our first camp at Kokonor in order to begin our projected journey round the lake. In the morning we already had a glimpse of the principal big game of the Kokonor area, the wild ass or Kiang, called Yeh Ma by the Chinese. To call this animal a wild ass is somewhat misleading, for it is very much larger, reminding us rather of a large mule. Neither is it really a wild horse, for its head is undeniably asinine.

We shot two kiangs on that day, a stallion and an older mare, intended for the Riksmuseum collections. We might easily have shot many more, as their curiosity exceeds their shyness, but when we had procured our two specimens I gave orders that the herds grazing along our route were not to be disturbed. In this way I had a unique opportunity during the following days of studying these interesting animals, which to my mind suggested prehistoric times when the Palaeolithic savage hunted on the plains of western Europe in districts as undisturbed as this. One day we saw around us more than 400 kiangs grazing in flocks, or slowly moving across the steppe. When I saw these animals silhouetted against the horizon I really understood for the first time the familiar contour pictures of herds of horses, drawn in rows, head to head, which we discover in the remarkably realistic artistic creations of Palaeolithic man.

At our third camp we made our first archaeological discovery at Kokonor, on July 30th. Away to the north, at the foot of the mountains, were visible some light patches, and through my Zeiss glasses I saw that they were sand-dunes beneath which prehistoric remains might be buried. I took one of my two soldiers and rode off to the sand-dunes.

It was not long before I found prehistoric artifacts. My soldier was a short distance away. I lay on the ground picking up chips of flint. As I turned round I saw a wolf sniffing close behind me. I had no time to rush off for my gun, but seized the first convenient stone and hurled it at the creature, which slunk away like a dazed, shamefaced dog.

FIG. 109.—" The Pillar ", the last remains of a Stone age deposit, in which we found painted fragments of jars and bone knives.

I now directed my attention to a detached pillar, 1·64 metres high and 3·7 metres broad, consisting of an old, now almost destroyed, formation of drifted sand (Fig. 109). In this little remnant of erosion I made useful discoveries, but just as things looked most promising it began to pour with rain and the soldier came and grumbled and wanted to return home. I told him I intended to remain and that he would have to do the same. Then he also began digging among the dark cultural remains and soon drew forth a painted fragment of a jar, which was of the utmost importance to me, as it was genuine Yang Shao and thus immediately settled the date of the deposit. I was naturally overjoyed, and took a bright dollar out of my pocket and gave it to the soldier. He looked doubtful and wondered if it was really the intention of Anlaoyeh to give a whole dollar for a bit of jar. When he had the dollar in his pocket, his joy knew no bounds, and the following morning everybody in the camp wanted to accompany me to the spot. I now took Liu with me and we dug out the whole pillar. Our best find was a bone knife with a notch on the edge, evidently for securing chips of flint, which formed the cutting edge. The same autumn we found a perfect knife of this kind, with the flints still in position, at Chu Chia Chai.

The main result of our investigations on this site was the discovery of typical painted Yang Shao ceramics, which showed that the enterprising people of the later Stone age had penetrated into these icy districts. One of the attractions had been, no doubt, the abundance of game, but the large number of flints which we found among the dunes may possibly indicate that this district was the source of flints, which are rare in China, but were highly esteemed by the peoples of the Stone age.

We now continued our journey round Kokonor and found in numerous places pieces of jars of a prehistoric type.

After a very adventurous crossing of the many branches of the river, swollen by heavy rainstorms, which runs into the extreme westerly part of the lake, we arrived at the southern shore. Here the mountains came close down to the shore and on the narrow strip of plain we saw several Tibetan camps, whose fierce dogs were a constant source of annoyance. We also met several herds of cattle which the Tibetans were driving from their summer pastures in the mountains to the plains around Kokonor.

From the time of my arrival at Kokonor I had naturally been keenly interested in the question of the water level of this great salt lake in earlier ages. So far as I could find, the lowest pass of the district is just on the route by which we had come from the valley of the Hsi Ning Ho to the Kokonor basin. On the whole of the northern shore of the lake I only found in one place—at the Kara Nor lagoon—traces of a higher water level. Here one finds small cobblestones to a height of about 10 metres above the lake level. Yet I did not find any real raised beach, and it is not entirely impossible that these cobblestones are due to descending streams rather than to the waves of the lake.

On the southern shore of Kokonor we followed for long stretches a shore wall of which the height was 3·3 metres above the level of the lake.

At the eastern end of Kokonor I found very interesting conditions, which require more detailed description.

The most easterly part of the lake is cut off by a strong lagoon wall. A river flowing from the east runs into the lagoon, and the country about the lowest reach of the river is full of small lakes with extraordinarily abundant bird life, which must have been a strong attraction to travellers to Kokonor in the Stone age. The inner boundary of the lagoon is the old shore wall, of which the extreme south-westerly portion will now be described in further detail.

FIG. 110.—Tibetans on the southern shore of Kokonor.

The shore gravel reaches a maximum height of 6 metres above the surface of Kokonor. On the southern part of the most westerly shore wall there is a place, square in shape, enclosed by an earthen bank and with sides about 150 metres long.

The eastern end of the wall is of special interest to our work. It is crowned by a horseshoe-shaped, closed, earthen wall with small cairns in four places. Within the space surrounded by the wall is a little circular wall of stone. Outside the western part of the embankment two piles of stones rise up, which may conceivably be graves. Near to them, and close to the northern edge of the shore embankment, is a group of roof tiles and burnt bricks of the usual Chinese type.

All the above-described remains of human activity are certainly quite recent. At a guess I should imagine that the horseshoe wall is of a somewhat earlier date and that the square " town wall ", as well as the heap of bricks outside the horseshoe, are evidence of the latest settlements.

But there exists also an older and much more important deposit, which we discovered under the horseshoe wall, on the northern side of the shore embankment, facing the lake. At two levels, one at 6 metres and the other at 7·2, we found dark cultural soil, in which we encountered unpainted fragments of jars, splintered bones, a couple of bone implements and the larger portion of a staghorn axe. Since we did not find in this place any fragments of the painted Yang Shao ceramics, it cannot be directly proved that these cultural deposits belong to the Yang Shao age, but there is nothing in the composition of the material discovered which contradicts such an assumption, and in any case we can safely designate these finds as prehistoric.

Thus if we assume that the cultural deposit on the shore embankment at the eastern end of Kokonor is at least three to four thousand years old, we are inevitably led to an extremely important conclusion, namely that the water level of Kokonor during the last three or four thousand years has never exceeded a maximum of 6 metres above the present level.

Nobody who has seen the surf on the shores of Kokonor, when the water is blown up by the swiftly rising local storms, can doubt for a moment that the prehistoric cultural deposits on the slope of the shore facing the lake would have been washed away if during thousands of years the waves had reached their level.

Observations in the Caspian Sea and in Chinese Turkestan seem to show that the great salt lakes in the interior of Asia have undergone great changes of level. As against these observations we are now able to place our own incontrovertible observation at Kokonor, which indicates that this great salt lake has for thousands of years been completely stationary.

As a guide to those who may in the future study the changes of the level of Kokonor I would mention that in the valley which leads down to the lake from the east I saw terrace formations high above the water level of Kokonor. But with the extensive experience which I possess of similar terraces in other places in Northern China, I believe I may draw the conclusion, with a high degree of accuracy, that these valley terraces, which are a good distance from

Kokonor, have no relation to the lake, but are river terraces of the same kind as we have already described in the chapter on " The Face of the Earthly Giant ", in the Chai T'ang valley, near Peking, and in Kuei Te in the valley of the Yellow River, not far from Kokonor.

FIG. 111.—The site of prehistoric discoveries at the eastern end of Kokonor.

Let us now sum up the results of two weeks' work at Kokonor concerning the prehistory of this lake basin :

1. In several places round about Kokonor we found fragments of jars of a prehistoric type.
2. On the northern side of the lake we found in a sand-dune district masses of flints, a bone knife of the Yang Shao type, and typical, painted Yang Shao ceramics.
3. At the eastern end of the lake we found in the old shore embankment, at a height of 6–7 metres above the present water level, dark cultural soil containing fragments of jars, bone implements and a staghorn axe. Since, to judge from all appearances, this cultural deposit is also prehistoric, we may conclude that the surface of Kokonor has never during three to four thousand years reached more than 6 metres above its present level.

These diffuse observations during a hasty reconnaissance are not sufficient to do more than to stimulate somebody who may be willing to take the trouble to inquire more exhaustively into the history of the Blue Lake and of the ancient dwellers on its shores.

FIG. 112.—The old madman and his companions.

CHAPTER FOURTEEN

THE GIFT OF THE OLD MADMAN

ON August 21st we departed eastwards over undulating steppes and low mountain ridges.

The interpreter Li took us by mistake too far south, but after the loss of a day we regained the road to Kuei Te. The detour to the south had given us as early as the morning of the 13th a wonderful view of the Yellow River about Kuei Te, a river panorama of over 60 miles in length and of the rarest beauty in the clear morning light.

The next day the bright sunshine glistened over the steppe, a herd of antelopes was in movement to the north and the Tibetans were tending their herds of sheep and cattle. Round about us was the charm of the wide, open steppe. Only in the far south a dark streak showed us where we might find the Yellow River.

But before noon the steppe came to a sudden, almost alarming end. We arrived at the brink of an abyss, 1,000 metres deep, and looked down on a new world, with narrow streaks of sunlit land and between them new abysses with deep umbrae, a boundless confusion of deep, narrow valleys and ridges, with walls which gleamed bright red and blue-green in horizontal, multi-coloured strata, and isolated plateaus which had evidently at one time formed a part of the unbroken steppe behind us.

I was well prepared for this sudden change in the type of

landscape by the excellent description of the Hungarian geologist Lozcy, but nevertheless this river landscape unveiled itself to my gaze with overwhelming magnificence. Lozcy has compared this valley landscape of the Yellow River at Kuei Te with the famous Grand Canyon in North America, and the resemblance is indeed striking. The frequently horizontal stratification, the architectonic structure of the ravines and of the buttresses of the canyon cliffs are all the same as in the Grand Canyon, and even as regards dimensions the canyon of the Kuei Te district is most imposing, for the difference of altitude between the surrounding plateau and the surface of the Yellow River deep down below amounts to almost a thousand metres.

We now advanced steeply, at times along narrow zig-zag paths, on which the pack mules had difficulty in finding a secure foothold in the sticky, salt-impregnated Tertiary clay. Far down in the valley we glimpsed a copse of trees and a valley terrace with cultivated fields. At three o'clock in the afternoon we had reached them and pitched our camp under the most idyllic conditions which have ever fallen to my lot during my eleven years in China.

Our camp lay at the foot of a 20-metre high terrace cliff in a grove of big leaf trees, between which a stream purled its way in many small branches. It was a delightful change after the recent weeks on the bare Kokonor steppes, but it was a dangerous place if we should get into trouble with the people of the village situated on the terrace above us. A few sharpshooters on the edge of the terrace would soon have rendered the place untenable for us.

This village, of which the Chinese name is Lo Han T'ang, is inhabited by settled agricultural Tibetans who are under Chinese jurisdiction, a circumstance which subsequently saved the situation for us, as we shall soon see. These Tibetan peasants had fine well-built houses and extensive cultivated fields, all situated, like the village, on a valley terrace which is shut in between the high, precipitous walls of the ravine.

We had scarcely pitched camp in this idyllic spot before one of my collectors, Chen, came and reported that up on the edge of the terrace, right over our camp, he had found traces of a prehistoric dwelling-site. Soon we were all busily engaged in digging in the gravel in order to find the fragments of jars, stone axes and bone implements left behind by the people who had inhabited this place 5,000 years ago.

The peasants from the village came down to the scene of our operations and there was lively discussion of our work. It was easy to see that our operations awakened their misgivings, which seemed to me perhaps natural, since these people are extremely superstitious and imagine that practically every stone and every tree is guarded by spirits who can avenge themselves on anybody who does anything to disturb them.

Among the men I noticed especially a little old man who talked eagerly with my interpreter Li, whilst at the same time pointing to the west with lively gestures. I took Li aside and questioned him concerning the old man. Li then told me an interesting story. The old man maintained that on the other side of the valley there was another place, only 2 km. distant from our camp, where we could find the prehistoric remains of which we were in search, and that there were far more large and finely painted fragments of jars and whole stone axes than there were where we were working.

I made Li fetch the old man and question him further concerning the new place. Whilst we sat talking with him several Tibetans came to us and began a loud and excited conversation with Li and the old man.

" They say that the old man is mad and is only talking nonsense," said Li to me. A couple of powerful fellows took the old man in their arms and carried him off into the village ; so there was no more talk about this mysterious story that evening.

But when I lay in my tent late at night and listened to the purling of the stream and the crunching of their night fodder by our pack animals, I could not help reflecting on the day's experiences. It seemed to me that this Tibetan village held great possibilities in store for us, both good and bad. The people evidently did not like our excavating, though there might be some truth in the old man's fantasies.

The following morning I had a private talk with Chen and ordered him very quietly to make investigations on the other side of the valley in the direction indicated by the old man.

Two days later Chen arrived, beaming with joy, with a collection of Stone age objects far finer than any we had yet found elsewhere in Kansu, and found in a position exactly corresponding with that indicated by the loquacious old man. The following morning I moved with the whole of our staff to this splendid new site, but I took care that our two soldiers kept guard over our camp, which lay in such an uncomfortably vulnerable position right under the terrace cliff, beneath the large Tibetan village.

That my suspicions were not unfounded appeared some days later when on returning home in the evening I received very disturbing reports from the soldiers : one of their horses had disappeared in the course of the day and one of our mules had received a nasty knife blow on the mouth.

There could be scarcely any doubt left that the village population wished to get rid of us by tactics which might best be described as sabotage, and it was evident that some energetic steps must be taken if we wished to remain on the spot without too much risk.

I held a council of war in my tent that evening together with the interpreter Li and my Peking boys, and when we broke up our plan of campaign was clear. In order that the effect of our measures may be understood I must preface some explanations.

This Tibetan village was in a Chinese district and was organized entirely on a Chinese model. Thus there was, as in all Chinese villages, a local official, a sort of magistrate, who, according to Chinese custom, is personally responsible for everything that happens within the boundaries of the village. It was on this circumstance that in substance I conceived my plan of action.

Another thing which should be mentioned is that I had obtained my two soldiers from the Mohammedan general Ma in Hsi Ning. Shortly before my departure he had undertaken a major punitive expedition against the defiant Tibetans around the great and famous temple of Labrang, and the manner in which the Mohammedan soldiers had advanced through the country had filled the Tibetans with terror far beyond the district into which the punitive expedition had advanced.

Let us now see, after these introductory explanations, how we settled up with the Tibetan villagers of Lo Han T'ang.

At six in the morning I sent Li, accompanied by the two soldiers, to the house of the Headman, with the message that I wished to call on him, and with orders to the soldiers to mount guard in his house and to see that he did not leave it before my arrival. This arrangement saved me the trouble of going there and finding the bird flown, whilst at the same time announcing to the whole village the demonstration which I had decided to make.

As soon as Li returned with the news that the Headman was at home and awaited me, I set out with my main forces, consisting of all my servants, except two men who were left behind to guard the camp.

We saddled all the horses and other hacks which were in any way presentable, and rode off, with all our weapons visible, slowly and with the utmost possible dignity, through the village street up to the Headman's door.

Here we were received with all the ceremony we could desire, and I and my men and my soldiers were conducted into a garden where a resting place had been prepared for me.

My own people on one side, and the villagers, of whom many were present, on the other, were ranged up in a semicircle around me, and then the negotiations began, with Li as an intermediary.

" I have come here as a Chinese official from Peking and I have not only the best recommendations and a passport from the central government in Peking, but also the special protection of the military governor in Lanchow and of General Ma in Hsi Ning, who has given me two soldiers as an escort."

I then took out my great passport, which was written in three languages—Chinese, Mongolian and Tibetan. One of my men read out the Chinese text, which, phrase by phrase, was translated by Li, and afterwards we called in a priest from a neighbouring temple to read the Tibetan text, so that the old fellows should clearly understand that the sense of the two texts was the same.

I now asked the Headman whether or not he realized that my papers were in order and that I was consequently fully entitled to his assistance and protection.

He made a profound bow and his assenting reply sounded quite Swedish, a repeated monotone,

" Ya, Ya, Ya ! "

" Well," I said, " You have nevertheless allowed this soldier's horse to be stolen and a mule to be badly slashed on the mouth."

" It is certainly nobody in the village who has done it, but some traveller walking along the road below the terrace cliff," the Headman answered.

" Is not our camp within the bounds of this village ? And don't you know that you as Headman are personally responsible for everything that happens there ? "

" Ya—Ya—Ya," answered the Headman with another bow.

" Well then, you and all your villagers assembled must hear what I demand of you as compensation for the damage done to us by your village. Before six o'clock this evening the stolen horse must be returned to our camp, together with 10 dollars as damages for the slash on the mule's mouth. If this is not done before six o'clock I shall send one of my soldiers to Hsi Ning to report that the horse, which belongs to General Ma, has been stolen in this village, and in less than a week you will find many soldiers here and your village will fare in the same way as did the temple at Labrang. Do you understand ? "

" Ya—Ya—Ya," mumbled the old man, and bowed several times at the thought of Ma's expedition to Labrang.

Then we went out in procession to the street, receiving many manifestations of politeness from the Tibetans. We mounted our proud steeds and rode back to our camp, with the same calm dignity as when we came.

We waited the whole day in tense excitement to see how the Tibetans would take my demands, but late in the afternoon one man arrived with the horse and another with 10 dollars, and finally the Headman himself arrived with some old men to pay a return visit and to ask if I were satisfied, which I declared I was, on condition that they did not play any more silly tricks.

After a week of peaceful and undisturbed work we left this idyllic camp and moved down to the district town of Kuei Te, in the neighbourhood of which we made some discoveries both of fossil mammals and prehistoric dwellings.

But on August 28th we were back at the " old madman's " site. This time I wanted to be safer and more independent of the village folk, so we pitched our camp right opposite the site on a somewhat raised part of the completely dried-up river bank. This new camp was situated within the edge of a small stream ravine, which, however, brought down such evil-smelling alkaline water that we were compelled to fetch our supplies from the large stream near our first camp. But we were all pleased to have our work so near our camp. In case the village folk should again become troublesome we were near to our belongings and our weapons and, best of all, had an open range to use the latter.

Nothing happened to us in our new camp except a small tragi-comic episode, in which we were rather the aggressors.

On setting out for Kokonor I had bought in Tangar a rough, dirty dog for 3 dollars. It was a big, strong and splendid watch-dog and under the care of my men he acquired, after some weeks, a most magnificent silky coat. There was something remarkable in the beauty of that dog which fascinated not only us but also all the amatory lady dogs, wherever we came. Our own dog was tied up at nights and dutifully barked as soon as anything moved in the vicinity of the camp. As bad luck would have it, a bitch from the neighbouring village had become enamoured of him. If the dog community had only agreed to conduct their night love affairs quietly, nothing would have happened, but the bitch never ventured to advance, and instead roved round the camp howling, whilst our dog stood and barked throughout the night. We were all furious, tired as we were, at being deprived of our just sleep. I sent a message to the village to tell them to keep their bitch at home. But nevertheless the duet in the abyss went on night after night.

Then one night all was quiet and the howling lady dog was heard no more.

A whole week of delightfully peaceful nights passed. But one morning as I was wandering about with my drawing-board in order to survey the environs of the dwelling place, I smelt in one of the small ravines near the camp the nauseating smell of a corpse. I looked down, and, woe is me ! there lay the bitch, already putrefying. It was immediately clear to me that one of my men had secretly kept a look-out and settled accounts with the night disturber of the peace. Fortunately the people of the village never made the reprisals which I feared. On September 10th my maps were completed and by extensive excavations we had collected such a wealth of material that I considered I might definitely turn my back on this splendid site, Lo Han T'ang.

The Lo Han T'ang dwelling-place is situated on an island

The Lo Han T'ang Dwelling Site

[*face page 240*

remnant of the Ma Lan terrace, 85 metres in a SW.–NE., and 65 metres in a NW.–SE. direction (Plate 22). This island portion of the terrace is irregular and lobed. Towards the valley it drops almost perpendicularly for 31 metres, and the lower part of the cliff consists as to two-thirds of the variegated Tertiary clays of the Kuei Te series, whilst the remaining third is gravel and loess-like material.

From the south-western cliff, which rises to a height of some hundred metres, there stretches a flat gravel cone down to the site of our discovery, but this boulder-strewn slope is separated from it by ravines, with the result that the site looks like an island entirely detached and cut away. One can see quite clearly that this topography existed even when the people of the Stone age settled here, and it is evident that they selected just this place because the small island plateau with its ravine sides constituted a natural fortress which could easily be defended against an attacking enemy below.

The cultural deposits are in most places very thin and reach, in places, a maximum of one metre. During our excavations we made a unique find here, namely the bottoms of two ovens in which the Stone age people probably burned their clay vessels. The larger of these was somewhat more than one metre in section. At the bottom lay a bed of flat rubble stones 10 to 20 cm. in section. Of the walls there remained only small fragments of the base with a maximum height of 22 cm. The walls and the bottom, over the bed of rubble, were formed of layers of clay, which were burned red-brown to a depth of 7–11 cm. Both the base and the walls consist in fact of several layers, and it looked as if from time to time the oven had been repaired by smearing a new layer of clay on the inside.

On the evidence of the painted ceramics, of which we collected a considerable number of fine fragments, I was immediately able to designate the dwelling-place as approximately contemporaneous with the Yang Shao Tsun dwelling-site in Honan. Here, however, one finds, together with the painted fragments, another group which reminds us strongly of the ceramics in the Ch'i Chia P'ing dwelling-site discovered by us in the summer of 1924, and described in Chapter XVI. The latter place, containing almost exclusively unpainted, but otherwise extremely fine ceramics, I consider the oldest of the late Neolithic sites which I discovered in Kansu. Since the Lo Han T'ang dwelling-site contains numerous remains of the Ch'i Chia period we may rightly designate it as *early Yang Shao*.

The bone implements from this site are in part very fine: pins, exceptionally well-shaped awls and bone knives, whose cutting edge consists of flint-like chips secured in a notch in the bone shaft. The stone objects are sometimes peculiar and interesting. In addition to the usual symmetrical long axes and the asymmetrical adzes and chisels we note certain types known only from this site. The usual rectangular knives here receive an additional decoration, in so far as their sides swell out at an angle (Fig. 113) and are often indented at the edge. Another peculiarity of this site is that stone bracelets, which are usually narrow, in certain cases are as broad as a loose cuff and are, in addition, made of white marble.

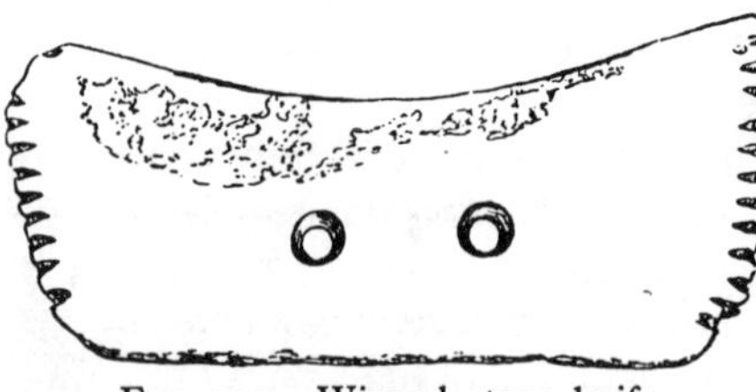

FIG. 113.—Winged stone knife.

A peculiar feature of this site is to be found in the flat, circular, roughly hewn stone discs, 10–12 cm. in section and 3–5 cm. thick. What the purpose of these roughly formed discs was, I do not know. Dr. E. Dahr, who has examined the bone fragments which we discovered, has given very interesting reports on the bones found at Lo Han T'ang. He points out that as regards the fauna of this place the composition differs from that of other dwelling-sites in Kansu. Distinctive of Lo Han T'ang is the fact that tame animals play a subordinate part and that wild animals, especially gazelles and stags, predominate. It is also a peculiarity of this place that pigs' bones are very rare. About 40 bones of cattle certainly belong to tame animals, and the same is probably true of sheep and goats. On the other hand the numerous gazelle and stag bones show that the inhabitants were successful in the chase of these animals. Of hares there are about a score of fragments preserved. Another rodent which played a certain part in the household of the Stone age people is the marmot, *Arctomys robusta*. There are about twenty bone fragments of tame dogs. It is quite probable that the dog was used in hunting by the Lo Han T'ang people.

The mammal remains from Lo Han T'ang are very shattered, and this is especially the case with the long extremity bones of the hoofed animals. In them the terminal pieces are always separated from the hollow middle section, which in turn was crushed in order to extract the marrow.

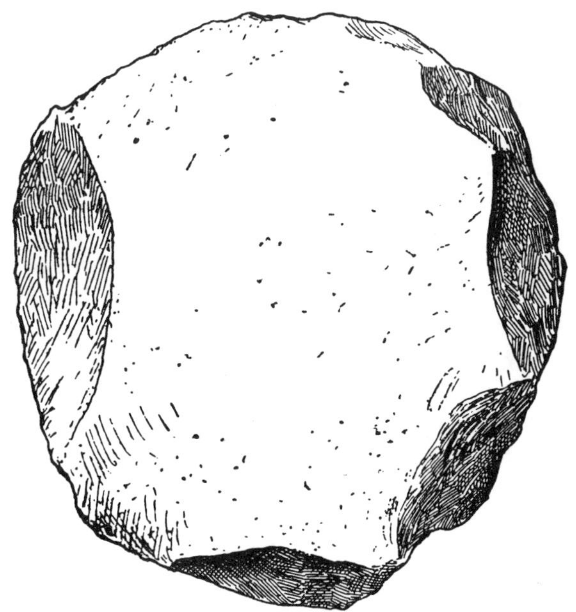

FIG. 114.—Disc-like stone slab, coarsely hewn out of a rubble stone.

The paucity of pigs' bones and, on the other hand, the abundance of remains of game ruminants and rodents shows that the inhabitants of this dwelling-place were predominantly hunters and cattle-raising nomads. The circumstance that Lo Han T'ang, situated quite close to the high Tibetan plateau, which still swarms with big game, has so abundant game bones, whereas the great discoveries in the lower river valleys show every sign of an agricultural population, is in full accord with geographical conditions. We may with justice say that Lo Han T'ang even to this day is on the boundary between the pastoral and the hunting regions on the Tibetan borderland.

CHAPTER FIFTEEN

ARCHAEOLOGY TAKES CHARGE

WHEN, on September 15th, I returned to my old quarters in Hsi Ning it seemed probable that the whole of my Kansu journey would be a comparative failure. I had organized this undertaking in the hope of making copious discoveries of fossil vertebrates in the thick clay beds of the Kuei Te series, as also in deposits of the cretaceous formation in Eastern Kansu. These hopes had almost completely failed. In the salt-impregnated Mesozoic districts of Eastern Kansu we had found practically no vertebrates, and the collections from Kuei Te were more imposing by their weight than by their wealth of form. I was therefore more or less prepared to return home and to acknowledge defeat by these formations poor in fossils.

The archaeological discoveries were, it is true, geographically very interesting, but there was only one site, Lo Han T'ang, which could in some degree vie with the wealth of the dwelling-sites in Honan.

I had, however, one more duty to fulfil to satisfy my conscience. On the way up to Kokonor I had seen by the roadside, in a cutting not far from Hsi Ning, some fragments which seemed to hold some archaeological promise, and I sent two of my servants there for a test excavation.

After some days they returned, bringing with them not only a large number of fine fragments of the Yang Shao type, but also several intact urns, bought from the peasants in a village called Chu Chia Chai. These urns were, it is true, both dirty and badly worn, but nevertheless they could be described as a remarkable promise of the possibility of better discoveries.

Instead of returning home we therefore prepared for a new expedition, and thus set out for Chu Chia Chai, which lies about 20 km. upstream, on the northern bank.

Chu Chia Chai is a medium-sized country village situated close to a small watercourse, which runs from the north into the Hsi Ning river. The village consists of a larger northern portion, situated between two temples, and a smaller group of houses 400 metres farther south. North-west of the village, which lies on the plain, there rises a hill 166 metres high above the plain in the southern part of the village.

In the north and south direction the site of our discovery has a length of nearly 900 metres, and its breadth from east to west is as near as can be 500 metres. In extent Chu Chia Chai is thus the largest of all the dwelling sites discovered and investigated by us. As regards volume it is, however, surpassed by Yang Shao Tsun in Honan. The deposits here are in most places somewhat thin, and there probably remain within its area large surfaces where no finds will be made.

The best places in the cultural deposits were in the northern part of the village, in many cases close to the houses, so that much care and tact was required on the part of my servants to dig them out without disturbing the occupants.

During the very first days we found some complete urns in the most southerly part of the site, and I then began to seek systematically for the burial-place of the district. On the northern edge of the southern group of houses there was a pit from which the villagers fetched earth for their compost. By carefully examining the sides of this pit I first found some small beads and then some other indications which led us to one of the richest, and in many respects most remarkable, of all the prehistoric burial-places of which I know.

It soon appeared that the graves were at a considerable depth below the surface, and we therefore had, after concluding a fitting agreement with the owner of the soil, to undertake comprehensive excavations before we reached the level of the ancient graves.

Here we dug out no less than 43 skeletons, together with, as we shall see later, a unique wealth of burial furniture. Topographically these graves showed a peculiarity which considerably increased the difficulties of our operations. It soon became clear that the objects had been moved some distance from their original position. Parts of one and the same urn were found at some distance from each other. It seemed scarcely probable that later burials had disturbed earlier ones. The disorder in the finds did not point in that direction. Neither was it probable that the peasants of more modern times had dug down to the level of the graves and disturbed them.

There exists in these districts quite a different and alternative explanation of such disturbances as we discovered there. Kansu is one of the earthquake centres of China. In 1920 a devastating earthquake passed over the country and there has since been at least one great earthquake there. I had myself had occasion to observe the catastrophic movements of the strata occasioned by the earthquake of 1920, and it seems to me far from improbable that the slight dislocations in the cemetery at Chu Chia Chai may be regarded as effects of such an earthquake.

As soon as we discovered the burial-place and were assured of its importance and wealth, we introduced a division of labour, so that all my servants were turned on to excavation work and to each one was allotted his special group of skeletons, for which he was responsible. There was a fine rivalry between them to work with a light hand and to observe carefully even the smallest indication of a new find (Plate 23). I myself was fully occupied with surveying first the whole site on a scale of 1 : 10,000 and then the cemetery, and finally separate skeletons 1 : 10. But this was not all: many of the objects which came to light were extremely fragile or constituted groups which should not be disturbed in their setting. It was here that we made the fullest use of the bandaging technique which I had learned from Dr. Walter Granger, the Chief Palaeontologist of Roy Chapman Andrews' great expedition. Skeletons and other coarser objects were bandaged in flour paste and coarse brown Chinese paper, whilst smaller and especially fragile articles were treated with Chinese cotton paper and gum solution. Cotton paper is a splendid bandage material. It is extremely thin and absorbs the gum solution, so that one can paint it with a brush from the outside, which is of the utmost importance when it is a question of loose pieces, such as fragments of jars, beads, etc.

Sometimes, as in the case of the bone knife with flint edges (Plate 24, 1) and the bone armour (Plate 24, 2), even the most skilful bandaging technique left me in the lurch. I then had to find another way out. The objects were cut away until they

Excavations at the burial place at Chu Chia Chai

[*face page* 246

were left on the top of a column of earth, which was then impregnated from above with a thin solution of gum, a process which was repeated many times, until the earth would absorb no more solution. In this way it became as hard as brick and could be cut away without risk, together with its precious contents.

Those were happy weeks of work at Chu Chia Chai, filled with the joy and excitement of discovery, without any disturbance from outside.

Yet there was one exception! One day I was to ride the 12 miles into Hsi Ning in order to get some money from the post office and renew our stock of provisions. I took Chen and Chuang with me. The district seemed so peaceful that I did not think of taking any weapons with me, but just as we were about to mount our horses Chuang came and begged me to take one of the big automatic pistols with me.

When we arrived at Hsi Ning we found that some of the Mohammedan soldiers had climbed over the roof and broken into the hotel room where I kept my paraphernalia. They had taken my typewriter into the garden, where they had been disturbed and left my machine where it was, much to my delight and with very little loss to themselves, since an American typewriter is not exactly ready cash in the town of Hsi Ning.

The reporting of this theft to the authorities, and other arrangements, took us some hours. The dusk descended rapidly as we rode out of the town in the evening, and we soon found ourselves in unusually profound darkness. The path was narrow and we relied mainly on the horses. Chen rode first, then I, and Chuang followed with the pistol. A couple of hundred yards behind us came a cart with our baggage, and a policeman whom the sub-prefect of Hsi Ning had given me as an escort.

Just as we were riding forward, step by step, in the inky darkness through a little gorge, I noticed that Chen's horse became restless.

"The pistol, quickly," cried Chen.

What now happened did not take one-twentieth of the time it takes to relate it. By accident I knew that we were only a few hundred yards from a large village inhabited by the Mohammedans, so much feared and hated by the Chinese. Like lightning the thought flashed through my mind: For God's sake no shooting ! I jumped off my horse, walked back a couple of steps and said half aloud :

" Give me the pistol."

Just as I took the heavy weapon in my hand I felt on my right elbow the pressure of the loin of a horse which was not one of our hacks. When I looked up I saw dimly in the darkness the trunk of a rider and was conscious of his felt-shod foot at my side. So it was not one of my people, who wore leather boots. In order to forestall him rather than be forestalled I dashed at the dark figure above us, pistol in hand, and felt the next instant a warm fluid pouring down on to my hand. At the second blow the fellow collapsed on the pillion. What followed was in the nature of a tragi-comedy. Like a couple of angry bears, my two men jumped on the arch-enemy lying on the ground and began to belabour him with their nailed shoes. After a moment I took them by the arm and said :

" Now he seems to have had enough ; take him to the side of the road so that he doesn't frighten our horses ! "

At this moment Chen pointed to the other side of the stream and cried out :

" Anlaoyeh, there is another ! ", and we could dimly perceive a second rider.

" Come along, and fetch your friend ! " I called to him, but instead of accepting my invitation, he turned his horse and rode away towards the village. We waited a little until the policeman arrived with our cart. He got out, lit a match and looked at the man by the roadside.

" Splendid," said he, " this is one of the worst of the Mohammedan petty robbers. Now he will keep quiet for a bit."

We hastened past the Mohammedan village before its inhabitants could be astir, and afterwards we never heard a breath of this night episode.

" *Hsiao tufei* ", petty robber, is a type which goes out in couples in the darkness of the evening to levy toll on simple unarmed travellers on their way home. I imagine that this pair were not at all expecting us, as we were well known to be a little troublesome.

When I travel in the dark it is my habit to remove my glasses and place them in my hat, as I can get on better in the darkness

1 2

Bone armour and bone knife from Chu Chia Chai graves

without them. During the few moments when I settled matters with this robber one thought alone possessed me—to forestall him so that he should not break my irreplaceable glasses.

Our discoveries at Chu Chia Chai confirm in every way that the burial-place in the most southerly part of the site and the dwelling place are contemporaneous (Yang Shao age) and belong to the same group of people.

The chief interest of the Chu Chia Chai discovery is connected with the finds of various sorts which we made together with the fragmentary and, in the light of our later discoveries, scanty, burial ceramics. I shall now with all brevity mention some of the most sensational of these finds.

Together with a skeleton we found a bone knife, which is common as early as the Lo Han T'ang dwelling-site, and is also to be found at Kokonor. This knife is made of bone and provided with a groove on one edge. When I made my first discovery I was fairly certain that this groove was intended for securing flint chips, which constituted the cutting edge of the knife, but it was a great triumph for us when we found in these graves a knife in which the flint chips were still intact in their original position (Plate 24, 1). Together with another skeleton we made an even more remarkable discovery. Close to the arm of a skeleton lay a whole group of carefully formed thin bone plates, on one side long lancet-shaped plates, and on the other, fitting into the bone lancets, short triangular bone plates (Plate 24, 2).

So also beside the other arm a similar group of bone plates probably existed, to judge by the fact that a long lancet-shaped bone splint of exactly the same shape as in the large group was found close to the bone of this arm.

The most natural interpretation of these bone splints is surely that they constituted a sort of bone armour, possibly sewn to the sleeves. Considering that these bone splints are very thin, this armour may have been rather ornamental than defensive. A closer examination of this remarkable discovery has not yet been made.

Perhaps the most important discovery of all at Chu Chia Chai were the groups (up to 7 pieces) of small, thin, rectangular bone plates, lying close together, 12–22 mm. long and 3–8 mm. broad.

Some of these plates are perfectly smooth, others have a hook on the edge and others again diagonal cuts across the plate. Here also the considerable quantity of material has not been examined in detail, but it seems quite reasonable, as I suggested in my preliminary report in 1925, to suppose that these plates represent some kind of primitive writing or at any rate a method of recording certain facts or ideas.

Finally, we should mention that at Chu Chia Chai we found for the first time quantities of beads, worn by the dead, and also simply carved pendants of a blue-green turquoise-like stone.

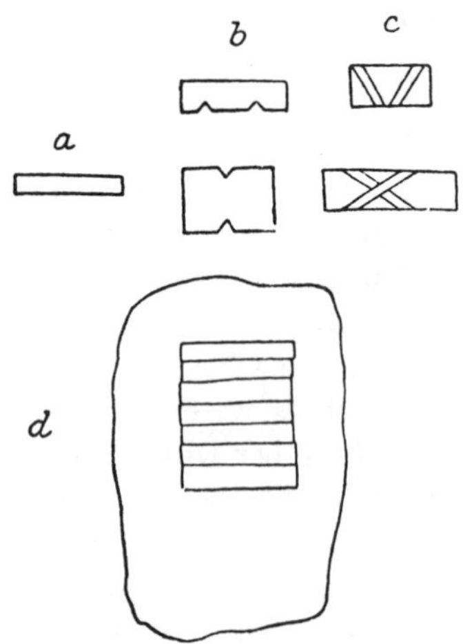

FIG. 115.—Writing tablets of bone (⅔ natural size).

FIG. 116.—We ride to the T'ao valley.

CHAPTER SIXTEEN

THE T'AO VALLEY

THE discovery of the rich, and in many respects unique, site at Chu Chia Chai in the Hsi Ning valley marks a turning point in my life. It determined me to remain in Kansu for one more summer, and it was the beginning of a series of great archaeological discoveries which caused me to abandon entirely my geological work in order to devote the rest of my life to archaeological research.

As soon as the Chu Chia Chai collections were finally packed, I moved my caravan by the shortest route to the provincial capital of Lanchow. On the outskirts of the town I rented a nice clean house, belonging to a Mohammedan of the name of Ma.

My position was now somewhat peculiar. The means which the Swedish China Research Committee had placed at my disposal were only sufficient for a summer expedition, and it was expected of me in Sweden that I would be back in Peking in the late autumn. None of the numerous proofs of goodwill and confidence which the Committee has shown me can be compared with the readiness with which it agreed, after I had explained the situation in my reports, to finance at any cost a second season in Kansu.

My abundant discoveries at Chu Chia Chai had convinced me that important prehistoric treasures in Kansu only awaited someone to discover them, but at the turn of the year I had no idea whither I should go. A kind fate then came to my assistance.

At that time there lived in the provincial capital of Lanchow a British missionary of the name of George Findlay Andrew. He was a man of about thirty-four, widely travelled, slim, and an enthusiastic explorer, who was most at home on the country roads and not adverse to adventure or danger. As a missionary he did not drink the excellent whisky for which his country is famous, but nevertheless he could stand on the table on festive occasions and sing the excellent Scottish songs as well as he could preach—as few others—in his church or missionary school. Owing to his cheerful, sunny temperament and his incorruptible honesty he was loved by foreigners and natives alike and, curiously enough, enjoyed the confidence both of the Chinese and of their arch-enemies, the Mohammedans. He was probably most interested in the latter and has written a book on the Mohammedans in Kansu.

When, in the latter part of November 1922, we returned to Lanchow, resolved to go into winter quarters in preparation for a new working season, Andrew invited me to give an address on our work to the schoolboys in his missionary school. I accepted the invitation in the hope of obtaining from the boys or their relatives information concerning the unknown sites of prehistoric civilization which more and more began to capture my interest. I consequently first gave an account of our geological and archaeological work and then asked the boys to make inquiries in various parts of the province as to the occurrence of burial urns and other prehistoric objects of the kind which we had found in the Hsi Ning district.

Some days later I received a short note from Andrew reading as follows :

" I have something which may interest you. Come and look at it when convenient."

There was something in the tone of his note which led me to believe that there was more behind this invitation than the mere words indicated. I therefore immediately ordered my *mafu* to saddle two horses, and some minutes later we raised the dust as we galloped off to the mission station.

When we arrived, my enthusiasm was somewhat damped. Andrew was in his school and could not be seen for another half-hour.

" But," added his wife, " there is something in the hut out there which you may care to look at while you are waiting."

I went out and saw something which almost made my knees give way beneath me ; a strange feeling, never experienced before, of astonishment, joy, fear and wild hope overwhelmed me.

On the table in front of me stood a perfectly intact burial urn with wonderfully well-preserved painting. The type was perfectly well known to me from excavations at Hsi Ning, and it was instantly clear that this was a burial urn from the close of the Stone age, 5,000 years old, though this specimen was larger, and in particular more richly and more finely painted than anything I could imagine in these parts. This was a find which fully equalled, if it did not even surpass, the best that had been found of the same period in the Near East or the Eastern Mediterranean. It was a magnificent discovery, and I stretched out my hands, trembling with eagerness. But it was much more than that—it was a promise, above all things, of untold possibilities of other discoveries.

Andrew told me that the urn belonged to an ex-official who had been taoyin in Chinchow in Southern Kansu and that he was reported to possess some more urns of the same kind, which he, Andrew, would arrange for me to inspect.

" But," said Andrew, " please come on foot, by the back door for preference. The more cautiously we approach, the better will be our prospects of gaining possession of the urns."

Andrew had not in any way exaggerated. The other urns were more than double the size of the first, and one of them is, in respect of character and richness of design, one of our greatest treasures, even taking into consideration that we subsequently obtained several hundreds for our collection.

I left the conclusion of the business in Andrew's hands and

he conducted the negotiations with the owner so wisely and so discreetly that within a few days the five superb pieces were our property at a price which must be regarded as very moderate. I cannot let this opportunity pass without acknowledging my great debt of gratitude to the Rev. G. F. Andrew, who subsequently on our account made a reconnaissance for a whole month, with exceptionally good results, and who, finally, took a large consignment of no less than 150 of our collection-cases safely and in good condition to Peking.

The acquisition of five magnificent burial urns spurred me on to further endeavours during the winter to make additional purchases and thereby to prepare for the coming working season. I visited all the dealers in antiques in Lanchow, but found that they knew nothing of the prehistoric burial urns. As a result of repeated inquiries, however, some further fine specimens came into my possession, and there gradually developed a formal trade in these burial urns, many of which had evidently been preserved for a long time in the homes of modern Chinese, to judge by the varnish and the dust with which they are covered.

The supply of these clay vessels—so important to me—was at first small, and prices rose higher every week, especially as Chinese officials and other private persons in the town had heard of my purchases and began to compete with me for the best pieces. A number of rare objects which I should extremely gladly have incorporated in my collection were lost to me, whilst at the same time my own purchases had made very serious inroads on my treasury. For a time things looked very black.

My utmost desire was, naturally, to discover the places from which these fine burial urns came, but all attempts to induce buyers to reveal their secret were unavailing. We soon discovered that all information on this point was, to say the least, unreliable. If a buyer said an urn came from the north one could be pretty certain that it had been found in the south, and we soon realized that there was no purpose in making such inquiries.

But then, at the beginning of March, much larger quantities of these urns began to arrive, and I could easily see by their appearance that many of them had been quite recently dug out of the earth. The supply of material had now become so abundant that I was able to choose and take only especially fine specimens or rare types. And I foresaw with certainty that one day I should be able to press down prices.

Every day there came to my house three or four different groups selling urns, and there was endless bargaining, whilst frequently in a single day thirty-odd urns or more would pass through my hands. I soon understood, however, that the various sellers had formed a syndicate, of which the members had undertaken not to accept any lowering of prices. I felt as if I stood before an insurmountable wall, and my money melted away with alarming rapidity.

Then one morning I had no less than six groups of sellers, representing at least fifty urns, in my house, and I thought the time had come to venture my coup.

I selected from the various groups a score of urns which I wished to acquire and offered for them prices which were very liberal, though somewhat less than the highly exaggerated prices which I had hitherto been obliged to pay. The Chinese looked questioningly at each other and shook their heads as a sign that my offer was not acceptable.

I made a little speech to them somewhat in the following terms :

" You know that these urns had no value till I came here. Nobody before me asked for them, and if I go away from Lanchow the demand will soon disappear, for the people in the town only buy them because I am interested in them. I am willing to pay you generous, but reasonable prices. If you don't agree I must leave the town and do some other work. Think it over and let me know what you decide."

I waited a little and then added :

" You must accept my offer or leave my house."

I saw a sign from the one who seemed to be the leader, and then they all nodded in confirmation that the matter was agreed and my price accepted.

During the following days the situation developed with the speed of an avalanche. My house was positively besieged by groups of men wanting to sell me urns. It was said that out on the roads men were seen time after time carrying urns to Lanchow. The sellers willingly admitted that there was a positive flood and that previous prices could not be maintained. On the contrary they were very pleased with my offers, for I did not wish to depress prices too much, as I wished to explore to the full this perhaps never-to-recur conjuncture in order to enrich my collection. But by degrees it became difficult for me, from mere considerations of space, to purchase any more, and my selection became more severe with every day that passed.

I now thought that the time had come to make a resolute attempt to discover where these quantities of large, superb, prehistoric burial urns came from.

I called in my most trusted man Chuang and had a confidential talk with him. I said:

"Chuang, here are fifty dollars; go and make friends with the urn dealers and their assistants. Urns are now so cheap that it will not be difficult to find out where they come from. Entertain the old fellows, if necessary, but don't come back until you can tell me where the place is."

Chuang vanished for two whole days, but then one morning he turned up looking pale and with trembling hands, but beaming with joy and eagerness.

"Anlaoyeh," said he, "now I want one of the horses and 200 dollars and I shall perhaps be away a week."

I knew my man and knew that he would not betray my trust. He got what he asked, and the strongest of our horses was put at his disposal, for I knew that it would be a testing reconnaissance.

Chuang was away a week; then he returned with a whole mule caravan laden with large and splendid burial urns, among which I noticed one of an entirely unknown type, which certainly belonged to a hitherto unknown prehistoric period.

He reported that he had journeyed over 200 Chinese li to the south to the neighbourhood of the town of Titao, in a district on the western bank of the T'ao River, populated entirely by Mohammedans. There he had been able to see the cemetery from which most of our fine large urns had come. Owing to the demand which we had created for these prehistoric relics, the Mohammedans had collected them in their hundreds in the old cemeteries. They had dug planlessly right and left, and when different parties came into conflict they had fought regular battles, in which one day a man with a spade had struck off the

The T'ao Valley

[face page 256

hand of his opponent. The consequence had been that the official in charge of the district in question had sent soldiers to see that no further excavations were made.

I now clearly understood that as a result of our purchases a most deplorable spoliation of graves in these prehistoric cemeteries had taken place, and in order to do what I could to prevent further violation I visited the governor and suggested that he should instruct the local authorities to see that the local population should not commit further outrages against these precious scientific monuments of ancient civilizations.

We prepared for several months' absence from Lanchow and broke up for the south on April 23rd, in order to explore this new site which the urn traffic in Lanchow brought to our knowledge.

Our road first followed barren mountain tracts, but on our second day's march we descended into the T'ao valley, a tributary valley of the Yellow River, and it was a great surprise to me to find at a height of 1,800 metres above the sea level such a rich and smiling landscape (Plate 25). It was a broad open valley, the flat bottom of which was perfectly watered by numerous irrigation canals, and in which every square foot of ground was cultivated to the maximum, thanks to the natural rainfall and to irrigation. This flat valley is bounded on both sides by terraces about 50 metres high, and on the terrace level there are small villages which support themselves by the cultivation of such crops, principally wheat, as are possible without artificial watering, and by the use only of the natural rainfall.

Lower down on the carefully watered river level they cultivate partly wheat and also, to a large extent, the opium poppy. It was an extremely lovely sight to see these fields of poppies in bloom, but the beautiful landscape had a gloomy obverse, in so far as the population, driven by the greedy officials, had extended the cultivation of the poppy to such an extent that there did not remain sufficient ground for the cultivation of the necessary cereal crops.

In this lovely valley apricots and peaches were also grown, especially the latter, of such a size and aroma as I have never seen before. The American missionaries who were stationed here also told me that the T'ao peaches could successfully compete with the best Californian. This beautiful valley is one of the most fertile and smiling districts I have seen in China and, despite its height above the sea level, it is much more productive than the Peking plain, which is at sea level.

During the later Stone age, when man occupied the T'ao valley, the river level was very different from what it is now. The river wound then, as now, in various branches across the flat bottom of the valley, but from all appearances brushwood grew on the islands between the streams and on the valley sides beyond the river area. In this primeval wood there was certainly an abundance of big game to hunt, especially deer, which were a favourite prey of the savages of the Stone age. But the brushwood was marshy and impenetrable, and beasts of prey rendered it dangerous. The well-stocked hunting grounds offered by the forest were thus not a safe habitation for human beings.

It is in this circumstance that we must seek the explanation of the fact that the old settlements were, topographically, quite different from the modern. The river plain is now a well tended and well watered garden. All the large villages are situated close to the main roads and have abundant supplies of water.

None of these attractions existed for the Stone age savage, who therefore chose his habitation on sites quite different from those of a modern man. On both sides of the T'ao valley, but more highly developed on the eastern side, there runs a terrace of 50 metres height rising steeply from the river plain. This represents the Ma Lan stage, of which we have made the acquaintance both in the Western Hills near Peking and in the Kuei Te valley. The Ma Lan terrace shows here the same topographical features as in the Peking district and in Kuei Te: it rises by a steep erosion slope above the present river level. The surface of the terrace is cut up into lobes, separated by small gorges, and here and there we find detached island remains of the former connected terrace. It was precisely these terraces which tempted the Stone age man to settle there. There they found on their arrival a natural fortress: a dry, flat surface on which it was easy to build their villages, and all round were inaccessible cliffs which were easily defended against an enemy. This type of terrace settlement we know already from Lo Han T'ang in the

Terrace landscape, Hsin Tien

[*face page* 258

Kuei Te valley, and here in the great open T'ao valley we find similar terrace islands at Ch'i Chia P'ing, the oldest of the prehistoric villages, at Hsin Tien, where first the Yang Shao people built a village and where, much later, the people of the Bronze age occupied the same place (Plate 26). Finest and most typical of all these prehistoric villages built on terrace islands is, however, Hui Tsui, the Bronze age village which yielded such rich discoveries.

When, on April 23rd, we rode across the T'ao valley, I was conducted by Chuang to the large village of Hsin Tien, in the neighbourhood of which, in the small village of Kuo Chia Chuang, we found simple but pleasant quarters close under the terrace cliff. During the weeks that followed we found the Hsin Tien district a veritable eldorado for archaeologists. The geologist P. L. Yuan, who accompanied me on this occasion, carried out during the month of May a detailed survey of the Hsin Tien district, which will be published in *Palaeontologia Sinica.* His survey, with 5-metre curves, gives an extraordinarily fine picture of the dependence of the prehistoric settlements upon the terrace topography.

A little south of Kuo Chia Chuang, where we lived, a little stream, Chi Chia Ho, runs into the main valley. On the southern side of the ravine rise up two terrace islands, the outer, westerly one being occupied by a large modern building (fortress ?), which I had no time to examine more closely. The inner, easterly terrace island, on the other hand, is completely covered by a cultural deposit, of which the main mass consists of Yang Shao material with a sprinkling of Bronze age fragments in the surface deposit.

On the northern side of the Chi Chia Ho ravine and directly east of, and above, our village of Kuo Chia Chuang lay a Bronze age cemetery—the richest of those which were known to us. A large part of the Bronze age graves had been excavated before our arrival and the vessels contained therein had been purchased by me in Lanchow. Happily there still remained a sufficient number of graves to give us an adequate picture of the burial customs of the Bronze age.

Farther to the east, in the interior of the terrace, the Chi Chia Ho ravine divides into two branches, and in the peninsula between them we found a third cultural deposit, quite different from the two already described and belonging to the first stage of the Stone age, Ch'i Chia, which we shall describe more fully in what follows.

The Hsin Tien district provides an excellent sample of the extraordinary wealth of our discoveries in the T'ao valley. Within an area only one hundred metres square we find here three productive cultural deposits, a dwelling of the first stage of the Stone age, Ch'i Chia, a dwelling of the Yang Shao period, and a very rich Bronze age cemetery.

Ten to twelve kilometres down the valley, but on the same side of the river, there lies, quite near the district town of T'ao Sha Hsien, another large country village, Sha Lêng Tzŭ. Here we found a terrace topography closely resembling that of Hsin Tien, but even more strongly developed. Two ravines here penetrate into the terrace area and form between them an island which is completely isolated, surrounded by immense ravines. This island was in the Bronze age (Hsin Tien age) a flourishing village. The discoveries which we made during our first reconnaissance in the cliffs bordering the terrace island were so abundant that I moved three of my collectors there, Pai, Chang and the little Korean Li. Whilst I was engaged in the detailed measuring of our finds at Hsin Tien I rode every second or third day to Sha Lêng Tzŭ to inspect the finds made by my three collectors in the neighbouring Hui Tsui dwelling-site. Afterwards I transferred the whole of my work to that place for a few days and surveyed the vicinity of the Hui Tsui find on a scale of 1 : 5,000, with 10-metre curves.

During this surveying work I was bitten by a dog. I was walking from the north along the road through the village of Sha Lêng Tzŭ with my drawing-board in my hand, when a dog came rushing out of a gate and bit me in the left thigh. It was a nasty bite, with a mess of trouser rags and torn flesh, and you never knew whether the dog was smitten with rabies. I now felt, as never before or since, that I held my life in my hands, and I acted accordingly. I went into the kitchen of the nearest house and politely asked the three women working there to leave me for a few minutes in sole possession of the kitchen and the fire. Then I took out my pocket knife, heated it to a glow and cauterized the wound. From the cauterization there came a thick, fatty, white smoke which was far from pleasant.

I thanked my hostesses, packed up my gear, mounted my horse and rode home 12 km. to headquarters at Hsin Tien. Arrived there, I examined the wound anew, together with my groom Chin. As we thought we could see deep down a spot which had not been properly burnt out, we again went into action, this time with a more suitable implement, the ramrod of a Mauser rifle, with which we succeeded in properly burning into the depths.

I have since consulted doctors, both in China and here at home, and the unanimous opinion is that with a risk of rabies I did exactly what I ought to have done. But the healing was a very slow process, during which my men excavated by themselves a Bronze age cemetery, Ssŭ Shih Ting, situated on the other side of the river, opposite the district town of T'ao Sha Hsien. During my convalescence I had clean and splendid quarters in a temple on the outskirts of the little town. I instructed the Korean Li how to make simple surveys of the graves on the scale of 1 : 10. He performed this task so faithfully that I was able to include 19 grave plans drawn by him in my topographical work " Prehistoric Sites of Northern China ", which is in course of publication in *Palaeontologia Sinica.* When we were finished with this cemetery we all moved some distance up the valley to the village of P'ai Tzŭ P'ing in the Ning Ting district, on the western bank of the river. On that side of the river the population is predominantly, if not entirely, Mohammedan. The population of P'ai Tzŭ P'ing was exclusively Mohammedan, and I now had an opportunity of seeing how they lived. They are all called Ma, which is rendered by the Chinese written character " horse ", which, however, is said to be derived from the first syllable of the prophet's name. There must be a strong Semitic strain in these Mohammedans of Kansu, for I saw in this village, as also elsewhere, many types which reminded me of Hedin's types of popular life in Chinese Turkestan, or still more of the pictures we have formed for ourselves of the Old Testament patriarchs. My host had on his wall a picture which, he said, represented Mecca, the Holy City, and which he showed me with great reverence. Moreover, there were constant prayer-hours, accompanied by sprinkling with water, laying out of mats and mumbling of prayers.

One day as I was going to a neighbouring site I met a small boy on the way to school, carrying his home lesson under his arm in the form of two shoulder-blades of a mule, or something of the kind, on the flat surface of which a passage from the Koran was written in Arabic.

I bought this quasi-schoolbook from the lad for 20 cents. Happy and relieved, he sprang on his way quit of his home-lesson but with the money in his pocket.

The most important discovery made during our stay in P'ai Tzŭ P'ing was the large dwelling-site, Ch'i Chia P'ing, situated to the north of P'ai Tzŭ P'ing, and, like so many other sites, situated on a small, entirely detached, terrace island (Plate 27).

FIG. 117.—Urn with a high collar and large handles ($\frac{1}{3}$ natural size).

Chi Chia P'ing is pre-eminently conspicuous for its extraordinarily fine and peculiar ceramics. When one speaks of the high quality of the prehistoric ceramics of China, one's praise applies almost exclusively to the beautiful painted vessels, and especially to the large burial urns. Our ideas would, however, be much more one-sided and limited than they are if we did not know of the Ch'i Chia P'ing find. Here we found practically no painted ceramics (some Yang Shao fragments on the surface of the site and a couple of vessels which we found with a few painted lines scarcely alter this view). Two ceramic types have rendered the Ch'i Chia P'ing site famous. One is, in general, a small urn of very fine pale brick-red ware with a high collar and handles which are either very large, extending from the edge of the collar almost to the top of the vessel, or else purely rudimentary. These vessels, of which the lower portion is covered by a basket pattern, are extraordinarily graceful and thin-walled, and it has excited general surprise that, in view of the circumstances of the discovery, we have put their age as early as before

PLATE 27

Excavations at Ch'i Chia P'ing

[*face page 262*

the Yang Shao age. The second ceramic group belongs to the large family called " comb " ceramics, of which it is characteristic that the decoration, consisting of dotted lines, was produced by a comb-like instrument. The Neolithic " comb " ceramics are widespread in Northern Europe and Northern Asia, but nowhere has the type of these ceramics attained such a refinement as characterizes those of Ch'i Chia P'ing, in which the dotted lines are arranged in graceful patterns, which, together with the careful modelling, make this elegant group of finds one of the most noble of prehistoric ceramics.

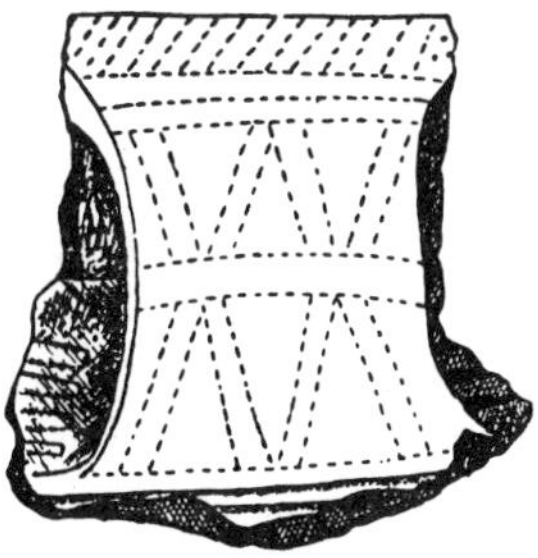

FIG. 118.—Fragment of " comb " ceramics.

FIG. 119.—Old Ma says " stop " to our excavations in the P'an Shan hills.

CHAPTER SEVENTEEN

THE LIVING IN THE VALLEY AND THE DEAD IN THE MOUNTAINS

IN the spring of 1924 I sent my little groom Chin up the T'ao valley to look for new prehistoric sites. He then made the greatest find of his life when, 15 km. south of the district town of Ti Tao Hsien, he discovered on the western bank, in a ravine close to the village of Ma Chia Yao, an immensely rich dwelling-site of the Yang Shao period. Even the first collection which Chin brought back to Lanchow at the end of his reconnaissance showed that we had here to do with something which never was seen before, and the subsequent excavations, in which some of Chin's comrades participated, brought to us material which in many respects rivals, and in some cases even surpasses, the great typical site of Yang Shao Tsun in Honan.

Ma Chia Yao is quite a small village lying on the present-day river level, right at the foot of the steep cliffs of the Ma Lan terrace, which is here 50–60 metres in height. Quite near the southern part of the village is the mouth of a fairly broad and open-sided valley, through which a small water-course runs down to the T'ao river. This valley is flanked by a lower terrace, 24 metres above the river level of the ravine, and it is on this lower terrace that the rich site is situated. The topographical conditions are here somewhat different from those in the other dwelling-sites in the T'ao valley, which are situated on the high

Dwelling Site. Ceramics of the Yang Shao Period, Kansu

[*face page 264*

Ma Lan terrace, as a rule on detached terrace islands. The site at Ma Chia Yao extends 350 metres in an east-west direction. In a north-south direction it is quite narrow.

In proceeding to examine the extraordinarily abundant material from Ma Chia Yao we are justified in beginning with the painted ceramics, represented by about 6,000 fragments and some intact vessels. This fine " everyday ware " of the Stone age people consisted partly of bowls—from quite small ones to large dishes —and partly of tall, slender urns with a narrow neck (Plate 28). In contrast with Honan, where the Yang Shao bowls were only painted on the outside, these bowls are in many cases painted inside and out. The decoration is painted quite freely, with varying patterns, among which curves predominate. Sometimes these curves assume such forms that one is tempted to imagine plants, algae or the like. Another group of patterns, which is certainly rare, but very striking, shows the " toad " motif.

The decoration of the urns consists of much the same patterns as those of the bowls, and here also groups of parallel curves predominate, though among them are interspersed toad patterns, such as that of the " swimming toad " and the " headless toad ".

As in all other prehistoric sites, so also here there exist beside the painted ceramics also coarser unpainted vessels, which, however, occupy a subordinate position in our collection, largely perhaps because my collectors had a pronounced preference for the more interesting painted ceramics.

The stone material from this site consists of the usual axes and chisels, as well as rectangular and oval stone knives. To these we must add coarsely hewn disc-like objects. These discs are only hewn at the edges and have always flat top and bottom surfaces, showing that they were shaped from disc-shaped pebbles as the raw material.

The bracelets in this case constitute an interesting chapter. They are either cut out of stone or modelled from clay. An especially elegant bracelet is seen in Fig. 120*c*, cut out of some black, laminated rock.

Together with the fragments of thin clay rings there also occur such clay objects as we see in Fig. 120*d*. These are slightly spiral and toothed like the horns of an ibex. As the base has in every case been broken off, I dare not express an opinion as to their function.

Among the smaller clay objects we find in this site a peculiar group, namely a few rattles. They are all zoomorphic. One specimen imitates the body of a small turtle. Its top side is painted with a typical Yang Shao pattern.

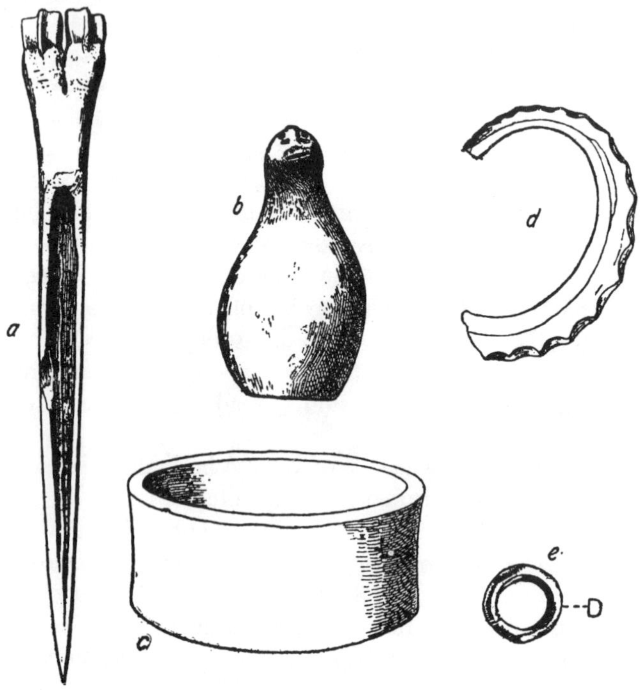

FIG. 120.—Objects from Ma Chia Yao: *a*, bone awl; *b*, clay rattle; *c*, stone bracelet; *d*, ibex (horn-shaped clay ring); *e*, bone finger ring (½ natural size).

Another rattle looks much like a long-necked clay cuckoo, with two holes in the sides and four in the somewhat formless face (Fig. 120*b*).

A third fragment must have belonged to a large turtle, prepared in clay. It is uncertain whether this object was a play rattle or not.

Bone objects from this site are fine and numerous: sewing

needles, awls, chisels and other objects of which the function is far from clear. Amusing and neat are the three bone finger rings (Fig. 120*c*).

We had now arrived at midsummer, 1924. We had already spent two months in the T'ao valley, working eagerly to establish order in the confusion of prehistoric sites, of varying age, which we here encountered. During the whole of this time as we worked up from site to site, I had always in mind the recollection of Chuang's lively account of the remarkable cemeteries from which we had purchased such quantities of large and magnificent painted urns in Lanchow. It was only on June 26th that I had an opportunity of myself visiting the sites.

We left our quarters at P'ai Tzŭ P'ing down on the Ma Lan terrace early in the morning, accompanied by Chuang and two Mohammedan porters and guides. All the cemeteries of the prehistoric period in question which we had hitherto examined had been situated close to their respective dwelling-sites, or in other words, the prehistoric habitations and cemeteries had lain side by side. It therefore seemed to us most surprising when our guides led us out of the valley higher and higher up the western slopes. We ascended hundreds of metres. The fertile valley bottom now lay far below us like a deep green ribbon, and the view began to extend over distant valleys which I had not seen before. I asked the men if we should soon arrive at the graves.

" No," they answered, " higher, much higher, up."

Two hundred metres higher up we rode along paths which wound in sharp curves up the steep valley side. We had now reached an entirely different landscape. There was an open view for 50 km. on all sides. I looked out upon a number of hills and ridges, all of about the same height, and thus constituting an old, but now broken, plateau, which in the east continued unbroken as far as the horizon, but on the south and west at a distance of about 30 miles was bounded by a high dark wall of mountains which marks the boundary of the Tibetan highlands. We were now 2,200 metres above the sea and the mountain wall to the south-west was between three and four thousand metres high.

We had reached a height from which we had a completely open view in all directions. Here I saw the traces of extensive excavations, and in the earth thrown up were visible everywhere fragments of painted vessels of the same kind as the magnificent, intact vessels which we had bought at Lanchow. It was evident that many vessels had been crushed in the graves by the pressure of the earth and that others had been broken in the competition of the villagers to despoil the old graves of their treasures.

The extent of the cemetery was clearly indicated by the recent excavations, which had fairly completely plundered the whole of the site. The cunning Mohammedans had made yard-long iron probes, with which they had dragged the ground and with striking accuracy localized every burial urn which was not more than one metre below the surface.

After we had hastily examined this first site, my guides conducted me to a second cemetery of the same kind, and it soon became clear to me how many hundreds of graves containing burial ware of unique size and beauty had been looted by a desecration which had for all time rendered impossible a scientific investigation of the connection between the various objects in the graves. It was poor comfort that we had been able to acquire by purchase almost all the more interesting burial urns. It is more important that, but for the large scale urn business in Lanchow, we should not have known at all of the existence of these remarkable sites.

When I had thought out, with very mixed feelings, the course of events, I sat down and tried to reconstruct the conditions under which these in many respects unique accumulations of graves had come into existence. Each of the five grave sites is situated on one of the highest hills in the district, surrounded by steep and deep ravines, 400 metres above the floor of the neighbouring T'ao valley. Continued investigation fully confirmed my first surmise that these cemeteries, situated on the highest hill-tops, must have belonged to the habitations of the same period down on the valley terraces. It then became clear that the settlers in the T'ao valley of that age carried their dead 10 km. or more from the villages up steep paths to hill-tops situated fully 400 metres above the dwellings of the living to resting places from which they could behold in a wide circle

The P'an Shan Hills. To the left Wa Kuan Tsui, in the centre P'an Shan, and on the right Pien Chia Kou

[*face page* 268

the place where they had grown up, worked, grown grey and at last found a grave swept by the winds and bathed in sunshine (Plate 29).

It must indeed have been a strong, virile and nature-loving people which was at pains to give to its departed such a dominating resting place, and as I sat there on a grave mound that sunlight day in June I tried in imagination to reconstruct the funeral procession which assuredly slowly wound its way with great pomp and now for ever forgotten ceremonies up the mountain sides.

It was now a question of saving what remained of undisturbed evidence of the old graves, and in order to facilitate my work, I removed the whole of my staff to the nearest farm where suitable quarters could be obtained.

This farm happened to belong to a rich young Mohammedan of the name of Ma, who was so exceedingly kind as to place his best house at my disposal and another at that of my servants and soldiers. He himself had previously lived in the large house with his two young wives and a whole bunch of little children, but he now removed the whole family to another much smaller house, and I greatly appreciated his kindness in giving up the best premises to me.

Ma's two wives were quite young and, as far as I could judge, of about the same age. They were pretty little creatures, but extremely shy. I only saw them properly on two occasions, once when I came home unexpectedly and found them in my house examining my things, and the second time when we left the place and they came out to nod farewell to us. But their seemly modesty was combined with considerable curiosity. The little ladies' window was diagonally opposite mine, and whenever I looked out in their direction I always saw a pair of interested eyes seeking a glimpse of the curious foreign devil. We used to call them Huang-Yang, gazelles, because they were so shy.

But there was another woman in Ma's house who was not at all timid, and that was his old grandmother. Ma's parents were dead, but his grandmother lived, and although she was old and wrinkled and hobbled about on a stick, she ruled the whole household. Not only did the two wives and the small children obey her least sign, but my men and my soldiers stood to attention when granny was hobbling around. She ruled and ordered even in my house, with the consequence that I had to pack up all my collections so that the old lady might not mix up my labels, for which she had very little respect.

For a long time we sought for graves which had escaped the ravages of the villagers. For several days it looked as if the whole district had been completely plundered, but finally Chuang made a magnificent discovery at Pien Chia Kou. It was, in fact, the most splendid grave which we found during the whole of the Kansu expedition.

One exquisitely painted jar after another was laid bare during our careful excavations, and in the end we beheld twelve burial urns placed round the skeleton of a full-grown man, who lay on his left side with his knees drawn up. Two polished stone axes and two whetstones close to his head completed the ample equipment of the grave.

It was not possible to complete the major excavation the same day as we made the discovery, so I had one of our small tents pitched on the spot and left the two soldiers to guard the site. Early the following morning I was up on the mountain, but found the situation changed in an alarming way. The whole slope was swarming with Mohammedans. One of the soldiers met me a short distance down the slope, evidently much perturbed.

" Anlaoyeh," he said, " many Mohammedans have come, more than 200. I am afraid they will make war on us. Cannot Anlaoyeh make haste with the old man's bones so that we can go back to Titao ? I think that would be best."

We had now reached the cemetery and I saw to my indescribable joy that nothing had been touched in the grave. But round about sat a couple of hundred men from the villages, looking very serious.

In the middle of the crowd, on one of our tarpaulins, which one of the soldiers had laid out, sat an old Mohammedan with large horn spectacles on his nose. He looked very venerable and pleasant. He rose up and advanced to meet me. We saluted each other according to all the rules of Chinese etiquette. Then we sat down together on the tarpaulin and began to talk.

He explained that our excavations had aroused general hostility in the neighbourhood and that he expected serious difficulties if I did not kindly abandon the work and leave the district.

I saw that there was little prospect of defying such a widely held opinion. I therefore decided to concentrate entirely on the unique grave which was for the most part laid bare before our eyes.

I told him that I was quite willing to agree with him and to undertake not to look for any more graves, but I made clear to him at the same time that under all circumstances and without regard to what the villagers proposed to do, I was resolved to complete the excavation which we had begun the previous day.

He explained that he fully understood my point of view and promised to order the men present to give me every assistance during the day on condition that this would be the last excavation. Thus we became good friends and in the end I took a photograph of the original old gentleman.

Towards midday we had the grave so cleaned up that I could take my photographs and make the necessary detailed measurements. Whilst I was doing this I saw a dark bank of cloud mounting up in the west and I knew only too well what that meant. We hurried on our work as much as possible, and just as we had collected the last bones of the skeleton the first raindrops fell. We then hastily retreated to the little tent, where we sat for several hours, packed like sardines in a box, among urns and packages of bones, with a torrent of rain streaming down around us. At dusk the rain abated somewhat and we wandered back to Ma's house over steep mountain paths, which were now so slippery from the rain that the men had to dig down to dry earth with their spades in the most difficult streams.

Just as the T'ao valley with its confusing maze of prehistoric sites will certainly one day in the future be regarded as one of the foremost fields of prehistoric research in the world, ranking with the rich sites of the Eastern Mediterranean, the Nile valley and the river areas of the Tigris and the Euphrates, so also we may say without the least exaggeration that the P'an Shan district, with its five cemeteries high up on the hill-tops, is one of the most magnificent burial-places left to us by prehistoric peoples. It is true that the graves were here invisible beneath their grass covering when the great spoliation began in the spring of 1924. No giant megalithic structures bore witness here to the industrious and virile people slumbering in the windswept graves. But in the majestic free situation of the cemetery, as in the perfect modelling of the burial urns and the finished beauty of their decoration, following inexorable laws of design, these

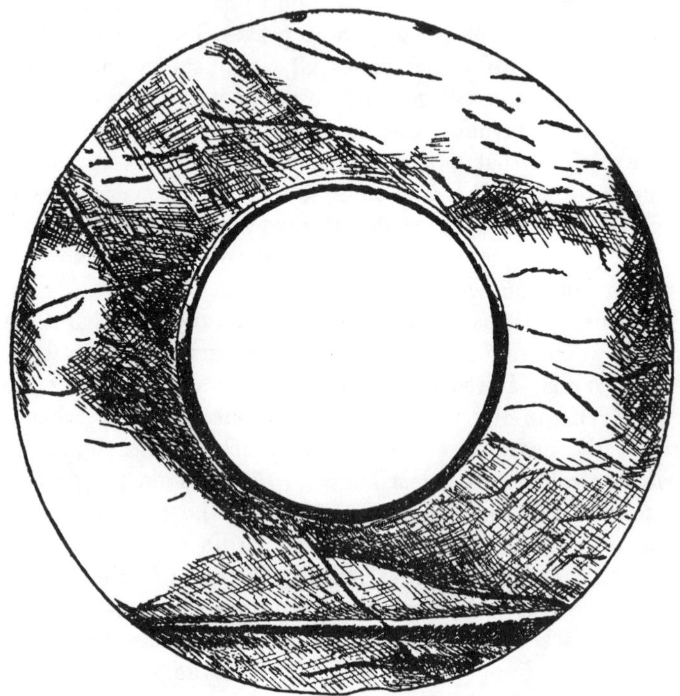

FIG. 121.—Jade ring ($\frac{2}{3}$ natural size).

burial-places are perhaps without parallel in the history of the human race.

Unhappily we know too little, owing to the great desecration, of the position of the dead in the graves, as also of the burial furniture surrounding them.

A man living in a little hut close to the richest of the cemeteries, Wa Kuan Tsui, had collected during the excavations, as he told me, a number of stone objects which I bought of him. Two of these are to be seen in Figs. 121–2. After careful considera-

The Pien Chia Kou grave

[*face page* 272

tion I think it is probable that the man's information was correct, for it is improbable that objects which in all respects bear the stamp of the Yang Shao period should have been transported from other places to this waste and remote spot in order to lure me to buy them for a very small sum. The price would in such a case have been quite different from that with which the old man was satisfied. I therefore regard it as highly probable that the objects really did come from the P'an Shan graves.

In addition to the objects illustrated I also acquired a considerable number of very large stone axes of exactly the type which we found in other Yang Shao dwelling-sites. These objects will be fully described in a monograph in *Palaeontologia Sinica*.

Among the objects illustrated we should in the first place notice a jade ring of the type which Chinese antiquaries call Yüan (Fig. 121). The stone is a flame green jade with rust-coloured veins and spots. The external diameter is 135 mm. The hole in the middle has a diameter of 65 mm. The actual breadth of the ring is thus 35 mm. The outer circumference is fairly well carved, whilst the inner shows traces of having been cut away somewhat uncertainly, from both sides. Also the cutting of the plain surfaces is very imperfect, with a large gash on either side. On the other hand the whole of the ring is well worn, with rounded edges, and one gains the impression that we have here an object showing signs of long use and wear.

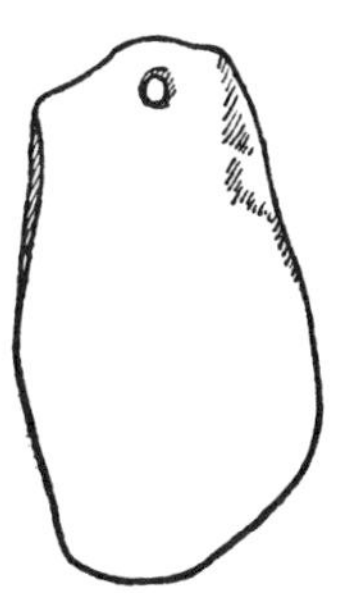

FIG. 122.—Pendant ornament (natural size).

There is also a smaller fragmentary ring cut from spotted green marble and a fragment of a ring, similarly in marble, with a large element of mica and some brown mineral.

Further we have a small chisel of agate and two pendant ornaments of some green stone (Fig. 122).

From the P'an Shan cemeteries, especially Wa Kuan Tsui, we also purchased several hundred splendid burial urns, which are now exhibited in equal numbers in the Geological Museum in Peking and the Museum of Far Eastern Antiquities in Stockholm. This unique and magnificent material is described in detail by Nils Palmgren in a large and profusely illustrated monograph which will be published by *Palaeontologia Sinica*. We shall leave aside entirely this rich ceramic material, since it is more fruitful for our purpose to make use of the discoveries, more limited, it is true, but also more decisive, made during my own excavation. Only in regard to two graves have I my own observations to report. The grave at Wa Kuan Tsui was very fragmentary. Of artifacts it only contained a stone axe and a fragment of a jar. Most important is the fact that the remains of the skeleton, though incomplete, show that we are here concerned with a so-called "hocker" grave, i.e. a grave in which the skeleton lies on one side, probably the left, with the knees drawn up.

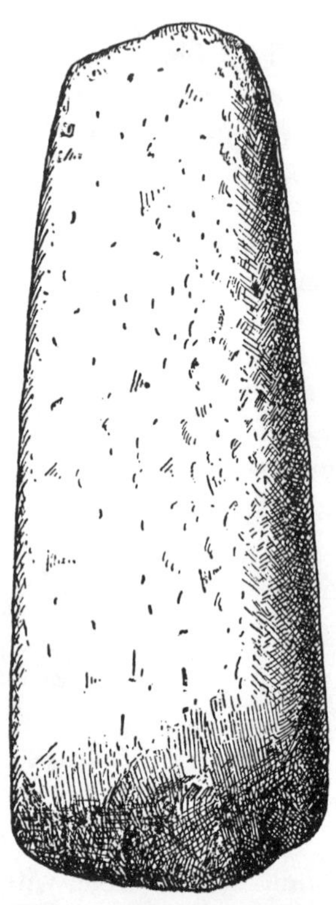

FIG. 123.—Greenstone axe. Pien Chia Kou grave ($\frac{2}{3}$ natural size).

This is also the case in the large grave at Pien Chia Kou, the very dramatic story of the excavation of which we have above described. Plate 30 gives us a very clear picture of this splendid grave.

The skeleton is that of a man of about forty years of age lying on the left side in a pronounced hocker position. Round about the body we find a rich collection of burial ware consisting of two greenstone axes (Fig. 123), two grindstones of light red sandstone and twelve burial urns, of which four are unpainted, of a grey, somewhat coarse flame ware, as well as eight urns of the elegant, fine, pale brick-red ware, painted in various patterns. Let us for a moment pause at the four unpainted vessels. It is striking that, though quite small in section, they are placed close above and in front of the head. In the largest vessel, placed in front of the crown of the head, we found a number of bone fragments which Dr. Dahr has identified as those of a

Two of the painted urns from the Pien Chia Kou grave

stag's skull. On the basis of this find there is reason to venture the surmise that there was once meat in this vessel. Above the crown of the head we found a little mug and beside it a larger vessel, and in the middle of the fragments of the larger vessel another little mug. It is conceivable that this larger vessel was a water jug from which the mug was to be filled when the dead man became thirsty—this also is a mere guess.

Right in front of the face, but at a considerable distance from it, stood an urn with a fine and well-preserved chess-board pattern (Fig. 124). Behind the body and down by the feet we found, in all, seven large painted urns. Four of these eight painted urns are illustrated in Plates 31 and 32. We find here for the first time a majority group of four large urns, of which the principal decoration consists of magnificent spirals covering the whole of the upper part of the vessels.

FIG. 124.—Small urn with chessboard pattern.

Another large urn is decorated with eight bottle-shaped, or rather gourd-shaped, figures, which are filled with a lattice pattern of two varieties (Plate 31, 1).

Then, in addition, we have a smaller urn, the decoration of which consists principally of six rhombs (Plate 32, 1) and finally we must mention a vessel with large black fields between horizontal red bands (Plate 31, 2). In the lower black field we find a row of large, painted, oval, oblique figures encircling a black contour, which approximately follows the light, painted oval contours of the figure. In the upper black field there are groups of light painted ovals without any black figure.

Among the eight painted urns we can thus distinguish five decorative types.

1. Four large spirals—four urns (Plate 32, 2).
2. Eight gourds—one urn (Plate 31, 1).
3. Six rhombs—one urn (Plate 32, 1).

4. Light painted ovals on black field—one urn (Plate 31, 2).
5. Chessboard pattern—one urn (Fig. 124).

A survey of the large collection of burial urns—amounting to several hundred specimens—which we acquired by purchase from these cemeteries will show that nearly all the urns derived from the P'an Shan district can be ranged under one or other of these types. This is an important observation, since the occurrence of the five leading types in a single grave shows with some degree of certainty that the P'an Shan graves came into existence during a comparatively short period of time and that consequently, archaeologically speaking, they represent one single period.

I have now concluded my description of the topography of the P'an Shan graves and will pass on to the at once difficult and interesting interpretation of the decorations of the burial urns. In order to motivate my view that these decorations originate in a highly developed death cult, embracing many magic elements, I was compelled to collect comparative material from widely separated parts of the world and from many different peoples. In the chapter on "Fecundity Rites, Hunting Magic and Death Cult" I shall bring together abundant folklore material in order to elucidate this problem, and in the following chapter on "Aphrodite's Symbol" I shall, in a general ethnographic survey, describe the symbolic significance of the pointed oval figures. Only then will it be possible for us, in Chapter XX, to disclose the symbolism of the P'an Shan graves.

FIG. 125.—Rest during the transport of the P'an Shan vessels to Ti Tao.

1

2

Two painted urns from the Pien Chia Kou grave

FIG. 126.—Chinese symbol combining the male principle *Yang* and the female *Yin*.

CHAPTER EIGHTEEN

FECUNDITY RITES, HUNTING MAGIC AND DEATH CULT

> FOR man in the natural state it was impossible, with his intelligence, to understand natural phenomena, especially nature's procreative work, otherwise than as the work of one or more hidden personalities. At an early stage two personified principles became more prominent than the others : a life-giving, procreative principle, and a fostering, nourishing principle—male and female. It was only later that the necessity arose of discovering among the phenomena of nature where these divinities had their being, and in this quest there undoubtedly arose differences of opinion under different natural conditions and at different stages of development. The life-giving god could be imagined in the skies, in the lightning, the sun, and so on, and the goddess of nourishment in the earth, the clouds or, in popular belief, in the moon, which yields the dew of life, or in the dawn, etc., and, indeed, where linguistic conditions, as in the case of the Germanic peoples and the peoples of the north indicated it, certainly also in the sun. Even to-day this goddess survives, in a manner, in thought, speech and writing, although most people are unconscious of her. She is now called Nature.

With this fine passage, supported by sure and meticulous evidence, our great folklorist, Edvard Hammarstedt, concludes his important dissertation, " Lussi ".[1]

In it he shows that the Lussi festival of December 13th, the festival of light which introduces Christmas and which in our mind is associated with the picture of the young girl with a wreath of burning candles in her dishevelled hair, does not merely go

[1] *Meddelanden från Nordiska Museet*, 1928, pp. 1–38.

back to the apocryphal Christian legend of Saint Lucia, who on December 13th, A.D. 304, was surrounded in Syracuse by burning pine torches and, when these failed to ignite her, finally suffered martyrdom at the hands of the executioner.

According to Hammarstedt's brilliant dissertation the Lucia celebration is rooted in primitive heathen conceptions.

> Lussi herself appears in Nordic popular belief as a beneficent virgin goddess of love who, dressed in white and surrounded by light, reveals herself at the darkest period of the year, distributing an elixir of life from a bowl. The cow, the goat and the cat are sacred to her, and a ship seems to have been added as an attribute or symbol. Offerings were made to her near a tree. She was the wife of the original ancestor of man, the first cultivator of the soil, whom primitive belief seems to have regarded as the ruler of the underworld and perhaps also the god of the morning star ; she was the ruler of the underworld and its inhabitants, as also over the priestesses of the cult of witchcraft. She was, though virgin, the mother of the personified forces of nature, elves and fairies, and in pre-Christian belief she was probably regarded, under another name, as all-mother.

The attributes which our ancient popular beliefs gave to this midwinter bringer of light and life remind us of those which were given to several of the goddesses of the ancient civilized peoples.

Especially in the Semitic Astarte do we recognize the prototype of the Germanic bringer of the elixir of life. " We find, for example, that the Semitic goddess of love, war, and culture was worshipped in the form of a tree ; that the cow was sacred to her and probably, on the Egyptian model, the cat or some animal belonging to the cat family ; that she was represented in some Phoenician Carthaginian monuments by the half moon with a star within it, or by a globe (the sun) in a half-moon or boat-like vessel as an attribute."

The planet Venus belonged to her and the Semitic women brought her bread as an offering.[1] Her beloved is Tammuz (Adonis), the god of vegetation.

Some years later Hammarstedt treated in his dissertation " Såkaka och såöl " another detail of the cycle of rites which the peoples of the north developed in support of their struggle with the winter darkness. During the Christmas baking the last dough

[1] Hammarstedt, *Meddelanden från Nordiska Museet*, 1903, pp. 235–77.

which could be scraped out of the trough was used for baking the so-called *yule cake.*

In order to understand the magic significance of this cake it is necessary to notice that it was made from the last remains of the Yule baking. This accords with the popular belief that the power of a thing is concentrated in the last remnant, thus " the power of the cultivated field in the last sheaf, the power of the plant in the last green branch, fruit, or seed, of the night mists in the dew, of the fire in the glow ".

The yule cake was borne out at the end of the holy festival to the granary and was buried in the seed, where it remained until the spring sowing began. When ploughing or sowing began in the spring the cake, now called " sowing cake ", was taken out, partly to be divided between the ploughman and the drawers of the plough, and partly to be mixed with the seed and harrowed in the soil. In certain districts it was portioned out at ploughing time as energizing bread to all members of the family and to the domestic animals. Thus the whole life force of the newly threshed seed was concentrated in the yule cake which was used with the spring seed in order to yield a good and abundant crop for the new year.

Originally the sowing cake was probably only a conveyor of plant life, but when it was shaped to resemble the disc of the sun or the sun wheel it became an element in the sun cult, just as the sowing ale, with which cattle were painted and the fields sprinkled, belongs to a rain ritual which was an element in the cult designed to safeguard the harvest.

Of great interest are certain ramifications of the cult of fertility, which found its material expression in the yule cake and the sowing cake. In certain parts of Germany the woman who had just kneaded the yule dough and who still had dough on her arms, was made to go out into the garden and embrace the fruit trees. In Finnish Österbotten the fishermen, in order to secure a good catch, used to throw a yule cake into the seine when it was first drawn in.

For comparison I would refer to the chapter on " Aphrodite's Symbol " in which another life-bringer, the cowrie shell, is associated with good fortune in fishing.

Long before our Swedish folklorist Hammarstedt began the

investigations to which I have referred, a German, Johann Wilhelm Emmanuel Mannhardt, fighting against illness, adverse fortune and lack of appreciation, had devoted decades to a profound study of the mythology of vegetation, and especially of agriculture. The progress of his studies is revealed in the works *Roggenwolf und Roggenhund* (1865), *Die Korndämonen* (1868), and his great work *Wald und Feldkulte* (1875–1877). Mannhardt shared the fate of many pioneers and died not understood and relatively little known.

It was only when the English ethnologist and student of religion, Sir James George Frazer, in his famous work, *The Golden Bough* (first edition 1890), again treated similar problems with much more comprehensive and varied material that the fundamental importance of Mannhardt's work was fully understood.

Frazer had originally attacked an apparently somewhat specialized problem, namely the interpretation of the legend surrounding the priest-king in Diana's grove on lake Nemi in the Alban mountains, who broke the " golden bough ", the mistletoe, killed his predecessor and subsequently had to lead a life of constant watchfulness until, one day, his life would be taken in the same manner, in accordance with the fateful tradition. From this starting-point Frazer examined the folk-lore of all peoples and ages and amassed an incredible amount of material, which he offered to his contemporaries in the splendid and brilliantly written work *The Golden Bough.*

Through Frazer's work we now know the innumerable varieties of magic rites by which primitive peoples invoked aid from the forces of nature. One of the leading principles in such popular beliefs has been the conception that resemblance, in many cases purely superficial, and according to our modern views, quite unessential, was sufficient to create the desired resemblance of effects.

In accordance herewith a Hindu custom prescribes that on the evening of a wedding day the newly married couple shall sit in the open air at sunset when the stars begin to appear in the evening sky. When the North Star becomes visible the man must show his bride this unchanging star and utter a prayer that they and their numerous children may be constant like it, and live for a hundred autumns.

In the same way it was imagined by ancient peoples that the fixity of the stones over which they pronounced their oaths would fortify their solemn oaths. Similarly Saxo Grammaticus relates of the election of the Nordic kings that the electors stood on stones in order, by virtue of their fixity, to emphasize the endurance of their oath to the newly elected king.

Especially interesting is an account which Frazer cites from Lumholtz concerning Mexico. The Huichol Indians greatly admire the beautiful design on the backs of snakes. When a Huichol woman begins to weave or embroider, her husband catches a large snake and holds it in a cleft stick, whilst the woman strokes the reptile down the length of its back. Then with the same hand she strokes her forehead and eyes in order that she may be able to produce patterns as beautiful as that on the back of the snake.

The rhythmic phenomena of space and their reflection of the life of the earth were an inexhaustible object of study and reflection among ancient peoples. Thus all sorts of phenomena affecting mankind were associated with the rise and fall of the tides. Frazer gives a number of references to this fact both from exotic races and from authors of antiquity. He also mentions that even at the present day, both in Portugal and on the coasts of Wales and Brittany, the people imagine that births occur when the tide flows in to the land and deaths when the ebbing water recedes from the shore.

The imitative magic which underlies the customs and conceptions described above has also been employed to a large extent to assist childless mothers to their longed-for firstborn. Among the Nishinam Indians in California the friend of a childless woman sometimes smuggled into her hut a doll made of grass. When the woman found this image of a little child she pressed it to her breast, pretended to suckle it, and sang cradle songs to it.

Among the Moab Arabs it is customary for a childless mother to borrow the clothes of a woman with many children, in the hope that the wearing thereof will help her to become pregnant. By another Arab custom a woman who desires strong children hastens to drink from a water trough from which a thoroughbred mare has just drunk.

Within the circle of this fecundity cult also falls the custom of

Chinese women of setting up in their Niang Niang Miao, the temples devoted to the god of fecundity, small votive gifts consisting of a small clay statuette of a woman who has bared one breast and holds the nipple with her fingers.

Customs used against the same imitative background are known from widely different peoples in connection with adoption and the resurrection of persons wrongly assumed to be dead.

It is not only the fecundity of women, but also, in perhaps an even higher degree, the fertility of the soil which is the subject of these groups of procreative rites, and not least interesting in them is that these two groups of procreative acts are often interwoven, in most cases with the purpose of making the woman, as the bearer of life fruit, stimulate the fertile fields. Thus in Sumatra it is customary for a woman far advanced in pregnancy to participate in the festival for securing a rich rice harvest. In Syria, gardeners, in order to induce a sterile tree to bear fruit, persuade a pregnant woman to tie a stone to one of its branches. The tree is then assured of a rich crop, but the woman runs the risk of misfortune, since she has in this manner transferred her fertility, or some part of it, to the tree.

The magic power of a pregnant woman over fruit trees was employed in Central Europe in such a way that the man gave to her the first fruit of a young tree, or, with a slight variation, gave the first apple to a woman with many children or the first cherry to a mother with her first-born.

Among the Nicobars it is held lucky to employ a pregnant woman and her husband for sowing in the gardens. The Greeks and Romans offered pregnant women to the goddesses of the harvests and the soil. The Galilareans think that if trees do not bear fruit it is because they are male. The remedy is very simple. They hang round the tree a woman's underskirt which transforms it into the fruitful female sex.

Among the Baganda people it is believed that a childless woman can infect her husband's trees, so that they no longer bear fruit. For this reason the husband prefers to separate from a childless wife.

A procreative rite which in an interesting manner combines women, fields and trees as creators of life has already been mentioned: the custom of making the woman who bakes sowing cakes at Yuletide go forth with dough on her arms and bless the trees for fruit by embracing their trunks.

Just as the imitative rites of abundance are found among all

FIG. 127.—Holy Tree. Province of Hupei. At the foot of the tree is a table for offerings, and on the trunk are secured tablets with invocations to the tree.

agricultural peoples, so we encounter analogous rites among hunting tribes and cattle-raising nomads.

The Indians of British Columbia live largely on fish. If this is lacking for a season, a sorcerer makes a model of a swimming fish and drops it into the water in the direction from which the fish usually come. The islanders of Torres Strait use models of dugong and tortoise in order to attract these animals. The Toradjas of Celebes hang jaws of stags and wild boar in their houses so that the spirits in their bones may lure living animals of the same kind into the path of the hunter.

That similar conceptions have survived in an ancient agricultural race like our own appears from Herman Hofberg's account of Ysätters-Kajsa's friend Bottorpa-Lasse, a great hunter who, together with his goddess of the chase, dwelt in the forests of Östernärke. " He was a great marksman, for if he only went out to the porch and called the bird he wished to shoot, or drew on the wall the animal he wished to slay, then it fell to the ground when the shot was fired."

That his friendship with Ysätters-Kajsa brought him luck in the chase may *possibly* be due to the fact that his patron was of the *female sex* :

> Once Lasse asked his neighbour to accompany him on the chase, and the latter, expecting a good bag, was not slow to accept the invitation. They went forth in the evening and built themselves a shelter of branches so as to start on the chase early in the morning. Later in the evening Kajsa came and visited the two hunters and asked them to show her their guns. First she examined the neighbour's gun, but immediately cried out " Fie ! ". Then she examined Lasse's gun, blew down the barrel, examined the priming powder and finally returned it, exclaiming, " Good, good, good, my lad ". What this meant soon appeared, when Lasse procured a plentiful bag whilst the other could not fire a single shot.[1]

That the luck of the chase might be jeopardized in a fatal manner by woman's influence appears from a number of instances collected by Frazer. Elephant hunters in East Africa believe that if their wives are unfaithful whilst they are out hunting, the elephants gain power over their pursuer and can kill or injure him. Consequently if a hunter hears evil rumours of his wife, he regards the chase as useless and returns home. Among the Moxos Indians in Southern Bolivia it is thought that an unfaithful wife may expose the hunter to the risk of being bitten by a jaguar or a snake. Consequently if such a misfortune should happen, the end may be that the woman will be slain without trial.

[1] Hofberg, *Nerikes gamla Minnen*, Orebro, 1868, p. 240.

In the chapter on " Aphrodite's Symbol " we shall relate how the cowrie shell, the special symbol of woman's fecundity, is used to bring luck in the chase and in fishing.

We should therefore be justified in concluding that these magic conceptions, which in various parts of the world are interwoven in a most significant manner with the life of present-day primitive peoples, also exercised a very deep influence in bygone times. Indeed, it may be extremely probable that prehistoric man at a very early stage began to develop magic rites as an aid in the struggle for food and as a guide in the terrifying and dark journey which lies beyond the greatest mystery of life—death. If such be the case, prehistoric discoveries should show remains which, correctly interpreted, may reveal to us something of the spiritual life of the prehistoric peoples.

It is a very alluring prospect which is here opened up to the archaeologist ; the possibility of reading in dead things something more than form, colour and pattern, of penetrating to the spiritual complexes which have set their seal on at least some prehistoric objects.

An epoch-making idea in the study of the magic of prehistoric peoples was given by the famous archaeologist Salomon Reinach in an essay, published in 1903, entitled " Art and Magic, with Reference to the Paintings and Engravings of the Reindeer Age."[1]

Reinach, in this little essay, gives an extremely probable interpretation of the wonderfully apt naturalistic art of the later Palaeolithic age, as it appears especially in the cave paintings of France and Spain and in the engravings on bone as well as in statuettes and other smaller objects created by the same artistically gifted race as produced the cave paintings.

It is mostly animal pictures which, often reproduced in a masterly manner, are found on the walls of caves on which artists of the later Palaeolithic age, contemporaries of the mammoth and the woolly-haired rhinoceros, worked. Reindeer and horses, bison and rhinoceros, as well as the mammoth, the giant of the Pleistocene big game, are the forms which he depicted by preference, with a knowledge of their structure and movements, as well as with a masterly sureness of delineation, which make this extremely early art one of the great mysteries in the history of art.

[1] *L'Anthropologie*, 1903, pp. 257–66.

It is remarkable that in most of these caves man is very seldom depicted, and the same is true of beasts of prey, although we know well from other sources that the cave bear, the cave lion, the cave hyaena, the sabre-toothed tiger and several other large beasts of prey were contemporary with Pleistocene man. It thus seems clear that the art of the later Palaeolithic age was predominantly occupied with the animal forms which were the chief objects of the chase. In this circumstance we find a clear indication that it was not art for art's sake, but the depicting of edible game for some definite purpose.

A further clue to the interpretation of these cave pictures, which so delight the modern art lover, is their occurrence in dark caves which we, of course, can easily illuminate with our electric torches, but which have always been in semi-darkness, however much the Pleistocene savage tried to illumine their rocky walls with his torches or smelly oil lamps. It is especially striking that in some cases pictures of animals were found far inside cave complexes, even in inaccessible passages.

These circumstances led Reinach to seek for customs among modern savages which might help to explain these primeval cave pictures. He then found that two English scientists, Spencer and Gillen, in a work published in 1899 on the tribes of Central Australia, had described certain usages which tend to throw light on the complex of ideas underlying the cave art of the Pleistocene age. It is the custom of these Australian tribes to depict those animal forms, such as the larva of a certain insect and the ostrich-like Australian emu, and its eggs, which play an especially important part in their domestic economy, and the purpose of this custom is, by means of imitative magic, on the one hand to promote the increase of these edible animals and on the other hand to obtain power over them in order more easily to capture them. It is also deserving of notice that these Australian paintings of game are often executed on the walls of cliffs, to which women, children and uninitiated boys are denied access.

In these comparisons Reinach finds a suggestion for an interpretation of the Pleistocene animal pictures in the caves of France, which he regards as being in the service of the magic of the chase for the purpose of increasing stocks of game and of obtaining power over them in order to facilitate their capture. On this interpretation it is easy to understand the presence of these pictures in remote and narrow passages in the interior of the caves : they were magic symbols for the use only of adult hunters, and were not supposed to be seen by women and children.

Not only the paintings on the walls of the caves, but also the small loose objects of bone and stone with images engraved by the same artists and depicting the same animal forms, are interpreted by Reinach according to a common formula. He dwells especially upon the pieces of reindeer antlers with animal engravings which are known as " bâtons de commandement ". These peculiar and often artistically decorated objects have been regarded sometimes as weapons, sometimes as insignia of chieftains and sometimes as dress ornaments, to mention only some of the thoroughly unsatisfactory explanations which have been given. These objects also are now regarded by Reinach as having been used in the magic ceremonies of the chase.

Direct evidence in support of the theory that the cave pictures are associated with the chase is to be found in certain pictures representing animals pierced by arrows. On the other hand certain recent discoveries showing reindeer engraved on small objects, and the famous pair of bisons at Tuc d'Audoubert in Ariége, sculptured in clay, may be interpreted as mating scenes intended to promote the increase of game.

A number of small statuettes in ivory, sandstone and steatite, representing women with a greatly exaggerated emphasis on the specifically female features, may most naturally be interpreted as representatives of the imitative magic which aims at securing the perpetuation of the race. " It is scarcely too far-fetched a suggestion that in these Palaeolithic female figures, which seem to speak the same language as Diana of Ephesus with her hundred breasts, from which the human race derives never-failing nourishment, we may also see a kind of goddess of fecundity," says Dr. Rydh in her *Grottmänniskans årtusenden*.

After Reinach had thus given a clue to the interpretation of the meaning of Palaeolithic pictorial art, his theory was applied to other groups of cliff paintings and stone engravings, such as those of Upper Egypt, which we know from Capart's work *Les débuts de l'art en Egypte*, 1904, those of Northern Africa in Frobenius and Obermaier's *Hadschra Maktuba*, 1925, and the stone engravings situated high above the sea in the Ligurian Alps, which were first studied by the Englishman Bicknell. During the last decades there have been found in Northern Sweden and Norway, and as far as the southern parts of the country, naturalistic cliff paintings and stone engravings which have been made known for all time by the work of Hallström and A. W. Brögger. In this case we are concerned principally with the magic of stags, in the far north of reindeer, in Central Sweden of elks, and in Southern Norway of stags. These two scholars regard it as probable that these Nordic cliff pictures are derived from Palaeolithic art, even though they cannot be older than the Neolithic age. Most writers who have dealt with this subject seem to be agreed that these pictures had their source in the magic of the chase, and it has been pointed out that their occurrence near waterfalls, marine cliffs and solitary inland lakes seems to indicate the ancient places where the ritual of the chase was practised.

The wide and extremely difficult problem of interpreting the immense stone engraving material of the Bronze age in Southern Sweden has been placed in a new light by Almgren's treatise " Hällristningar och Kultbruk ", *Vitterhets Historie och Antikvitets Akademiens handlingar*, 35, Stockholm, 1926–7.

Everybody who knows this modest and learned archaeologist, equally original and fertile as a teacher and as a scientist, and the harsh fate which compelled him prematurely to moderate his zeal for research, will receive with reverence this masterly work, in which he announces his abandonment of scientific work. There is something monumental and profoundly touching in the infallible sureness with which this aged, and now blind, scholar dominates from memory the immense pictorial and literary material, and it almost seems as if the physical darkness in which he is now compelled to live has bestowed on him the opportunity for that deeper contemplation which has given to us an interpretation of this obscure material which is at once consistent and convincing.

Characteristic of the rapid development of prehistoric Nordic research in our day is the radical transformation which the problem of the stone engravings has undergone in the last twelve years. Scholars such as Montelius and Eckhoff, who were until quite recently still among us, represented the earlier historical view, which saw in the cliff engravings a pictorial language with an historical content, telling us of sea journeys, battles and other events. By his " The Scandinavian Rock Engravings and their Significance ", *Ymer*, 1916, and a series of subsequent essays, Ekholm paved the way for new conceptions. He advanced numerous parallels between the Nordic cliff pictures and the Egyptian death cult, and by means of these comparisons came to the conclusion, which he afterwards consistently developed, that the stone engravings are connected with the reverence for the dead of the people of the Bronze age.

An essentially similar theory was developed by Nordén in his research into the Bronze age in Östergötland, and by his especially important discovery of engravings in the Norrköping district he was able to furnish an account of their connection with the cultivated soil, an account which is of great importance in the attempt at a solution of the whole problem of rock engravings which will be briefly surveyed in the following paragraphs.

FIG. 128.—Chinese Bronze-age jar, of which the neck is decorated with zig-zag signs, which are the archaic forms of the Chinese character " lightning ".

In his desire to include all the phenomena of rock engravings under a common formula Almgren proceeds from the " älfkvarnarna ", or elfin mills, to use a name established in popular speech. These are the oldest of the varied pictorial elements of the cliff pictures, in so far as groups of only elfin mills occur as early as in connection with the latest Stone age graves.

Almgren considers that these simple circular cavities in the rock are, as it were, the root symbols from which the whole of the complex pictorial script developed.

Just as ritual boring is used among primitive peoples as a symbolical expression for the human act of coition, and this action of the cult may be subsequently employed with a transferred meaning in the service of the general cult of fertility, so Almgren considers that analogically the elfin mills symbolize the marriage of the male force, cloud-thunder-rain, and the female, mother earth.

From these simple symbols, which, if this interpretation be correct, embrace the fundamental element of the fertility cult, the whole of the richly developed harvest cult of the Bronze age was, according to Almgren, developed, especially by borrowings from the cult of fertility which was developed in the countries around the eastern Mediterranean. The most important element in the large Bronze age pictures is the *ship*, which was taken by representatives of the older school as essential evidence in support of their historical interpretation. Since, however, the ship of the rock pictures sometimes shows symbols well known in the Orient, such as the *tree* and the *wheel*, they can scarcely represent sea journeys, but rather refer to cult customs, as in the case of the tree of life and the sun-wheel. In this question we derive even greater certainty from Almgren's observation that in individual cases the engraved ship is borne by a man, exactly in the same way as in pictures of Egyptian cult scenes.

FIG. 129.—Bronze rattle, with sun-wheel on top and bull's head on the base (*Crown Prince of Sweden's Chinese collection*).

In the ancient religion of Egypt the ship played an important part as the bearer of the sun during its nightly journey from evening to morning, just as in the death cult it bore the dead. In the same way Almgren believes that the ship, which demonstrably also plays a large part in our Nordic burial cult, was, on the evidence of the rock pictures, found far from graves in the middle of the old cultivated fields, a dominating element in the harvest religion of the Bronze age.

From these two starting-points, the *elfin mills* and *the ship*, which constitute a large part of the material of these rock pictures, Almgren proceeds to classify the remaining elements, such as, for example, pictures of ploughing (ritual ploughing), love scenes (the marriage of the god of fertility), battle scenes (the struggle between the powers of summer and winter), etc., under the general fertility cult.

Almgren, however, does not neglect the force of the evidence which Ekholm advanced for his theory of the connection of the engravings with the death cult. The truth is probably to be found in a combination of the two views expressed in Almgren's theory (p. 157). " Since it is manifest that the sun and fertility engravings were originally devised to promote the harvests and fecundity in human beings, and only afterwards, by analogy, were used to give new and continued life, it is natural to suppose that the custom, for purposes of magic, of engraving pictures of these rites was also at first and most generally adopted in the service of the general cult and only as a special case in the death cult."

In the hasty survey of a great amount of varied folklore and archaeological material which we have just concluded, we find as a consistent leading motive the imitative acts, intended, by way of resemblance, to promote the survival of the species, whether the endeavour is directed towards making women pregnant, game numerous and easily captured or the powers of the seasons and the weather bestow a rich harvest.

These fertility rites, which primarily envisage the welfare of the living, were transferred by a simple process of thought to the dead member of the family who is about to set forth on the long and dark journey and who will require all the help which his relatives can give him.

In this chapter we have made the acquaintance of the general mentality of imitative magic. In the chapter on " Aphrodite's Symbol " we shall find how in this field imitative magic operates under numerous forms, but with the consistent endeavour to dominate the world of the living and the dead by the same magic symbols.

In connection with Almgren's inspired and broadly conceived attempt to interpret the engravings of the Bronze age in Sweden, I would wish to furnish some notes on the occurrence in the Far East of some of the cult symbols found in the Swedish rock pictures.

In proportion as one penetrates deeper into the study of folk magic, religion and cults, we find more and more numerous and surprising examples of how religious conceptions and the symbols representing them crop up amongst peoples far apart. It is probably in many cases too early to discuss the origin and dissemination of these widely practised customs. Only when the material is much more plentiful and better sifted can we hope to succeed in our attack upon the great final problem. It is only as a very modest contribution to this collection of material that I have written the following notes, which are inspired by reading Almgren's suggestive work.

Cult boats.—During the festival of the dragon boat, which is celebrated on the fifth day of the fifth Chinese month, i.e. at the beginning of the period of vegetation, it was customary in China to arrange processions on the water, with boats adorned with a dragon's image in the bows, and the sides of which gave a suggestion of a dragon's body.

In this connection it is worthy of mention that the acrobats whom one often sees wandering from house to house in the streets of Peking showing their simple tricks, also carry a little boat among their paraphernalia.

Since in the Swedish rock pictures, as also in other pictorial representations and cult customs in Europe and South-western Asia, the sacred boat and the sacred tree are combined in such a manner that one or more trees are borne by the ship, it may be of interest to mention that in the Museum of Far Eastern Antiquities there is a Japanese postcard showing a tree which has been clipped to represent a boat bearing a tree.

The Tree of Life.—For anybody who may have the opportunity it will doubtless be an extremely profitable undertaking to make a thorough investigation of the extraordinarily widespread and varied cult of the tree in China.

During a railway journey through the province of Shantung one need only look at the beautiful cypress groves hedging in the cemeteries and so characteristically adorning the otherwise treeless plain to understand the part which the *arbor vitae* plays in Chinese religious life. It would be interesting, among other things, to discover whether certain trees providing valuable drugs of the Chinese pharmacopoeia, such as the chaulmoogra tree of Southern China, which provides mankind with the only remedy for leprosy, has contributed largely to the development of the Chinese tree cult.

In the case of the dead, certain kinds of trees play a very important rôle. The immense and incredibly thick coffins are made by preference of certain kinds of wood which are especially rich in life-giving substance. On two occasions, in 1918 in Honan and in 1920 in Hupei, I have had occasion during my travels in China to see trees which were the object of a local cult and on the trunks of which were affixed prayers for a cure for disease and other afflictions (Fig. 127, p. 283).

The Sun-wheel.—I do not know to what extent the sun-wheel enters into Chinese decorative design. On the other hand I think I ought to mention in this connection the circular symbols, with spokes in a diagonal position, which I found on burial urns in Kansu of the Hsin Tien period (Bronze age).

One prehistoric object which is possibly an image of the sun-wheel is the bronze rattle which is not infrequently found in small Chinese bronzes and of which H.R.H. the Crown Prince of Sweden possesses a very fine specimen, in which the lower part is decorated by two bulls' heads on each side (Fig. 129).

Cult Axes.—Pictures of axes are not uncommon in Swedish stone engravings and play an important rôle in the rock pictures in the Ligurian Alps. That cult axes were common in ancient China appears from the magnificent bronze axes, which can scarcely have been real weapons, and from the daggers (ko) which have been found in early historical graves.

Sacred Ploughing.—To judge from the rock carvings, ritual ploughing was an important element in the harvest ritual of the Nordic Bronze age.

In this connection we should remember the well-known ritual action performed every year by the Chinese Emperor, when he ploughed a furrow in a field near the Temple of Agriculture in Peking.

FIG. 130.—Dragon Boat. (*After Allom, " China "*).

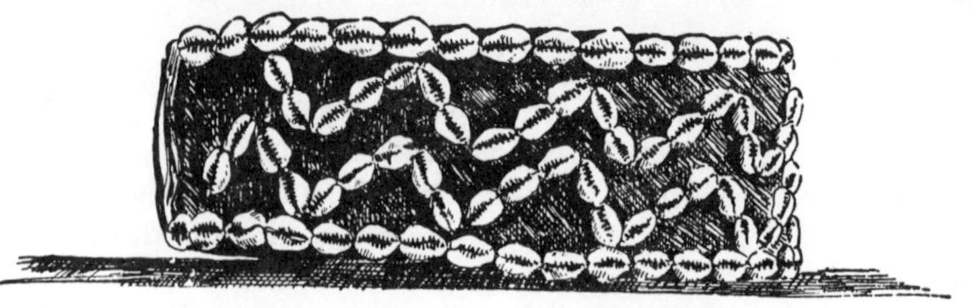

FIG. 131.—A woman's cap with cowrie shells, used by the Hottentots.

CHAPTER NINETEEN

APHRODITE'S SYMBOL

THE seashore has always been a playground for mankind.

It was there that we learned to listen to the breathing of Nature in the murmuring of the waves on the wet sand, or, in a larger and more mysterious cycle, in the rising and falling rhythm of the tides. But when the ebb sucked the water away from the cliffs, there was revealed in crevices and pools an alluring world of brightly coloured things. Under the slimy branches of the brown sea-weed shone the pale rose-coloured calcareous algae, the beautiful orange chalices of the sea anemones and thousands of graceful shells.

This boundary line between two worlds, which for most modern civilized peoples is a place only for play, recreation and rest, was to prehistoric peoples the most productive of all places for the collection of animal food. To hunt the big game of the forests and steppes was accompanied by danger, to go out on the open waters to catch fish required apparatus which primitive man only gradually learned to master. But on the sands at ebb tide and in the pools by the cliffs there were edible gastropods and mussels ready for eating, and whole groups of people became in this way consumers of shells, as the remains of their shell heaps bear witness.

The molluscs of the shore fauna were not only edible, their graceful shells furnished to the mothers of our race beautiful necklaces and pendants. Beautiful small shells such as *Nassa*, *Oliva* and *Olivella* were available for this purpose, without further treatment than preparation for threading on a string, to adorn the throat of a beauty.

But this was not all. Large mussel shells, such as *Tridacna*,

Venus and various others were broken up and shaped into beads and other objects for use and decoration.

In certain mussel shells were also found natural pearls, which not only became the most precious objects of adornment, but were at the same time a convenient means of accumulating and preserving wealth. They also came to play a characteristic part in the development of the earliest civilization.

Another early discovery which helped to bestow beauty on the lives of the ancient peoples was the observation that certain molluscs produce a certain secretion, which could be worked up into a splendid dye, purple. Great heaps of the shells of these purple molluscs, *Purpura* and *Murex*, have been found from ancient times, "shell dumps", consisting of a single species, with the shell opened in a characteristic manner, showing that it was only the purple gland which was sought for.

The purple industry is in a manner connected with another use of the large mollusc shells, namely as trumpets for war and ritual purposes. The *Murex* shell, like the shells of other large-sized gastropods, *Triton*, *Buccinum*, *Strombus*, *Fusus*, etc., are admirably suited, if a hole is bored through the tip, for producing a strong and penetrating note, and thus became one of the earliest musical instruments.

The seashore was in many ways an inspiration to the ancient peoples. The aureole of the sun, as it rises from the sea, gave rise to one of the oldest forms of natural religion, and one of the first personal divinities, the goddess of love and fecundity, rose from the bosom of the sea and was created from the foam of the waves.

But if Elliot Smith is correct in his attractive theory of the connection between the goddesses of fecundity of the ancient peoples, the Assyrian-Babylonian Ishtar, the Egyptian Hathor, the Greek Aphrodite and the Roman Venus, they have all developed from ideas associated with the cowrie shell. In any case the folklore complex which has its centre in this shell is so varied and of such ancient origin that it is necessary for our present purpose to survey the field. The most important data in what follows are derived from Stearn, *Ethno-Conchology : a Study of Primitive Money*, 1889; O. Schneider, *Muschelgeldstudien*, 1905; and, above all, J. W. Jackson, *Shells as Evidence of the Migration of Early Culture*, 1917, with an extremely interesting introduction by Professor G. Elliot Smith. In order not to overload my survey I shall not give detailed references to these works, but refer only to data derived from other sources.

My account of the folklore of the cowrie shell scarcely contains anything new, but I have arranged the material in a manner different to that of other writers, as my purpose is not so much to enter into geographical details as to throw light upon the changing facets of the ethnology of the cowrie.

The Distribution of the Cowrie Shell.—There exist in tropical seas a large number of kinds of the genus *Cypraea*, among which some of the larger and beautifully coloured ones were much valued as ornaments. But there are a couple of the smaller forms which have come to play a vast and peculiar rôle in the history of the human race. Foremost of these in importance is *C. moneta*, which obtained its name from the great part which it played as money among primitive peoples. A closely related form is *C. annulus*, which, though to a less extent, came to share the fame and popularity of the money cowrie.

Jackson, on page 124 of his book, gives a map of the distribution of these two kinds of cowrie, and according to this map they live in the littoral belt of the Indian Ocean and in the western part of the Pacific Ocean. They also occur on the east coast of Africa and in the islands of the Pacific. On the other hand they are entirely absent from the coasts of America, which should be carefully noted, since cowrie shells, as we shall see, have been found among the remains of American Indians, possibly also in a pre-Columbian find. It is of interest that both *C. moneta* and *C. annulus* are found in the Red Sea, since the ancient Egyptians and the Mediterranean peoples of antiquity probably obtained their supplies from that source.

As regards the provision of cowries for China and Japan there are two circumstances deserving of mention. Marco Polo relates that he (in the thirteenth century) found cowries in use as money in Yünnan and that they were brought from the Pulo Condore islands off the south coast of Cochin China.

The cowrie, *C. moneta*, is also said to occur in the Liu Kiu islands connecting Japan and Formosa.

The catch of cowries seems to have been especially important in the Laccadive and Maldive islands. According to two reports, one from the tenth and one from the seventeenth century, the catch appears to have been made by women, and only at new moon and full moon. We may possibly wonder whether these provisions are in any way connected with the cultural complex surrounding the cowrie shell.

Cowries in Graves.—In Chapter XX we shall see how extensive is the use of cowries, real or imitation, as burial ware in China from the Yang Shao age until at least as late as the beginning of the Christian era. A survey of the connection of the cowrie

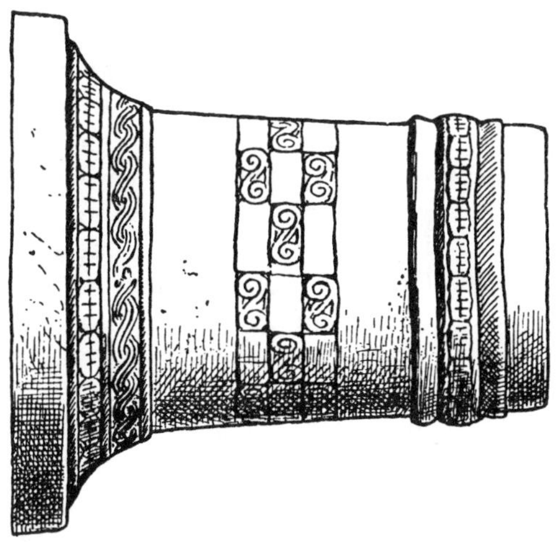

FIG. 132.—Chinese axle-mounting in bronze, decorated with rows of cowrie images (natural size).

with burial rites in other parts of the world will show how this little mollusc shell has deep roots in the early pre-history of the human race.

One of the earliest discoveries of cowries as burial ware originates from the later Palaeolithic age. In the Laugerie-Basse cave in the Vézère valley in Dordogne a number of cowries belonging to two Mediterranean species, *C. pyrum* and *C. lurida*, were found together with a skeleton. It is a remarkable fact that they were found in pairs, four on the forehead, one close to each upper arm, four near the knees and thighs and two on each foot. Through every shell a hole was bored.

Also belonging to the later Palaeolithic age is the cave discovery, Grotte des Enfants, at Mentone (Riviera), in which were found a *Cypraea* and *Cassis rufa*, a mollusc which is indigenous to the Indian Ocean. In another Mentone cave (Barma Grande) a pierced cowrie was found in a grave beside each thigh-bone.

In the pre-dynastic graves in Egypt there have been found both *Cypraea moneta* and *C. annulus*, and it may be added that these forms, together with several others, especially species living in the Red Sea, have been found in later graves in Egypt and Nubia.

In Crete there have been found black cowries, probably *C. pantherina*. As the discoveries were made in the ruins of Minoan houses we are in this case not concerned with burial ware.

A cowrie discovery which in a most remarkable manner throws a bridge between the great European-African cowrie area and that of our discoveries in Eastern Asia is the cowrie shells which were found during the excavations of the Pumpelly expedition at Anau in Russian Turkestan. In this case there is no indication that the finds were made in graves. Curiously enough, these extremely important shells are mentioned in the learned report of the expedition merely as " mussels ". If Pumpelly had imagined that he had discovered a marine mollusc, he would hardly have advanced his theory of the Anau Kurgans as monuments of an isolated oasis civilization.

In India there are several cases of the discovery of *C. moneta* in prehistoric deposits, together with stone implements, fragments of flint, agate, metal, and of jars.

It is remarkable that the cowrie is here everywhere associated with the trumpet shell, *Turbinella pyrum*, which played so important a part, in India, in the ancient ritual acts.

Cypraea moneta was also found in the famous Kuban necropolis on the northern slopes of the Caucasus. This cemetery dates from the end of the Bronze age and the transition to the Iron age (1300–1700 B.C.).

In the neighbourhood of Kiev cowries have been found in Scythian graves.

In the Ananino civilization—in a cultural region contemporary with the civilization of the Scythians of the Black Sea—near the

Kama river, west of the Urals, cowries (*C. moneta*) were found in graves H and K in the Ananino necropolis. Both of these were graves of women.[1]

These discoveries in the widespread regions of the steppe nomads throw a bridge over to my discoveries in Chen Fan (south-western part of the Gobi desert), which belongs to the most south-easterly steppe province (Ordos).

Numerous discoveries of *C. moneta* and *C. annulus* have been made in prehistoric and early historic graves in Bosnia, France, England and Germany, especially in the old amber region of the Prussian Baltic coast.

A discovery of *C. moneta* of especial interest to us Swedes is that at Birka, of the tenth century. Together with Kufian coins, Silurian fossils from Gothland, Cretaceous fossils from Scania and mollusc shells from the west coast of Sweden, were found five shells of the *C. moneta*.[2]

A cowrie discovery in a grave removed from the chief area of its use, in Eurasia, constitutes one of the connections between the Old World and America which it is difficult to interpret.

In a grave in the Roden Mounds in Tennessee, possibly dating from the period before the Indians came into contact with the whites, five shells of *C. moneta* were found. Jackson, from whom I derive this information, considers that the cowrie and the ideas associated with it came to America long before the arrival of the white men, but other scientists, such as the eminent expert on molluscs, W. H. Dall, consider that the Roden Mounds discovery may contain cowries brought over in one of Columbus's ships !

Having now in all brevity, and far from completely, surveyed the finds of cowries in ancient graves, it is time to collect information concerning the use of the cowrie shell in association with modern burial rites.

In this connection we would first advance a report from India that in funeral processions cowrie shells are strewn along the road from the house of the dead to the grave, a custom which

[1] A. M. Tallgren, " L'époque dite d'Ananino ", *Finska Fornminnes-föreningens Tidskrift*, XXX, Helsingfors, 1919, pp. 28–9.

[2] *Congrès internat. d'Anthropol. et Archéol. Préhist. 1874*, Stockholm, 1876, Vol. II, pp. 619–29.

has its parallel in the Chinese custom of strewing paper imitations of copper money along the funeral route.

From Africa come many reports throwing light on the rôle of the cowrie at burials. It appears to have been the custom there to place on the grave of the dead larger or smaller quantities of cowries. Thus it is reported from the Niger district that a young chieftain caused much annoyance by opening his father's grave in order to take the cowrie hoard which had been bestowed upon the dead.

According to another account it was customary at the interment of a chieftain to lay beside his mouth a calabash filled with beads and cowries in order " to pay travelling expenses ".

From Togoland we have an account which points to the same background as in the last instance. It is customary at burials there for relatives and friends to place in the grave quantities of cowrie shells in order that the dead may be able to buy food and palm wine and to pay the old ferryman Akotia, who will take him in his boat over the broad River Assisa to the country of the dead.

A peculiar and circumstantial form of magic is reported from Uganda. Five months after the burial of a king the grave is opened and the head is separated from the body. The lower jaw is removed and placed in an ant heap for cleaning, whilst the skull is re-interred by itself near to the original grave. When the ants have cleaned the jaw, it is washed in ale and milk, wrapped up in fine bark cloth, smeared with butter and adorned with beads and cowries. Finally the jaw thus adorned is preserved in a special temple built for the purpose.

The Cowrie as Money.—At the beginning of the Chinese historic era, during the Yin dynasty, this shell was the commonest form of money. Later on the natural cowrie shell was replaced, first by metal imitations, and later by metallic money modelled upon other objects. Nevertheless the cowrie retained its position as money for centuries in remote parts of the country. Thus we have already referred to the fact that as late as Marco Polo's time the cowrie was in use at Yünnan. There is a further report that in 1578 this province paid a tribute of 5,769 chams of shells and that in the same century the cowrie was officially demonetized.

Whether or not the cowrie was ever used as money in Japan

I do not know, but the Japanese name "Takaragai" (takara = wealth and gai = shell) points to the same association of the ideas of value and shell as in the Chinese "Pei".

There is a report from modern Indo-China of the use of the cowrie as money in quite modern times, for it was seen in circulation in Luang Prabang in the latter part of the nineteenth century.

At the end of the seventeenth and as late as the middle of the eighteenth century the cowrie was used as money in Siam, but in 1881 it was no longer in use in Bangkok.

In the island world of the Pacific Ocean the cowrie has been widely used as money, as is shown from reports from the Bismarck archipelago, the New Hebrides, New Caledonia and Hawaii.

In India the cowrie was probably used as money as early as the beginning of our era. In any case we can cite the Chinese traveller Fa Hsien of the fourth century. In the thirteenth century the cowrie was in common circulation in Bengal and in the middle of the eighteenth century it was in use in Hindustan. As late as that century the cowrie has been seen in native retail trade in India.

In Equatorial Africa the cowrie was widely used as money until quite modern times, and in this connection Schneider in his *Muschelgeldstudien* has given a great deal of interesting information which cannot be reproduced here. In any case, from this wealth of data we are enabled to make two definite observations which are of importance to our present purpose, namely that in West Africa the monetary area of the cowrie is much more restricted than the area in which the cowrie is used as an ornament or an amulet, and also that its use as an ornament survived after its use as money had ceased.

The Cowrie as an Ornament.—In the work just cited Schneider contrasts the use of the cowrie as money and as an ornament, but he remarks that at the same time we must not overlook the rôle of the cowrie as an amulet, in which capacity it acquires "an even greater and deeper mystical significance". This latter aspect of cowrie folklore has been treated in an entirely new way by Elliot Smith and Jackson. There is very good reason to suspect that nearly all the uses of the cowrie which at first sight appear purely decorative are really based upon ancient magical conceptions, and that the decorative element only predominated in modern times after the magical complex of ideas had been dimmed and forced into the background.

After I had convinced myself of this truth I thought that for my present purpose it would be of less importance to describe in detail the use of the cowrie as an ornament, and consequently in what follows I shall endeavour group by group to trace the magic conceptions which underlie the widespread and varied uses of this mollusc as an ornament with an *essentially mystical emphasis*.

The Cowrie and Woman.—The cowrie has been used by widely dispersed peoples as an ornament for women.

There is no evidence of this use from China, but Dr. Thompson, an English missionary doctor who accompanied General Pereira on his last journey to the frontier territory between Western China and Eastern Tibet, has told me that among one of these frontier tribes he saw a girl wearing cowries as an ornament in the hair.

In Burma the women of the Taungtha tribe wear a skirt adorned with a broad belt of cowrie shells.

From India there is much evidence. In the province of Nagpur the Brinjari women wear cowries sewn on their dresses. In the Punjab the *Cypraea annulus* is worn by native women. In the Nilgiri mountains of Southern India the Toda women wear bracelets and necklaces adorned with cowrie shells.

The Bedouin women of Southern Arabia adorn their girdles with cowrie money.

Among some of the Volga peoples, such as the Cheremisses and the Mordovins, cowrie money was used for necklaces and to adorn the breast and forehead. The Bashkir women wore cowries in their peculiar head ornaments and the Kirghis women also adorned themselves with the shell.

From Africa there is much evidence: in the Cameroons the women wear as many as 200 cowrie shells in their hair ornaments. In Morocco the daughter of a chieftain was adorned by these shells; the women of Tibesti wore them and the Joloff women fastened them to their girdles. The Kufu women bound cowries to the fringes of the goatskins and sheepskins which they wore round their hips, and so on.

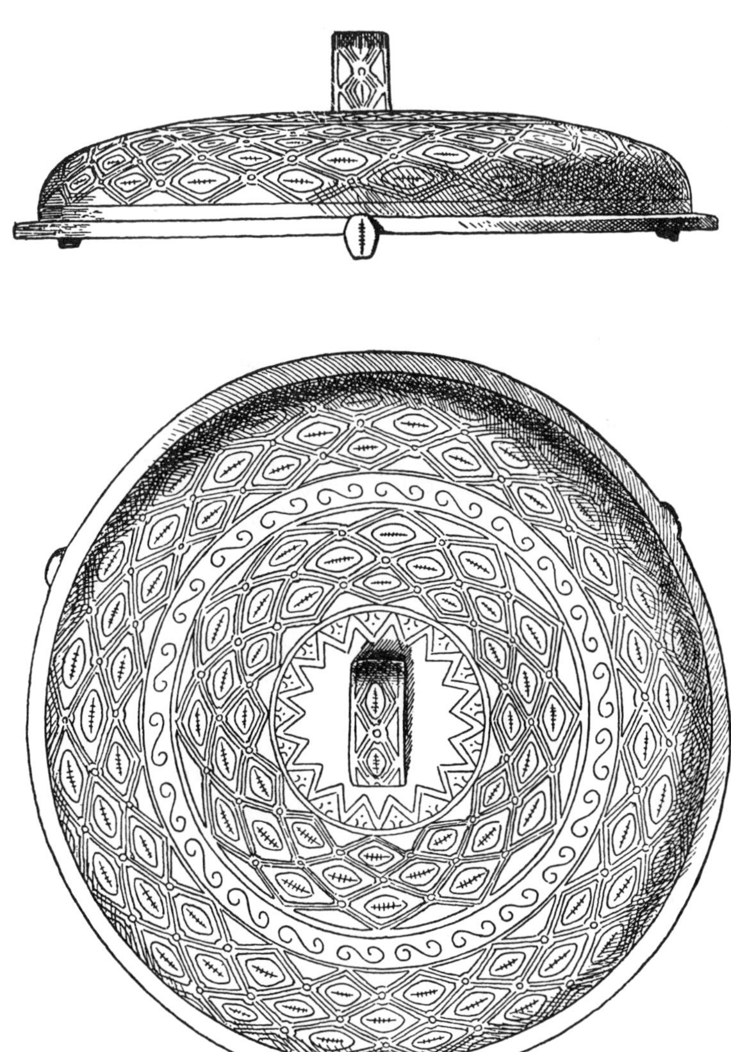

FIG. 133.—Chinese bronze lid with copious cowrie embellishments. Probably Han dynasty (⅔ natural size).

It deserves mention that the use of the cowrie as a personal ornament is not restricted to women. In the Haussa country the Kado men wore a leather apron hung with cowries and the Kavirondo men of East Africa are known for their peculiar and carefully worked hair ornaments made of these shells.

But if we return to women we need not seek far to find this wearing of cowries associated with a very specific complex of ideas.

The Tiagy girls wear a mollusc shell, probably a cowrie, as a symbol of their virginity, and in the event of a wrong step they must remove this symbol of honour.

In many places the cowrie is associated with betrothals. Among the Jur people beads and cowries constitute an indispensable part of the bridal gifts. The Akamba women wear belts and aprons decorated with beads and cowries, but these are removed after the birth of the first child. The Masai girls wear a band covered with cowrie shells round their heads during the period of their engagement. In Benin, among the Bini people it is customary among the upper classes to give cowries and kola nuts, and palm wine, as betrothal gifts.

Among the Chitti in Southern India the unmarried women wear cowrie shells.

The cowrie is associated with pregnancy. If we return in the first instance to Africa, from which continent data are abundant, we shall find that in Togoland numbers of cowries are worn by pregnant women as a protection against danger.

Among the Bini (Benin) one often sees a tree planted by the roadside, near which is an earth mound. This tree has been planted in memory of a woman who bore a child on this spot. So also in India the cowrie is associated with pregnancy and there is interesting evidence of the same kind from Japan. In connection with child-birth the cowrie acquires a special name, "*Koyasu-gai*" (easy birth shell), and Japanese women are accustomed to hold a *Cypraea* shell in their hand as a support during the hours of pain.

The women of Pompeii wore *Cypraea* shells as a remedy for sterility.

The Cowrie as an Image of the Vulva.—In his suggestive introduction to Jackson's book Elliot Smith writes: "The whole of the complex shell cult seems to have sprung from the resemblance which a group of primitive men believed they saw between the cowrie and the female vulva."

To support this he quotes the authors of the eighteenth century, and in this connection the following extracts from Adamson's *Histoire naturelle de Sénégal* deserve to be mentioned: "Concha Venerea sic dicta quia partem foemineam quodam modo repraesentat: externe quidem per labiorum fissuram, interne vero propter cavitatem uterum mentientem . . . Sunto igitur dictae Porcellanae (id est Venereae) ob aliquam cum pudendo muliebri similitudinem."

FIG. 134.—"Easy birth" shell used in Japan ($\frac{2}{3}$ natural size).

For the proper understanding of this passage it should be added that the word cowrie is derived from a Greek word which means "a little pig"[1]; that the name given by the Romans to this shell was "*porci*", or "*porculi*", whilst a modern French name is "*porc de mer*", which is closely related to "porcelain", "porcelain shell".

In Japan the conception of the cowrie as an image of the female vulva appears still to survive. It is also quite probable that the same association exists among some primitive peoples, where the cowrie is connected with fecundity magic. It will be an important task for ethnographers to examine this subject. It is of an urgent nature, since under modern conditions the cowrie is rapidly falling into disuse.

Association with Children.—Having become familiar with the internal connection between the cowrie and woman as the mother of the race, it is scarcely surprising that this object is sometimes

[1] According to another writer the word is derived from India: Skt. "*Kaparda*"; Mahratti "*kavari*", Hindi and Urdu "*kauri*" (*kaudi*).

worn by children as an amulet to protect them against the " evil eye ", or against misfortune or sickness.

Thus the cowrie is worn by children in present-day Egypt as a protection against the " evil eye ". In Corfu children wear the cowrie in combination with a Christian medal, and similar usages exist in Montenegro. In Togoland (Africa) the children wear a couple of cowries in their hair as a protection against evil.

In the same way I would interpret an observation which I made in Northern Kansu in July 1924. I was then travelling between Liangchow and Chen Fan and stopped for lunch at a small Chinese inn on the road. To my considerable satisfaction I noticed that the landlady's little boy was running about with a cowrie shell fastened in his hair. I offered her a dollar for the shell, but she rejected my very generous offer with a decision which gave me the impression that she would not at any price deprive her boy of his precious amulet.

Circumcision.—Interesting evidence comes from Togoland. In circumcision the operator takes a cowrie, puts it on the brow of the boy to be operated and buries the excised foreskin together with the cowrie shell. As a reward for his work he receives 81 cowries.

Initiation Rites.—In two widely separated parts of the globe the cowrie is associated with mystical initiation rites.

Among the Sierra Leone cannibals of West Africa cowries were included in the medicine bag used in the Human Leopard Society.

Similar usages occur among the Ojibwa and Menomini Indians of North America, in whose great Medicine Society the *Cypraea moneta*—not a native of America and consequently a very rare shell—was included in the contents of the medicine bag.

In both cases Jackson, who associated these curiously identical rites, speaks of the cowrie as a " symbol of life ".

Gods and Fetishes.—We obtain from Togoland a fairly detailed picture of the connection of the cowrie with religious customs. At the entrance to villages there are in many places idols with cowrie shells for eyes, and before them are placed offerings in the form of bottles and calabashes filled with cowries.

Among Ewe negroes in Togoland the cowrie is used not only

for the eyes of the Begbowo idol, but fetish priests and priestesses also adorn themselves with cowries for their ritual dances. When a girl seeks admission among the Ewe priestesses her relations pay a fee in cowries.

The resemblance of the cowrie to an almost closed eye must have been the origin of the use of the shell for the eyes of fetishes. In addition to the case already quoted it may be mentioned that in the Congo we also find similar fetishes, human figures, carved in wood, with cowries for eyes.

Similarly it is reported from New Zealand that a species of cowrie, *Cypraea asellus*, is used for the eyes of idols.

In Benin (West Africa) the large houses contain an altar for the worship of the river god Olokun, and here also the cowrie is an object of the cult. In an Olokun temple there is a wooden image of the river-god, in front of which sits a priest half hidden by long strings of cowries suspended from the roof.

The custom of offering cowries to the gods is found in more than one place in Africa. In one place the negroes made this offering to their god because he gave them water, seed and yam roots.

In another case cowries were offered to the fetish which protects against smallpox.

Administration of Justice.—In Africa (Togoland) the cowrie is also taken into the service of the administration of justice. In trial for murder the priest blows poison towards the sun through a pipe decorated with cowries. If the suspicion is justified, blood issues from the pipe. In the trial of a thief two pieces of wood are used with a cowrie at each end.

Augury.—For this purpose the cowrie is used in several places in Africa, such as Liberia, Togoland and Uganda. Among the Egba people this shell was used for auguries. The war priest threw 16 cowries into the air; if the majority fell with the opening to the ground it meant war. Among the same people the custom existed of heaping up masses of cowries on prisoners of war, after which they were made drunk and then killed. In this way it was thought that not only messages but also the cowrie treasure could be transferred to the dead of those who executed the cult.

Games.—In places in Africa the cowrie was also used for a

very simple game of chance. In one case 4 cowries were thrown on the ground. If the majority fell with the opening upwards it was said that the " cowrie smiled ", and this smile meant a win.

Hunting and Fishing.—Another field in which the cowrie was used as a lucky medium was in hunting and fishing. In the Pacific islands, for example in Ohau (Hawaii Islands), cowries are hung in the fishing nets in order to bring luck to the catch. Some ethnologists have described these objects as " sinkers ", but the interpretation here given has more in its favour.

In Togoland (Africa) the hunting fetishes were adorned with cowrie shells.

Among the remarkable bronze relief plates which the English discovered in Benin there are also pictures of leopard hunters with immense helmets decorated with cowries.

Amazons and Head-hunters.—In Dahomey the King's Amazons dwelt in a house which was richly decorated with human skulls and cowrie garlands. It was their custom to dip a cowrie in the blood of the slain enemy and with the congealing blood as a sort of cement to secure the cowrie to the stock of the gun as a symbol of triumph. Sometimes they instituted the " battle for the cowries ", the result of which was that the person on whom the cowries were thrown was killed, and finally cowries were thrown on the blood-drenched soil.

In Assam, among the Naga people, head-hunting was a pre-condition to taking a wife. The warrior who killed his enemy had the right to wear a shirt and a collar decorated with cowries, red-coloured tufts of goat hair and locks of the hair of the dead enemy.

Among the Patosiwa people of Seran, who were also head-hunters, a man might not marry until he could show the head of a slain enemy. As evidence of his bravery he wore round his neck or arm as many cowrie shells as he had slain enemies.

A curious analogy has been adduced from Africa, where the head-hunting Djibba people wear not only cowries, but also the hair of the heads of the slain enemies.

Offerings to Rivers, Springs and Trees.—Cowries have been offered to the spirit of the trees, as also to rivers and springs, in order that the rivers may continue to flow and the springs to gush. This connection is of especial interest, as primitive peoples attributed life-giving power to all of them.

Horses and other Riding and Pack Animals.—The Arabs of North-western Darfur weave cowrie shells into the manes of their camels and horses. In India elephants are decorated with cowrie shells.

In Morea in Greece a traveller in 1907 saw a horse which bore an amulet consisting of the jaw of a wild boar from which hung a cross consisting of four cowrie shells sewn on leather.

The custom of decorating the harness of horses with cowrie shells extends from Persia through Hungary up to Germany and Scandinavia. As early as 1741 German hussar horses bore this decoration and as late as 1905 it was customary with the horses of officers.

So also this custom of decorating harness with cowries penetrated as far as Sweden. Major D. F. Kuylenstierna, formerly Director of the Artillery Museum, has kindly informed me that in the nineteenth century and possibly earlier, hussars and the mounted artillery used this decoration, though probably only on the horses of officers.

In the Nordiska Museum there is a cowrie bit, once in use among the people. Both Baron Rudolf Cederström, Chief of the Armoury, and Major Kuylenstierna were of opinion that the people borrowed this custom, and a great deal more, from military uniforms.

We have now followed through time and space the wanderings in human hands of the little cowrie shell.

As early as the first known appearance of *Homo sapiens* this shining little shell was a thing of value, as appears from the Cro-Magnon graves at Laugerie-Basse. On the other hand the writer of these lines also had direct evidence of the survival of the use of the cowrie in our day in the Chinese boy who wore a cowrie woven into his hair.

From its place of origin in the Indian Ocean cowrie money penetrated into far-distant lands. The peoples of antiquity fetched it from the Red Sea. It spread to Central Asia as early as the Stone age. It reached the American continent, where it is a stranger, and was highly esteemed there, perhaps before the time of Columbus. Even as far away as Scandinavia there were visible some of the undulations of the wave of cowrie customs, first in Ansgar's time and again in the mounted uniforms of the last century.

What is the reason why this little mollusc, selected from many others, of which some are more graceful and more beautifully coloured than it, should have played such a unique rôle in the history of the human race ?

By its form, which resists wear, by its thickness and hard polish of surface, the cowrie is no doubt admirably suited for use as money. But its use as an amulet and as an ornament extended far beyond the areas where it was in use as money, and the experience of Africa shows that it is still esteemed for certain purposes, though it has ceased to be used as money.

All the objects first chosen as standards of value were objects of use in some form or another : cattle, knives, spades, beads, etc. This circumstance alone renders it quite probable that the adoption of the cowrie as money was a secondary step and that long before it was used as such it was highly esteemed for some other purpose.

It is therefore probable that Elliot Smith is right in his theory that the demand for cowries for other purposes, such as betrothal gifts and burial ware, gave to this shell, especially in places remote from the coasts where it lives, an increased value, which led to its adoption, secondarily, as a measure of value.

What was it in the cowrie shell which from the beginning fascinated the primitive peoples ? To us who have learnt in the chapter on imitative magic how fertility rites of various kinds occupied a central and comprehensive place in the world of ideas of primitive peoples, it is easy to accept Elliot Smith's view when he states the formula that " the whole of the complex cowrie cult sprang from the resemblance which a group of primitive people thought they saw between the cowrie and the female sex organ ". The large group of fecundity rites which Almgren has collected with such great erudition and interpreted in such a masterly manner in his *Hällristningar och Kultbruk* presents such striking analogies to Elliot Smith's line of thought that it is sufficient to refer to Almgren's book and our quotations from it.

If, therefore, we attach ourselves to the brilliant English

anatomist and conceive the use of the cowrie as a symbol of fecundity as the primary idea in the complex group of conceptions woven round this little shell, it will be easy to derive the various uses of the cowrie shell from this primary conception.

The whole of the large group of conceptions which includes woman as the mother of the race (virginity, betrothals, bridal gifts, remedies for sterility, aids to child-birth) is immediately and directly intelligible from our primary conception.

The causes of life and death, so contrary in our modern thought, were less so to primitive peoples, who conceived death as the entrance through a gate to a new form of existence, a critical change in the existence of the individual, when it became necessary for the relatives to send with the departed all such life-giving substances as might assist him on his journey. Therefore it was obvious that they should place symbols of fertility in his

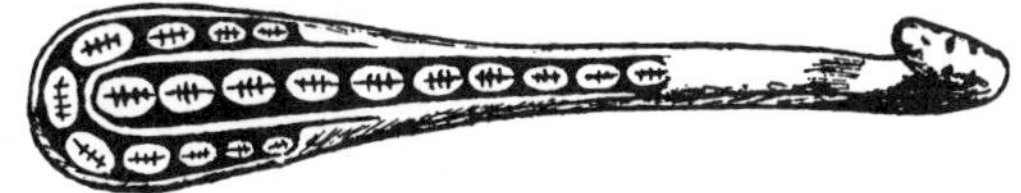

FIG. 135.—Chinese buckle of bronze, with cowrie ornament (natural size).

grave or in some other way transfer elements of the fertility cult to the burial cult. If we interpret the occurrence of the cowrie in different ages and in the burial ware of different peoples in this way, it will be easy to range this use of the cowrie under our primary conception: the life symbol. In this case also Almgren's work presents striking resemblances as regards the connection of the fecundity cult and the death cult.

When the cowrie was thus established, probably at an early stage of the Stone age, as a power which bestowed life and helped the dead in their new existence, it was an obvious development to use this luck-bringing object as a protection and an auxiliary in the affairs of daily life. Thus it came to be worn as an amulet by children, horses and other valuable domestic animals as a protection against the "evil eye" and other unlucky influences. The cowrie then became a means of bringing luck in games, hunting and fishing, a medium for discovering crime and divining the future, a gift which the gods graciously accepted and which brought to the giver the blessing of the spirits of the trees, the rivers and the springs.

No other point of departure than that of Elliot Smith makes it possible to range under one single point of view all the varying uses of the cowrie. At any rate we must accept as a working hypothesis his interpretation of the folklore rôle of the cowrie as beginning far back in the early Stone age when it was adopted as a symbol of fecundity and transferred to the burial cult in order to ensure a new existence for the dead.

It was thus a conception thousands of years old which the people of antiquity found when they associated the little sea shell with their goddesses of fecundity by names such as " Concha Venerea ".

J. C. Melville in his monograph on the genus *Cypraea* gives the following derivation of the name : " Cypraea, or, more classically, Cypria, is derived from one of Aphrodite's many attributes, due, no doubt, to the fact that the worship of her not only originated but was for a long time centralized in Cyprus, at that time a luxuriant and smiling island, full of riches. Horace greets her, 'Thou Goddess who rulest over Cyprus', and Tibullus addresses her, 'And mayst thou show thyself gracious, Cypria, borne by thy shell' ".

Like glittering dew we see the little sea shell shimmering everywhere in the history of our race as a symbol of life's force, taking personal shape both in the New Hebrides, where it is believed that the first woman came from a cowrie, and also in Cyprus where she took the beauteous form of Aphrodite, rising from the foam of the waves and borne by a shell.

Fig. 136.—Burial urn from the New Stone age in Denmark.

CHAPTER TWENTY

THE SYMBOLISM OF THE P'AN SHAN GRAVES

Let us now, after our prolonged excursions in the last two chapters into the perplexing field of popular superstition, return to the P'an Shan graves and the dwelling-sites of the Yang Shao period in the T'ao valley.

We have already shown in Chapter XVII that the P'an Shan graves, on the evidence of the great grave of Pien Chia Kou, are probably representative of a comparatively short period of time and that, archaeologically speaking, they may be regarded as belonging to one and the same period. We shall now advance a step further and easily prove that the graves on the P'an Shan heights are contemporary with the Ma Chia Yao settlement. At first sight the ceramic material of the Ma Chia Yao terrace appears quite unlike the stately burial urns of the P'an Shan mountains, and we shall, indeed, find in what follows a fundamental opposition between them, though the essential difference relates to *custom* and not to *age*. In a comparison of the two ceramic groups we are immediately struck by the fact that in both cases the ware is the same, as also the black pigment used in both cases for the decoration of the vessels.

Definitive in the determination of their age is the fact that in the overwhelming majority of the 6,043 fragments of vessels which we brought home from Ma Chia Yao there occur a very small, it is true, but also significant minority of fragments of P'an Shan urns. These consist in the first place of a large part of a badly painted vessel, which was perhaps for that reason rejected as useless. In addition we have six small pieces of a finely decorated urn of the P'an Shan type.

By means of this comparison we obtain a clear insight into a circumstance which we consider of fundamental importance. We have to do here with two ceramic groups of the same age, on the one hand a plentiful fund of domestic ceramics, such as we know best from Ma Chia Yao, and on the other hand a more stately group of burial urns, represented by hundreds of complete and well-preserved vessels. The scarcity of discoveries of P'an Shan fragments in the Ma Chia Yao settlement may probably with justice be attributed to the fact that some at least of the potters making P'an Shan urns dwelt within the Ma Chia Yao settlement and had their workshops there. Now and then an accident occurred, an urn was occasionally broken, and the pieces were carried about the settlement by playing children, just as happened on a much larger scale to the pieces of pottery of the settlement itself. If this interpretation is correct, we shall find in the few fragments of P'an Shan urns at Ma Chia Yao a proof that this settlement represents one of the villages which buried their dead up on the P'an Shan mountains.

We are then confronted by the interesting fact that the people of Yang Shao in Kansu had two kinds of pottery, one kind for living beings and a totally different kind for the dead.

The pottery of the settlement is distinguished by groups of wavy lines and other freely drawn figures, among them some which recall floating water plants and frogs. As regards form, there are on the one hand bowls richly painted inside and out, and on the other hand tall slim urns painted in much the same patterns as the bowls.

The burial ceramics of the P'an Shan mountains consisted almost exclusively of urns, usually with a very narrow neck. Bowls also occur, but with quite inferior, relatively careless, painting. The large burial urns are painted with strictly determined patterns, among which we distinguish the following main groups.

1. Horizontal, concentric bands.
2. Four large spirals covering the whole of the upper half of the vessel.
3. Large gourd-like figures in the same position as the spirals.
4. Large rhombs.
5. Fields filled with a check pattern.

A remarkable and consistent feature of these burial urns is the fact that however the various patterns are arranged, all of them contain a common element to which I have given the name " death pattern ", because it is restricted to burial ceramics, in contrast with domestic ceramics, in which this pattern is entirely missing.

The characteristic features of the " death pattern " appear best from Fig. 137. From two black fields saw teeth project towards each other, but between the saw teeth there is a red or violet band which is just touched by the tips of the saw teeth. Thus we may say more concisely that the death pattern consists of two opposite rows of black saw teeth with an intermediate band of red. It may be specially mentioned here that neither of these two elements of the design is to be found in the domestic ceramics of Ma Chia Yao, and it is especially striking that the red colour appears to be strictly forbidden to the living and to be exclusively reserved for the cult of the dead.

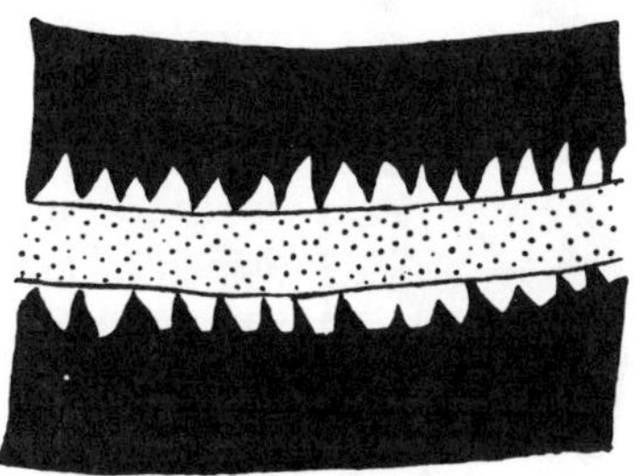

FIG. 137.—Death pattern; the red central band is dotted.

Let us now attempt to interpret the meaning of this death pattern. We shall begin with the black saw teeth.

In a work entitled " Symbolism in Mortuary Ceramics ", published in the first volume of the *Bulletin of the Museum of Far Eastern Antiquities*, Dr. Hanna Rydh has shown that similar patterns occur also in burial urns in the late Stone age of the Scandinavian North. Especially remarkable is the stately vessel from Skarpsalling in Denmark (cf. Rydh's work, Plate 1, Fig. 3, and compare the vignette at the beginning of this chapter), which in many details resembles the decoration of burial urns from Kansu, with the difference that the Chinese urns are painted and the Danish vessels are decorated with impressed or engraved patterns.

Dr. Rydh has with great erudition collected much literary material with the object of illustrating the extent of the use of the "triangle" pattern in prehistoric finds and she attempts with the help of her studies to interpret the symbolic meaning of the triangle pattern.

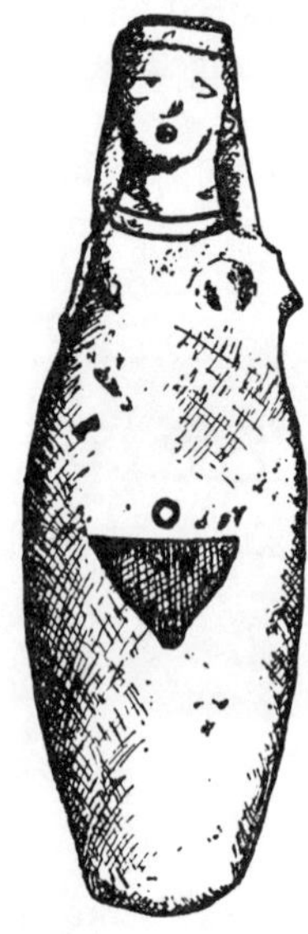

Fig. 138.—Female-shaped mortuary urn, Egypt.

Her presentation may be summarized in the briefest form by saying that the triangle pattern is a symbol of female fecundity, or, what is the same thing in the magic of primitive peoples, of fertility. She deduces the female character of the triangle pattern from the *quinta essentia* of womanhood, which remains on figurines or other female representations, in which all anthropomorphous features have disappeared by progressive simplification, with the exception of a downward pointing triangle, which in figurines is often filled with dots to indicate the hairy covering of the female *mons veneris*.

Dr. Rydh is of opinion that this female symbol of fecundity or fertility was multiplied into whole rows of triangles in order by mass effect to intensify the lucky effects of the symbols.

I can scarcely say that I am convinced that Dr. Rydh's elegant and learned theory could be applied without question to such tooth patterns as the double rows of the P'an Shan urns. It is quite possible that other magic motivations can be advanced with equal justification. Thus two Swedish folklorists, Sune Ambrosiani and Louise Hagberg, have connected the prophylactic function of the tooth pattern with certain primitive folklore conceptions, such as sharp steel as a magic talisman.

Here I would only add that the development of the tooth pattern may be interpreted in quite a different way, namely as a derivation from the protective walls and fences by which primitive agricultural peoples sought to protect themselves against beasts of prey, and their small cultivated fields against wild cattle. Whoever has travelled in the interior of China will certainly have no difficulty in following my line of thought. Where stones are available the farms and fields are encircled by stone walls, upon which are laid networks of thorny bushes. The thorns of these bushes are sometimes inches long and are very strong. It seems to me far from improbable that this may be one of the contributory causes of the adoption of the tooth pattern as a means of protection.

Let us, however, return for a moment to Dr. Rydh's theory of the triangle or tooth pattern as originally a symbol of *female* fecundity. It is an amusing coincidence that whilst Dr. Rydh endeavoured to show in our first *Bulletin* that the triangles were feminine symbols, Professor Karlgren attempts in *Bulletin* No. 2, in an essay "Some Fecundity Symbols in Ancient China", to show that during the early Chinese dynasties triangles were *male* symbols of fecundity. He proceeds from the archaic Chinese written character for progenitor, i.e. the root of the race, the procreative force in its most monumental form. Many of these variants of written characters are simply triangles, or else triangles constitute the top element of the character. Karlgren propounds that these characters in the Chinese pictorial writing go back to an ancient phallus cult. In this connection he also reminds us of similarly shaped wooden symbols which in the Chinese ancestral temples represent the various male members of the earlier generation of the family.

FIG. 139.—Painted urn. Egypt.

These two scholars, Rydh and Karlgren, may with perfect right emphasize their own equally justified views of an ancient fecundity cult. The fact is that not only in the Yang Shao ceramics, but also in the symbolism of the Near East, we encounter images which sometimes resemble a double axe and possibly relate to the function of the axe as one of the symbols of fecundity (cf. the hammer which Tor laid on the knees of the bride). This image contains two opposite triangles with their apices touching. Dr. Rydh has considered the question whether this double triangle is a symbol of fecundity of a higher order, in which the male and female forces meet, or, in brief, a schematic picture of the act of procreation.

Pursuing this line of thought we might further ask ourselves whether the still surviving Chinese symbol Yang-Yin (see vignette at beginning of Chapter XVIII) is not possibly a variant of the two triangles, which have been remodelled in order to fit into the circular framework.

If this view is correct, it is conceivable that the two rows of teeth of the death pattern represent in the one case Yang and in the other Yin, the male and the female principles opposing each other in an endless series of ritual marriage scenes.

Nobody is more fully aware than the writer of these lines that the whole of this symbolical structure is an excursion on very thin ice, in which a catastrophe threatens at every movement. But it is a hazard well worth venturing upon in view of the possibility of finding at the end a solution of many of the riddles of primitive times, of finding a clue which will teach us how to read the magic conceptions which ruled the primitive races.

The chain of thought which we have just forged seems, however, hopelessly weak in face of the objection that the symbols which we have interpreted are all strong manifestations of life, whereas in the P'an Shan graves we are concerned with the cult of the dead. But whoever has had occasion to study and familiarize himself with the nature and method of magic will soon recognize that the implied contradiction is only apparent. Death appears to primitive man quite different to what it appears to us. It is by no means the end of material existence, but only the fateful journey through the gates of death into the great unknown, to which the surviving relatives look with wonder and trepidation. According to primitive conceptions the dead have much the same needs in the new life as here on earth and the same desire for wealth and all the other good and pleasant things which this life offers. For this reason they give to the dead weapons like the two stone axes in the Pien Chia Kou graves. They are also given meat and water, and probably a generous measure of seed, which was contained in the large burial urns.

But, in any case, the journey through the gates of death was a difficult affair. The relations who stood sorrowing and perplexed round one who had but recently moved and worked among them knew above all things that they must give him every form of vital force.

It is deeply interesting and in the nature of imitative magic that it works along several lines of communication. Thus we have seen in the preceding chapter how cowrie shells, in origin one of the most significant symbols of fertility, yet in other hands bestowed wealth, good fortune in hunting and fishing, luck in games, etc., and we also found that this powerful symbol was often given to the dead as one of the burial gifts.

We have also seen how woman, the mother of the race, in a transferred meaning bestowed fertility on the tree in the field and participates with man in the ritual marriages which were performed in the fields and which had the purpose of bringing a rich crop in the ensuing summer. Here also a bridge is thrown between life and death, in so far as female representations of many kinds, often strongly emphasizing woman's creative rôle, are included in the burial gifts. Under such circumstances we find nothing surprising, on closer observation, in the fact that the Yang-Yin symbols meet each other from the two sides of the red middle line of the death pattern and speak in the grave of the mighty force of life.

And now we have cleared up, or at least imagine we have done so, one element of the death pattern, the rows of teeth. It remains to consider the other, the red central part. Undoubtedly there is something attractive and mysterious in the circumstance mentioned above that the red colour was strictly forbidden in the decoration of the everyday ware of the villagers of Ma Chia Yao.

What is the meaning of this red colour? Students of folk life will certainly unanimously reply that the red colour is a symbol—according to the principles of imitative magic—of the most important of all life-inspiring substances, blood.

The savage slays an enemy or a beast of prey. The spear or axe strikes a vital spot, the blood flows, and with the warm red vital fluid life also runs out.

The same mysterious connection between life and blood meets primitive man not only at the end of life but also in its first beginning. The menstruation blood disappears as a first sign that a small new member of the family is on the way from the mysterious world from which little children come. The blood dries up and life is born, the blood dries up and life dies. This is the mysterious framework within which all human life is lived.

It would be easy to fill a small volume merely with reports on blood as a life substance in the conceptions of primitive peoples. According to Spencer and Gillen the Australian negroes gave the old men young men's blood to drink in order to give them new strength, and according to Trumbull the Chinese smeared blood on their doors in times of plague as a protection against infection. The Vikings smeared the keels of their ships with blood before launching them, and even in our time blood is called " power " by the peasants. The royal purple and the Cardinal's red are probably expressions of the same thought.

On the lines of association which are universal in imitative magic the transition was made from human life to crops. Thus, according to Karsten the Peruvians sprinkled human blood on their fields. Elliot Smith also relates that the Nile during its fertilizing floods is sometimes coloured blood red, and I may be permitted to mention an observation made during my journeys in China which made a deep impression on me, even if at the time I did not realize the folklore possibilities of the phenomenon. I therefore take the liberty of quoting from page 357 of my book *The Dragon and the Foreign Devils.*

> After a week's journey through extremely arid, almost desert-like tracts we arrived on the morning of June 21st at the Yellow River. Here I saw again an old acquaintance, for I had worked for long periods on the lower course of the Yellow River in Honan and Shansi. Here the mighty and famous river presented itself in a new and assuredly very strange guise. The water of the Yellow River was *blood red.* At first this curious spectacle was quite incomprehensible to me, but it gradually became clear that the preceding night, or early the same morning, there had been higher up the river a shifting of the loose, deep red clay deposits which form the bed of the river.

> Beyond the blood-red waves of the Huang Ho extended a smiling picture of open and luxuriously fertile land forming a framework round a wall-encircled town, the first goal of my endeavour, Lanchow, capital of the province of Kansu.

It should be noted that this blood-red flood of the Yellow River occurred at the height of the season of the growing crops, when, with the assistance of direct irrigation and "Persian wheels", the flood waters are conveyed to the thirsting fields.

The "bloodstone", or hematite ore became, as the name indicates, a symbol of blood, and this mineral substance was used to a very large extent by prehistoric peoples to transfer the beneficent powers of blood to the cult of the dead.

Even during the Old Stone age we find a number of graves in which the red ochre, i.e. pulverized hematite, plays a striking rôle. Thus in the Cavillon cave at Monaco there was found the skeleton of a full-grown man on a bed of powdered red ochre which stained to a deep red both the legs and the burial ware.

In the Barma Grande cave in the same neighbourhood was found a male skeleton of which the skull was covered with red ochre. Farther in the cave were found the skeletons of a man, a young woman and a fifteen-year-old youth in an artificial cavity strewn with red ochre.

In the neighbouring Baousso da Torre cave were found two skeletons coloured with red ochre.

The Cro Magnon discovery (Dordogne) comprised the skeleton of an old man, two grown men, a woman and a foetus. They were partially dyed by red ochre.

A famous find is the Englishman's "Red Lady", discovered in a cave at Paviland in Wales, a male (!) skeleton with an extraordinarily rich covering of red ochre.

Similarly from later prehistoric times we can adduce a number of cases of graves in which red ochre is included in the burial ware. In the graves of the Copper age at Kuban, on the South Russian steppe, where red ochre is included in the burial ware, the dead were found to be buried in the hocker position and coloured with red ochre. In the graves at Maikop three skeletons were found in the same position with uplifted hands, covered with red ochre.

From China we note especially the plentiful grave finds at

Hsin Cheng in Honan, where a red pigment forms a complete deposit in the grave. It should be noted, moreover, that early Chinese antiquities which came into our hands through the instrumentality of Chinese antique dealers often show traces of cinnabar. It is true that all these cinnabar coverings are not authentic, but they show beyond doubt that red pigment is associated with burial gifts from the early dynasties.

I myself found red pigment in some of my Kansu graves, partly as a covering of bones, partly, in one case, in the form of whole lumps of hematite, which were found inside the pelvis. A detailed account of these will be given in the monographs in *Palaeontologia Sinica*.

After these excursions into various fields we are well equipped to return to the red central band of the death pattern on the P'an Shan urns. The general and extensive use of red ochre in the service of the cult of the dead in many countries and in widely separated periods of time must predispose us to accept the interpretation of the red band of the P'an Shan urns as a symbol of life given to the dead. To what extent red ochre was used otherwise in the P'an Shan graves we are not in a position to decide, as nearly all the graves had been plundered by the Mohammedans before I arrived there. In the Pien Chia Kou grave we saw no trace of red ochre except in the death pattern on the urns, but it is quite possible that in other cases loose ochre was placed in the graves, since such was the case in other prehistoric graves in Kansu.

On one of the Pien Chia Kou urns we find rows of pointed ovals, of which the lower and larger ones have an inside black contour approximately like a section through an apricot. At first I was doubtful of the meaning of these figures, but a comparison of all the Kansu urns, both from the Yang Shao period and from the next succeeding Ma Chang period, has convinced me that we are here dealing with a picture of the objects which we described in Chapter XIX under the name " the symbol of Aphrodite ", the cowrie shell (*Cypraea moneta*). In the interpretation of such figures as those on the Pien Chia Kou jar in question we must bear in mind that the cowrie shell obtained its unique significance owing to its resemblance to the female vulva. We must, however, always remember that primitive peoples either copied the cowrie shell or, alternatively, the original, which is more probable in the case of the Pien Chia Kou urn. So far as the magic effect is concerned it is obviously a matter of indifference whether the picture on the urn reproduces directly the female vulva or does so indirectly via the cowrie shell.

In the graves of the Yang Shao age we sometimes found cowries, as for example at Yang Shao Tsun, in which the genuine cowrie shell occurred in association with a skeleton, and at Chu Chia Chai, where it had been found necessary to use a substitute carved of bone, probably because the supply of the original shells was inadequate.

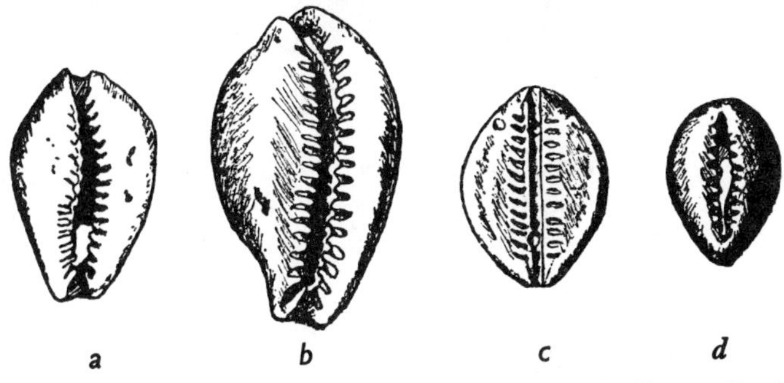

FIG. 140.—Cowries from China: *a*, from the Stone-age dwellings at Pu Chao Chai; *b*, unknown Chinese origin; *c*, cowrie imitation in bone; *d*, imitation in bronze.

In the graves at Sha Ching in the Chen Fan desert we found numerous genuine cowrie shells. Similarly they occur in the famous grave at Hsin Cheng in Honan, which contained so unusually many large bronze vessels. Both of these groups of graves probably belong to the centuries immediately before the birth of Christ. In the Museum of Far Eastern Antiquities we possess rich material of cowrie shells, imitations in stone, bone and bronze (Fig. 140), as well as pictures of cowries on various bronzes.

If we compare the rows of cowries on the bronze lid (Fig. 133) with the design on the Ma Chang jars (Fig. 141), we shall certainly find the resemblance striking, and we shall easily agree that one of them copies cowrie shells just as much as the other.

And where we find cowries in the Yang Shao graves, either genuine cowries (Yang Shao Tsun), bone imitations (Chu Chia Chai), or copies on a burial urn (P'an Shan), we can agree,

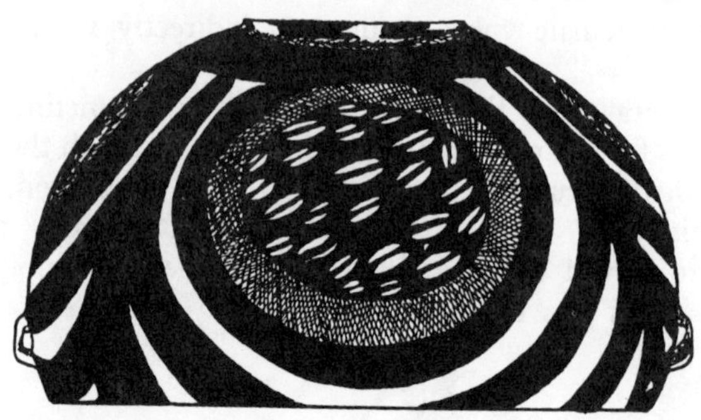

FIG. 141.—Details of an urn with cowrie pattern. Ma Chang period, Kansu.

especially after our abundant experiences in Chapter XIX, that in this case one of the most potent life symbols of imitative magic has been given to the dead in their graves.

We now come in due order to the figure which dominates the design of the P'an Shan urns, the four magnificent spirals, which cover the whole of the upper part of four of the painted vessels in the Pien Chia Kou graves and which are repeated on hundreds of urns from the P'an Shan district. As we have already discovered that the double row of teeth of the death pattern, the red middle band and the cowrie (vulva) features are pictorial signs with symbolic meaning, it is extremely probable that this is also the case in the predominant element of the P'an Shan design, the great spirals.

A very attractive suggestion for the interpretation of this element is to be found in Donald E. Mackenzie's *The Migration of Symbols*, 1926, in which the second chapter, " The Spiral ", and especially the second section, " Whirlpools and Whirlwinds ", is devoted to this problem. Unfortunately this author is not always reliable, though if we also consult such specialized Chinese works as those of C. A. S. Williams, *Outlines of Chinese Symbolism*, 1931, and De Wisser, *The Dragon in China and Japan*,

1913, we shall find indications that in this case Mackenzie is possibly on the right track.

In his view the spirals may represent an extremely striking and sometimes terrifying atmospheric phenomenon, the water spout or the local whirlwind. In Northern China, the region in which the Yang Shao civilization developed and flourished, two types of climate merge into each other in the cycle of the seasons. From August to June, over large parts of Northern China, there prevails a desert type of climate, with very little rainfall and successive dust storms. If this type of climate were also to extend to the three summer months, Northern China would of course revert to the steppe or desert stage, in which the Eolian forces would entirely dominate.

FIG. 142.—Whirlwind.

But then there come as China's salvation the life-bringing, though sometimes in their violence devastating, summer rains. At the end of May the heat has already laid its hand upon the land. The soil is burning hot owing to the insulation, but the heat is easy to bear, thanks to the dryness of the atmosphere. Then one day in June the new regime begins. The air is troubled. The clouds bank up darkly on the horizon and over the glowing plain there pass the dust-laden whirlwinds, capricious and destructive. This spectacular prelude does not last long. The blanket of clouds passes over the land. Lightning illumines the wall of clouds and the torrents begin, as a sign that the summer monsoon rains have arrived, bringing green and a rich harvest, but perhaps also floods and devastation.

FIG. 143.—Dragon in the clouds.
(*After an original which in his day belonged to the Klaes Fåhræus collection.*)

It is natural that this stupendous atmospheric drama should have made a profound impression on the people of the Stone age, both by its magnificent and dramatically swift action and by its profound significance as a life-bringer to the crops. It was no doubt by this vast early summer festival of nature that the legend of the mighty dragon king, so well disposed to lesser men, was created. From his winter palace in the depths of the lakes, rivers and seas the great rainmaker ascends the spiral steps of the whirlwind, rolling across the plain until he reaches his summer workshop in the clouds, and sends down over the thirsting earth the lightning and thunder, but also the life-giving rain.

Let us listen to what Okakura has to relate in *The Awakening of Japan*, pp. 77–78, of the lord of the rain :

> The dragon of the far East is not the same grim monster that we know from the Middle Ages of the West, but is a being characterized by strength and goodness. He is the spirit of change, and therefore represents life itself. Hidden in caves in the highest mountains or coiled up in the measureless depths of the ocean he bides his time until he returns to work. He ascends in the storm clouds, he washes his mane in the darkness of the seething whirlwind. He plunges his claws into the lightning, his skin gleams like the bark of the pine trees when the rain runs down the trunks. The tornado is his voice, which, resounding through the mouldering leaves of the forests, heralds the new spring.

De Visser introduces Chapter VIII, which treats of the phenomenon which the Japanese call *tatsumaki*, by the following words: "The mighty whirlwinds which call forth dust spouts and in a moment destroy human works and all else that stands in their way, are regarded as made by the Dragon when he ascends into the 'heavens'."

Then follow numerous accounts of dragons which in the splendours of remarkable happenings rose up into the clouds on the rolling stairs of the dust spout.

We willingly admit that we do not at present possess any proof that the great spirals on the P'an Shan urns are a part of the cult of fertility personified by the Dragon King, but on the other hand the reader will certainly agree that the association of ideas which we have here suggested seems far from improbable.

It remains for us to mention briefly three further motifs which are probably symbolic and which we find on the P'an Shan urns. As regards the check pattern I refer to Hanna Rydh's above-mentioned work, in which she adduces numerous examples of the check pattern as an element of the death cult among different peoples.

The large gourd-like figures which replace the spirals on many of the P'an Shan urns probably also occupy a place among the old symbols. The gourd is a favourite motive in Chinese art. Li T'ieh Kuai, one of the eight immortals of Taoism, holds in his hand a gourd, from which there radiate spirals of smoke, which indicate his power to free his spirit from his body.

Old men are accustomed to carry gourd flasks, either natural or made of copper or wood taken from the coffins of other old men, and these amulets are thought to bestow long life.

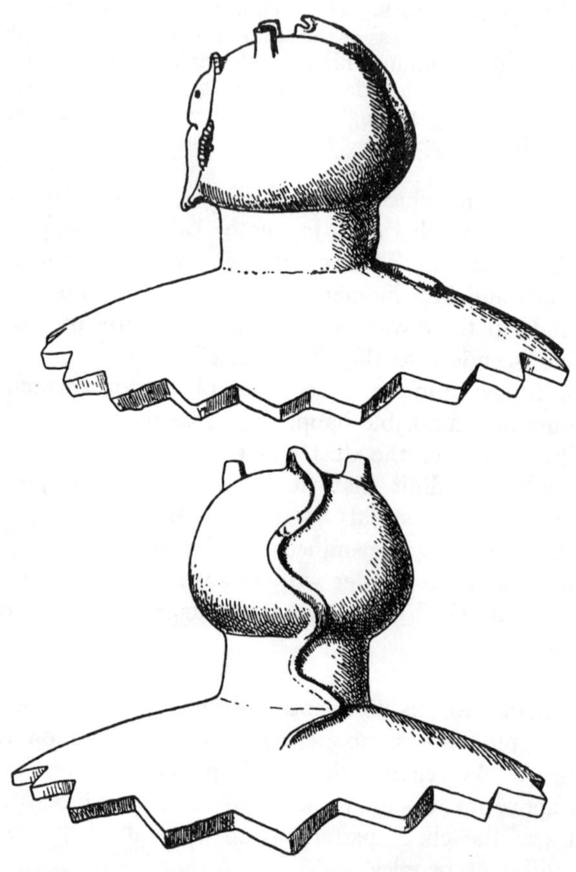

FIG. 144.—Ceramic piece, probably a lid, crowned by a human head, on the top and neck of which a snake is coiled. It is decorated with the typical P'an Shan pattern and certainly belonged to this group.

Doolittle says in *Social Life of the Chinese*, page 566, in speaking of the gourd: " Gourd skins, a picture of a gourd on wood or paper, a small piece of gourd carved in wood, a piece of cardboard so cut that it resembles a perpendicular section through a gourd, or a paper lantern in the shape of a gourd, are often used to avoid death or misfortune."

Frazer mentions that in South Africa dolls are made of gourds in order to render childless mothers fertile. According to the same author gourds are associated in Japan with the married woman's desire to be blessed with children.

Last, but not least, I must draw attention to the object which we have used as the subject of the final illustration to this chapter. It is an object of the usual P'an Shan ware and painted with the orthodox P'an Shan pattern, a human head with an enormous serrated collar. Possibly this piece served as the lid of a burial urn. In any case it is certainly one of the most remarkable magic productions of P'an Shan ceramics, in which the ritual character is emphasized by a snake which coils itself upon the neck of the image with its head on the crown and its mouth open. In another connection I shall return to this snake cult, which is an element in the religious customs of prehistoric peoples as widespread as the use of the mystic rows of triangles, of red ochre and of cowrie images.

A rich field is here opened up for the study of the death cult of the Yang Shao civilization. It is necessary to follow the history of the spirals, gourds, check pattern and similar images as thoroughly as we have already done with Aphrodite's symbol. But even now we are able to glimpse a broad connection of life symbols, all of which were enlisted in the service of the cult of death, certainly the rows of teeth, the red colour, and the cowrie images, probably also the spirals, the gourds, the check pattern and the snake image—a many-toned orchestra, attuned to a resurrection symphony intended to make it easier for the departed to take the fateful step through the gates of death.

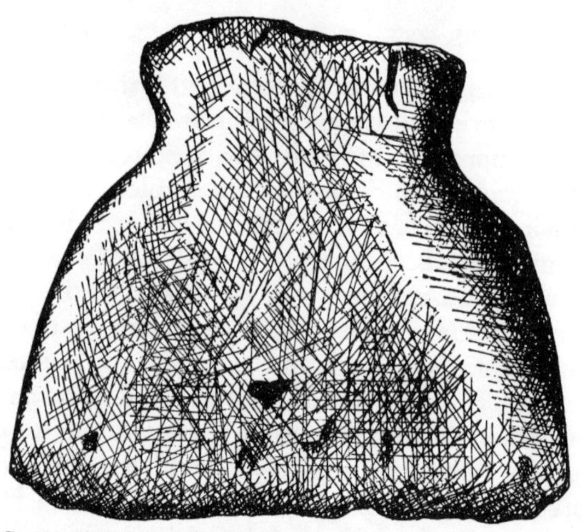

FIG. 145.—Stone pick from the Kalgan district ($\frac{1}{3}$ natural size). As this type has never been found in the Yang Shao dwellings, it may possibly belong to an earlier stage of the Stone age.

CHAPTER TWENTY-ONE

THE YANG SHAO CIVILIZATION

THREE times during the continuation of our wanderings through prehistoric China we have met the human beings who at widely different periods lived in the country. On the first occasion, in Chapter VI, we made the acquaintance of the Peking man, one of the earliest, if not absolutely the earliest, of the hominids which deserve the name " man ". *Sinanthropus pekinensis* was a savage on an extremely low level of development, and it probably cannot properly be said that he succeeded in taking possession of the land. A varied, and in parts terrifying, animal world, including rhinoceri, numerous beasts of prey, and especially the sabre-toothed tiger, competed with him in the consumption of the available resources of the country in edible plants and acceptable game. If the Chinese geologists had not recently discovered the simple implements of the Peking man and, together with them, thick beds of ashes, we should have been very uncertain of the part played by *Sinanthropus* in the Chou K'ou Tien cave. But now it seems to be proved that the Peking man was for a long time sufficiently master of the cave to be able to make fire and to keep there his simple implements.

Long ages pass. The climate and the appearance of the country change. Of the part played by man in China during these long periods of time we know nothing.

But then once again a broad beam of light penetrates the darkness of unwritten history. This time it is far away, up on the borders of the Mongolian desert, that the first great discoveries are made for science.

In Chapter VIII I have told of the Jesuit Father Licent and Professor Teilhard de Chardin who, in 1923, in the gravel deposits below the loess, as well as in the bottom layers of the loess, found numerous and unequivocal remains of Man of the Old Stone age. The conditions of stratification show that the early Stone-age savage lived in a country quite different from that of to-day, and the bones of the animals which we encounter in heaps in his old dwelling-sites show a fauna somewhat resembling the modern Mongolian, it is true, but yet comprising many forms—an elephant, the woolly-haired rhinoceros, etc., which have long been extinct. The savage of the early Stone age was certainly still at a very low stage of development in the human family. It is not even certain whether he could lay claim to be included in the modern genus of man, *Homo sapiens*. But on the other hand it is quite evident that our race has made great progress since the early beginnings of the Peking man. The man of the Old Stone age of the Ordos desert was certainly a strong and purposeful hunter, who ruled freely and successfully over the abundant big game which the steppes of that day afforded him.

Long periods again elapse during which the history of China is shrouded in complete darkness. When we again find settlers on the wide plains of Northern China the sunlight of prehistoric research falls full and clear over the land.

It is the age of the Yang Shao civilization. The country teems with busy cultivators of the soil, living together in large villages. There are certainly already quite competent woodmen. Their ceramics are the finest to be found in any part of the world during the Stone age.

The skeletons in the Yang Shao graves, in Honan and Kansu, have been designated by Davidson Black as proto-Chinese. It appears therefore that we here encounter the original ancestors of the modern Chinese. Up to this point our studies have referred to China's pre-history. From the Yang Shao age until the beginning of historical time, about 1,500 B.C., we are concerned with the still more alluring problem of *the beginning of Chinese civilization*.

Before we begin to survey this great problem we would first attempt to reply to a question which I will formulate as follows: How is it that at the present moment, when we well know of about 40 sites of the Yang Shao period in Northern China, we have not found a single dwelling site which can bridge over the period between the Early Stone age discoveries in the Ordos desert and the much more numerous discoveries of the Yang Shao period? Or, in other words, the Yang Shao period, which is so abundantly represented, itself represents the close of the latest Stone age and perhaps even the beginning of the Metal ages. Why have we never made a single discovery of the actual New Stone age, which is so copiously represented in other parts of the world? We must admit that we have no answer to this mysterious riddle. It is certainly true that the loess period, the steppe period, when the whole of Northern China became covered by a carpet 50–100 metres thick of the yellow Eolian earth, was a period of such drought that human beings, who on the evidence of the Ordos discoveries were demonstrably numerous at the beginning of the loess period, were driven out, so that Northern China either became depopulated or at best was inhabited by small groups of men who survived here and there on the steppes where the supply of water was more or less adequate.

But after the loess period came a great climatic change in the P'an Chiao age which we have described in Chapter IX. The rainfall again became copious and collected in new rivers, which cut their way through the carpet of loess and gradually discovered their old river courses. Indeed, the erosive power of these rivers was so considerable that it in places carved out deep precipitous channels in the solid rock. There is no doubt that the P'an Chiao age must have been quite favourable to cultivation. The climate was certainly mild and the great river erosion testifies that the rainfall was plentiful. This must have been the real Neolithic age, the New Stone age, and it is especially remarkable that we have not yet discovered any dwelling from this period. To some extent the explanation may be found in the fact that the work of the rivers largely destroyed the once-existing dwellings. It is possible, moreover, that we do possess some isolated discoveries from this first stage of the New Stone age, especially a large stone blade (Fig. 146) and a broad, coarse, triangular stone pick, such as we never found in the cultural deposits of the Yang Shao age, but of which we possess a few isolated examples found in Northern China. (Cf. the vignette at the head of this chapter.)

FIG. 146.— Stone blade from the Kalgan district (½ natural size). Since this type has never been found in the Yang Shao dwellings it may possibly belong to an earlier stage of the Stone age.

In any case, the scarcity, or rather absence, of traces of the real New Stone age seems to indicate that the population of Northern China was not then very numerous. Possibly the population at that time consisted mainly of hunters and fishermen who wandered about in small groups in the forests and along the river valleys. The absence of settled villages and the paucity of population would thus give a reasonable explanation of the few and uncertain finds which have been made.

In strong contrast are the very abundant remains of the Yang Shao age. My experience seems to show that the Yang Shao dwellings must be counted by the thousand. Our searches during a period of a few years were only in the nature of pioneer work. We assuredly stand only on the threshold of exploration of this rich and splendid prehistoric stage, which constitutes the foundation of Chinese civilization.

Everything, therefore, seems to indicate that the Yang Shao period heralded a new age, with a greatly increased population, which became possible owing to the introduction of higher forms of agriculture, handicraft of many kinds, and the aggregation of the population in large, permanent villages.

Both in Honan, where we made our first considerable Yang Shao discoveries, and in Kansu, where they were still more numerous, we recognize cultural groups lacking the painted ceramics which are the finest hallmarks of the Yang Shao age. In Honan, Pu Chao Chai, a site situated only a few miles west of Yang Shao Tsun, represents such a predecessor of the real Yang Shao age. There can scarcely be any great interval of time between the two sites, for we may sum up briefly by saying that Pu Chao Chai resembles Yang Shao Tsun except in the one point that it lacks the painted ceramics.

In the same way in Ch'i Chia P'ing in Kansu we have a discovery which is almost entirely lacking in painted ceramics. It betrays no noticeable resemblance to Pu Chao Chai in Honan, but it seems probable that Ch'i Chia P'ing is somewhat older than the great Yang Shao sites in Kansu.

These circumstances suggest the thought that the painted ceramics came to Kansu and Honan as a finished art, which in its—to us unknown—homeland must have required a long time to reach such perfection. The painted ceramics of Yang Shao Tsun in Honan, Ma Chia Yao in Kansu, as also the great P'an Shan urns, reveal a striking resemblance to the painted ceramics excavated by the Pumpelly expedition at Anau in Russian Turkestan, but especially do they resemble the abundant discoveries in Southern Russia, especially in the area of the town of Kiev (Tripolje civilization).

The usual theory of the experts is, of course, that these painted ceramics came to China through Central Asia from the Near East and Eastern Europe. The local conditions of Kansu and Honan, indeed, also suggest that the painted ceramics came to China suddenly as a finished and highly developed art. On the other hand we should remember that such thin-walled, exquisitely shaped and beautifully decorated vessels as the P'an Shan urns and such graceful and in surface treatment perfect ceramic products as the painted dishes at Yang Shao Tsun are scarcely to be found in any other area of painted ceramics of the latest Stone age and incipient Metal ages. In this case we are only at the beginning of a great period of research, in which everything points to Central Asia as the Promised Land.

In speaking of painted ceramics one is almost inclined to see in their rapid and complete disappearance the fact that they were to the proto-Chinese an alien imported art. It is true that we have in Kansu, which always lay on the confines of the Chinese empire towards Central Asia, an echo of the Yang Shao ceramics in the closely related, though on the whole degenerate, painted vessels of the Ma Chang age, and similarly in Kansu (Hsin Tien) and the western Gobi desert (Chen Fan) in the painted ceramics both of the early Bronze age and the transition period between the Bronze age and the Iron age. But all this relates to the remote western boundaries, the home of the western barbarians, and it is improbable that Hsin Tien and Chen Fan were genuine Chinese cultures. In Eastern China we find no descendants of the magnificent painted ceramics of the Yang Shao age. The few specimens we possess of painted objects from the Chou and Han dynasties have no proved connection with Yang Shao.

But side by side with the painted ceramics, which possibly represent an art borrowed from the west which reached a high stage of development in China, the Yang Shao civilization embraces a number of elements, the sickle-shaped and rectangular knives, the asymmetrical stone chisels, tripods of the Ting types and especially Li, which have persisted into our times. First and last comes the remarkable Li tripod with its bulging hollow legs, so characteristic of the whole of Northern China that we may reasonably regard it as a symbol of Chinese civilization.

When, in 1925, I wrote my *Preliminary Report on Archaeological Research in Kansu* the idea hovered in my mind that perhaps the higher stage of agriculture, represented by *wheat* as the principal and most suitable crop, had come to China from the west at the beginning of the Yang Shao age, together with the painted ceramics. But the first kind of crop which we were able to identify points in a totally different direction. One day during the early years of our work here in Stockholm we happened to examine more closely a fragment of a jar from Yang Shao Tsun. It was unusually thick in the wall, porous and full of plant imprints. Two Swedish botanists, G. Edman and E.

Söderberg, examined this small fragment and their examination led to the most important discovery in this field since the discovery in 1921 of the Yang Shao dwelling-site. It could be shown with certainty that the plant imprints in this fragment were husks of cultivated rice (*Oryza sativa* [1]). The discovery was in a high degree sensational not only because it sets back the history of rice an immense distance in time, but also because it points, not to dry Central Asia, but to rainy Southern Asia, which is the homeland of rice.

Time after time the pertinent question presents itself: how old is the Yang Shao civilization? In 1923, when I published my first work, *An Early Chinese Culture*, I estimated the age of the Yang Shao period, on the basis of somewhat uncertain comparisons with the Near East, at about 3000 B.C. In his *Weltgeschichte der Steinzeit*, O. Menghin wishes to advance the Yang Shao culture to about 2000 B.C. I note with interest this view, advanced by a great pioneer of comparative archaeology, but I reserve myself in anticipation of the attempts at a chronology which I shall endeavour to establish when the whole of our prehistoric material has been described in detail.

FIG. 147. — Ivory carving from An Yang (about 1500–1000 B.C.), one of the earliest historical relics of China.

Our knowledge of the archaeology of the Near East is overwhelming, but we who work in Eastern Asia are only on the threshold of a period of research which will require decades to accomplish, though it may possibly lead to radical re-adjustments in prehistoric chronology.

The Yang Shao age stands out as a rich and brilliant episode, not only against the genuine Neolithic age, which is dark and unknown, but also against succeeding ages. When next we encounter definite remains of the ancient Chinese we arrive at a period about 1500–1000 B.C. This occurs with the discoveries

[1] Edman and Söderberg: " Auffindung von Reis in einer Tonscherte aus einer etwa fünftausendjährigen chinesischen siedlung ", *Bull. of the Geol. Soc. of China*, Vol. VIII, No. 4, 1929.

at An Yang in Northern Honan, the capital of the small kingdom which, towards the end of the Shang dynasty (Yin), was the origin of the power which, a thousand years later, was to become the empire of the Han age.

The discoveries at An Yang consist partly of short texts, engraved on pieces of bone and bronze vessels and bronze weapons, partly, and not least important, of exquisite carvings in bone, stone and ivory. Here we find the historic Chinese culture complete in its main characteristics: statesmanship, religion, literary language, a calendar, and an art which comprises all the motives which we call archaic Chinese. Concerning the 1,000–1,500 years between Yang Shao and Yin we know at present nothing. A great and important cultural development lies between these two milestones, but concerning the road which runs from the one to the other I hope to advance some guesses in a future work.

THE MOST RECENT GEOLOGICAL HISTORY OF NORTHERN CHINA

	Land Deposits.	Land forms.	Civilization.
PLEISTOCENE	Peat		Yang Shao culture
	Redeposited loess	P'an Chiao canyon formation, on a smaller scale	
	Loess with *Struthiolithus*, *Elephas cf. namadicus* and *Rhinoceros tichorhinus*	Ma Lan: Valleys filled with gravel and loess inlays.	The Old Stone age man of the Ordos area.
	Cave deposits at Chou K'ou Tien.		*Sinanthropus* with stone implements and ash deposits.
PLIOCENE	Gravel and sand with fresh-water mussels: *Lamprotula*, *Cuneopsis*, etc.	Fen Ho: Carving out of canyon valleys.	
	Loess-like red clays with *Paracamelus* and *Proboscidipparion*. / Lake deposits at Ni Ho Wan with abundant mammal fauna.	Pao Te: Deposits of red clay and gravel on a "mature" land surface.	
	Red clay with *Hipparion*, etc.		

INDEX

Actinoceras tani, 14
Adamson, 305
Adonis, 278
Adzes, 181–2, 209–12
Agnostus hoi, 14
Akamba, 304
Alligator, 73
Almgren, 288–91, 310–11
Amazons, 308
Ambrosiani, Sune, 316
Amulet, Cowrie as, 301–2
Amynodon sinensis, 53
Ananino civilization, 298–9
Anau, 165, 166, 185–6, 224, 298, 334
Andrew, Geo. Findlay, 252–4
Andrews, Roy Chapman, 35
Andropogon sorghum, 204
Annularites, 20
An Yang, 72, 207, 216, 337
Arctomys robusta, 242
Armour, Bone, 249
Arrowheads, 182, 213–16
Art, Primitive, 285 ff.
Artifacts, 181 ff., 192 ff., 200 ff., 229 ff., 242–3
Assam, 308
Astarte, 278
Astrocupulites, 20
Augury, Cowries and, 307
Aurignacian culture, 153
Australians, 286, 320
Avebury, Lord, 210
Awls, 182, 226, 242
Axes, 181, 193–4, 209–12, 216
Axes, Cult, 293

Baganda, 282
Baiera cf. australis, 42
Baousso da Torre cave, 321
Barbour, Geo. B., 92, 159–61
Barma Grande cave, 321
Bashkirs, 302
Bâtons de Commandement, 287
Beads, 194, 250
Bedouins, 302
Belt District, N. American, 11
Beltia danai, 11
Benin, 304, 307–8
Bibos geron, 102
Bini, 304
Birka, 299
Bismarck Archipelago, 301
Bithinia mengyinensis, 36
Black, Davidson, 104, 107–9, 116–118, 123, 167, 189, 197–8, 331
Block-faults, 60
Blood, 320
Bloodstone, 321
Boats, Cult, 292
Bohlin, Dr. Birger, 85–7, 106–8
Bos primigenius, 151–2
Brachyphyllum multiramosum, 42
Brandt, 133, 135
Breuil, Abbé H., 121, 125, 154
Brinjari, 302
British Columbia, 282–3
Bubalus wansjocki, 151–2
Burial Urns, 253 ff., 273 ff., 313 ff.
Burma, 302
Buttons, 194

Cache-pits, 173
Cambrian system, 11, 14
Camelus knoblochi, 151–2
Cameroons, 302
Canis cfr. dingo, 102
Canis lupus, 152
Cannibalism, 197–9
Carboniferous system, 15
Cave paintings, 285 ff.
Cavillon cave, 321

Z

Celts, 211–12
Cephopoalds, 14
Ceramics, *see* Pottery
Cervus elaphus, 151–2
Cervus megaceros, 151–2
Cervus Mongoliae, 151
Chaggan Obo, 207
Chai T'ang, 23–4, 59, 156–61, 233
Chalcedony artifacts, 192
Changshania conica, 14
Chang Sin Tien, 51–3
Chang Yi Ou, 3–4
Chansitheca, 20
Check pattern, 328
Chen Chia Yü, 19
Chen Fan, 221, 299, 335
Cheremisses, 302
Chiang Chün Ting, 46
Chi Chia Ho, 259
Chi Chia Kou, 80–2
Chi Chia P'ing, 241–2, 259, 262, 334
Chicken Bone Hill, 95 ff.
Chichou, 79
Chi Ku Shan, 95
Children, Cowrie and, 305–6
Chilotherium, 85
Chinese civilization, beginnings of, 332 ff.
Ching Kou, 135–6
Ching Pai K'ou, 214
Chingshan series, 44
Ching Yang Fu, 82, 147
Chin Wang Chai, 219
Chisels, 181–2
Chitti, 304
Chleuastochaerus stehlini, 85
Choei Tong Keou, 148 ff.
Chou K'ou Tien, 23, 58, 66, 93, 95 ff.
Chow, T. C., 42
Chu, T. O., 27
Chu Chia Chai, 170, 230, 244–50, 323–4
Chu Hsi, 16
Circumcision, 306
Coal mining, Chinese method, 24
Collenia, 10–11, 13, 60
Colquhoun, A. R., 210
" Comb " ceramics, 263
Congo, 307
Cordaites, 22
Corfu, 306
Cowries, 294 ff.
Cretaceous age, 27, 47–8
Crete, 298
Cro-Magnon caves, 321
Cryptozoon, 10
Cuneopsis, 140
Cyclophorus, 44
Cypraea, 296 ff.
Cyrena, 44

Dahomey, 308
Dahr, Dr. E., 242
Dall, Wm. H., 140, 299
Darfur, 309
David, Armand, 147
Death and Primitive Man, 318–19
" Death Pattern ", 315
De Groot, 72
De Visser, 327
De Wilde, Fr., 148
Diceratherium palaeosinense, 84
Dicerorhinus orientalis, 84
Dinosaurs, 34 ff.
Djibba, 308
Doolittle, 328
Dragon-Bone mining, 81–2
Dragon's Bone, 74–6
Dragons, 70 ff., 327
Drills, 209
Dryopteris, 28
Dubois, Eugen, 110
Du Halde, Fr., 147

Earthquakes, 65–6, 246
Eastman, 133
Edelstein, J., 27
Egba, 307
Egypt, 298, 306
Ekholm, 289
Elaphurus davidianus, 147
Elasmotherium, 84–5
Elephants, 135–6, 140
Elephas cf. namadicus, 151–2
Elfin mills, 289
Emplectopteris, 20
Eoanthropus dawsoni, 111
Eocene Age, 48–51
Eolian Theory, 128–31, 134–5
Epirusa Hiltzheimeri, 92
Equus cf. prjewalskyi, 151
Equus hemionus, 151–2

Equus sanmeniensis, 121
Erh Liang Kou, 144
Erikson, C. F., 2–4
Ertemte, 95
Esteria middendorfi, 42
Euryceros, 115, 121
Ewe, 306–7

Fagus feroniae, 29
Fa Hsien, 301
Fecundity rites, 277 ff.
Fen Ho, 157, 159
Figurines, 195, 316
Florin, R., 27, 29
Folding, 55 ff.
Forrer, 172
Frazer, Sir J. G., 280 ff., 329
Fushun, 26–7

Gazella prjewalskyi, 151
Gazella subgutturosa, 151
Germany, 309
Gibb, J. McGregor, 95–6
Gigantopteris nicotianaefolia, 19, 20–2
Gingko, 25
Glyptostrobus europaeus, 28–9
Gourd pattern, 328–9
Grabau, Amadeus W., 1, 10, 12, 16, 36, 105–6
Granger, Walter, 33, 35, 97–8
Gymnosolen, 10

Haberer, K. A., 76
Hagberg, Louise, 316
Halle, T. G., 18, 20, 24–5, 30
Hammarstedt, Edvard, 277–8
Haussa, 304
Hawaii, 301, 308
Hedin, Sven, 216
Helicidae, 130
Helopodidae, 37
Helopus Zdanskyi, 32, 37–40, 44, 46–7
Hematite, 321–2
Hipparion fauna, 84 ff., 147
Hoes, 182
Hofberg, Herman, 284
Holtedahl, 10
Hominidae, 110
Homo neanderthalensis, 110
Homo sapiens, 110
Hooton, E. A., 173–4
Hopei, 163, 204
Ho Ti Tsun, 140
Ho Yin, 184
Hsien, 222
Hsi Kou, 168, 174
Hsin An, 77–8
Hsin Cheng, 322, 323
Hsi Ning, 64, 218, 226–7, 247
Hsi Ning river, 161
Hsin Tien, 259–60, 335
Hsin Yao, 4, 60–2, 131
Hsi Shan, 58–9
Hsi Tzŭ Kou, 168, 180
Hsüan Hua, 206
Hsüan Hua Fu, 4–5
Hsüan-Lung, 4, 6–7
Huai-Ho, 214
Huai Lai, 66
Huailai plateau, 8–9
Huang Ho, *see* Yellow River
Huang T'u, 127–9
Huichol Indians, 281
Hui Tsui, 259–60
Hulutao, 188
Human sacrifices, 197–9
Hung Cheng, 148
Hun Ho, 8–9, 23
Hyaena sinensis, 102, 140
Hyaena spelaea, 152
Hyaena ultima, 140

India, 298–301, 309
Initiation Rites, 306

Jackson, J. W., 295–6, 299, 301, 306
Japan, 301, 304–5
Jesuits in China, 146–7
Joloff, 302
Jur, 304

Kado, 304
Kaiping, 12, 16, 55–7
Kalgan, 206
Kaoliang, 204
Kao Ti, Emperor, 71
Karlbeck, O., 208, 214
Karlgren, 317
Karsten, 320
Kaschel, Fr. Alfred, 35
Kavirondo, 304

INDEX

Keith, Sir Arthur, 119
Kellergruben, 172
Kiang, 228
Kidney Ore, 6
Kiev, 298
Kirghis, 302
Knives, 202 ff., 242, 249
Ko, 212–3, 293
Ko Hung, 16
Kokonor, 226, 228–33
Kou Yü Kou, 133
Krystofovich, A. N., 35
Kuban, 298, 321
Kuei Te, 64, 233, 234–5, 239
Kufu, 302
Kuo Chia Chuang, 259
Kurgans, 170
Ku Tzŭ Tang, 120

Laccolith, 58
Lacroix, Alfred, 105
Lai Yang series, 42
Laiyangia paradoxiformis, 42
Lanchow, 161, 225, 251
Lan Kou, 92
Lao Niu Kou, 98
Larson, F. A., 5
Laugerie-Basse cave, 297, 309
Lei Hiao, 75
Leptestis chingshanense, 44
Li, C., 106
Liang Chi Chao, 103
Licent, Emile, 92, 104–5, 131, 147 ff.
Limestone, 14
Limnaea, 42
Lingulella dimorpha, 14
Lithostrotion kaipingense, 14–15
Li T'ieh Kuai, 327
Li-Tripod, 220–3, 335
Liu Chang-shan, 164
Liu Pan Shan, 65
Loess, 127 ff., 158–9 ; formation, 130 ff.
Lo Han T'ang, 203, 235 ff.
Lophospira morrisi, 14
Loulan, 216
Lozcy, 235
Luang Prabang, 301
Luan Ho, 57
Lung Kuan, 206
Lung Shan, 65
Lung Wang, 71–2
Lung-Yen Company, 6
Lussi, 277–8
Lu Tzŭ Kou series, 81
Lycoptera, 36, 42
Lygodium, 28

Machairodus, 88
Ma Chia Yao, 264–6, 313 ff.
Mackenzie, Donald E., 324–5
Madisonville, 173–4
Magdalenian culture, 153, 209
Magic, Imitative, 280 ff.
Magic, Primitive, 200–1
Maikop, 321
Ma Lan, 158, 258
Mannhardt, J. W. E., 280
Masai, 304
Mathiesen, F. C., 1–4
Meles taxus, 152
Melville, J. C., 312
Menghin, O., 216, 336
Meng Yin, 32–3, 36
Menomini Indians, 306
Mentone, 298
Mertens, R., Fr., 35
Metailurus, 88
Mien Chih Hsien, 79, 133, 167
Moab Arabs, 281
Money, Cowrie as, 300–1
Montelius, 211
Montenegro, 306
Mordovins, 302
Morea, 309
Morocco, 302
Mostaert, Fr., 148
Mousterian culture, 153
Moxos Indians, 284
Mukden, 26
Mycetopus mengyinensis, 36

Naga, 308
Nankou pass, 10
Nan P'iao, 189
Nan Shan mountains, 225
Needles, 182, 195
New Caledonia, 301
New Hebrides, 301, 312
New Zealand, 307
Niang Niang Miao, 282
Nicobar Islanders, 282
Niger district, 300

INDEX

Ning Chia Kou, 34, 36, 40
Ning Hsia Fu, 148
Ni Ho Wan fauna, 92–3, 115, 141
Nishinam Indians, 281
Nordén, 289
Nordenskjöld, Otto, 30–1
Norin, Erik, 19–20, 22
Norinia, 20
Nystroemia, 20
Nyström, E. T., 4, 19

Obolus luanhsiensis, 14
Ochre, 321–2
Odhner, Nils H., 49–50, 141
Ojibwa Indians, 306
Okakura, 326–7
Ordos desert, 148 ff.
Ordovician system, 14
Ornament, Cowrie as, 301–2
Ornithopoda, 44
Oryza sativa, 186
Osmunda, 28–9
Ostrich eggs, 165
Ovens, 218, 241
Ovis ammon, 151–2

Pagodispira dorothea, 14
Pai Mai Ssŭ, 227
P'ai Tzu P'ing, 261–2
Palaeanthropus heidelbergensis, 110–111
Palaeocyparis cf. flexuosa, 42
Palander, Louis, 88
Palatin, J. V., 27
Palmgren, Nils, 273
P'an Chiao, 159
P'ang Chia Pu, 4, 6
P'an Shan, 271–6, 313 ff.
Pao Te Hsien, 80, 91, 157
Paracamelus gigas, 92
Patosiwa, 308
Paviland cave, 321
Pei, W. C., 108, 115, 120–5
Peking, 22–3
Peking Man, 95 ff., 330
Pen, 209, 211
Permocarboniferous system, 15
Peruvians, 320
Pettersson, Maria, 78
Pien Chia Kou, 270, 274, 313, 322
Piltdown skull, 111
Pithecanthropus erectus, 110–11, 118
Place-names, 200
Planorbis, 49
Pleistocene Man in Ordos, 146 ff.
Pliopithecus, 95
Ploughing, Ritual, 293
Polo, Marco, 296
Pompeii, 304
Populus glandulifera, 28
Pottery, 182–6, 195–7, 218–23, 262–3, 265–7, 274–5, 313 ff., 334 ff.
Proboscidipparion sinense, 92, 168
Productus, 15
Proteroscarabaeus yeni, 42
Protoceratops andrewsi, 35
Pu Chao Chai, 178, 218, 226, 334
Pseudaxis grayi, 102, 121
Pseudomonotis Mathieui, 15
Punjab, 302

Quadrula, 140

Rattle, Knife-grinder's, 205–6
Rattles, 266, 293
Red colouring on Burial Urns, 319 ff.
Regenrillen, 66
Reinach, Salomon, 285–7
Religion, Cowrie and, 306–7
Rhinoceri, 84
Rhinoceros tichorhinus, 140, 151–2
Rice, 186–7, 336
Richert, Gösta and Mrs., 7–8
Richthofen, Ferd. von, 10–12, 67, 127–31
Rings, 182, 194, 267, 273
Ringström, Torsten, 84
Roden mounds, 299
Rosenius, Elsa, 167
Rydh, Hanna, 287, 313–6, 327

Samarura gregaria, 42
Samotherium sinense, 88
San Men, 93
Sanmenian series, 93
San Men rapids, 140
Sauropods, 44
Saxo Grammaticus, 281
Scaptochirus primitivus, 102
Schall, Adam, 146

Schlosser, Max, 76–7, 88
Schmidt, Hubert, 166
Schneider, O., 295, 301
Scythes, 206–7
Sequoia gigantea, 30
Sequoia langsdorfii, 28–9
Sequoia sempervirens, 30
Seran, 308
Seymour Island, 31
Sha Ching, 323
Sha Kuo T'un, 188 ff.
Sha Lêng Tzŭ, 260
Shang Yin Kou, 78–9, 91
Shells, 294 ff.
Shih Huang Ti, 71
Shih Li P'o, 226, 227
Ship, in rock paintings, 290
Shui Tung Kou, *see* Choei Tong Keou
Siam, 301
Sierra Leone, 306
Sinanthropus pekinensis, 95 ff., 330
Sinian system, 11, 13
Sinoblatta laiyangensis, 42
Sinotherium lagrelii, 84–5
Sjara Osso Gol, 148, 150–2
Sloping strata, 55 ff.
Smith, G. Elliot, 118, 295, 301, 304–5, 310, 320
Snake cult, 329
Sollas, 209
Sphenolepis arborescens, 42
Spiral designs, 324–7
Spiriferina chuchuani, 15
Spirifer mosquensis, 15
Spirocerus kiakhtensis, 151–2
Ssŭ Shih Ting, 261
Stearn, 295
Stegodon, 102
Stegosaurus, 40
Stromatolitic Ore, 3, 7
Struthio camelus, 135, 152
Struthiolithus, 133–5, 152, 168
Sumatra, 282
Sun, Y. C., 14
Sun-wheel, 293
Sus lydekkeri, 102
Sus scrofa, 151
Sweden, Bronze Age engravings in, 288–91 ; cowries in, 309
Sweden, Crown Prince of, 102–3
Synamia Zdanskyi, 36
Syria, 282
Tai An, 33
Tai Shan, 33
Taiyuanfu, 19
Tammuz, 278
T'an, H. C., 33 ff., 46–7, 63–4
Tangar, 228
Tanius sinensis, 44–7
T'ao river, 161, 256 ff.
T'ao Sha Hsien, 260–1
Tartoux, Fr., 146
Tatsumaki, 327
Taungtha, 302
Ta Yao Kou, 189
Tertiary Age, 27–31, 48
Textiles, 216–7
Theropoda, 44
Thinnfeldia, 42
Thompson, Dr., 302
Tiagy, 304
Tiaochishan series, 59
Tibesti, 302
Ting, V. K., 88, 93, 106, 123, 140
Tingia, 20
Ting-tripod, 222
Titao, 256
Todas, 302
Togoland, 300, 304, 306–8
Tongshan, 14, 17–18
Toradjas, 283
Torii, R. and K., 201–2, 204
Torres Strait, 283
Transport in China, 33
Tree of Life, 292–3
Triangle Pattern, 316–7
Trinil, 110
Tripolje, 186, 215, 224, 334
Trugor, 39
Tuc d'Audoubert, 287
Tung Kou, 168, 174
Tung Tzŭ Kou, 169
Turbinella pyrum, 298

Uganda, 300
Unio cf. menkii, 36
Unio johanböhmi, 36
Ursus arctos, 102

Valvata suturalis, 36
Verbiest, Ferdinand, 146

Wa Kuan Tsui, 272–4
Wangshih series, 44
Wan Hsien, 102
Waterspouts, 325–7
Wen Hsi, 48–9
Western Hills, 22–3, 58–9, 214
Whirlwinds, 325–7
Whorls, Spinning, 182, 217
Willoughby, 173
Wiman, C., 36 ff., 47, 82–4, 103
Woman, Cowrie and, 302–4
Wong, James, 189
Wong Wen-Hao, 33, 103, 123

Yang Shao, 92, 133, 143, 164 ff., 215 ff., 230 ff., 331 ff.
Yang-Yin principles, 318
Yao, Emperor, 70
Yellow Earth, 127 ff.
Yellow River, 67, 132, 142, 179, 320–1
Yen Shan folding, 60
Yen Tung Shan, 5–7, 61–2
Yih, L. F., 59
Young, Dr. C. C., 108, 123, 155
Yü, Emperor, 143
Yüan, 273
Yuan, P. L., 166, 259
Yuan Chü, 49–50, 62
Yule cake, 279, 282–3
Yü T'ai Shan, 60

Zamites, 42
Zdansky, Otto, 33, 35–8, 47, 51, 53, 80–2, 97 ff., 166, 174, 180
Zikawei Museum, 147

PREHISTORIC SITE

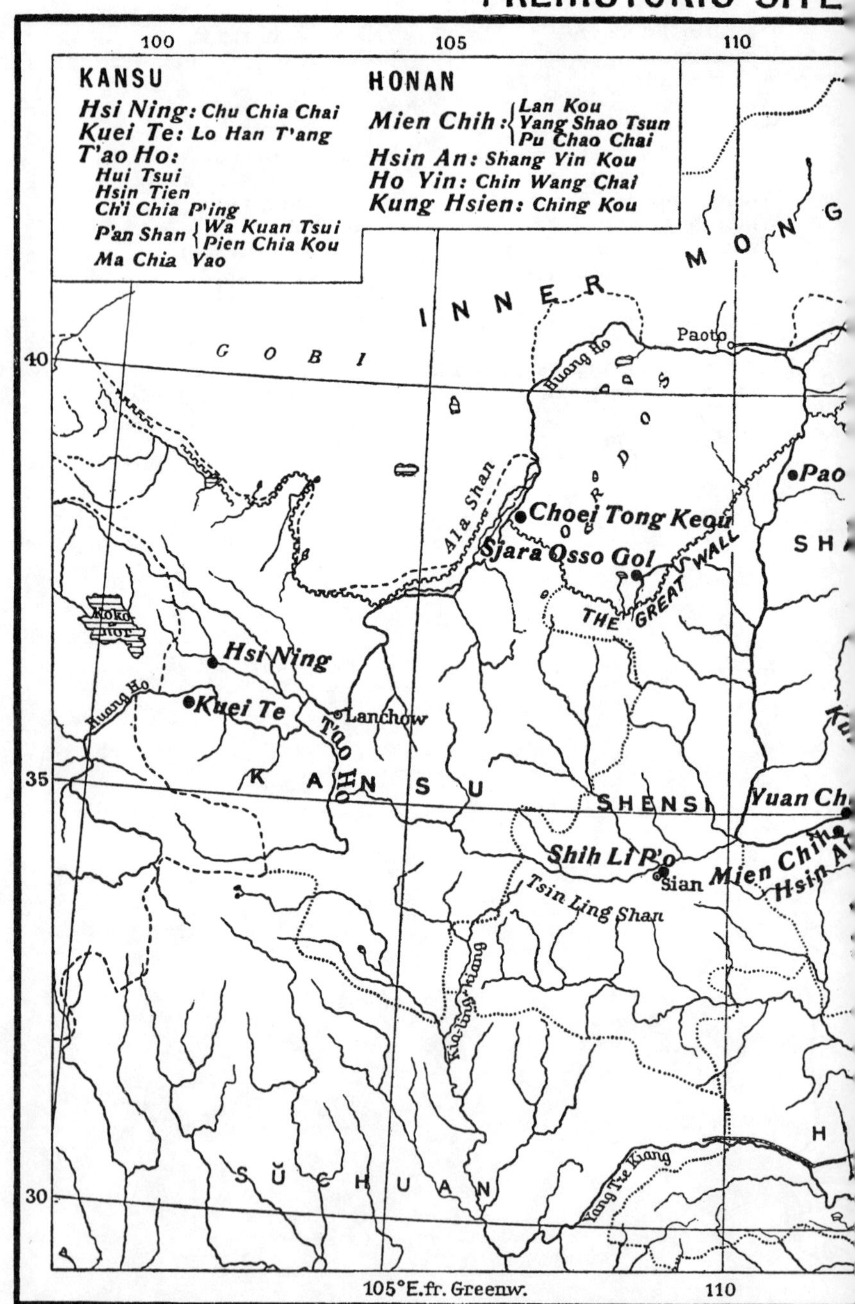

Scale 1:10 millions

0

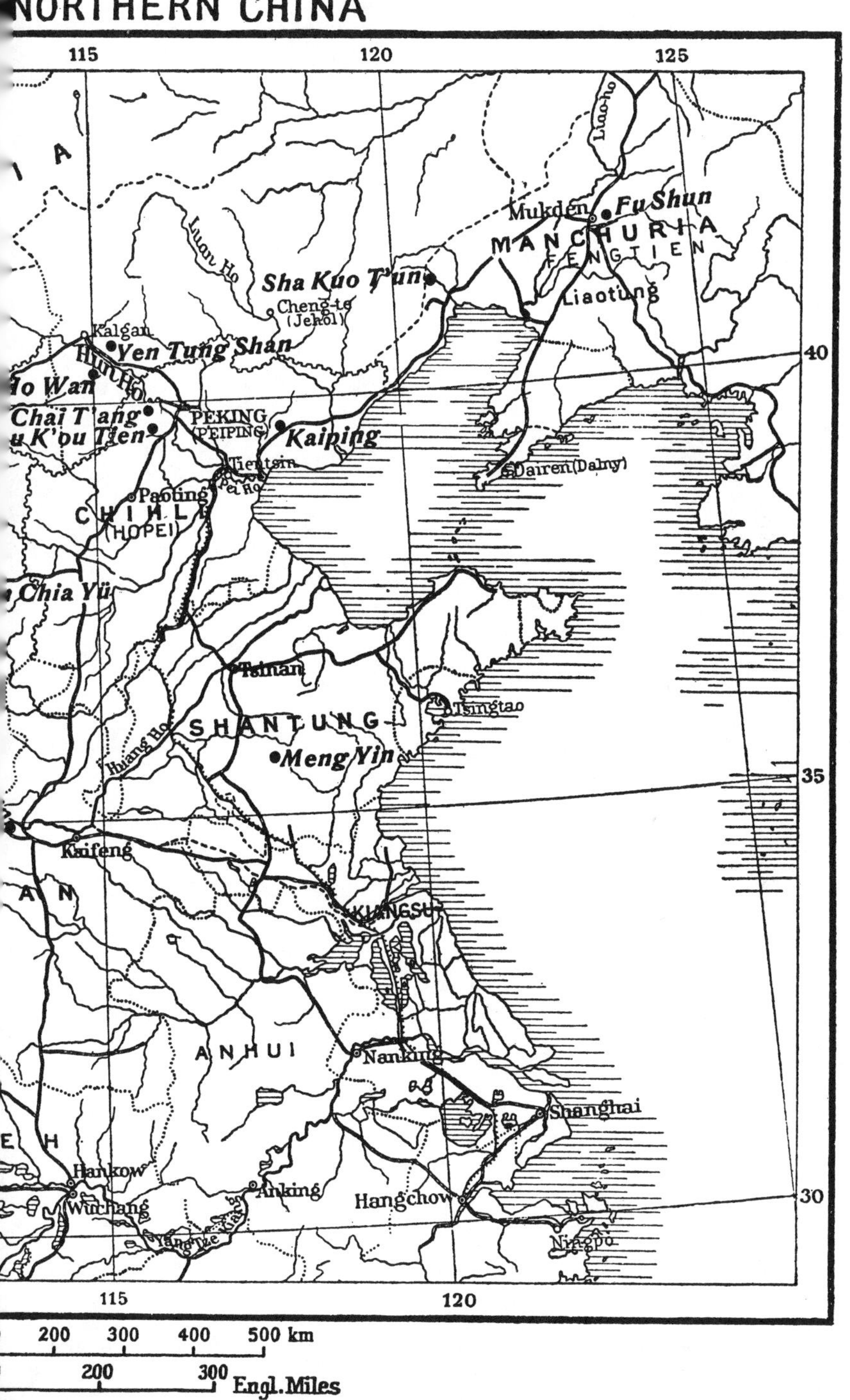
NORTHERN CHINA
115
120
125
Liao-ho
Mukden
Fu Shun
MANCHURIA
FENGTIEN
Luan Ho
Sha Kuo T'un
Cheng-te (Jehol)
Liaotung
Kalgan
Yen Tung Shan
Hun Ho
PEKING (PEIPING)
Kaiping
Tientsin
Pei Ho
Dairen (Dalny)
Paoting
CHIHLI (HOPEI)
Chia Yü
Tsinan
Tsingtao
SHANTUNG
Huang Ho
Meng Yin
Kaifeng
KIANGSU
ANHUI
Nanking
Shanghai
Hankow
Wuchang
Anking
Yangtze Kiang
Hangchow
Ningpo
40
35
30
115
120
200
300
400
500 km
200
300
Engl. Miles